More praise for *California*

"[Thurston Clarke's] use of history complements his travels superbly.... Clarke spends much of his trip in the company of good hearted Quixotes, tilting at the forces of greed and commercialism. In them he finds remnants of the California Dream, and sees hope in a society shaking itself to rubble."

—*Los Angeles Times*

"A book to savor ... Clarke's acerbic wit and vivid description are a pleasure throughout, but his admiration of 'eccentric community builders' gives the book its heart."

—*The Seattle Times*

"This is a brilliant, mordantly funny book, and Clarke's vision of the San Andreas Fault is powerful and true. He's a dark millenarian who's given us a beautifully complex metaphor, and if California at century's end is America's future, then we're all living on the Fault, and the Big One's due any minute."

—Russell Banks
Author of *Continental Drift*
and *Rule of the Bone*

"I lived in the Golden State in the Seventies, just before the tarnish, the fool's gold, and Proposition 13. Now comes Mr. Clarke, an adventurous investigator. In his persistent wandering he uncovers a cornucopia of America's disappointed dreams. We hear the voices of wanderers, settlers, ex-communards, and working philosophers. The closeness of dream and dread is still thrilling and comes through. I wiped my eyes."

—Andrei Codrescu
Author of *Road Scholar*
NPR commentator

"[Clarke] has a nice touch and a close eye. Like novelist John Updike, he has the ability to raise the stature of the mundane and to make an interesting prose purse out of a sow's-ear situation."

—*The Philadelphia Inquirer*

"*California Fault* is a vivid, witty, tremendously enjoyable journey through the most beautiful but potentially lethal landscape on earth. Clarke weaves together earthquakes, flying saucers, and disoriented homing pigeons. He introduces us to a memorable cast of eccentrics and dreamers and has given us a golden book about the golden state. A classic in travel literature."

—Nicholas Pileggi
Author of *Wise Guys* and *Casino*

CALIFORNIA FAULT

Searching for the Spirit of State
Along the San Andreas

THURSTON CLARKE

BALLANTINE BOOKS   NEW YORK

http://www.randomhouse.com

Library of Congress Catalog Card Number: 96-97130

ISBN: 0-345-40908-6

Cover design by Carlos Beltran
Cover photo courtesy of Photonica

Manufactured in the United States of America

First Hardcover Edition: April 1996
First Trade Paperback Edition: July 1997

10 9 8 7 6 5 4 3 2 1

FOR JAMIE AND DAMARIS

Contents

Map of California and the San Andreas Fault   xi

INTRODUCTION

1. Fandango Pass   3
2. The Shadowy Scar   12

PART ONE
TRIPLE JUNCTION

3. Eureka!   25
4. Seth Kinman's Scalps   34
5. Seth Kinman's Homestead   42
6. Jerry Hurley's Headaches   47
7. The Valley Grocery   52
8. The Function on the Triple Junction   60
9. A Million Miles From California   65

PART TWO
REDWOOD EMPIRE

10. The Trees of Rondal Snodgrass   77
11. "Fanning the Flames . . ."   85
12. "Our Children, Our Resource, Our Future"   94

Contents

PART THREE
DOWN THE NORTH COAST

13.	At Home in Mendocino	109
14.	The Raven and the Wizard	120
15.	Living Light on the Land	129
16.	"Wildlife Observation Area"	138
17.	Earthquake Bay	149
18.	"Good-bye, Sea Drift"	160

PART FOUR
SAN FRANCISCO

19.	The Wizard of Sutro Heights	169
20.	"The Day Our World Shook"	174
21.	Lotta's Fountain	183
22.	Purported Earthquake Shacks	192
23.	The Death Lady	200

PART FIVE
SOUTH BAY

24.	Alive in Daly City	213
25.	Dream House	223
26.	The Ghost of Toys "Я" Us	228
27.	The Fast-Food Flasher	236
28.	Lost Cats and "Smashed" Pigeons	244

PART SIX
SANTA CRUZ TO PARKFIELD

29.	Holy City	261
30.	Eye of the Beast	272
31.	Greywolf	277
32.	Quake City	286
33.	Vehicular Recreation	297
34.	"Be Here When It Happens"	304

PART SEVEN
TO THE SALTON SEA

35. "Master-Planned Community" 321
36. Family Values 330
37. Some "Doggone Individualists" 338
38. The Rebus Letter 349
39. The Integraton Prepares for Takeoff 355
40. Cabot Yerxa's Eyesore 368
41. In the Vicinity 379
42. "A Real Happening Place" 391
43. Back Along the Fault 397

POSTSCRIPT
At Bruff's Camp 405
Bibliography 415
Acknowledgments 418

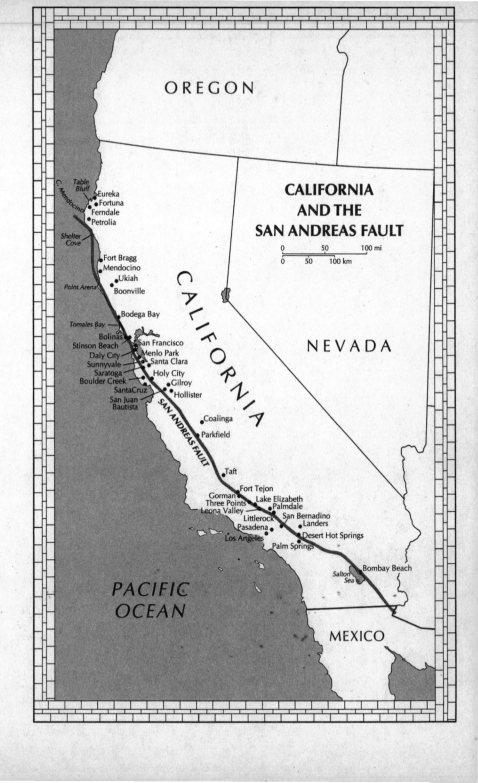

CALIFORNIA
AND THE
SAN ANDREAS FAULT

INTRODUCTION

1

Fandango Pass

I became interested in earthquakes when one almost killed me, and in California when I discovered it almost killed my ancestor J. Goldsborough Bruff, whose last name is now my middle.

The earthquake struck Ecuador on the morning of March 5, 1987, and had I not changed my itinerary the week before, it would have caught me on an overnight bus traveling a highway twisting down six thousand feet from the Andes to the Amazon. The epicenter was several football fields from this road and the death toll of five thousand included three hundred bus passengers swept by landslides into Amazon tributaries or entombed in ten feet of mud.

After convincing myself I would have been among the lucky survivors (a typically Californian attitude toward seismic risk, although I did not know this at the time), I felt strangely disappointed at having missed the experience. After all, earthquakes are the Bigfoot of natural disasters, resistant to prediction, manipulation, or control, the only ones still defying both the imagination and the photograph. A hurricane's giant waves and black skies send witnesses dashing for cameras, but the first tremor of an earthquake sends them running for their lives. Earthquake photographs show an aftermath of fissures, landslides, and pancaked expressways—but those of the event itself are invariably disappointing, just blurred buildings or panicked shoppers caught by a security camera. People *say* their refrigerators danced and their palm trees kissed the ground, but where is the proof? The National Geographic Society has installed video cameras aimed at bar stools and couches in earthquake-prone Parkfield, California, setting them to begin filming at the first nudge, but film what? Crashing gin bottles and falling chimneys? And how will this help anyone imagine an earthquake?

Even Californians blasé about the kind of moderate earthquake measuring 6.0 on the Richter scale have trouble imagining the 8.2 that shook San Francisco in 1906, or the 7.4 hitting the Mojave Desert town of Landers in 1992. Each point on this logarithmic scale represents a tenfold increase in energy as measured by the ground motion recorded by a seismograph, so a great earthquake measuring 8.3 is more than one hundred times stronger than a moderate 6.0. If you have felt the 40 mph winds and ten-foot waves of a moderate coastal storm, you can probably imagine a great hurricane three times as strong, with 125 mph winds and thirty-foot waves. But can you imagine one a hundred times as strong, with 4,000 mph winds and thousand-foot-high waves?

When I was growing up near Long Island Sound I followed the swirling little hurricane eyes as they slid up the eastern seaboard on newspaper maps, rooting for them to come ashore in southern New England for the same reason I rooted for blizzards and baseball-sized hail—because I wanted to witness the storm, snowfall, or disaster of the century. So after being cheated out of that earthquake in Ecuador, I stayed on the lookout, and two years later in Honolulu, while watching a film in a high-school auditorium, I felt a slipping and shaking so gentle it set the audience murmuring instead of screaming. You might compare it to a ferry leaving a dock, but it was really a sensation unlike any other, like sex for the first time; and like sex, it left me hungry for more.

Professor William Jarvis of Stanford popularized the concept of "earthquake love" after the Great San Francisco Earthquake of 1906, defining it as a "tenderness" toward others who shared the experience, and an "uplift from the common lot that briefly banished loneliness." The author William James, who was lecturing at Stanford in 1906, wrote afterward of waking to his shaking bed, feeling "pure delight and welcome," and a "gleeful recognition of the nature of the movement." He hurried to the station and caught the only train making a run into San Francisco that day. For hours he wandered through the rubble, impressed by the "universal equanimity" of the survivors, and reporting that "the terms 'awful and dreadful' fell often enough from people's lips, but always with a sort of abstract meaning, and with a face that seemed to admire the vastness of the catastrophe."

John Muir enjoyed an earthquake's "strange thrilling motion" on a moonlit night in Yosemite when he dashed from his cabin shouting, "A noble earthquake! A noble earthquake!" He reported its roar was "tremendously deep and broad and earnest." It provided the "sublime spectacle" of an avalanche of boulders pouring onto a valley floor in "an arc of glowing, passionate fire," perfumed the air with crushed spruce, and blanketed the valley with a luminous, moonlit dust cloud. This proof of the "orderly beauty-making love-beats of Nature's heart" left him "both glad and frightened."

Before I went searching for what had so delighted James and Muir, and intrigued Charles Darwin, who after surviving an earthquake in Chile marveled at the "strong idea of insecurity, which hours of reflection would not have produced," I ordered a cassette tape of earthquake sounds from the Seismological Society of America. They had been recorded by chance and compiled by a structural engineer named Karl Steinbrugge. I played them and thought, "This is what I would have heard seconds before that mountain slid onto my rattletrap bus—first a distant rumble, then a low-pitched moan, a roar, screaming, then silence."

Mr. Steinbrugge's taped quakes all sounded like world-enders, capable of rearranging lives and landscapes as fast as the Old Testament God. The most chilling let me eavesdrop on the niece of Mr. Ervin A. Hadley as she was playing with her son in a two-story frame house in Eureka, California, on the morning of December 21, 1954. There was a click-clack of blocks, a voice saying, "Well, how about that? That's fine!" then a rumble, then an avalanche of explosions, as if a speeding train had slammed into the house, or a mountain had buried it. The most satisfying Steinbrugge recording was of a courtroom of medical malpractice attorneys being silenced in middeposition by the strongest earthquake in U.S. history, the 8.4 that sent the jerry-built subdivisions of Anchorage sliding down cliffs in 1964. The most terrifying showed how the moderate Daly City earthquake of 1957 affected seven hundred students gathered for a choral concert in the auditorium of Sequoia High School. An authoritative male voice was explaining Tchaikovsky's *Legend* when a lone student cried out. Within seconds, kids were screaming like passengers in a plunging aircraft, or falling bus.

When I listened to this particular segment, which I did often before leaving for California, I thought, "This is how it will sound: the end of the world, or of Palm Springs, San Bernardino, or whatever town near the San Andreas Fault is next," and then wondered if I would be lucky enough to be there.

My ancestor J. Goldsborough Bruff left Washington, D.C. (then Washington City), for the California goldfields on April 2, 1849, in command of sixty-six men ranging in age from fifty-nine to fifteen who called themselves the Washington City and California Gold Mining Association. A Washington newspaper described "truly a well-chosen band, handsomely uniformed and well-equipped for the dangers they might have to encounter." Bruff praised them as "energetic gentlemen," joining the Gold Rush to enrich themselves "by every honorable means."

Their departure was an event. Bruff had drilled them to the standard of light infantry and dressed them in gray frock coats with gilt eagle buttons, black-striped pantaloons, and forage caps. Each man carried a rifle, two pistols, a bowie knife, and belt hatchet. Led by a military band, they marched across Lafayette Square to the White House. President Zachary Taylor shook Bruff's hand and praised his men's "courage and enterprise." Bruff assured him they were all men of "strength and character," adding, "As we are on the eve of an extraordinary journey, of great extent, and which must be fraught with arduous trials, most probably many of us will never again have the pleasure of greeting you."

Bruff's only qualifications for guiding this band of civil servants through deserts, mountains, and hostile Indian territory were a West Point education cut short when he wounded a classmate in a duel, followed by seven years as a merchant seaman that his wife claimed had provided him with "many wonderful adventures, full of thrilling escapes," and left his brain "stored with anecdotes of his travels." For the previous twenty years he had worked as a draftsman at the Bureau of Topographical Engineers, sometimes reproducing maps of the American West drawn by pioneers and explorers. The year before joining the Gold Rush he had copied Captain Frémont's maps of California, his hand tracing, although he did not know it at the time, the tangle of mountains where he would soon prospect for gold, the squiggly rivers whose headwaters he would discover, and possibly, the remote ridge a plaque still identifies as BRUFF'S CAMP, where six months after leaving the White House, with winter approaching, his well-chosen band of honorable gentlemen would leave him to starve within sight of the Sacramento Valley.

This betrayal has remained a family mystery ever since. Had it happened in the goldfields, or had he been a cruel or incompetent leader, it might be understandable. But according to historians of the California Trail, he was "a man of strength and courage" who possessed "natural ability as a leader," commanded "with skill and authority," and was "one of the very best Captains of the whole year . . . [an] officer of the type who keeps his men together because he takes good care of them." He combined "the military man's dedication to duty with a reflexive kindness," "demanded that the strong help the weak, particularly women and children on the trail," and was "a soft touch for anyone in need." He distributed food to starving Pawnees, denounced a squaw's rape as "villainous conduct," and condemned emigrants who defaced rocks with graffiti and whipped their oxen. Their beasts' eyes spoke "eloquently," he said, and "if any four-footed animal has soul, it is an ox."

Most paramilitary companies squabbled on the trail, dividing assets and dissolving constitutions before reaching California. But Bruff kept his men together, and for six months and two thousand miles they passed the smashed wagons, discarded supplies, and crude headstones of less well-commanded outfits. Because he insisted on nightly guard duty, the only scalp injuries to his men occurred when they rolled over upon waking on cold mornings, yanking out patches of their hair frozen to the ground.

Certainly the Washington Miners' Fourth of July celebration on the banks of the Platte River did not foreshadow what was to come when they reached California. The men covered wagons with tent cloths to make a banquet hall, raised Old Glory through a roof, donned uniforms, and dined on "luxuries of the season," Bruff reported. After toasting "California—El Dorado and Pacific Emporium," he delivered a grandiloquent speech praising their "spirit of daring adventure and indomitable enterprise," promising "the trials of this travel will serve as amusing tales for our children and friends," and extolling their "bravery, judgement, patience, and perseverance." They were, he said, "the right kind of people for California."

Six weeks later they halted near the Idaho–Wyoming border for a formal reelection of officers as mandated by the company constitution. Every man was voted out except Bruff, who was reelected unanimously. Soon afterward Bruff, like many emigrant leaders that summer, made the mistake of taking the Lassen Trail, a cutoff from the California Trail that meandered north through Nevada's Black Rock

Desert before looping back into California near the Oregon border. The Danish settler Peter Lassen had promoted it as having a lower altitude and milder weather than the route across the Sierras, which had claimed so many members of the Donner Party in 1846. But it had the disadvantages of adding hundreds of miles to the journey and traversing a terrain so forbidding that emigrant graffiti and wagon ruts remain untouched to this day.

When the veteran guide Captain Milton McGee chose the Lassen Trail in mid-August of 1849, every large emigrant party behind him followed suit. The earliest found barely enough grass and water for their oxen, while later parties like Bruff's, who traveled it in mid-September, found less. Some Lassen Trail stragglers abandoned their possessions along the way, others burned the grass to reduce competition in the goldfields, and still others, displaying the fusion of materialism and optimism that would become characteristic of their new state, buried them in "graves" marked by bogus headboards, convinced they would soon be returning to collect them.

The forty-niners on the Lassen Trail became true Californians when they reached the Fandango Pass that crosses the Warner Mountains just inside the state line. Its last two hundred yards rise steeply and diaries of the time describe emigrants wrapped in blankets and shivering with fevers, clinging to the necks of skeletal donkeys. At the top, they could simultaneously see where they had been—a wasteland of black rock and barren hills—and where they were going—dramatic waves of thickly wooded mountains. "What a scene from here!" Bruff wrote in his diary, marveling at "the Snow Butte [probably Mount Shasta], and his blue neighbors, deep vales, silver-thread like streams, near mountains, dense forests, bright deep valleys," and stunned by a landscape created by one hundred million years of earthquakes.

His men crossed the Fandango with famished oxen and reduced supplies, but not in extremis. His first wagon planted the Stars and Stripes at the crest where a sign indicated Peter Lassen's ranch and fresh provisions were another 228 miles. "At least 150 miles longer than we all thought it would be," Bruff wrote. "Well, here are the facts, and they *are* stubborn things!"

Three weeks later, the Wolverine Rangers of Michigan became the last organized company to cross. Unlike Bruff's men, they disbanded and divided their stores when they saw California, then fed their constitution to a bonfire and danced a fandango around it with the daughters of a straggler, giving the pass its name. Other emigrants reported wild figures throwing huge shadows against the rocks and mistook them for Indians celebrating a massacre. Later, it was said the Michigan men danced because the daughters were beautiful, because they were striking out for the goldfields on their own, or because with winter approaching, they expected to die; they danced naked, to keep warm, or to celebrate California.

While they danced, Bruff's company was making camp several hundred miles west on a ridge only two days' walk from the Sacramento Valley and Peter Lassen's ranch. Although their rations were low and many animals near death, they had fared better than other emigrant groups, losing only one man, the least of any organized party that year. Bruff volunteered to guard the company property while the others descended into the valley with the surviving mules, six wagons with bare necessities, and his horse. His men, Bruff reported, "were delighted, and they immediately set about the task, selecting indispensable articles to pack in etc.—They promised most faithfully to come out with my team and my horse." The Western historian George Stewart has called Bruff's decision "a final demonstration of his responsibility as a captain," adding, "However ... [his company] may even be said to have deserted him."

As his men departed, Bruff was astonished that the man riding his horse, already packed with the remaining food, "entirely forgot to offer me either flour or bread as he rode by."

A week later, six Washington Miners sneaked back into his camp at dusk. "My own comrades, for whom I had done so much did not ask me how I had subsisted," he noted. They cooked themselves a hearty meal. When he inquired after his horse he was told "in a tone of indifference" that it was "in the valley." As his comrades well knew, Bruff was incapacitated by rheumatoid arthritis, barely able to walk. Finally he saw the truth. "You came for me!" he snapped. "No sir! You came for these wagons, and their contents, that's what you came for!—take the plunder and roll on. I'll not disgrace myself by further companionship with you!"

The next morning they demanded his tent, arguing it was company property. He watched them "avariciously" pile their wagons and wrote, "Thus ends my connections with the Washington City Company, as an organized body, and with some of them, all future acquaintance."

Bruff was stranded in the mountains six months. His sufferings almost equaled those of the Donner Party, and had he eaten a companion he might be a household word, too. He hunted deer and assisted stragglers who found in him "a kind friend." He sent desperate notes to the settlements, begging his comrades for "provisions and tea, or at least a riding animal." He suffered "infirmity, cold, dampness, starvation, and yelping of my cur, and howling of wolves." He slept in an open wagon, waking up buried under drifting snow, and was "in a snap truly, without food, helpless, and subject to spells of prostration," with "apprehensions of insanity." He hallucinated he was sitting at home, his son "parting my long matted hair with his little hands." He shared a diet of candles, coffee grounds, and woodpeckers with a four-year-old boy abandoned by his father, until the boy died. He refused to butcher his dog—"my faithful watch . . . who has shared my sufferings." When he stumbled on the footprints of an Indian—"pigeon-toed and I judge small," his mouth "watered," and he imagined "a good broil." He tracked him for miles, but in the end, "could not shoot the poor wretch in the back."

During an early April thaw he gathered his strength, buried his diaries, and staggered into the valley, collapsing a hundred yards from the first homestead. He stayed a year in California. His diaries are largely silent about prospecting, but filled with ecstatic descriptions of a "wild," "beautiful," and "remarkable" country. He discovered Indian hieroglyphics, drew panoramas of mountains never visited by whites, named a lake after a friend, was assaulted by bears and wolves, drew plans for a small city, watched Sacramento burn to the ground, stumbled on a lynched corpse, and was shocked by a small earthquake, the only adventure I could duplicate.

At other times, and in other places, such experiences would have guaranteed several biographies, perhaps a county named in your honor, but they were so commonplace in 1849 California that after returning East, Bruff failed to find a publisher for his diaries and sketches. Columbia University Press finally published them in 1944 and I read them when I was twelve. The story seemed obvious: a noble man betrayed by scoundrels. It did not occur to me to wonder why Bruff had been unanimously reelected along the trail in August, and unanimously abandoned in California in October. The editors of his diaries offered no explanation. They had not researched the lives and motivations of his comrades because, as they delicately put it, "Their descendants, if any, might not welcome the attention."

I took the Washington City roster with me to California so I could check it against telephone books and historical-society membership lists. If I found a Capron, Coumbs, Fowble, or Moxley, or any of the more unusual names, I planned calling to ask if Goldsborough Bruff had led their relations across the Fandango Pass, if they had any diaries or letters, and if they cared to meet; but not asking them, at least over the telephone, to speculate why their ancestors had left mine to starve, and why California appeared to have worked on them such different magic.

2

The Shadowy Scar

The historian Hubert Howe Bancroft called the Gold Rush "the first general disruption of home circles since our government was formed, the effects of which are destined to reach down to future generations." If Bruff's adventures reached me, it was to make me even more bewitched by California than a normal boy growing up during the fifties and sixties on the East Coast, and at the same time, slightly more wary.

My grandparents Bruff lived in a hilltop town in Southern California. We never visited them, but thanks to the photographs in their Christmas cards, I knew you could see orange groves, the Pacific, and a range of snowy mountains from the terrace of their glass-and-redwood home. As a boy growing up in suburban Connecticut, I believed most Californians lived this way—high up, with a great view, eating outdoors under a cloudless sky, surrounded by gardens, picking fruit from their own trees, and enjoying an endless Technicolor spring. That was also pretty much how the whole state looked in the copies of *Sunset* magazine we received from them each month. When I imagined California I saw a *Sunset* family vacation in a wood-paneled station wagon, wicker basket picnics by a Yosemite lake, Spanish missions haunted by Zorro, and driving through giant sequoias. During the 1960s, that great California decade of the Beach Boys, Free Speech Movement, Monterey Pop Festival, and Summer of Love, when the state promised generous helpings of music, beaches, sex, convertibles, and money, I became a confirmed, yet cautious, Californiaphile.

I realize now that this greedy, optimistic teenage dream of a place where people lived in glass houses surrounded by spectacular vistas and spent their lives being paid handsomely for surfing, making love, and demonstrating for noble causes, yet also managed to be laid-back, forward-looking, and amusingly eccentric, was in its essentials the "California Dream" of natural beauty married to extraordinary freedom and opportunity that inspired Bruff, and generations of emigrants who followed. It is there in the letter he wrote before his departure: "I cannot be very unfortunate in California, and if the gold shall have vanished, my abilities will guarantee a handsome salary," and there in that Independence Day speech on the plains, when he praised California as "rich in commerce, and agriculture; and destined to become the grand emporium of vast trade of the Eastern hemisphere. . . . Enterprise . . . prosecuted by the right kind of people, must be successful."

It is also in the California books filling the five-foot-long shelf over my desk. For the Depression-era authors of *The WPA Guide to California*, California was "perpetual summer," "orange groves in sight of snowy peaks," "oil wells spouting wealth," "real estate promising fortunes," and "cinema stars and bathing beauties." It promised "a new start, a kinder providence, a rebirth of soul and body." Four decades later, a new introduction to this same guide declared it "a divine inspiration from nature," "a land of exceptional opportunities," "limitless possibilities for individual expression and . . . social transformation," and "a break from the constraints of the East Coast."

But despite my own Californiaphilia, I seemed unable to make the break. A teenage friend of mine went to Los Angeles to visit his father during the surfing-craze summer of 1963. He stayed, enrolled in high school, and returned for Christmas taller and suddenly handsome, with sun-bleached hair and toes bent crooked by surfboards, proficient in dances that did not hit New England until spring. He asked me to visit him during the summer but I dithered and our friendship ended.

Ten years later, two friends surprised me by suddenly moving to Los Angeles. He was a filmmaker who despaired of finding work in New York. She was a teacher tired of catching her students' winter colds. As their taillights disappeared in westbound traffic I wondered, "Why not me?" They called from a bungalow deep in a canyon, surrounded by coyotes and chaparral, praising the sharp light and luminous nights, and I thought, "Why not go?"

Then there was my English friend who attended graduate school at UCLA. His wife surprised him by winning enough money on a quiz show for a down payment on the house outside London where they still live. I felt a flash of "gold fever" when I heard this. I knew that program, its questions were easy. I told myself, "If I lived in Los Angeles, I could have won that money," and wondered why I did not.

But still I resisted. Perhaps because of the shadow cast by Bruff's story; perhaps because California struck me as a card you only played once and I was afraid of wasting it. You went there at a natural crossroads, after graduation, a wedding, or the army, or you went impetuously, to heal a bad marriage, recover from tragedy, or change your luck. You went to walk Pacific beaches, become a Sierra hermit, or find God in the Mojave, for sun hot enough and landscape awesome enough to cauterize grief and inspire art. You went because it was rich in the clay from which new lives are fashioned: optimism and opportunity. You either went and never returned, or like Bruff, came home and never went back.

I did not set foot in California until I was thirty-two. But it hardly counted. I went only because my wife's company transferred her temporarily to San Francisco. There, by force of habit, we lived like New Yorkers: in a doorman apartment building on Russian Hill, walking everywhere, driven by the rain into secondhand bookstores and revival cinemas. I never saw that *Sunset* magazine California of drive-through trees, Spanish missions, and orange groves running into walls of snowy mountains. We stayed only three months, but for the next ten years discussed moving back. Then suddenly, in the early 1990s it appeared that saving California for later was like saving a fast-devaluing currency that might soon be worthless.

Like everything in California, this reversal of fortune happened fast. The *Economist*'s 1984 survey of the state was headlined "The Optimists." The one in 1990, "They Paved Paradise and Put Up a Parking Lot," announced, "One of the most striking things about California is the state's dispirited mood." A 1985 poll reported 78 percent of Californians believing it was "one of the best places to live." Four years later, a *Newsweek* cover story, "California Dream, California Nightmare," quoted one Californian as saying, "California is not where the dream is anymore—it's not a wonderful place to live."

Suddenly, only 51 percent of Californians believed themselves living in "the best place," and Peter Ueberroth, a symbol of California success and optimism since the 1984 Olympics, was warning that "things are much worse than we expected. Things are much worse than you know."

Suddenly the lowest unemployment rate of any industrialized state had become the highest, the highest per capita spending on highways the lowest, and the best pupil-teacher ratio in the nation the worst. Over 55 percent of California's business leaders claimed to be planning to relocate or expand out of state, and a 30-percent increase in population during the 1980s, from twenty-three to almost thirty million was accompanied by a 200-percent rise in the inmate population of maximum and medium-security prisons now being ringed with "death fences" to electrocute escapees.

I read the principal planner for the Southern California Association of Governments was predicting, "Those who are able to take their skills and move will be increasingly likely to do so." The president of a Los Angeles manufacturing concern believed the state was "right on top of a cliff." The editor of the *San Diego Tribune* detected "a deep disenchantment . . . a dejection born of overblown dreams." "This dream of California as a golden place has now turned sour," a Hollywood agent said. "Half my friends now own guns."

The *California Dream Report,* a telephone survey of 632 Californians conducted in 1992 by the San Francisco office of the advertising agency Young and Rubicam, reported 65 percent of all Californian heads of households believing "the best time to achieve the California Dream was in the past." Only 19 percent considered it "alive and well."

The most offbeat stories and statistics were the most telling, and depressing.

In 1991, U-Haul reported 10 percent more people renting vehicles to leave California than returning them from other states. Yet during this same year, more people moved to California than left, indicating those leaving the state had enough possessions to fill a modest trailer, while those arriving, did not. Hundreds of Los Angeles residents attended a course at The Learning Annex titled Escape from L.A., during which an instructor recommended becoming involved in the community affairs of their new hometowns, in order to stop them becoming too much like California. Surfers complained overpopulation was forcing them to surf at night and even then, one said, he went out at one A.M. and found people competing for waves. Lifeguards in Los Angeles carried handcuffs.

A newsletter for people fed up with California, *The Greener Pastures Gazette,* ran classified advertisements for bargain properties in western Kentucky and Gold Beach, Oregon—"like Carmel, 20 years ago." A display advertisement for Bartlesville, Oklahoma, proclaimed, "We want you here!"

Had it really come to this? A reverse migration of the children and grandchildren of the Okies? Were their roots in California so shallow they could yank them up at the first bad news in 150 years, returning to the dust bowl with their one-way U-Hauls stuffed with booty accumulated during the golden years?

Even the celebrities were bailing out. Called to explain her move from an idyllic small town in Washington to New Mexico, Shirley MacLaine, evidencing an eagerness to vilify the place where she had prospered that was becoming typical, remarked, "There are too many Californians now in Washington. . . . I didn't go from California to be with Californians."

On a flight to San Francisco I read an article in *House and Garden* by Joan Didion and John Gregory Dunne describing their new New York City apartment. Their dining-room table had once sat in their Brentwood patio, and their favorite piece of furniture was a partners' desk from the state capitol at Sacramento. A Lucite box preserved a wreath of dried santolina from their garden. They sounded like White Russians in Paris decorating rooms with icons and portraits of Romanoffs. "We moved back to New York City on a whim," they wrote. "We had lived in Los Angeles for twenty-four years, but neither of us was working on a book. We felt stale, settled, restless." But before, when Californians became "restless," they moved to another part of California.

The bad news about California was infected with a nostalgia that reminded me of Hawaii, another endangered paradise whose residents have cultivated the selective memories of exiles and refugees. A University of California regent missed "vast areas of orange groves and open space." A Los Angeles artist missed "a sense of neighborhood . . . and ocean air that doesn't smell of sewage." The former owner of the San Francisco Giants missed "freedom of movement . . . the ability to get in one's car and drive someplace in a reasonable amount of time."

I called the filmmaker whose Los Angeles move had made me so envious in the 1970s. He said I should hurry if I wanted to find him in Pacific Palisades, because "I'm getting the fuck out of this place as soon as possible." He and his wife were considering Virginia, perhaps northern New England. "Hey, what's it like up where you live?" he asked.

I found the pessimism unsettling. I had always wished California well, if only selfishly, because someday I might need it. So I took no pleasure in discovering the newest California fad was leaving it, in seeing headlines like "CALIFORNIANS BET ON LAS VEGAS, ARIZONA — SPIC 'N'

SPAN COMMUNITIES ARE LURE," or in reading that 49 percent of Californians believed another state or country was the "best place to achieve the California Dream."

The most sinister document I found before leaving for California was a 1972 report of the California Tomorrow Foundation titled the *California Tomorrow Plan*. CALIFORNIA ZERO was the California of 1972 (now widely considered a golden age). Its environment was being misused "to the point where amenities are rapidly disappearing, social order gives way to turmoil. . . ." It was threatened by air pollution, expensive housing, excessive water use, "signs of educational failure," depletion of physical resources, and increased population—"a contributing cause of every environmental and social problem in the state."

CALIFORNIA TWO was the "thriving, beautiful" California that might emerge by the year 2000 if the foundation's recommendations for strict statewide zoning and planning, and "rational limits" on population growth were adopted.

The alternative, CALIFORNIA ONE, was "the logical future consequence of CALIFORNIA ZERO," a "tortured place" that would "surely come to pass" by the year 2000 if present policies continued. It was described as follows: "Cities have spread out and joined together north and south, taking over thousands of square miles. . . . The agricultural character of many regions disappears entirely. . . . The state continues to assume a responsibility to provide water to match or even to encourage growth or development. . . . Remaining salmon and steelhead fisheries are destroyed. . . . People continue to rely on the automobile. . . . Traffic congestion increases even with additional freeways. . . . Run-down core areas have expanded—accompanied by crime, drug problems, discontent, and a near-paralysis of public services. . . . Natural disasters are still not rationally planned for. . . . Seismic dangers are acknowledged by adoption of statewide building-code standards. But there is no serious seismic zoning. Fires continue to be an annual, late-summer trauma in southern California. New tract development continues along tinder-dry hillsides and canyons. . . . An increasing number of crimes involve the use of guns. . . . Private security services expand, and closed-circuit television and other alarm systems are used increasingly by small businessmen and householders to prevent robberies. The threat of crime has grown to the point where night time foot traffic in major cities has almost ceased. Protective fortifications of various kinds surround many areas. . . . The failure to solve the problems of political social inequities, or to meet urban and environmental problems, causes sporadic demonstrations and riots."

At the time, this pessimistic scenario was attacked for being alarmist, but if you believed the scary literature I was reading, it rather accurately described the California of the 1990s, a place where the California Dream had been stood on its head.

The Dream was supposed to mean outdoor living, natural beauty, and drawing inspiration from nature, but I was reading about high-school athletics scheduled in the evening when cooler weather chased away smog, and about how only 4 percent of California household heads had included "the Beauty of Nature," "Mountains," or "Redwoods/Beautiful Trees" in their dream. Twice as many mentioned a new television or "major appliance," and the *California Dream Report* summarized, "We found that the California Dream is defined in materialistic terms."

The California of my dream was friendly and open, but I was reading that the San Fernando Valley, which ten years ago had not had a single gated or guarded community, now had over a hundred, that 16 percent of all Californians were said to live in a "secured dwelling," and that the Los Angeles County Dispute Resolution Service reported quarrels between neighbors rising from 10 percent of their caseload in the mid-1980s to 30 percent by 1992.

My California meant mobility and cars, particularly convertibles. But a carjacking epidemic hit San Francisco after I arrived and according to the "crime-stopper tips" only an idiot parked next to a car with people in it, traveled in a curbside lane after dark, or failed to check the backseat and undercarriage before climbing in. "Drive with the car locked and the windows rolled up no matter what the weather is," one chief of police advised, "close the sunroof, and if you have a convertible keep your roof up at all times." If these were the rules, what was the point of California?

Once the main threats to the Dream had been drought, wildfire, and earthquakes. But with the Dream turned upside down, a few Californians longed for an earthquake to wipe the slate clean. The remedy was not new, although the emotions behind it had become less playful.

According to historian Kevin Starr, the architect Arthur Page Brown was so discouraged by the inferior nature of San Francisco's buildings that in 1894 he suggested a great earthquake and fire as its best hope for rebuilding as a distinguished seaport. After the 1906 earthquake, Ambrose Bierce wrote, "Of all the Sodoms and Gomorrahs in our modern world, [San Francisco] is the worst. There are not ten righteous (and courageous) men there. It needs another quake. . . ."

And after the 1989 earthquake that struck Northern California during the World Series and became known as "Loma Prieta" for the mountain near its epicenter, T-shirts and bumper stickers proclaimed NATURE BATS LAST! and San Francisco author Marc Reisner argued in *The New York Times Magazine* he would not be "staring at unseen corpses" on the collapsed Oakland freeway if such elevated highways and other "gargantuan wizardry" had not been constructed to "snub nature." He asked Los Angeles residents, "How many more people are you going to squeeze into your deadly arid little basin? What are you going to do when your aqueducts are destroyed? When your freeways come tumbling down? When the mobility you have so assiduously pursued bites you back, paralyzing you?"

While I was in California I ran into people hoping for the Big One. They all said, "only if no one's killed," although they knew this was an impossible condition. Many applauded Loma Prieta for mortally wounding the detested Embarcadero Freeway, succeeding where years of petitions and lawsuits had failed in opening San Francisco's waterfront to sunlight. At least an earthquake proved that underneath the asphalt nature was alive. If you believed in God, well, here was His handiwork continuing. If you believed environmental catastrophes more threatening than economic ones, why not root for an earthquake to burst an aqueduct and impose some rationing, or bring down some interchanges and encourage mass transit, and give Californians the opportunity to rebuild paradise.

My head told me the California declinists were right, and that adults do not wish for what could be the greatest national disaster since the Civil War unless they already consider themselves facing a catastrophe; but my heart wanted to believe their pessimism was another California fad, the surf music of the nineties. My head said these were facts; my heart said that in California I would discover other ones, perhaps less stubborn, but more true.

To find them I needed a route, preferably one that would impose some discipline and prevent me from stacking the deck for or against California. I imagined the ideal one resembling the hollow knife a cheesemaker plunges into a round and withdraws with a sample, deep from the heart.

I stared at road maps and relief maps, maps of climate, topography, and population, maps drawn by Frémont before the Gold Rush, and by Mexican padres before Frémont. Nothing grabbed me. The equator had jumped off the globe, an obvious around-the-world route. But the obvious Californian ones were all flawed. Its rivers were short, and silted by logging or shriveled by dams. Much of its coast was too rugged to support a large population. If I took Interstate 5 down its middle, I would see truck stops, agribusiness, and mountains. U.S. 395 down the east side of the Sierras promised ranches sucked dry to water Los Angeles.

When a friend suggested the San Andreas Fault I ordered the *Fault Map of California (Fourth Printing, 1988)* from the state Division of Mines and Geology. It unfolded to the size of a small rug and showed the San Andreas to be a graceful curve, instead of the brutal straight line I had imagined. It flirted with the north coast from Cape Mendocino to San Francisco, left the Pacific for the last time south of San Francisco at Daly City, then continued for five hundred miles under tract houses and reservoirs, garlic fields and oil fields. It threaded two mountain passes, nicked the edge of the Los Angeles sprawl, and split into two branches that squeezed Palm Springs. At the Salton Sea it fractured like a car's windshield before disappearing into Mexico.

I decided to follow its 750-mile length from north to south, starting in the small north-coast city of Eureka and ending at Bombay Beach on the Salton Sea. Where it was underwater, as it mostly was north of San Francisco, I would stick to the coast. When it came ashore, I would take whatever roads paralleled it, stop in the closest towns, and seek out people living over it.

When I settled on this itinerary I had imagined an underground line as invisible as the equator, only revealed when an earthquake plowed trenches or cracked asphalt. But after Loma Prieta a television network filmed the fault from a plane and I saw a shadowy scar, as if God had slashed California with a knife. Like every great travel route—like the Amazon, Pan-American Highway, or Trans-Siberian railway—the San Andreas had transformed what it touched, in its case creating the razorback ridges, folded green hills, soaring sea cliffs, pink mountains rising from desert floors, and jumbled, wine-friendly valleys—in short everything that made California beautiful. It had also littered the landscape with surprises: rivers paralleling the ocean instead of draining into it, zigzagging creeks, and straight lines of palm trees marching across desert floors.

Its main drawback was that although you could see its effects, it was not always an easy route to follow. What is known as the "San Andreas Fault zone" is a broad, complex zone of parallel cracks, ranging in width from a few hundred feet to almost a mile and forming a continuous break in the earth's crust between two of its tectonic plates— the Pacific and North American. These continuously moving plates of rock float on an underground sea of hot, soft rock known as magma. They are constantly shifting, usually so slowly their motion is imperceptible. It is estimated that the normal movement of the plates along the San Andreas is about two inches a year, the same as a human fingernail. In some places the Pacific plate slides easily north in relation to the North American, producing a phenomenon known as "creep" that manifests itself in cracked sidewalks and offset fences. But in others, the plates are locked, their rock no longer capable of bending to accommodate this natural movement. Pressure builds until the underground rock breaks. The suddenly unlocked plates surge past one another, releasing energy, and causing the vibrations that travel beneath and across the earth's surface in a few seconds, producing an earthquake. The "fault trace" is an earthquake's footprint, showing where it has broken the earth's crust.

I decided a single fault trace would be too narrow a road. Instead, I would follow the fault zone, calling it simply, as most Californians do, "the fault." I could see that although its physical landscape would be typically Californian, its social landscape would be somewhat more rural and less diverse. But no route is perfect, and the fault also offered the best place in the world to hunt for an earthquake. The one I missed in Ecuador had wiped out families down to fifth cousins, ending the histories of whole villages. A 1976 earthquake in China had killed 750,000, and in 1993 another threw a tidal wave at the Indonesian island of Balai Babi, drowning most of its one thousand residents and leaving few behind to mourn. But in California, where reinforcing bars and bracing are thought to guarantee mourners, temblors are less lethal, and the emotions surrounding them more complicated. Earthquakes seldom appeared high on the list of woes persuading people to leave California, but even before I left my home in upstate New York, I began wondering if they might explain the sudden repudiation of a state that no matter how beautiful, might suddenly, while you opened the cereal, combed your hair, or bathed the baby, strike you dead.

The paradox was this: The seismic forces making California so beautiful and prosperous had also made it spectacularly dangerous. A hundred million years of California earthquakes had created the soaring mountains where Bruff almost perished, the jagged coastal ranges that snagged Pacific rainstorms, and the jumble of rich-soiled valleys. Without the San Andreas Fault system there would be no Yosemite, agricultural industry, or vineyards, or as many people at risk. California would be safe, but flat.

I expected to find people along the fault struggling to reconcile this paradox, balancing the pleasure of living on a mountainside against the risk of it sliding into the valley, oscillating between imperturbability and panic, like the Palo Alto woman who told a *New York Times* reporter she never worried about quakes, then admitted accelerating and thinking, "Not now, please," whenever she jogged under a freeway overpass.

I expected the kind of denial resulting in California's first geological map being issued in 1916 without a single fault, and in the insouciance shown in 1906 by Alice B. Toklas's father, who, when told San Francisco had been rocked by an earthquake and was on fire, replied, "That will give us a black eye in the east," and went back to sleep.

ONE

TRIPLE
JUNCTION

❖

3

Eureka!

Past the *Eureka . . . You've Found It!* sign I drove up a steep bluff to Fort Humboldt State Historic Park for a view of a landscape dreary enough to provoke alcoholism on a Scandinavian scale. The fort was a threadbare attraction, a few reconstructed white clapboard buildings facing a parade ground. Drizzle fell from a low sky. Below, mudflats and warehouses circled a polluted bay. A pulp mill on a distant sandspit pumped white spirals of effluent. The low hills, a patchwork of second-growth timber, scrub, and meadow, resembled the fur of a sick cat. Houses sat on treeless lots because the sun shone so seldom no one wanted to block it with even a twig.

This was the view, and the weather, that prompted Ulysses S. Grant to write his wife on arrival in 1854, "I cannot say much about this place." A letter sent soon afterward began, "You do not know how forsaken I feel here!" After one famous drinking binge he fell off his horse and passed out in the underbrush. One Humboldt County historian blamed his mood on "leaden skies overhead, mud and flood underfoot, the great bay in front and the dismal forest behind." After four months he resigned his commission and returned to Illinois. There is no mention of Eureka in his otherwise detailed memoirs, and according to one of his biographers, the view from Fort Humboldt "can still send a chill of loneliness to the modern viewer."

Besides Grant, Eureka is famous for spectacular maritime disasters, the first skid row, and Bret Harte. The three years he spent in neighboring Arcata have been called the "three lost years" of his life and he left fleeing a lynch mob.

I fingered the keys of my rented Tempo and worried about what lay ahead. If Eureka was, as I had heard, the new Promised Land, the place to which people fled hoping to reassemble the California Dream, then what could it be like farther down the fault? I had come here on a whim, why not leave on one? The fault first came ashore in Northern California fifty miles south at Shelter Cove, but I had decided to start here because "Eureka!" was the state motto, carved into the seal, stamped on school textbooks, and shouted by pioneer James Ryan when, so the story went, he discovered the only stretch of solid land along Humboldt Bay's marshy shore. It meant California delivering the goods and was now on the lips of a new kind of pioneer. While unpacking in San Francisco, I had overheard a television news story describing former Bay Area residents finding a better life in Oregon and along this "unspoiled" north coast. Some had chosen Eureka, trading their suburban quarter acres for stately Victorians, and still having enough cash left to start a small business. The two news anchors followed this story with, "There go the moving vans" and "I can hear suitcases closing all over the Bay Area." *Eureka!*

Bruff had visited these north-coast counties in 1851 to pursue rumors of a shoreline strewn with gold nuggets. Instead he found damp weather and hemorrhoids that prostrated him on clammy beaches. His descriptions included: "drizzly all day and night," "cold and disagreeable weather," and "this is a very muddy place." He also encountered a former comrade, and I hoped that if that man's descendants had settled in this underpopulated county they might be easy to find.

Eureka also promised earthquakes. *Peace of Mind in Earthquake Country* by engineer Peter Yanev included a map showing "Seismicity and Tectonics of the Pacific Northwest" in which black dots of increasing size indicated the location and magnitude of previous temblors. Just thirty miles offshore Eureka, something resembling a giant oil slick marked the Mendocino Triple Junction. Here the splintering, dying San Andreas Fault met two others—the Mendocino fault and the southern boundary of the Cascadian Subduction Zone. Here the North American and Pacific plates separated by the San Andreas collided with the smaller Gorda plate. The result was one of the most seismically active, and arguably most dangerous, places on the West Coast. A damaging earthquake had struck Humboldt County, of which Eureka is the seat, an average of once every three years since 1906. Although several towns along the fault have declared themselves California's

"Earthquake Capital," Humboldt County offered the best odds for finding a quake.

I knew Gary Carver was a geologist before I met him in his office at Humboldt State University, but I would have guessed anyway. Not so much because of his muddy boots, or the powdered rock covering his clothes like dandruff, or the cracked hands that appeared tattooed with dirt, although these were all clues, but because of his manner. Like it or not, seismologists and geologists in California are authority figures. Although Carver had the enthusiasm and friendliness common to people who believe themselves to be living in the right place and devoting their lives to the right thing, and although the tangle of gray-streaked hair and pronounced features made me think of a Greek Orthodox monk, he still had the *gravitas* of a physician who knows that predictions, hope, miracles, and life-and-death decisions are expected. I was instinctively deferential, asking a few respectful questions, acting like a patient granted fifteen minutes with a medical specialist.

His subspecialty was paleoseismology, the study of fossilized phenomena left in the rock by earlier earthquakes. He was an expert in the Cascadian Subduction Zone and its Triple Junction. The San Andreas Fault was "small fish" by comparison, he said. His zone could produce a monster earthquake over 8.0, like the 9.6 striking Chile in 1960 that resulted in aftershocks five or six times greater than the great San Francisco quake of 1906. His excavations of saltwater marshes along Humboldt Bay had uncovered submerged tree stumps and whole fossilized forests that had once been above the high-tide mark but were now entombed in mud. They were persuasive evidence that Eureka had already experienced great Cascadian earthquakes and that its coastline had once dropped like an elevator.

"It's all brand-new stuff and I've only been working on it the last six or seven years," he said, his voice quickening and becoming less clinical as he explained a Cascadian Subduction Zone quake could mean flooding in low-lying areas, prolonged ground motion, and most scary of all, a tsunami, a giant wave rushing ashore and breaking thirty feet above the high-tide mark. "There aren't any sirens like in Hawaii," he said. "So we'll have little time to flee for higher ground. Just minutes." He had advised farmers to keep life vests in their barns and cautioned residents of remote Cape Mendocino towns to expect being cut off for weeks. If the shaking lasted over thirty seconds he recommended running uphill.

Everyone wanted Carver to make a prediction, at the very least the vague kind the United States Geological Survey (USGS) issues for segments of the San Andreas Fault along the lines of "a 30-percent risk of a 7.0 or greater in thirty years." But he would only say the risk of a subduction-zone quake in any given year was low, but present. Radiocarbon dating had placed the last one at the beginning of the eighteenth century. He seemed to anticipate a subduction-zone quake with shifting amounts of dread and excitement, and said the next one could strike in the next century, next year, or the next minute.

His findings had unsettled Humboldt County's emergency services. Their tsunami planning anticipated long-traveled waves of the kind sweeping southward after the great 1964 Alaskan quake, but a subduction-zone wave might begin only several hundred miles from Eureka and could come ashore in minutes. A draft supplement to the *Humboldt State University Multihazard Emergency Plan* he had helped write said, "This type of event would have the potential for being truly devastating for the Humboldt Bay region." It mentioned "the additional hazards of widespread liquefaction [the soil becoming liquid]" and the "destruction of even well-built structures."

"It's not inconceivable it might happen tomorrow. I would be surprised, but not overwhelmed," he told me. "Of course, if you look a hundred years ahead, then the probabilities *have* to creep up."

He had less to say about the San Andreas, only that its northern segment was an enigma, more complex and not as well defined as farther south, and harder to pinpoint because it was offshore. He was not even sure if it first hit the continent at Shelter Cove or farther south at Point Arena. The prevailing wisdom was Shelter Cove, but he had been unable to find conclusive proof. But regardless of where it ran, if I wanted to feel a shake, I had picked the right place. The last temblor had been only three days ago, and on average there was a "felt quake" in Humboldt County every three weeks.

Eureka was not ready for Gary Carver's tsunami, but at least it was trying to prepare for the sort of moderate earthquake that shook it every decade. Some downtown stores displayed printed signs in their windows—not voluntarily, I supposed, since they declared, THIS IS AN UNREINFORCED MASONRY BUILDING. UNREINFORCED MASONRY BUILDINGS MAY NOT BE SAFE IN THE EVENT OF A MAJOR EARTHQUAKE.

Downtown Eureka did not need this extra bad news. U.S. 101

funneled traffic from the only coastal route between Oregon and San Francisco through its heart on one-way streets. Half the storefronts were empty and their former names appeared in faint outline above their MOVING TO THE MALL placards like photographic negatives. I was told their former owners now worked as clerks in the Bayshore Mall. The big holdout was Daly's, a turn-of-the-century department store on three floors belonging to a five-store chain stretching from Fort Bragg in the south to Oregon. It was a courageous emporium, but an empty one. Its small departments carried well-chosen toys, housewares, and fashions. Its veteran clerks kept their eyes trained on the doors, watching for customers and I suppose wondering how long this dinosaur could last. Tim Daly of the founding family said the Bayshore Mall had hurt Eureka's downtown, but the new state seismic regulations would deliver the coup de grâce by demolishing more venerable buildings than any earthquake. Thirty-six unreinforced masonry ones (including half his store) needed retrofitting within the next two years to meet state standards. The average cost was $200,000 and no one could afford it, not the city, and certainly not the struggling merchants and owners. To demolish a building cost only $20,000, and its antique bricks, redwood interiors, columns, and cornices could be sold to newcomers fixing up Eureka's Victorian neighborhoods. Most of downtown Eureka was worth more down than up, so it would probably come down.

I checked my roster of the Washington City Miners against the motel telephone directory and made some calls, but no one had heard of Bruff or the Washington Miners. I took it to the Humboldt County Historical Society, hoping to match it with Eureka's pioneers, but instead found Helen Yunker, who had a mad crush on Ulysses Grant. "He was never a boozer, *never*!" she said, her voice rising. "All right, maybe he sometimes drank to excess, but so did everyone at that fort. He missed his family terribly, and those letters from his wife, they made him so sad. My goodness, what a love story!"

She had written to the *Reader's Digest* to complain about a quiz asking, "Which president was a boozer?" She was a docent in the local museum, where she sometimes hovered around Grant's portrait, listening for disrespectful comments. One day she noticed a stocky man with a scraggly beard admiring it. Her heart leaped. He resembled a young Ulysses and admitted being a distant relative. She had read every Grant biography, even his wife's, "because a wife will tell you what a man is like," and she was jealous, saying, "Mrs. Grant wasn't really *that* good-looking." She lowered her voice. "Her eyes were crossed and she wanted to have them fixed. But Ulysses said, 'No! I fell in love with you the way you are. Don't touch them.' " She corresponded with his biographers and delighted in every detail. Did I know he was deathly afraid of hospitals? That he turned his wineglass over at banquets because he knew his critics were watching? That his sister once said, "Oh, he's such a doll!" She slapped her desk with her palm. "What a modern thing to say. Oh, he's just such a person to me!"

I thought Grant would have liked her. Like him, she was stocky and handsome and had crammed several lives into one. She had migrated from Oklahoma, raised a family, sold real estate, opened a day-care center in Southern California, moved to the north coast after brain surgery to live with her son, and at the age of seventy was raising her eight-year-old granddaughter. Her family had expected her to watch soap operas. Instead she had explored the coast, looking for a good place to live. She had found it here. *Eureka!*

After several days in Eureka, it looked better to me. There were some fine blocks of restored Victorians, and an infrastructure of schools and parks that would have made it a celebrated urban treasure in a smaller state. Still, was this enough to compensate for the winter rains? The summer fogs lingering past noon and the coldest summers south of Juneau? I asked a bank executive why thousands of downstate Californians had abandoned families, friends, secure jobs, and sunshine to move here, calling themselves "pioneers," but having more in common with refugees. He said the explanation was downstate crime. When I asked the same question of the vice president of the chamber of commerce, who had just returned from promoting Eureka in Los Angeles, he said every businessman he met wanted to abandon California because of regulations, taxes, and quality-of-life issues. He was pushing Eureka as a "great second choice."

(No one would admit choosing Humboldt County because it was one of the state's last Caucasian redoubts, but I suspected this was also a factor. It was 92 percent white, less than 10 percent Hispanic, and 1 percent black. Its Asian population had been minuscule ever since a stray bullet fired during a late-nineteenth-century tong war had killed a beloved city councilman, and vigilantes tacked a sign onto a hangman's noose warning that any Chinaman staying in the county would be hanged. As late as 1937, the *Humboldt Times* boasted of the "unique distinction" of being the only California county without a single Oriental.)

A cheerful real-estate agent compared the housing market to waves from a typhoon breaking on a distant beach. The typhoon was Southern California, the waves were buyers fleeing to Eureka. Each wave was larger than the one before, and ready to pay more. Because people down south were having trouble selling, he was in a temporary trough between waves. He was not concerned. Every week brought inquiries from people desperate enough to leave their houses unsold. In the last two months, four families had walked into his office who were victims of drive-by shootings, including a father shot because his daughter had dated a member of the wrong gang, and a family sprayed with bullets in a fast-food restaurant. Their stories meant Eureka's boom was just beginning.

The heart and engine of this boom was Old Town, a twenty-three-block neighborhood of nineteenth- and early-twentieth-century commercial and residential buildings containing fine examples of Greek and Renaissance Revival, cast-iron, and Victorian architecture. It was a National Register Historic District and its cheap rents and generous spaces had attracted artists and entrepreneurs, helping to give Humboldt County the highest per capita number of artists in the state. Some newcomers were known as "equity refugees," because after cashing in their tract homes in the south and buying a Victorian, they had enough left to buy a business, or live as remittance men. Besides capital, they brought their obsessions with food and children, so Old Town had trendy restaurants and a vast storefront kids' gym. When I asked the proprietors of Old Town stores why they had moved here, they rattled off the predictable reasons—crowding, crime, pollution, freeways, bland suburbs, shopping malls, and high housing costs. Even the scruffiest-looking artists said they were searching for "values."

Lanell Haysmer, the "owner/artist" of the Many Hands Gallery, had arrived six months before from Santa Cruz, a city many Californians still consider paradise, but which she and her husband saw becoming an expensive bedroom community for San Jose. They had planned their move carefully, first listing the characteristics of an ideal small town: live theater, arts, affordable housing, on the ocean, fresh bagels, and good coffee. When she said it had also been important, "essential," they stay within California, I at first dismissed this as nostalgia, only later understanding it was also testimony to the vitality of the Dream, and its ability to reinvent itself.

Marty L'Heurault, who drove tourists through Old Town in his horse-drawn carriage dressed in black cape and top hat, said I would be amazed how many of his customers were Angelenos staying an extra day to investigate real estate. Before moving to Eureka, he and his wife had driven carriages through Central Park to support fledgling theater careers. When they had had enough of New York they headed west across the George Washington Bridge, taking their harnesses and life savings. "It was a big risk because we were unsure if the city council here would approve carriage rides, but we were pioneers."

Pioneer was a word falling from the lips of Eureka newcomers almost as easily as *values*. Once it had meant people who civilized a wilderness, now it connoted fresh bagels, good coffee, and antique carriage rides. None seemed aware, or to care, that they had picked Eureka for small-town "values" presumably in place when they arrived, or that their word *pioneer* had somewhat insulting connotations for those already living in a pioneering destination, particularly when they were frequently dismissed as "rednecks." (Although the fact that some of these Eureka "rednecks" were descended from real pioneers, who had in turn dismissed the original Native American inhabitants as "savages," did lend the situation a certain satisfying irony.)

This "redneck" epithet was everywhere, uttered in the same reflexive and offhand way the n-word once was in the South. I was not surprised to overhear an over-the-hill hippie in the Arcata environmental center curse "the fucking rednecks." But I paid attention when a liberal clergyman, a leading businessman, an artist, real-estate agent, and a journalist muttered about "rednecks." It could be a crude shorthand for people who disagreed with the speaker, or delivered as a statement of fact ("You have to understand, Thurston, this is redneck country"). It was usually just a casual slur.

The redneck/newcomer divide was social, cultural, economic, and even culinary. At a redneck restaurant I ate fried clam strips, coleslaw, and cream pies served by a grandmotherly fussbudget; at a newcomer eatery, a distracted young woman with modeling clay under her fingernails delivered a small portion of Thai chicken, brown rice, and spinach salad in a bitter vinaigrette. The newcomers went to Old Town, the rednecks liked the mall. It was art deco collectibles, jazz festivals, secondhand bookstores, natural-fiber clothing, and community theater groups versus greeting cards, country music, Sears, and multiplex movies. The newcomers came to escape the material world the rednecks longed for, and brought poetry readings, left-wing politics, expensive restaurants, health-food coops, alternative schools, and boutiques, nothing the rednecks wanted.

This one word, *values*, was where they met, although few realized it. When newcomers attributed Eureka's appeal to "traditional values," they meant multigenerational families, a commitment to neighborhoods and community institutions, and happiness derived from family life and friendships—which were all, whether they recognized it or not, redneck values.

4

Seth Kinman's Scalps

The historical marker set into a boulder on the shoreline of Woodley Island was so stingy with the facts it made me suspicious. It said only, INDIAN/GUNTHER ISLAND, SITE 67 (TOLOWOT) HAS BEEN DESIGNATED A NATIONAL HISTORIC LANDMARK (FOR IT) POSSESSES NATIONAL SIGNIFICANCE IN COMMEMORATING THE HISTORY OF THE UNITED STATES OF AMERICA.

Woodley and Indian islands were low, marshy ovals floating off Eureka's waterfront. While Woodley had a marina and an exit from the causeway connecting Eureka to the Samoa Peninsula's pulp mills, Indian Island was mostly a wildlife refuge and accessible only by boat. At first I thought this might explain why this enigmatic marker was here, instead of on the island it commemorated. No one at the marina knew what of "national significance" had happened on Indian Island. The *Eureka! Visitors Guide* praised the "miners, loggers, and fishermen [who] made their mark in this unsettled wilderness," but ignored Indian Island. The *Eureka Visitors Map* identified among the "Things to Do and See," the Fishermen's Memorial Statue on Woodley Island. This was a fifteen-foot bronze fisherman with a plaque listing all twenty-eight Eureka fishermen lost at sea since 1951 by name. One could easily have left Eureka without learning anything about Indian Island. Perhaps that was the point, since, as I discovered at the Humboldt County Library, the event of "national significance" was among the cruelest Indian massacres in U.S. history, one earning Eureka the nickname "Murderville."

Indians died fast in California, where their population fell from 100,000 in 1848 to 50,000 by 1870, and even faster in Humboldt County,

34

where 10,000 perished between 1850 and 1860. The earliest massacres were revenge for a specific Indian crime, imagined or real. By the end of the decade they had become more cold-blooded. Settlers along the Eel River just south of Eureka held the Indians collectively responsible for cattle thefts, hunting them like deer and offering ten dollars for a scalp, "a most effective and economic remedy to get rid of the hated savages," one correspondent wrote the *Humboldt Times*. Meanwhile, Eureka's sheriff, district attorney, county treasurer, and the editor of the *Humboldt Times* formed a committee to support the vigilantes, urging them to engage in "active operations."

At the time, the Wiyot people of northern Humboldt County lived in isolated settlements along bays and river mouths and numbered about seven hundred. They ate seafood, wove baskets, worshiped shell mounds, and were never accused of stealing property or murdering a settler. A San Francisco newspaper called them "friendly Indians, the most defenseless and degraded of the race, entirely destitute of the bold and murderous spirit which characterizes other red men." The army commander at Fort Humboldt praised them for "acting as spies upon the mountain tribes . . . who might come for spoilation and murder."

During the last week of February 1860, several hundred Wiyot had gathered on Indian Island for their annual religious festival. Following tradition, the men departed camp after the final ceremony, leaving their women and children asleep. Before dawn, seven white vigilantes crept ashore and swept across the island swinging axes, knives, and clubs, killing at least sixty Wiyot, mostly women and children. This was one of three coordinated massacres occurring that same morning. Settlers also attacked Wiyot camps on South Beach and at the mouth of the Eel River, in both cases singling out women of childbearing age. People living near Eureka's waterfront awoke at four A.M. to the cries of dying Indians. Robert Gunther, who had just purchased the island, sacred to the Wiyot for centuries, from a sea captain who had himself only recently staked a claim, reported, "a scream went up from many voices."

At first light, he rowed across to the place where he would soon build a three-story house praised as "the picture of Victorian elegance." He saw "corpses lying all around, and all women and children, but two. . . .One old Indian, who looked to be a hundred years old, had his skull split, and still he sat there shivering." The only survivor was a baby boy whom he found lying in his dead mother's arms, suckling her breast. "On the way home, we planned to bring the parties to justice," he wrote, "[but] we soon found that we had better keep our mouths shut."

Other whites toured the killing grounds. The commander of Fort Humboldt, Major G. J. Raines, called it "a spectacle of horror, of unexampled description—babes, with brains oozing out of their skulls, cut and hacked with axes, and squaws exhibiting the most frightful wounds in death which imagination can paint . . . an atrocity and horror unparalleled not only in our own country, but even in history."

Bret Harte, then an unknown reporter for a weekly paper in neighboring Union (now Arcata), watched corpses being laid out on a pier. He saw "old women wrinkled and decrepit by weltering blood, their brains dashed out and enveloped in their long grey hair. Infants scarce a span long, with their faces cloven with hatchets and their bodies ghastly with wounds," and could think of "no wrong that a babe's blood can atone for." After his article appeared, a cavalry detachment had to rescue him from a lynch mob.

The *Humboldt Times* justified the massacres as the "fruits" of men made desperate by "degraded diggers [Indians]," and denounced Indian lovers like Harte who "shed crocodile tears." The sheriff of Humboldt County wrote to the *San Francisco Bulletin*, arguing the perpetrators had been made "desperate" by attacks on their cattle. (Major Raines called him a "spokesman" for "the assassins.") A grand jury announced itself unable to identify the perpetrators. One member, a rancher named Hank Larabee, identified by an army report as "an accomplice and actor in the massacre at Indian Island and South Beach," later boasted of killing sixty Indian infants with his own hatchet at various slaughtering grounds. "Indian bodies came down the river [Larabee Creek] like driftwood," his neighbor reported, "all with Larabee's mark on them: ripped and slit open from their throats to their bellies."

Learning about this massacre in the town where it happened made it seem more immediate, particularly since Humboldt County still had a Larabee and Larabee Creek, while Van Dyke Court in Eureka was named after the newspaper editor who called for the "extermination" of local Indians. Feese Avenue honored the county treasurer who founded the committee to equip "Indian volunteers," and Hadley Peak was named for A. A. Hadley (perhaps an ancestor of the Hadley whose house shook on my earthquake tape?), who organized Indian hunts the army condemned as "outrageous and murderous." The failure to indict the perpetrators in 1860 tainted anyone claiming a pioneer ancestor. In-

stead of looking at elderly men and wondering what they had done between 1939 and 1945, as I did in Germany, I wondered where someone's
great-great-grandfather had been at four A.M. on February 26, 1860.

I searched for Wiyot artifacts at the Clarke Museum, a splendid
marble-and-granite Italianate Renaissance palace that congratulated itself for being "noted statewide and nationwide for Native American
Indian basketry and other artifacts." It featured the artifacts of two vanished cultures: pre-1960 urban Eureka, and pre-1860 Northern California Indians.

The tributes to prewar children's toys and vanished Eureka movie
palaces depressed me. The sturdy metal tricycles reminded me of my
daughters' plastic three-wheelers, scruffy and cracked after six months.
The usherettes photographed in front of art deco cinemas, wearing air-
line-hostess uniforms and holding flashlights, made me think of the
sticky-floored multiplex in the Bayshore Mall.

The Native American annex displayed scores of baskets, canoes,
dance regalia, eating bowls, and clothing from across the continent. But
the only Wiyot objects, in a museum built on their former lands, were a
doll basket and ceremonial hat. A faded card identified them as
"Wyiot" [sic]. When I complained, a docent said in five years no one
had noticed the misspelling.

The museum also had on permanent exhibit the moccasins and
buckskin jacket of Humboldt County's legendary frontiersman Seth
Kinman. His portrait showed a hulking man in a long white beard
who, except for the cold, shrewd eyes, resembled a Victorian Santa
Claus. He had arrived in California the same year as Bruff, also showing considerable bravery during the overland journey. Neither found
gold in the Sierras and both were lured north by rumors of gold strikes.
Then their stories diverged. While Bruff behaved as if he was in a
Washington with mountains, Kinman reinvented himself, changing in
a flash from a Midwestern farmer into a buckskin-clad hunter. Bruff
refused to publish his memoirs except in their unedited entirety and rejected an offer of $10,000 to turn his sketches into a popular entertain-
ment of the time called a panorama; Kinman turned a pile of elk horns
into a gold mine of publicity. Bruff refused to shoot an Indian; Kinman
used them, dead or alive, as bear bait. Bruff returned East to obscurity;
Kinman stayed to become famous and prosperous. A decade later,
while Kinman was being entertained at the White House, Bruff was
back on his high stool at the Treasury Department, copying blueprints
and paying off his California debts.

Kinman had the good fortune to arrive in the Eel Valley when it was thickly populated with trusting elk who were easily butchered. He supplied meat to Fort Humboldt and set a local record by shooting 240 in ten months, so many their antlers littered the ground around his cabin, becoming a nuisance. He fashioned them into a fence, then into chairs. When James Buchanan, a fellow Pennsylvanian, was elected president in 1856, Kinman built him an elk-antler chair that was "unequalled in any part of the world," according to the *Humboldt Times*. He traveled to Washington to present it in person and "woke one fine morning to find myself famous," he said. A New York newspaper praised his "rich, picturesque hunter's dress." Buchanan extolled him as "honest, sincere, and brave," and made him a salaried Indian agent.

He returned to California to become one of its first professional eccentrics, appearing everywhere in fringed buckskins with "Ole Cotton Bale," a rifle reputed to have fired the shot killing the commanding British general at the Battle of New Orleans. According to county historian Lynwood Carranco, he "sometimes" regarded Indians as human, sometimes as "predatory animals to shoot at." He admitted scouting for parties of vigilantes who "slaughtered and captured Indians," and his favorite story described a wounded grizzly charging him and his Indian guide. When he saw the bear gaining, he tripped the Indian. "The bear chewed him up a while, and then left him, and the Injun finally got well," he reported. "Injuns can stand a great deal of hurtin' and not die."

His Table Bluff Ranch overlooked Humboldt Bay and the site of one of the three 1860 massacres. His neighbors must have been among the vigilantes; there were simply not that many whites along the Eel River, and if he missed out on the butchery, it was probably due more to chance than scruples. Shortly afterward, he opened a small museum in San Francisco praised by the *Bulletin* as "an instructive place of amusement." It had bearskins, elk chairs, and a collection of Indian scalps. When he told an audience how he had sawed them off, the ladies "looked horrified and aghast."

He returned to Washington to present two elkhorn chairs to President Lincoln. Headlines announced EVEN THE LADIES HELD UP THEIR CHILDREN TO LOOK AT THE FRONTIERSMAN, and when he fiddled "Root Hog or Die," a witness remembered, "It took old Abe so down that he laughed until his stove pipe hat fell on the floor." He stayed for months, becoming a frequent dinner guest at the White House and a persistent salesman for photographs of himself from a stand outside Congress. He posed for Civil War photographer Matthew Brady and was at Ford's Theater the night Lincoln was shot. When he returned home the *Humboldt Times* said, "He has made a lion of himself, and we hope he will live long enough to enjoy the reputation which he has been smart enough to win." He spent the remainder of his days running a saloon on Table Bluff, delighting customers with a stuffed grizzly bear mounted on wheels, and his scalps.

Andrew Genzoli, Humboldt County's most prolific historian, wrote in 1971 that "the Indians of northwestern California knew about earthquakes. Their experiences are to be found in some of their traditional stories and songs. They can be regarded as our first 'observers,' but few people ever bothered to ask what they knew about the trembling earth."

Gary Carver's wife, Debra, had made herself an expert in Native American earthquake legends. By scouring century-old anthropological treatises and newspapers, she had uncovered evidence of north-coast earthquakes and tidal waves predating the first written records. She found Yurok myths recorded at the turn of the century by the Berkeley anthropologist A. L. Kroeber, including "How the Prairie Became Ocean," which went, "The land sank . . . [where] earthquake ran about, then the water would fill those [depressed] places." After this quake, animals that "had lived on the prairie where the ocean was now" disappeared, replaced by salmon and whales.

In a Tolowa legend, a man warned his son, "When the earth shakes, look at your canoe. If it's sinking, get up on the reefs and run for high ground." The son later remembered this advice and survived a tidal wave that left the corpses of wild animals floating in meadows.

Her Wiyot earthquake material appeared more sketchy. She had found an 1855 newspaper article that described a small earthquake that shook Humboldt Bay, and reported how afterward the Wiyot warned settlers that a tidal wave might follow (proof their legends connected earthquakes to tidal waves). After the whites convinced them this was superstition, they remained in their camps along the shoreline, performing ceremonies to quiet the earth.

I thought it was not impossible that among the Wiyot massacred at Indian Island were storytellers who knew legends that might have narrowed or expanded the timetable for the next Cascadian Zone quake. Nor impossible that in killing so many Indians, pioneers across California had destroyed centuries of seismic history.

The great-granddaughter of the massacre's sole survivor—the boy found suckling his dead mother—was a woman named Cheryl Seidner who worked in the student-aid office of Humboldt State. We ate lunch in the student union surrounded by the usual multiracial California student population, but no one looked remotely like her, heavy-set but graceful, with fine features and all-American freckles. She spoke with the careful diction of an African schooled by missionaries, making every word seem important. When she held my eyes and said, "Listen, I did not even *know* I was an Indian until I was seven years old," it seemed to take her forever to complete the sentence.

She first learned about the massacre when her grandmother described how her great-grandfather's father swam to the mainland after watching from hiding as the whites butchered his family. No one accused him of cowardice. If he had not escaped, her family would have lost all knowledge of itself.

She said the surviving infant took the name "Jerry James" and died in 1929. His son, her grandfather, was typical of his generation. He refused to teach his descendants Wiyot because he feared it might prevent them succeeding in white society. She was certain their surviving culture did not mention earthquakes. Most of the old stories had died at Indian Island, and the only legend she knew was a Pomo one about how five great turtles lived underneath California, causing earthquakes by rubbing their shells together.

She considered the massacre a simple land grab. Many prominent Eurekans had participated, and covered it up. Their descendants continued the conspiracy. Why else had the "historical turnout" onto Indian Island been deleted from the original plans for the Samoa causeway? Why else had most Wiyot, herself included, never set foot on Indian Island? Why else had the Woodley Island marker remained in storage for twenty-seven years before Wiyot complaints got it erected? Talk of a new Indian Island marker made some white Eurekans uncomfortable, particularly those believing themselves descended from the murderers. A city official of pioneer stock had reportedly said, "I'm not going to let the Indians make me feel guilty."

The Wiyot and their supporters were raising money to build a more informative memorial. It would cost $10,000, resemble the interpretive signs at national parks, and have fiberglass panels describing the massacre. Seidner daydreamed about the dedication. No bands or feasts. Instead, the Wiyot would circle Indian Island in boats and conduct ceremonies for the dead. The guests of honor would be descendants of the three men who witnessed the massacre from hiding. It would happen on Columbus Day.

When we began lunch she had been cheerful and slightly amused by my search for a Wiyot legend that might help predict an earthquake. When she started off saying, "I don't mean to be bitter or hostile, but I have to state the facts, sometimes without a smile," she was smiling. But after describing the massacre again, she had stopped. "The fact is that white people killed my family," she said, pausing almost a second between each carefully enunciated word. "It happened, like the Holocaust, and I can't forget it. It wasn't really that long ago. Like, I mean we're only talking great-grandparents here.

"Did you know that during the floods of 1955 and 1964 my father risked his life rowing out to save people. No one thanked him for it, not the Coast Guard, not the mayor. He was also a fantastic baseball player for the Crabs. Do you think he got any publicity or credit? No. The Wiyot are still invisible."

She was right. An hour later I found the index for volumes one to sixty of the *California Historical Quarterly* in a Eureka secondhand bookstore. There was not a single entry under "Wiyot." But for J. Goldsborough Bruff, who had been a Californian for less than two years, there were twenty-three.

5

Seth Kinman's Homestead

Before leaving Eureka, I visited the rancheria near Table Bluff where two hundred Wiyot lived in a boggy hollow beneath a windswept plateau. Stripped cars sat on cinder blocks, mongrels strained against frayed lengths of gray rope, and houses looked slapped together from driftwood. A hand-lettered sign on a rust-streaked trailer identified it as TRIBAL HEADQUARTERS. Inside I met Albert James, the rancheria's chairman and Cheryl Seidner's uncle. He worked in an office so stuffed with files documenting Wiyot sufferings there was scarcely room to swivel a chair. I displaced a stack of injustices in order to sit down, sending up plumes of dust.

Hanging over his left shoulder was a blurred 1920 photograph credited to "U.C. Berkeley Department of Anthropology," the only known one of his grandfather Jerry James, the infant survivor of Indian Island. Its placement made it impossible not to compare the two men, which was perhaps the point. Both had broad faces, widow's peaks, looked younger than their ages (James was seventy but his crew cut was only flecked with gray), and stared at you with the exhausted eyes of a POW.

James said of course there must have been earthquake legends. They had been part of religious ceremonies, although thanks to the massacre and theft of Wiyot regalia, this religion was "just about gone." The killers and their accomplices had looted the Wiyot camps, hauling away treasure by the wagon load. The stealing continued today. White families went to South Point on Sunday outings, bringing metal detectors, shovels, and packed lunches. Off-road vehicles churned up Wiyot

burial sites on the northern spit of the Samoa Peninsula, while a homeless encampment defiled sites on the southern one. His people had once
picnicked there, but there were shootings and rumors of tuberculosis,
and they were saddened to stumble on the excavations of the weekend
treasure hunters. A retired city councilman had earned the nickname
"digger" for his skill at unearthing Wiyot sites. A dentist bragged of
excavating 382 graves. "That's right," he said, "we know the exact
number."

Was I aware, he wondered, that his grandfather's village, a Wiyot
cemetery, and the site of the corral where soldiers gathered the survivors of Indian Island for relocation to distant reservations were all beneath the Bayshore Mall? He had argued that the noted anthropologist
Llewellen Loud had found a Wiyot village there in 1918, but the city's
anthropologist claimed the village was only nearby. Now that a Super
Safeway was planned for *that* spot, they were saying the Wiyot had
lived somewhere else. James shopped in the mall anyway. "We all do."
But when he browsed in Payless Shoes or Radio Shack he never forgot
he was walking over the corral where his ancestors had died of cholera,
or that when he ate pizza in the atrium, he dined over their graves.

On weekends and holidays he and his wife searched for Wiyot
possessions in museums across California. In Sacramento they had
found bones, perhaps from Indian Island. He had written the Smithsonian demanding a list of its Wiyot holdings. "I wish I could show you
how short it is," he said, shuffling through his files. "We know darned
well they're not going to tell us everything they've got."

He did know Wiyot possessions had decorated Humboldt County
curio cases for generations. Many white families considered them heirlooms, but he suspected they knew their provenance. One pioneer descendant had told him his wife's grandfather had been asked to join one
of the murder parties, but at the last minute his wife persuaded him to
stay home. "Oh yes, you can count on it," he said, "these pioneer families, they know their history."

What did I think of this? And this? And this? he asked after
every example of the white man's injustice. What I thought was that
perhaps he was including me in the ranks of the grave robbers, here to
make off with a piece of Wiyot culture, and even if an earthquake legend was buried in his files, he was unlikely to share it. But I still asked if
any Wiyot songs mentioned tidal waves or earthquakes.

He said turn-of-the-century anthropologists had gathered songs
on cylindrical records. He had spent hours trying to decipher the

words, but the static was overwhelming. His father had taught him some songs, but none mentioned earthquakes. When they visited Indian Island, he and his wife sang them to the shell mounds and he imagined his grandfather as a baby, screaming under the weight of his dead mother.

Did I know Eureka's mayor lived on Indian Island? They got along. "Although that's about all you can say." He handed me, without comment, an article in which the mayor was reported as saying, "To me, living on the island is like living at the turn of the century, in the 1880s."

Did I know that he had to ask for permission to visit the island? He had tried to reclaim the island for his people, suggesting a museum there to attract visitors. When the city rejected the idea he proposed a recreated Wiyot village. It would be closed to the public, but visible from the causeway. He imagined tourists saying, "Gee, I guess Indian people lived there once," then wondering why they did not anymore. When this, too, was rejected he joined Cheryl Seidner in demanding a sign. He reckoned if the federal government could spend millions erecting a Holocaust museum in Washington, then the Wiyot could have fiberglass panels on Woodley Island.

Like Seidner, he offered no apology for making whites feel bad, and after an hour of listening to him, I was feeling good and guilty. Had the ocean been less stormy when Bruff sailed down this coast after abandoning his gold diggings on the Trinity River, his sloop might have entered Humboldt Bay as scheduled, and he might have disembarked and stayed, sending for his family and making a life here like Seth Kinman. I wondered if his generous attitude toward Indians would have survived a decade in Humboldt County.

James had saved his best story for last. Had I known that in 1960, the centenary of the massacre, the federal government had declared the Wiyot a "non-tribe," too small to be recognized by the Bureau of Indian Affairs and qualify for financial aid? The Wiyot sued and for twenty years he and his wife had haunted libraries and county courthouses, collecting proof of their existence. But even after they won their lawsuit in 1980 and collected $1.3 million in damages in 1990, the struggle was not over.

You might think whites would be sympathetic to Wiyot turning up, cash in hand, to purchase land once theirs. Instead, the Wiyot plan to build a new rancheria had outraged nearby Loleta. Residents protested, signed petitions, and wrote to newspapers, raising objections on environmental grounds and forcing James to hire attorneys and consultants. Newcomers to Humboldt County were his fiercest enemies. He promised the rancheria's population would be under a hundred, but they feared crime and graffiti and were unmoved. They had seen this happen downstate. The Wiyot were obviously building a ghetto.

"Finally we gave up," he said. "We preferred to be near town but they didn't want us, so we proposed building up here on Table Bluff, but even then they objected." A retiree living on the adjoining property protested to the State Historic Commission that the new rancheria would have an "adverse impact" on her house. It was an "historic site," she explained, the original homestead of Humboldt's most famous pioneer, Seth Kinman.

The state ordered the Wiyot to prepare an "Historical Impact Assessment" and James and his supporters spent weeks in libraries and public-records halls, collecting material to blacken Kinman's reputation. The state functionary called upon to make a decision professed to be in a quandary. Both sides had merit, she said, "On the one hand we have these Indians who want to move here; and on the other we have this home of an early pioneer."

Remembering the hearing made James furious. "This Kinman guy bragged about killing Indians, and because of him an Indian people have to stay where they are. No, I don't think so. I don't think that's right!"

Finally the Wiyot won a partial victory. They could build, but only if they planted rows of trees to spare Kinman's old homestead the upsetting view of their new rancheria. When James explained this he stared at me like Seidner, unblinking, with his grandfather's vacant eyes, finally asking, "I wonder if you find this as amusing and ironic as we do?"

I drove up to the Table Bluff plateau and parked above the construction site. It was spectacular but lonely, with an unimpeded view of the bay and ocean. Because it was one of the last buildable coastal sites in California, downstate refugees often stopped to ask for a prospectus. The houses nearing completion were typical tract ones, comfortable but not ostentatious. By comparison, Kinman's former house was a shambles.

Tomorrow, next year, or sometime next century, whenever Gary Carver's Cascadian Subduction Zone earthquake strikes, perhaps surprising Humboldt County slightly more than if Wiyot oral histories had survived, the Wiyot will have a grand and relatively safe view of the disaster from their new rancheria. They will watch a giant wave rolling across the Samoa Peninsula, submerging the pulp mills, then sweeping across Humboldt Bay, over Indian Island, and into downtown Eureka. They may even see the homes and farms of the descendants of their ancestors' murderers being washed out to sea, while their owners swim for their lives.

6

Jerry Hurley's
Headaches

Californians grumble about the lack of short-term earthquake predictions, but I thought the scientists of the United States Geological Survey were performing quite a feat by offering the odds for a major earthquake in a certain location within a twenty-to-thirty-year window, particularly considering how many centuries can pass without one striking a particular segment of a fault. Nonetheless, a forecast of a 60-percent probability within thirty years was not going to lead me to the next California earthquake. To find one in the next few months I could not depend on traditional science. Instead, I had to consider any theory, no matter how crackpot it seemed, including claims that earthquakes were routinely foreshadowed by geysers, advertisements for lost pets, an increase in roadkill, UFO sightings, high tides, full moons, a surge in AM radio waves, disoriented homing pigeons, apparitions of the Virgin Mary in the Egyptian village of Zeitun, and Jerry Hurley's headaches.

I stopped in Fortuna just south of Eureka to ask Hurley if I should hang around Humboldt County waiting for an earthquake. He is an earthquake "sensitive" who believes he suffers headaches, ringing ears, and an irregular heartbeat in the weeks and days preceding a significant earthquake and credits himself with predicting Loma Prieta.

I expected a hypochondriac or dreamy psychic, perhaps a crafty old hippie charging for consultations; I found an open-faced high-school mathematics teacher in his midfifties with the earnest manner of a young Mormon missionary. I wanted to believe his migraines would point me to the next earthquake, so I was delighted when he described himself as "a registered Republican, open-minded but not counterculture," adding he was a veteran of the air force and IBM, and currently a member of MENSA, the organization for people with high IQs. "I understand we're talking 'out-to-lunch' stuff here," he said. "But I don't read tea leaves and I've never seen a UFO or Elvis."

His headaches started in 1983, after a bad divorce and a case of pneumonia. His first wife had taken their furniture and sons, leaving him with a mattress. He faced it north because he had read that Thomas Edison believed that stimulated the brain. He dreamed of tremors and fissures and woke with headaches so excruciating he smelled burning rubber and wrote a will. A few days later an earthquake shook Idaho. Next he imagined his classroom rocking like a storm-tossed ship. He felt seasick and went outside, where the utility poles appeared to be swaying like palms in a hurricane. Two days later a moderate earthquake shook Hawaii.

A friend suggested he try predicting the next earthquake. When his headaches started he rotated like an antenna, stopping when the pain became unbearable. "Central America," he said. "Somewhere north of the Panama Canal." Before the end of the week, a 6.8 struck Nicaragua. His physician listened to his heart and said yes, it *did* race when he turned a certain direction.

The direction of the next earthquake, Hurley said.

On December 6, 1983, he felt as if someone was punching his stomach. When he faced southwest the pain increased. He warned his congressman to expect a 6.2 seventy miles southwest of Fortuna before Christmas. On December 23, a 5.8 hit the Mendocino scarp. I measured the distance on my road map, seventy miles. Afterward he enrolled in Project Migraine, an unfunded research project into earthquake premonitory behavior by Christopher Dodge, a Washington biochemist in the Science Policy Research Division of the Library of Congress. He has earthquake and volcano sensitives report headaches, intestinal upsets, or ringing in their ears, and grades them for accuracy. He praised Hurley to me as skilled at predicting magnitude and pinpointing epicenters. "A nine-out-of-ten," he said, "a member of my varsity."

Hurley thought he was so accurate because his symptoms were so severe. They began with a "feeling of dread" and "an emotional beat in the abdomen." As an earthquake approached, his heart pounded and his headaches worsened. Then his legs tingled, jagged streaks of light flashed across his eyes, and he buzzed like a power drill. When the earth broke, his symptoms vanished.

In August of 1989, he told Dodge, "Something's coming down the road." He called twice in October to report worsening symptoms. On October 13 he went to a chiropractor for his stiff neck and ringing ears. Three days later he returned in agony, reporting the worst symptoms he had ever experienced and saying he feared a great earthquake in the Bay Area. The next day Loma Prieta rocked Northern California from Hollister to San Francisco.

The few scientists who place any credence in sensitives like Hurley believe they are sensing shifts in the geophysical environment preceding a quake, including changes in radio waves or electric or magnetic fields caused by the increased grinding, shifting, and squeezing of underground rock on either side of a fault. Sensitives "hear" this activity because abnormal quantities of magnetite in their inner ears make them human radio receptors. Anecdotal evidence suggests animals are also affected, and since antiquity, carp leaping from ponds, chickens flying into trees, and snakes slithering from burrows to freeze on snow-covered ground have been staples of earthquake lore. Hours before the 1906 earthquake, witnesses described the thunder of hooves crashing against the stalls of a San Francisco livery stable, and before a 7.4 shook Tianjin, China, in 1969, its zookeepers observed bolting deer, twitchy swans, and a giant panda holding his head in his paws and wailing in pain, much like Jerry Hurley.

The Chinese government analyzes abnormal animal behavior at ten seismological research stations and once distributed millions of paper fans showing rearing horses and roosters perched in trees, urging people to report such phenomena. Chinese seismologists credit animal observations for contributing to their first successful short-range prediction, a twenty-four-hour warning given in 1975 to Liaoning Province that enabled residents to move cars, trucks, and valuable objects from houses and garages. A 7.3 struck the next morning, but in this densely populated province where in some cities 90 percent of the buildings collapsed, the death toll was under five hundred. Still, most U.S. seismologists remain skeptical of animal observations, arguing the evidence is anecdotal and circumstantial, that earlier Chinese warnings were false alarms, and that the Liaoning prediction also depended on traditional predictive techniques such as ground tilting, changes in water levels, and the measurement of electric currents running through the earth.

Hurley believes a ferrous material in the magma flow preceding an earthquake carries an electromagnetic charge that affects him as it nears the earth's surface. "Right now the magma's really flowing," he said. Headaches plaguing him for five months had worsened this week and he was "tracking" a quake twenty miles southwest of Fortuna. It might strike Cape Mendocino near the mouth of the Mattole River at Petrolia, or just offshore. He had warned his students to expect a 5.8, but he feared it would be several decimal points higher.

I wanted to believe him. He considered his gift a social responsibility, had checked into major medical centers to find a cure, never charged for an interview, and at his own expense returned calls from anyone asking if it was safe to drive the freeways, jack up a house, or work under a car. When he leaned forward in his Archie Bunker armchair and said, "No one in their right mind would choose this," and "Earthquake sensitivity is a real lonely lifestyle," I thought I should stick around a few more weeks for his earthquake. But when he mentioned an "internal voice" saying "earthquake, earthquake . . .", speculated about UFOs, or wondered if he had inherited his fear of earthquakes from his great-great-grandfather's Cherokee wife, since her people had lived in Arkansas and experienced the Great New Madrid earthquake of 1818, an experience he sometimes relived "as if it were a movie," well, then I had my doubts, and when I asked Gary Carver how much credence he put in Hurley's predictions, he answered, "That's easy, none whatsoever."

Had Hurley remained in Dodge City, Kansas, where he was raised, his symptoms, if they are related to earthquakes, would have been milder and he would have been told to live with the pain. (And if the uncontrollable movement of tectonic plates *is* causing Hurley's afflictions, one wonders how many other untreated and undiagnosed maladies they are behind.) But in California he had found not only the faults to irritate his symptoms, but a climate so tolerant it encouraged him to draw a connection between them and earthquakes.

Had I met him farther down the fault, I would have dismissed his mild and charming eccentricities as the custom of the country. Had I met more seismologists and known that they admit their theories are untested, disputed, and constantly changing, and that they are still arguing over what triggers a quake, I might have found Carver's dismissal less convincing. Had I considered the odds more carefully, I might have realized that while conventional seismology offered a 66-percent chance of a 7.0 earthquake or greater somewhere in the Bay Area sometime in the next thirty years, Project Migraine promised a 90-percent chance of experiencing at least a 5.6 earthquake if I just listened to Hurley and hunkered down in Cape Mendocino for a few weeks. But I was so tired of the drizzle and low sky I decided to believe Hurley enough to stick around Humboldt County for another week or so, but not another month. It turned out to be a stupid compromise.

Ten days after I finally left the county, and seventeen hours after he called Project Migraine to predict an earthquake twenty miles west of Fortuna, one struck near the Triple Junction. Afterward he sent me an article headlined, 5.2 LEVEL TEMBLOR HITS COAST — EPICENTER SOUTH-WEST OF EUREKA, writing at the bottom, "A good hit on the above quake," but adding that his symptoms continued and he believed another was possible in roughly the same place. I was impressed, but not enough to double back. (And if I was unwilling to risk the economic disruption and boredom of waiting around for Hurley's prediction to be realized, no wonder the California Office of Emergency Preparedness was wary of issuing earthquake alerts.)

Hurley's second earthquake struck six weeks later. The week before he had predicted it during a taped radio interview, written 6.0+, 20 MILES WEST OF FORTUNA on his classroom blackboard, called Christopher Dodge to report killing headaches and vision problems, and told his wife he was walking on Jell-O. It was a 6.9, the largest onshore Humboldt County earthquake of the century. The epicenter was eighteen miles southwest of Fortuna, and it caused heavy damage to the commercial districts of Ferndale, Petrolia, and Scotia. It caught Hurley and his wife shopping in the Bayshore Mall, midway between Sears and JC Penney. Windows shattered and mirrors rippled like a pond. They dashed back through Penney's, long-jumping fallen mannequins and shoppers. The headaches continued and he feared aftershocks. When he turned to the west his heart leaped and his body "boiled." He felt "as if a doctor was shining one of those bright flashlights into my eye."

That night he woke his wife and said, "Pray for me. I don't think I'm going to make it." She prayed, "Dear God, please let this guy shut up so I can get some sleep."

He insisted they camp in the car. A third aftershock struck two hours later and Hurley's 1980 Cadillac absorbed the shock.

Headlines afterward in Sacramento and San Francisco newspapers proclaimed, TEACHER'S DISCOMFORTS SOUND QUAKE WARNINGS, and NORTH COAST TEACHER PREDICTED QUAKE. He became briefly famous, but remained unspoiled. Before appearing on *Oprah* he recited the Lord's Prayer and asked God not to let him say anything untrue.

7

The Valley Grocery

Five miles west of Fortuna in Ferndale, and two months before Hurley's earthquake, Wayne Sedam, the world-weary chief of Ferndale's three-man, two-car, one-room police department, told me earthquakes were "no big deal." After all, Ferndale had suffered no serious damage since 1906, although every month a small tremor did knock some cans off shelves at the Valley Grocery. He preferred to worry about ten thousand people bringing their "big-city bullshit" to Ferndale's county fair every year, and about floods like the 1964 one that swept cows out to sea. Right now his mind was on tonight's basketball game. When the same teams met last month in Eureka there had been a "riot," and he planned having his entire force at the high-school gym.

He listened poker-faced as Officer Bob Johnson, a recent recruit, insisted Ferndale was the best small town in California. Johnson's hometown had once been like Ferndale. Now it was ruined by drugs, crime, and squabbles between old-timers and Humboldt State environmentalists. When he had worked in the Eureka Police Department, the other kids picked on his teenage son. In Ferndale they shook the boy's hand and welcomed him. When kids saw a cop in Eureka they flipped him the bird. In Ferndale they shouted, "Hey, Officer Bob, what's happening?" "If you've got to be a cop," he said, in a voice suggesting it was perhaps not his first choice, "you couldn't be one in a better town."

Sedam flashed a tight smile. "Let's just say this town gets real small. Let's just say if people don't have a problem they make one. I guess after so long I'm getting kind of sour on it."

But how could anyone get sour on Ferndale? It rested against a green wall of coastal mountains and at the end of a broad valley blessed by some of the richest soil and finest pastures in the West. It was as compact and cozy as a Swiss village and many kitchen windows looked out on mountains, church steeples, and cows. Residents sat on their front porches, clipped their hedges and cypress into whimsical shapes, and painted their restored Victorians Caribbean carnival colors—pinks, lime greens, and deep purples. Main Street was a handsome four blocks of false-front nineteenth-century buildings whose unprotected plate-glass windows said this was a town without vandals or public drunks. One of the state's best small repertory theaters was a few doors from a café catering to retired farmers. Boutiques had yet to elbow out the feed store, hardware store, old-fashioned pharmacy, and the Valley Grocery.

Citizens were a lively hybrid of ranchers, artists, and downstate refugees. Some ranchers sold jewelry and watercolors, some artists wore boots and drove pickups. A spring art festival exhibited pottery, sculpture, and New Age jewelry, as well as weaving, knitting, and other endangered household skills. Guidebooks and travel supplements called it "timeless," "a showcase," "a photographer's dream," and "out of a fairy tale." Walter Cronkite had broadcast from it, and the state had declared it an historic landmark. The Rockefellers had considered turning it into a West Coast Williamsburg.

It was certainly pleased with itself. "Not an artificial gingerbread-plastic town," an ex-mayor said in one laudatory article, adding that its dairy farmers' thrift and hard work gave it "a real-life kind of feeling."

When I walked up and down Main Street, asking pedestrians and shopkeepers to explain Ferndale's success, I heard about houses being sold to the children of other Ferndale residents at below market prices, and merchants staying on Main Street because landlords like Viola McBride, the beloved descendant of a pioneer, were not greedy. It boasted the highest per capita income in Humboldt County, and perhaps more artists per capita than any town in the world, 100 out of a population of 1,100. Grown children found jobs near their parents, and grandchildren were minutes away. People watched one another's kids and there was no drug problem. The school had won state awards, the band was excellent, and piano teachers were so busy people had to drive children to Fortuna for lessons. Relations between old-timers and newcomers were good because the fifth-generation ranch families were land-rich and laid-back. Danes, Portuguese, and Swiss had united to create a community here in the nineteenth century, and now the same thing was happening again between locals and suburban refugees from the south.

When I asked old-timers about the newcomers they said, "He came to town wearing a ponytail and now he's one of our most prosperous businessmen." "It was a real culture shock when they arrived, and we called them hippies, but now they're our most conservative citizens."

Newcomers said, "Even the old-timers whose grandfathers lived here are incredibly tolerant of newcomers." "If you shake hands with multimillionaires and there's cow shit on their callused hands, it makes their wealth a lot easier to take."

I never heard the word *redneck*.

Ferndale certainly seemed blessed. The art in the galleries was good, no crying clowns or wide-eyed urchins. The pharmacy's cabinets could have been exhibited in the Smithsonian. The Valley Grocery, one of California's last independent Main Street supermarkets, was an airy emporium with wide aisles and high ceilings that encouraged customers to linger and chat. The elderly were the attractive, vigorous type you see advertising the over-the-counter medications on television. A bulletin board displaying photographs of Ferndale's youngsters showed handsome boys and pretty girls with creamy complexions and expensive teeth. The teenagers hanging around the variety store smiled and spoke to strangers. The boys wore clean blue jeans, sweaters and sweatshirts that were not black—real kid clothes. They did not look like basketball rioters but some ninth graders told me, "Whoooeee, better hold on to your hat. It's the last, biggest game of the season and the police are putting on souped-up security. Hey, sure hope you'll root for us."

Some things were California cute. Did the grandmother sitting in the window of Trudy's Sweets and Treats hand-dripping truffles and waving at passing children really need a sign saying LET'S SEE THEM GET A COMPUTER TO DO THIS? Were the gaudy Victorians trying too hard? And was there something unsettling about so much praise lavished on good schools, polite children, friendly neighbors, and safe streets, things recently considered commonplace, even outside museum-quality towns?

My favorite store was Ferndale Books, the best of several dozen used bookstores I visited in California. Too many offered paperbacks with loose bindings, deaccessioned library books dumped in barrels, and shelves of underlined college reading, but the books in this cavernous

Main Street emporium were meticulously cataloged and carefully displayed. Its owner, Carlos Benerman, was an owlish former Berkeley student who like many sixties veterans was gently and offhandedly pessimistic about the future. Books were long, but the attention span of most Americans was shrinking, and he realized retailing well-priced and well-selected used editions was not enough. So he sold travel and local history to tourists, rare works about South America to collectors, and books by the foot to Los Angeles interior decorators. They had already stripped stores farther south of the leather-bound ones they needed to fill the shelves of rooms architects persisted in calling libraries. "I charge them ten dollars an inch or a hundred dollars a foot," he said, smiling as if this somehow proved the thesis on which he based his life, "and of course the author and subject are totally irrelevant."

Some of his patrons were more interested in browsing for real estate. They came in the summer on a family vacation with two kids and a pet, driving slowly up from San Francisco, "searching for the town Walt Disney had told them to want." They asked for the name of a good real-estate agent, and if he liked them, he told them.

Ferndale's old-timers believed their rich soil and sleek cows were enough to protect them, but new arrivals fretted that each new boutique would tip the scales. Some had already moved twice to escape the "California disease" of overpopulation and overdevelopment, and they clung to every Ferndale building and custom with the ferocious love of newlyweds. Jere Bowden, who managed the Eureka branch of Benerman's bookstore, expected the worst. He had the neat gray beard and round wire-rim glasses of a fussy family attorney in a *Masterpiece Theatre* production and chose his words carefully, as if they were an epitaph. He introduced himself by saying, "You see before you just one of the many fools who invested their lives on the Southern California coast, telling themselves their town would escape the ruin visited on the rest." In his former hometowns of Austin and San Antonio, they had torn down every building he liked. When he had moved to Laguna Beach in the 1970s, it had been a sleepy seaside village where people of all ages and races mixed in beach parks, and everyone knew the downtown merchants. A decade later it was a traffic-choked suburb where "you could still have a great view if you lived above the pollution."

He had the traditional refugee's worry that the calamity he had escaped would find him again. How could someone not be pessimistic, he wondered, when the great rule of California life was "the fucking car wins every time"? He had seen Eureka's downtown destroyed when "the local merchant princes spread their legs for development" and supported the Bayshore Mall. He thought Ferndale could be "swept away in a minute," because its patriarchs, "the ones who knew where their food came from," were dying and their children seemed more interested in boutiques and pickup trucks with big wheels. Last year a pasture had been subdivided for new houses and each one was a dagger in his heart. Just this week the planning commission had approved a mini-mall on a vacant lot between two downtown Victorian inns and the developer had told the *Ferndale Enterprise* there would be no butcher shops or pet stores, just places selling "upgrade" goods for tourists.

He was one of many who told me Viola McBride had saved Ferndale. After the 1964 flood ruined dairy farmers and closed the Main Street stores depending on their business, the surviving merchants wanted to "modernize" by replacing their bay windows and gingerbread facades with yellow stucco. McBride had persuaded them to reconsider, encouraged a townwide "paint-up," and bought empty buildings to rent cheaply to artists. She was the granddaughter of Ferndale's earliest resident, and probably the richest woman in Humboldt County, and although she had single-handedly rescued Ferndale, it could change overnight if her sons raised commercial rents after her death. She knew "the history of every tree, fern, and brick in town," Bowden said, and the Russ fault (part of the San Andreas zone) that ran west to east just south of the village was named for her great-grandfather Joseph Russ, who in 1876 had built the Valley Grocery.

In a history of Ferndale, I read that when an earthquake struck in 1877 the only damage had been a four-foot-long fissure at the rear end of the Valley Grocery, then known as "the brick store," and that after the great 1906 earthquake, "Russ, Early and Williams' new brick store, the best in Ferndale, valued at $30,000 and only completed last Christmas, is nearly a wreck—the whole front, brick, glass, and all, fell into the street and the side walls are cracked." A new one, also constructed of unreinforced masonry, was erected immediately, on the same lot.

Joseph Russ had come around the Horn by ship in 1849, a route presenting fewer physical dangers than Bruff's overland route, but leaving emigrants sickly, flabby, and unprepared for the hard work of the goldfields. He brought sacks of flour and a prefabricated house, selling them for the capital that helped to make him one of the wealthiest men in Northern California. He arrived in Table Bluff in 1852 and quickly became friends with two brothers named Shaw, who had followed an elk trail up a creek and found open ground at the base of a hill notable for its six-foot ferns. They built a cabin here on the site of present-day Ferndale, and Russ became a frequent visitor. It is known that all three men became acquainted with Seth Kinman and purchased elk meat from him, and that Russ lived near Kinman on Table Bluff, near one of the massacre sites. Although there is no evidence of Russ participating in the killing, considering where he lived and the small size of the white pioneer community, he could easily have been involved, if not as participant or supporter, then as someone who might have identified the guilty parties.

When I met Viola McBride in her family ranch office, I planned on dancing around the subject of Indian Island, perhaps tricking her into admitting a relationship between Russ and Kinman. But once she proved she indeed *did* know the history of every rock in Ferndale, even pinpointing the creek that provided the mud for the bricks that tumbled off the Valley Grocery in 1906, and once she had said she avoided raising rents on her commercial blocks because it would drive out the genuine artists and she had seen Carmel and, "Hoot! You can't even find a grocery store there," and once I saw her handsome long brown face framed by white curls—well, I was as infatuated as a man in his forties can be with an eighty-seven-year-old woman, and I shut up about Seth Kinman and Indian Island.

Instead, we passed the time agreeing that Ferndale was wonderful. She made it sound simple—you painted up some dirty white buildings, kept the franchises out of town, and shopped on Main Street. Ferndale's charm depended on it being ringed with pastures, and if these were lost to sprawl the town would become less appealing. What had ruined other cute small towns was "too many people moving in because it's a nice small country town, then deciding they need big-city things." She was optimistic because "a big faction here doesn't want it to change—including me." This sounded great, but I worried for the future when she mentioned that a twenty-seven-house tract had risen in a former pasture on the edge of town.

I went to Ferndale's museum several times to stare at the needle of its antique seismograph and wonder if I would be lucky enough to see it slash across the graph paper. The elderly docents obliged me with tales of recent tremors. One had shaken the town at three P.M., throwing schoolchildren into hysterics, another smashed figurines in a curio cabinet, another threw a ceiling tile onto a glass display case. Last week a couple from Reno became frightened when they saw the seismograph. "But we told them we barely notice earthquakes here," one lady said with a sweet smile.

Nevertheless, the Great Earthquake of 1906 had damaged Ferndale more severely than any town in the county. Its rich alluvial soil had magnified the tremors. Small volcanoes erupted along riverbanks, and chimneys flew fifteen feet. The most dramatic photographs of the damage showed two salesgirls peering from the doorway of a Main Street building. The quake had shattered its display windows and peeled bricks from its facade and cornices. It had been the most severely damaged structure in Ferndale. I looked closely. It was the Valley Grocery.

The museum also displayed small-town treasures like blacksmith tools, barber poles, photographs, and heavy glass bottles. I was impressed by how many were "on loan," and had recently been in service, such as the frayed wires of the "Last Cord Board of the Pacific Telephone System in California." It had linked Ferndale's residents until the end of Ronald Reagan's first term, when its retirement threw fifty out of work. I liked it that almost no one in the nineteenth-century group photographs of farmers and schoolchildren was labeled "unknown." (In Eureka's curio shops you could buy whole albums of someone else's deceased forebears to give your weekend country house a lived-in look, and I sometimes wondered if some smart young couple had, without knowing it, decorated their guest bathroom with a photograph of their own relatives.)

That evening I sat in the Ferndale gym surrounded by the sweet-natured, cowboy-preppy sons of Ferndale's ranchers. Their mothers had pressed creases in their jeans, but they claimed to be hoping for a riot. They said fights between the Ferndale Wildcats and the Crusaders of St. Bernard's, a Eureka parochial school, were a tradition. The Crusaders were "stuck-up rich kids" because they went to a private school. But I thought the Eureka kids and their fans looked stringy and pale compared with the buttery Wildcats. A riot was difficult to imagine in a gymnasium where Chief Sedam stood by the entrance, arms folded, and teenagers sat with their grandparents. When an overweight cheerleader tripped, no one whistled or laughed. Four Main Street merchants and two boys who remembered me from the variety store said hello.

When Ferndale lost, the cheerleaders threw their pom-poms into the crowd because it was the last game of the season. Big kids who caught them gave them to the little kids. The students around me muttered about the Crusaders. "Dorks! Damn rich kids." But no one made a move. I asked what had happened during last month's riot. Were punches thrown? Well, not exactly. Had the teams wrestled on the floor? No. Had the stands emptied? No again. Finally one boy said, "But the benches emptied and everyone kinda pushed each other."

Afterward I walked down Main Street to Benerman's store. He had left some books outside on a card table, along with a chair for browsing and a sign announcing IT'S YOURS FOR A DOLLAR! The air was balmy, almost tropical, and I sat outside for an hour, skimming a James Bond thriller and one of Nixon's early attempts at rehabilitation. The names on the bookplates and Christmas inscriptions were mostly Danish, Swiss, and Portuguese. I recognized one from the basketball program and wondered if it was bad news that these dollar books had survived one or two generations only to fall into the hands of one with less compunction about selling them.

In the moonlight Ferndale's false-front stores resembled a Hollywood back lot, just flimsy facades propped up with planks. By comparison the Valley Grocery appeared stolid. I compared it in my mind's eye with its 1906 photograph in the museum. The bricks that had once exploded off its facade, spraying the street like grapeshot, had been collected and reattached. Even I could see why the slightest tremor might disturb the cereal boxes. It had a "soft" ground floor with large plate-glass windows. It was a different height from the adjoining structures, meaning they would respond to tremors at different frequencies, slamming into one another. The unreinforced brick facade was the kind *Peace of Mind in Earthquake Country* held responsible for many California earthquake deaths.

Two months later, Ferndale was rocked by its strongest earthquake since 1906, the 6.9 that was the second of two predicted by Hurley. I saw the Valley Grocery in a downstate newspaper, its windows shattered, its bricks sprayed onto the street—a dead ringer for the 1906 photograph in the museum.

8

The Function on the Triple Junction

Jerry Hurley's headaches had pointed to the Cape Mendocino region as the site of the next earthquake, so I drove there from Ferndale on a nineteenth-century road Chinese coolies had hacked over the coastal range before Humboldt County expelled them. It still felt hand-made, climbing steeply through dense fog banks and twisting over sky-scraper mountains and past WATCH FOR FALLING ROCKS signs that for once made sense. At Cape Mendocino it dropped to the Pacific and fol-lowed a beach that would soon rise several feet, leaving seaweed and starfish baking in the sun.

The wind rocked my compact and covered its windshield with spray. This westernmost point in the lower forty-eight states was how I imagine Patagonia: exhilarating but lonely, not a ship on the horizon or a car on the road, cows on emerald meadows and ranches tucked into hollows, pounding surf and smooth boulders, a landscape for sheep and penguins.

Cape Mendocino was no exception to the rule that anywhere beautiful and empty usually gets pressed into service as a military test range or a dump. Local protests barely stopped the navy from scuttling a hundred decommissioned nuclear submarines here in the 1980s and soon afterward a Scientology front, the Church of Spiritual Technol-ogy, bought a three-thousand-acre Mendocino ranch, stripped the top off a knoll, and filled a forty-foot trench with a two-story-high steel cylinder designed to withstand nuclear explosions and earthquakes. "The most impregnable repository known to man," a spokesman said. Its titanium time capsules were designed to hold "the wisdom of the ages" on indestructible gold disks, this wisdom being L. Ron Hubbard's cuckoo science-fiction religion.

I drove inland to the Scientologists' locked gate and NO TRESPASS-ING VIOLATORS WILL BE PROSECUTED sign and saw the kind of bleak terrain that conceals missile silos in North Dakota. Which was worse? The slight risk of a nuclear submarine fuel leak, or the certainty of L. Ron Hubbard outlasting Shakespeare? The only hope was that an earthquake might bury his gold disks under a new mountain range or drown them in a new estuary. After all, the 1964 Alaskan quake had registered between X and XI on the Modified Mercali Scale, a measurement of an earthquake's intensity. An XI could bend railroad tracks and cause huge landslides. It is conceivable the next subduction-zone quake will produce a XII, which is officially described as "damage nearly total," including the displacement of large masses of rock.

Petrolia was a few miles inland, and small and remote even for Humboldt County, just a fire station, church, and some bungalows. Life centered around the post office and a general store *The New York Times* would soon be describing as "a heap of moldering rubble."

In many rural Humboldt towns the telecommuters, aging hippies, loggers, environmentalists, and ranchers were at odds, but Petrolia struck me as an easygoing place where they had discovered common ground, or at least called a truce. I saw evidence of cross-pollination in the Hideaway, which offered both draft sake and chicken fried steak. At the bar, ranchers and middle-aged longhairs were having a jolly time excoriating the federal government's search-and-destroy antimarijuana campaign. They agreed the IRS was the most socialist organization in the USA, and that last summer's 6.0 quake, the strongest since 1906, had been no big deal. A tourist in the store had suffered a nervous breakdown, but the bartender had caught the Hideaway's television set. An hour before, fishermen had noticed the Mattole River running ten degrees hotter. "Guess they should call us next time that happens," a rancher in a white hat joked. The others fell silent for the first time, perhaps thinking, "Yeah, that might be a good idea."

A hawk-faced woman said they were bullshitting. Instead of jumping under tables, standing in doorways, or "doing all the little things you're supposed to," they had run for their lives. She called over her daughter, a pale and solemn little girl who had been wading with friends in the river when the quake struck, and ordered her to tell me what happened.

"The river started bubbling and I started sinking."
"No, I meant about the other kids."
"The guys were more scared than the girls."

A former student of Gary Carver's named Thomas Dunklin was teaching mathematics in Petrolia while studying the Triple Junction on a National Science Foundation grant. He lived in a small, tumbledown shack near a larger one surrounded by gutted pickups and slavering dogs. There had been a party last night and he was still asleep, so I talked to his landlady, a twitchy long-faced woman who made puppets and performed marionette shows. She had lived here since 1974, but had the remnants of a wisecracking, urban attitude and called herself "a ranch dudette extraordinairé." Petrolia's earthquakes had usually been outdoor ones, and "watching the fence posts dance was awesome," she said in a dreamy voice. But last August's 6.0 caught her indoors, making her feel like a spectator to her own death. Afterward she sold her most fragile possessions and scattered cans of food around at ground level so she could reach them if the house collapsed and she was trapped. She assumed another quake was imminent and never slept in her bedroom because it was too far from the front door. I took pity and kept Jerry Hurley's headaches to myself.

Dunklin was a charming earthquake fanatic who had written an article for the Ferndale newspaper describing Petrolia's location near the Triple Junction as its "good fortune." He lived like a Peace Corps volunteer, among good paperbacks and the tatters of well-made clothes. His sister Annette was spending the weekend mothering him and taking a break from a similar life in the Sierras. She fried up a breakfast of mushrooms and potatoes, then washed his hair and braided it into a coolie's pigtail. He wore the wire-rim glasses and knit watch cap of a sixties radical and spoke about earthquakes with the passion of a campus agitator. He said Cape Mendocino was an exciting geological frontier, in part because even the location of the San Andreas Fault and the Triple Junction were in dispute. A minority opinion placed the fault onshore, and running underneath the Mattole Valley and Petrolia. The Triple Junction might also be onshore, perhaps under Honeydew or Petrolia, and he dreamed of finding it. Carver had promised to mark it with a barber's pole and throw a black-tie party—the "Function at the Triple Junction."

Dunklin had wallpapered the cabin walls with computer printouts of earthquake swarms, and woke every morning hoping for an

Kø Яń

earthquake. When he left Petrolia he became nervous about missing a big one. He admitted there was "glee and ecstasy" at the Humboldt State Geology Department when earthquakes struck, although of course no one wanted casualties. I told him about meeting two women at the Arcata environmental center who wished for an earthquake as a warning, and as punishment for California's environmental sins. He gave a shy laugh and said, "Well, I kind of espouse that view, too."

Petrolia was a relatively safe place to root for earthquakes. The Red Cross had warned that after a subduction-zone earthquake it might be accessible only by helicopter for weeks, perhaps months, but most people had wells and generators and grew their own food. Some would welcome the solitude: after all, being cut off from California was no hardship if you had come to Petrolia to escape it. But even Dunklin was not hoping for an 8.5-to-9.0 subduction-zone event. He said it would be so extreme and destructive it seemed like a fantasy, and some scientists avoided discussing it. The shaking would be measured in minutes instead of seconds. The ground could rise or fall twelve feet. Bridges would collapse and landslides cover highways. Depending on its epicenter, Portland, Seattle, or Eureka could be devastated. The tsunami could kill thousands. Carver wanted an early-warning system of sirens, like those in Hawaii, but no one was listening.

"We're talking big things here: uplift, mountain building." His eyes glistened and one leg jiggled as he spoke. "It's not just talk. It happened three hundred to five hundred years ago and it will happen again. Last summer's 6.0 could have been a warning. That's what we're looking for—the precursor."

Two weeks later, Jerry Hurley's 5.4 hit Petrolia. I called Dunklin the next day. His voice was high-pitched. The quake had struck after dark, catching him inside. It felt like a huge fist slamming into his cabin. Pickup trucks bounced on driveways and buildings slid off foundations. Ever since, he had been talking to reporters, the USGS, and Humboldt State. Everyone wondered if it was a precursor to a great subduction-zone quake. "To be honest," he admitted, "I enjoyed this one a lot less."

On the one-year anniversary of the 6.9 that had also been predicted by Hurley, I returned to Humboldt County and met Dunklin at a student bar in Arcata. He said he was still "jazzed," and had "visual flashes," enabling him to relive it. The day had been clear and sunny. He felt a strong jolt, then a swarm of aftershocks. He threw himself on the ground and rode them like surf. Afterward people asked what to expect next. He told them the Triple Junction was so mysterious and complex even geologists had trouble explaining or visualizing its movements. He drove the back roads for days, searching for surface ruptures, cracking, and uplift, "things other geologists only dream of seeing." The shaking had made him realize he loved earthquakes, but others took it less well. One longtime resident moved out and a ranch family was talking about Montana. Drug use had increased, particularly speed. But most of the social aftershocks had been positive. It had been a community-building event, bringing ranchers and environmentalists closer. Lots of earthquake love.

He had no idea why the 6.9 had not unlocked the subduction zone, producing an 8.5, but he knew it made him nervous, and excited. He was on his way to a conference in Oregon, but when I told him Jerry Hurley's headaches had started again, he fell silent, perhaps wondering whether to return to Petrolia or keep driving north; to bet on intuition or science.

9

A Million Miles
From California

My geologic map of California and the 1908 report of the California Earthquake Commission agreed Shelter Cove was where the San Andreas first came ashore, slicing across a plateau that stuck into the Pacific like a clubbed thumb. The road connecting it to U.S. 101 corkscrewed through a jumble of thickly forested mountains and dived into valleys little more than dark slits.

For some reason, perhaps because my car seemed the only one on the road, I took pity and picked up a hitchhiking couple. His greasy ponytail had gray streaks and he was starved and jumpy as a greyhound. He had pinwheeling eyes, a jack-o'-lantern grin, and was a dead ringer for Charles Manson. Two decades of subsistence farming had given his woman the shriveled, nut-brown campesina grandmother face to match her peasant dress. They were traveling to the former mill town and now semi–ghost town of Whitethorn to collect a free kitten. Yesterday a dope grower's pit bull had eviscerated their cat. "They need them to guard their patches," he explained. "Hey, what can I say? It happens, man."

They whispered, ate balls of brown rice, and filled the car with a stink of whiskey and wet wool. Elsewhere I might have avoided them, but in Humboldt County, their sort packed these remote valleys. The people they called "rednecks" called them "hippies or "longhairs." They called themselves "hill people" or "people of the Mateel," a combination of the Mattole and Eel rivers. Many had bought forty-acre lots of logged-out timberland in the early seventies and survived on welfare, odd jobs, and family charity, until the Humboldt County high-grade

65

marijuana boom of the eighties. Most were environmentalists and bitter enemies of the logging companies, although had their land not been clear-cut or overcut during the postwar lumber boom, they could never have afforded it or grown dope on it. Timber logged from here in the fifties had built the subdivisions of their youth, and who knows, perhaps some lived on land cleared to build the same middle-class ranch houses they had escaped.

If they seemed so cheerful and fulfilled, perhaps it was because they had realized their dream of becoming third-world peasants. They grew their own food and were first-class cookers of beans and lentils. A subcontinent smell of curry and incense surrounded them and they kept yard dogs who fell somewhere between pets and wild animals. They showed an almost Micronesian interest in each other's children and were as skilled as Egyptian mechanics in keeping their rattletraps on the road. They gathered for the kind of marathon luaus that delight Polynesians and, like Haitians and Filipinos, lived in a wounded landscape.

The couple in my car slouched so low they disappeared from the rearview mirror. Was everything all right? I asked.

"Yeah, great!" they chorused, but I imagined them rifling my duffel bag, or unsheathing a knife.

When I dropped them at a crossroads, he said, "Hey, man, hold out your hands."

"Why?"

"Just do it."

When I hesitated he placed a stack of quarters and dimes on the dashboard and asked, "Hey, man, okay if I keep the pennies and nickels?" They had slid from my pockets into the backseat, and he had collected every one.

The first thing I noticed from an overlook high above Shelter Cove was a runway big enough for commercial jets. It shot down the center of a grassy plateau surrounded on three sides by ocean, giving it the appearance of an aircraft carrier. Scattered around it, and spreading like a rash into the hills and higher meadows, were houses resembling the model homes of several dozen Southern California subdivisions. Had this gimcrack development been almost anywhere else, it might have been forgivable, but in these surroundings it was like a boil on a prom queen's forehead.

The first white man to set eyes on Shelter Cove was a surveyor who described it as "a weird place . . . well-calculated for a seaside resort." One hundred and fifty years later it had become a very weird seaside resort indeed—a small, ill-conceived holiday village defacing the most inaccessible coastline in the lower forty-eight states. Nowhere, not even in Big Sur, was the landscape so rugged, beautiful, and untouched. What you saw was no different from what Indians had known 500 years before, or what Bruff had seen 150 years earlier from the deck of a boat taking him back to San Francisco after one more unsuccessful prospecting expedition. To the north and south, mountains shot up from the ocean at almost ninety degrees, providing the most stunning example so far of the fault's beauty-making powers. They were out of a children's book about dinosaurs, almost too green and dramatic to be real. You expected pterodactyls to glide above their cliffs and virgin forests, tyrannosaurs to disappear into their fern-choked gorges, and sea monsters to emerge from the thunderous surf and sun themselves on the black sand beaches.

Shelter Cove came with a typical California history of booms, busts, and land scams. It had been where Indians escaped the heat and gathered seafood, their summer resort. Then frontiersmen shot its elk, loggers harvested its trees, and ranchers grazed cattle on the cleared land. At the turn of the century, a tanbark boom turned it into a busy port with a hotel, warehouses, and a thousand-foot pier. Loggers in the interior stripped bark off tan oaks, boiled the pulp, and sent the extract from Shelter Cove to San Francisco tanneries. Once the accessible oak was felled, the boom ended, leaving tangles of rotting naked logs said to resemble skeletons.

In the 1920s, it became an entrepôt for bootlegged liquor. In the 1930s, it enjoyed a salmon boom. The postwar lumber boom briefly revived the interior. The booms were a tight little narrative, each literally preparing the ground for the next. The tanbark lumberjacks left roads for the bootleggers' trucks and a pier for the salmon fishermen. The lumber boom left the cheap logged-out land that ushered in the hippie land boom of the 1970s, and the marijuana boom of the 1980s. Instead of peaks and valleys, the booms plot as a downward curve, a narrowing of possibilities. The lumber boom meant rivers too silted to support another salmon boom. The hippie land boom precluded wilderness preserves, and only an earthquake could reverse the 1964 subdivision boom that had produced the Shelter Cove Sea Park.

Before this boom, the cove had two farms, twenty people, a dirt landing strip, and a marina renting boats to sport fishermen. Then a Los Angeles developer embarked on what a brochure now describes as his "vision." He laid down forty-three miles of asphalt and promised every lot owner "unrestricted access" to a paved road. He expanded the dirt landing strip into a 3,400-foot runway, making it possible for buyers to visit the site without understanding its isolation. He subdivided the plateau into 4,200 lots measuring an average of fifty by one hundred feet, each zoned for a single-family dwelling.

Some lots sat directly over the San Andreas Fault, others were steep and eroded. When the plan was submitted, the county engineer praised it as "engineered by some of the finest people in the business," but unhappy buyers later wondered if a checkerboard had simply been drawn over an aerial photograph. A fawning article in the *Humboldt Times* said a nationally known architect from Beverly Hills was responsible, and quoted him as saying, "Every effort has been made to retain the land in its natural and primitive character."

The development company sold almost four thousand lots in this seaside suburb during the first year. Members of the armed forces stationed abroad purchased many sight unseen. By 1974, only thirty owners had built houses. Others discovered their lots were unbuildable, that bringing supplies and workers over the mountains from Garberville was prohibitively expensive, that the nearest doctor or supermarket was an hour's drive, that there was no school or television reception, and that the promised golf course had somehow become a "greenbelt." Perhaps they wondered how they would amuse themselves in a resort without golf, tennis, or swimming; perhaps they gave up after a taste of the summer fogs, winter storms, and high winds, or became frightened when a DC-3 operated by the development company smashed into offshore rocks, killing seventeen passengers.

Interest in the development increased in the mid-1980s after the California Coastal Commission, which had been created to save the coast from more Shelter Coves, lifted a seven-year building moratorium. Because the commission had severely restricted new coastal development, and because Shelter Cove's lots had already been zoned and approved, they immediately became valuable. When I arrived, 176 houses had been completed in four years and land prices had quadrupled. The new buyers were younger and wealthier than the retirees and seasonal vacationers who had purchased lots in the sixties. Their boom had a certain backyard-bomb-shelter-survivalist atmosphere to it, and I discerned a rough correlation between pessimism about California's future and construction at Shelter Cove.

The manager of the motel told me real-estate agents and prospective buyers filled her nine rooms every weekend. At first their interest had baffled her. "I mean, sure, it's pretty here, but sometimes the wind is so bad I can't get into my car." Then, for the first time in many years, she visited relatives in Sacramento, and understood. "Poor things, who wouldn't want to escape *that* mess."

I went to the Shelter Cove Sea Park real-estate office on a busy Friday afternoon. The names and hometowns of prospective clients filled its blackboard. Some were coming from Napa and Sonoma, counties people escaped *to* a decade ago.

The young agents had the enthusiasm of campaign workers. They wore colorful parkas, and back in Santa Rosa or San Francisco where they lived during the week, they were probably cyclists, recyclers, and professors of keen environmental sensibilities. Many were in their twenties and early thirties, a good age for this job, since with grandparents dead and their own parents only in their fifties, they were less likely to pity the elderly. As they huddled around blond wood tables planning their strategy, I overheard: "Encourage them to tell you about themselves and their families, become their confidants." "The selling point is scarcity." "The key phrase is *a million miles from the rest of California.*"

I thought that was precisely what Shelter Cove was not. Its grandiose plans for an instant city of several thousand combined the features of a classic California land diddle with the reckless optimism that had succeeded in building the state.

The virgin forests and empty coast surrounding it had survived for reasons equally and classically Californian. Most of the land to the south lay within the Sinkyone Wilderness State Park. It had recently doubled its size, adding seventeen more miles of coast and more acres of virgin redwood groves purchased from Georgia Pacific, thanks to the efforts and funds of the Trust for Public Land, the California Coastal Conservancy, and the venerable Save-the-Redwoods League, all organizations whose environmentalism was uniquely Californian in its passion and determination.

One of the agents circled some lots on a map for me. A "blue water" ocean view cost $50,000. A "white water" view of surf was twice that. "It's your last chance to own your piece of the California coastline," she said, handing me a brochure promising a place with "all the physical characteristics of a seaside resort" that was "little changed since man first found it." The most generous explanation for these statements was that the publicists had never seen the place, or had so little under-standing of what a real wilderness was that it really *did* strike them as "the World of Xanadu." How else to explain the agent proudly report-ing "thirty to forty takeoffs and landings on an average weekend," or the brochure superimposing this quotation from Thoreau—"We need the tonic of wilderness. . . . We can never have enough of nature"—over a photograph of the airstrip?

Next morning I cruised Shelter Cove's forty-three miles of paved roads in the backseat of "Sally" and "Virgil's" overheated Taurus, its windows shut tight against the gale-force winds of a winter storm. They had bought their lot sight unseen for $7,500 in 1965 and built their retirement home in 1979. Shelter Cove had been "the most mar-velous place," she said, "a Carmel for common people like us."

She was chatty and cheerful. He was sweet and frail. She often squeezed his hand. He ran around to open her door and help her into a coat. Sometimes the wind blew him back a step, and whenever we walked to a bluff to marvel at a tidepool or black beach, she gripped his arm as if he might fly off like a kite.

We drove down wide curvy streets that in subdivision custom were named for whatever natural life they had eradicated or displaced. Some led to a scattered house or two. The others ran through empty lots marked by gray utility boxes and WILL BUILD TO SUIT signs. The wind and salt defeated landscaping, so even older homes looked stark. Instead of trees you saw satellite dishes. Because the ocean view was everything, nothing had been fitted into the natural contours of the land. Decks perched on double- and triple-story pilings, skylights rose like periscopes, and picture windows met like the prow of a ship. It was all glass and stilts, a spectacularly unsuitable architecture for the San Andreas Fault.

Although Virgil and Sally claimed to love Shelter Cove, almost everything on their tour came with a sad story. They showed me lots too steep for a driveway that owners had abandoned to foreclosure, a house being constructed on a cliff Virgil said would soon slide into the Pacific, and an eroded bluff where, he said glumly, "they promised to build a fancy restaurant. It was one of the selling points." As we passed a line of houses wedged between the airstrip and ocean that were as prominent as Stonehenge, he admitted being "kind of sad" they dominated the view. When a corporate jet came screaming in overhead for a landing, she complained the wealthy were taking over Shelter Cove now that the first generation of middle-class retirees had died or moved closer to hospitals. I sensed the newcomers landing in private jets were uninterested in Virgil and Sally, who were beginning to feel the loneliness and isolation common to the elderly in any gentrified neighborhood.

They were defensive about how they filled their hours. "Living here is Virgil's dream come true," she snapped. "I don't think we've ever been so busy." They boasted about playing bridge, acting in amateur theatricals, and belonging to a civic association, but I shared the backseat with a dog-eared satellite-TV guide. (The wife of a Shelter Cove manager once wrote in its newsletter there was so much to do that most residents wished "that days were longer!" She recommended visiting neighbors, entertaining, and bingo or just talk, as typical Shelter Cove activities, also candlemaking, tin-craft, needlework, string art, and model-making—all the traditional prisoner pastimes.)

There may be a fortune in gold coins from the wreck of a Spanish galleon hidden in these rain-soaked sea cliffs, or perhaps on the fault itself. I am such a sucker for buried-treasure legends I once went to Zimbabwe half hoping to find the lost hoard of King Lobengula in less than a week. The Shelter Cove one is particularly convincing because of its details. The gold coins are said to be triangular and the Mattole Indian children said to have used them in their summer beach games. The reason for their disappearance is also believable. The story goes they were lost for a second time when landslides caused by the great 1906 earthquake sealed the caves where the Indians stored them, more proof, if any is needed, of how quickly an earthquake could change Shelter Cove.

Virgil and Sally could not understand my interest in the fault. No serious earthquake had hit during the fifteen years *they* had lived here, so why worry? To humor me they drove along a former wagon road following the San Andreas, or perhaps a lesser fault, if you believed Gary Carver. I was astonished at how easily I could make it out. Centuries of faulting had thrown up two low escarpments, creating a ditch so pronounced it looked man-made, as if press gangs of Chinese coolies had hacked it out of the earth at the same time they were building the county's treacherous roads.

We drove up the fault to high ground and peered down into Dead Man's Gulch. A notch in a cliff to the south showed where the fault reentered the Pacific after running a mile across Shelter Cove. The cut was so sharp it appeared someone had tried to slice off the plateau with a knife. Farther down the fault, houses and thick forest sometimes made it difficult to pinpoint, but here it was impossible to miss. A marker almost directly over it said SEQUENCE #18 / LOT 6. "Oh, don't tell me," Sally said, waving a hand at the rows of utility boxes. "Even up here, more lots."

Squalls swept the ocean like brooms and a windblown drizzle hit our faces like needles. Virgil held his hat. Sally gripped his arm. "Just look at that view!" she said. "Isn't it beautiful?"

"Nowhere like it in California," he said. "*And* no crime; nothing to fear."

I drove back an hour later by myself, eating a sandwich and eyeing the fault through the rain-streaked windshield, willing it to open. Why not? I was in a car on high ground, with no buildings or trees nearby. Thanks to the original developer's "vision," even the utility lines were buried, and thanks to his landing strip, the cove could be supplied and evacuated by air. A moderate San Andreas temblor was unlikely to produce a wave tall enough to submerge the airport and plateau. But the tsunami after the 1964 Alaskan subduction-zone earthquake that slammed into Crescent City near the Oregon border had crested at eighteen feet, traveled a quarter mile inland, and flooded thirty city blocks. A similar wave would easily wash over Shelter Cove's nine-foot cliffs. After Crescent City, Berkeley seismologist Bruce Bolt reported the town was rezoned and its waterfront area developed into a public park, making it "a more attractive and safer place to live."

The next morning I called on Mario Machi because he had lived in Shelter Cove longer than anyone. He remembered his arrival in 1930 with the passion and detail of someone recalling their first affair. He had come from San Francisco at fifteen to work during the salmon boom. As he stepped off the pier he noticed three men digging clams. One look into their buckets and he was staggered. "The size of those clams! The size of the cliffs and mountains! Right away I fell in love."

He was one of several teenagers hired for the summer. They fished, lugged salmon to the icehouse, drank with cowboys, rode bulls in nightly rodeos, met bootleggers carrying machine guns, and saw a dead man pulled from Dead Man's Gulch. At night they played accordions and waltzed with the daughters of ranchers and loggers. It was the summer most men chase for a lifetime.

During World War Two he was captured at Bataan and spent three years in a Japanese prison camp, dreaming of Shelter Cove. After the war he and his brothers bought its derelict warehouses and opened a fishing resort, a move both brave and foolhardy in a place where he admitted that, "if you saw a car in two weeks it was a big event." They struggled through the 1950s, taking odd jobs and renting surplus life rafts. They tied ropes around their waists and waded into the surf to rescue customers. Sometimes they pulled lost fishermen from fogs so thick only lit cigarettes gave them away. They turned the tanbark warehouse into a tackle shop and garage, and the abandoned hotel into a green-shingled bar and restaurant with low ceilings and picture windows overlooking the surf. They laid out fifteen lots, but left the oceanfront empty. A fleet of commercial dories began fishing the cove, and by the end of the 1970s Machi was buying 200,000 pounds of salmon a year. But every year the state shortened the commercial season and this year it had been canceled. He blamed the timber companies for destroying the spawning grounds and leaving him with a fishing resort without fish.

He had not opposed Shelter Cove Sea Park. To prevent others enjoying what he loved so much would have been selfish. Nevertheless, he had chosen an aerial photograph predating the resort for the cover of his self-published book, and as we stood at his picture window admiring the landscape, he gestured to the line of houses sandwiched between the airstrip and the ocean and said softly, "Those houses, I guess they do spoil the view."

Afterward I knocked on one of their doors. A sign said SHELTER COVE BED AND BREAKFAST, but I chose it because the tricycle on its lawn was the only toy I had seen in town. It belonged to the daughter of Summer Read, who had moved here six months ago from a San Jose suburb to manage the inn and escape pollution, and her husband. People who never looked you in the eye and poisoned Halloween treats, they at first, had tried to escape together to a double-wide on a remote lot in the Santa Cruz Mountains. It sure looked like wilderness, but there were always planes overhead. Finally a pilot showed them his map. Their mountain was underneath a flight path and a favorite marker for low-flying jets.

She thought Shelter Cove was "a happening place." Her inn was part of the action. Besides being within walking distance of the airport, it offered Jacuzzis and "a full country traditional vegetarian breakfast." The Santa Cruz developer who owned it was planning a convention hall, right where we were standing (we were a few hundred yards from the fault). What she liked most about the cove was that "when you're here, you're in a real wilderness."

Her metamorphosis had a remarkable velocity, even for California. Six months ago she had been designing and constructing "wearable art" and fantasy costumes for Renaissance fairs and the Miss California pageant from Mylar, metal, fiber optics, phosphorescent paints, and strobe lights. After her Golden Gate Bridge hat, lights and all, won first prize at the San Jose Museum Headdress Ball, a Santa Clara Arts Council functionary had declared "Summer was the central planet or sun and we were all caught up in her orbit." The *Mercury News* reported that her "personal color preference" was black, and it was "evident in everything from her clothing to her fingernail polish." Now she was wearing frilly country frocks, painting her nails orange to match her hair, and instead of bending Mylar, whipping up exotic waffles.

She credited Loma Prieta for the speedy transformation. When the shaking began she had been in a glass cubicle applying metallic makeup to an actress starring in a science-fiction production of *A Midsummer Night's Dream*. Her sharp-edged costumes flew across the room, almost impaling her. Structural damage closed her store, she went into premature labor, and sickened from contaminated water. Worst of all was finding a stew of food, utensils, and smashed wedding presents on the kitchen floor. When she said, "What an amazing feeling, to lose 75 percent of your possessions in an instant. After *that*, I had to leave," her voice broke and her eyes watered. At the time I discounted her tears as artistic temperament. Instead, she was the first of many quake survivors still grieving for dishwashers, Hümmel figurines, and tissue-wrapped wedding presents. They told journalists earthquakes had taught them human life was more important than possessions, but they grieved for their belongings long and hard. That was fine with me. The heirlooms represented an irreplaceable family history, and when they mourned a new VCR they also mourned the hours worked to buy it. Losing one was a small death.

Six months later, when a frustrated urban refugee in Desert Hot Springs told me, "The mistake I've made is not understanding that to escape California, you really *do* have to leave it," I thought of Summer Read. After all, she had traded living under a flight path for living on the edge of a runway, a crowded South Bay suburb for 4,200 empty lots awaiting a convention center, and a house ten miles from the San Andreas Fault for one just yards away. She had felt some small quakes since moving to Shelter Cove, but figured she and her daughter could always run into the meadow—the same meadow that might be underwater minutes later.

TWO

REDWOOD EMPIRE

❖

10

The Trees of
Rondal Snodgrass

They say earthquakes and Californians are well matched; who better to live in the constant shadow of an inescapable catastrophe than a population heavy in laid-back optimists. The state's traditionally casual attitude toward seismic danger makes a certain sense, since once you have retrofitted, hung a wrench by the gas line, nailed down mirrors, stockpiled bottled water, and put a pair of sneakers in the car trunk so you can walk home over shards of glass, what else can you do? Besides, the California Special Studies Zones Act of 1972 seems to protect Californians from their own insouciance by requiring anyone selling property within a known active fault zone to warn a prospective purchaser.

The California Division of Mines and Geology publishes maps of these hazardous zones, and like the long-range predictions by the Working Group for California Earthquake Probabilities, they are grounded in the theory that since the slippage between tectonic plates along an entire fault is constant over time, earthquakes will recur on various segments with a certain rough regularity. If, for example, quakes have struck both north and south of a particular segment of the San Andreas, and that segment remains tightly locked, it is only a matter of time before one unlocks it, too. Places where the plates are locked and overdue for an earthquake are known as "seismic gaps." The problem for California with even this admittedly imprecise forecasting method is that to determine the location of these gaps, and fix the probability they will rupture in the near future, you need to know their seismic history. In fact, the more you know, the more precisely you can forecast the location and date of the next earthquake. This dependence on history made me realize that, contrary to conventional wisdom, California and earthquakes are actually a rather unfortunate combination.

California's written history is less than two centuries old, but great earthquakes often strike at much longer intervals. This makes paleoseismic evidence discovered from excavations of fault zones and the examination of tree rings even more crucial. But as California's population expands and every year more trees are felled and more ground disturbed, more clues to the seismic timetable are being lost.

In the 1980s, geologists sampling trees along a seven-mile segment of the San Andreas east of Los Angeles pointed to thin or missing rings as evidence that a traumatic event, probably an earthquake, had happened between 1812 and 1813, causing decades of stunted growth. Drought was eliminated as a cause since only trees near the fault were affected. These rings indicated an 1812 quake had occurred along the San Andreas. Until this study, it had been assumed a lesser coastal fault was responsible for this earthquake reported by Spanish missions, and that the San Andreas had lain dormant for 330 years before producing the great Fort Tejon quake of January 1857. Two great earthquakes on the southern section within forty-four years cast doubt on the conventional wisdom that it seldom experienced great earthquakes, and suggested even the calculation of a 60-percent probability for one earthquake in the next thirty years might be too optimistic. Had trees along the fault been clear-cut, this evidence would never have been found.

I met Rondal Snodgrass, who has made it his business to save as many of Humboldt County's trees as he can, after Sunday mass at the Redwoods Monastery in the former mill town of Whitethorn, seven miles east as the crow flies from where the fault crosses Shelter Cove. A sculptor and a Hollywood set designer constructed the monastery's main building in the 1950s, and old-timers remembered the men tying bells around their livestock so the meadows could tinkle like wind chimes. After the sculptor married, the set designer had joined an abbey and gave the Whitethorn property to an order of Cistercian nuns fleeing the Congo. A redwood trunk fills the high window behind what is now an altar, dwarfing a modest cross and making it possible for even a nature worshiper to feel comfortable here. When I asked a beak-nosed sister who had survived the horrific Kisangani massacre if she noticed earthquakes, she smiled and said, "We felt the ground tickle with the magic of the earth."

Snodgrass had a formal telephone voice, so I easily picked him out as the distinguished, straight-backed man with a gray mustache. His business card said RONDAL SNODGRASS, ENVIRONMENTALIST, EXECUTIVE DIRECTOR OF SANCTUARY FOREST. His strategy was to buy tracts of endangered old-growth redwood forest, then resell them to the state or a "conservation owner" who logged them according to principles of sustainable forestry. He was a modest environmental saint, preserving a few acres at a time. He lived on little, and admitted envying the rich counterculture types who grew dope. Their sudden embrace of the consumer society had disgusted their more principled neighbors, and he refused to save redwoods with drug money.

Driving with him through the Mattole Valley was like touring Virginia with a Civil War buff. Every road led to an old battlefield. We bumped to the end of a logging track, then stumbled through a stump-and-scrub wasteland where environmentalists had retreated before bulldozers after giving every tree a hug and naming it after a Greek god. We paused in a weedy field where rust ate at the peace signs and psychedelic rainbows of abandoned hippie cars. As a scrap dealer's flatbed truck lumbered down the road with a cargo of burned-out Valiants and Darts harvested from defunct communes upstream, he spread out a five-year-old aerial photograph of these once thickly wooded hills so I could compare them with the brutal clear-cut before us. He described the battle in the hushed voice of a soldier remembering a rout. Two weeks of sunrise prayer vigils, attempts to convert loggers, and sprawling in front of bulldozers had failed. The loggers called it a "rehabilitation cut," but it left the hills naked except for a line of trees parading the ridge like skeletons. "Exquisite hardwoods," he said in a dreamy voice, as if he could still see them. "The oak topping that knoll was exceptional. I begged a forester I knew to spare it as a personal favor, but it went down with the rest."

To reach the eighty acres of virgin forest Snodgrass wanted to save we had to cross an abandoned marijuana farm, picking through collapsing sheds and garden hoses he thought would outlast the trees. The doper had been a troubled man who was arrested for killing a bear and jailed on drug charges before disappearing. His mother had recently hiked through this forest, nailing posters to trees carrying a blurry mug shot and beginning HAVE YOU SEEN . . .

A stark boundary separated the logged-out pot farm and the virgin forest Snodgrass hoped to buy. You stepped across it and left a faded landscape of stumps, scrubby trees, and hills threatening landslides, for one of giant ferns, moss, and Douglas fir. Sounds became muffled and light softened, as if filtered through a stained-glass canopy. The squishy ground bounced back like a trampoline and my glasses fogged. It was a mixed forest, with single redwoods towering over tan oak, madrone, and fir. Foresters had already been through, tying blue tape around the trunks of trees marked for harvest, spray-painting those to be spared with a red *L* for "Leave."

Snodgrass stopped opposite a blue-banded virgin redwood and whispered, "Oh no! Too close to the stream. I can't help myself. I see a tree like this and imagine how many people you'd need to hug it."

"Suppose you don't buy it in time?" I asked.

"I get queasy thinking about it."

Although I was raised on 1950s social-studies texts portraying loggers as Paul Bunyans and timber companies as planters of handsome tree farms, and although I live in a wood-paneled house in the Adirondacks where trees seem to grow as fast as weeds, and I recently cleared an acre of land to improve my view, this blue band made me slightly queasy, too.

The logging of old-growth redwoods was the most contentious issue in Humboldt and Mendocino counties, dividing communities and sometimes leading to protests and violence. For decades environmental groups and the timber industry had been arguing over how much logging practices such as clear-cutting contributed to erosion, silted waterways, the destruction of the salmon industry, and floods like the one almost sweeping away Ferndale, over how many timber roads should be built, how close they should be to watersheds, how many trees should be left and how many taken, and how many years should elapse before a second-growth harvest.

Environmentalists believed clear-cuts were an indisputable atrocity; the industry countered that they produced the sunny conditions that encouraged stumps to sprout new trees. Environmentalists trumpeted a government study reporting that space photographs of the Pacific Northwest revealed a greater level of logging damage than in the Amazon; the timber industry denounced it as badly flawed. Environmentalists pointed to the thousand years needed to replace a 300-foot redwood; the industry responded they were the fastest-growing conifers in the nation, sometimes soaring 150 feet in their first fifty years. Environmentalists mourned the 90 percent of California's virgin forests lost since the Gold Rush; the industry said look at how many acres were preserved up in state and national parks. Environmentalists charged companies were closing north-coast sawmills because they had overcut inventory and moved their operations to lower-cost countries; the companies blamed logging restrictions meant to protect the spotted owl. But no one, as far as I could see, worried about losing part of California's seismic timetable.

In the end, where you stood on timber issues, particularly on the emotional issue of harvesting old-growth redwoods, was more a decision of the heart than the head. Either you were moved by the beauty of the tallest and oldest living things on earth, or you were not; appalled by the battlefield landscape of charred earth and stumps left by a clear-cut, or considered it an efficient technique leading to lower consumer prices. You believed every generation should preserve biological diversity for the next and that land had rights sui generis, or you were moved by timber workers abandoning communities where their families had lived for generations. You thought a tree farm's identically spaced and sized rows were an acceptable replacement for a redwood grove, or you saw a sterile plantation. You found redwood groves dank, monotonous, and claustrophobic, or places of mystery and wonder. You agreed with University of Oregon professor Ed Whitelaw that "clean air, forested mountains, and pristine beaches" had a dollar value because they attracted new enterprise, or with the chairman of a timber industry organization who called this "lunacy and fantasy economics." You thought, here is a tree that creates its own climate and was alive at Christ's birth, or thought, God has given us a miraculous building material with a clear straight grain and wood that resists rotting for centuries.

I saw evidence of both reactions while heading down U.S. 101, the "Redwood Highway" connecting Eureka to San Francisco. The hills flanking it in southern Humboldt County looked as exhausted as the towns responsible for them. Clear-cuts had left a patchwork of bald clearings and scrubby second growth. The muddy Eel River flowed back and forth underneath bridges, pinched by expanding banks of gravel and sending more silt downstream than the Mississippi. For most of its distance the highway was a brutal four-lane freeway. It had been built to accommodate lumber trucks in the mid-1960s, a time when California considered such roads so indisputably worthwhile that the Division of Highways (now Caltrans) had proposed naming one slicing through the coastal hills of suburban Contra Costa County the "John Muir Freeway."

Snodgrass's cheerful mixed forest had not prepared me for the thick redwood groves lining the thirty-three-mile-long "Avenue of Giants" in Humboldt Redwoods State Park. Although it was already a dark and drizzly March morning, the moment I entered the groves the temperature and light dropped so dramatically I turned on my heater and headlights.

I spent a day walking through the groves more because I felt I should than because I wanted to. I admired the trees, but their mass and humidity were smothering. I felt trapped in a somber, muffled Amazon without heat or parrots, and could understand the urge to open a sunny clearing. But when I flew over Humboldt County more than a year later, heading for another meeting with Jerry Hurley and a visit to Bruff's camp, I realized the groves I had seen were a redwood Potemkin village, just a thin green snake wrapped around the highway, a viewshed for tourists. Elsewhere, logging roads penetrated remote hollows, rivers flowed brown and sluggish, and a chessboard of cuts and second growth stretched to the horizon. The eroded slopes reminded me of Haiti, or Pacific battlefields where marines had incinerated holdout Japanese with flamethrowers.

Those photographs of a 1950s family driving a wood-paneled station wagon through a hole in a giant redwood had been among my first California icons, but when I finally eased my Tempo through the 315-foot-high Chandelier tree at the Leggett Drive-Thru Tree Park to the accompaniment of Waylon Jennings blaring from a loudspeaker, I felt like a fool. My two dollars also bought the right to carve my initials into a log, and patronize a gift shop selling bathroom jokes carved into plaques that because they are made of redwood, will survive centuries without rotting.

I sat watching in the drizzle as five cars navigated the Chandelier tree. Kids looked bored and wives sheepish, but the men insisted on circling it for a second go. One ordered his wife to videotape their Winnebago squeezing through the tunnel, and a man in a cowboy hat boasted, "I just drove that great big Cadillac through it!" They posed for photographs leaning against the tree, grinning in triumph, and pointing to a sign announcing its weight and height, like mountain climbers at a summit, or big-game hunters with a kill. I noticed the same poses and smiles on lumberjacks in the antique photographs in logging museums and gift shops. The men leaned on Bunyan-sized axes before fallen trees, painted their names on the end of a log, extended their arms to indicate its circumference, and sat in lines dangling their legs over a gargantuan stump. From the beginning, the impulse to turn a redwood into a freak had been irresistible. In 1853, five men spent twenty-five days cutting down a three-thousand-year-old sequoia before using its stump for a dance floor and its fallen trunk as a bowling alley, and a tree so huge it was called "Mother of the Forest" was felled intact and loaded on a flatcar for a tour of Eastern cities where gawkers decorated it with initials carved in intertwined hearts.

At the World Famous Tree House ("Tallest One-room House in the World"), I stood in the middle of a gloomy, fire-blackened redwood trunk and stared hundreds of feet up into a yellow bulb that glowed like a gorgon's eye. It debouched into a gift shop with displays of rabbits' feet, cuckoo clocks, and more redwood slices decorated with vulgar jokes. Identical crap could be had at the Shrine Drive-Thru Tree, "a natural gap . . . once used by Indians for smoke signals," Chimney Tree/Hobbiton USA, where redwood dioramas depicted scenes from *Lord of the Rings*, and the Tour-Thru Tree, where "a man-made cut through this 700-year-old redwood allows passage of most vehicles."

The nearby towns were as melancholy as their attractions. Weott was a huddle of the few clapboard houses to survive the great flood of 1964. Rio Dell's ramshackle main street would soon be consumed by fires caused by aftershocks of Jerry Hurley's earthquake. Only Scotia, a company town with the largest redwood mill in the world, was thriving. Until 1985, it had belonged to the famously paternal Pacific Lumber Company, noted for, among other things, providing every worker's child with a college scholarship and serving only the best spirits in the company saloon in the belief that expensive brands were less likely to cause hangovers. A 1950 travel article said its hospital was as modern as any in California and its baseball park the equal of San Francisco's. The *Saturday Evening Post* called it "paradise without a waiting list."

Its enlightened owners, the Murphy family, had phased out brutal clear-cutting after the development of the diesel-powered tractor in favor of selective logging practices that left forests more intact. They balanced mill output against the ability of their forests to regenerate trees, and preserved extensive stands of virgin redwoods, holding twenty thousand acres in trust until the state or a private conservation group could purchase them. In the 1940s, A. S. Murphy noted in his diary that his grandfather had stood in the pinewoods of Maine, and his father in the forests of Michigan and Wisconsin. "Those other forests are gone," he wrote. "These towering redwoods are the Murphys' last timber holdings and I feel a responsibility to use them wisely."

This attitude resulted in Pacific Lumber having the largest private inventory of virgin redwood on earth, making it an asset-rich takeover target criticized as "sleepy" for not maximizing its profit. In 1985 it was acquired by Maxxam, a revealingly named company controlled by a

Houston investor named Charles Hurwitz. Michael Milken financed the takeover with junk bonds, while minority shareholders, including the young Murphy heirs, charged the company was "sold down the river" by senior executives and board members seduced by Maxxam's stock-option and retirement plans. Warren Murphy warned that Humboldt County had lost "something money can't buy . . . a quality of life and a commitment to maintaining our natural resources."

Who, knowing this history, could resist examining Scotia for signs of decay? At first I noticed only the hallmarks of any company town: the dun-colored junior-officer bungalows and whiff of fear in the too tidy front yards. No one in the Scotia museum, on the street, or in the Ben Franklin store soon to be consumed by Hurley's earthquake would discuss Maxxam, and I received the hard stares and head shaking once greeting Westerners trying to initiate conversations on the sidewalks of Moscow or Tirana. The WE SUPPORT TIMBER signs in windows all came from the same printer, like the slogans and photographs of Kim Il Sung in Prongyang. A poster in the coffee shop declaring REDWOOD SUMMER COST YOU THE TAXPAYERS $252,000—$100,000 JUST FOR HAIRCUTS! referred to the expenses of a lawsuit brought against the county sheriff for shaving the heads of environmental protestors.

When I saw a flyer advertising the Fifty-fourth Annual Redwood Region Logging Conference and Equipment Show at the Redwood Empire fairgrounds in Ukiah, I decided it would be a better way of meeting timber workers and hearing their arguments than having some public-relations man lead me through a tree farm or mill. The flyer promised an equipment show, lumberjack feats of endurance and skill, and a gin-fizz breakfast during which former Washington governor Dixie Lee Ray would be delivering an address on "Environmental Myths and What They Cost." I was still suspicious of my sympathy for tree huggers like Snodgrass, and suspected I liked his redwoods for the same sentimental reasons one likes elephants—because they are big, valuable, and attract determined hunters.

11

"Fanning the Flames . . ."

I drove to Ukiah for the logging conference through the narrow, rolling Anderson Valley, where Bruce Anderson (who is unrelated to the valley's discoverer) edits the *Anderson Valley Advertiser (AVA)*. This is probably the funniest, nastiest, most high-minded and vulgar, entertaining and addictive small-town weekly newspaper in the nation, provided you are not among its targets, which is difficult for anyone living in Mendocino County. It has an old-fashioned look, with political cartoons instead of photographs, and contains twelve or fourteen oversized pages crammed with enough rage, enthusiasms, and grievances to fill a small city instead of an isolated agricultural valley of 1,500.

I became an *AVA* addict after reading a discarded copy in a Eureka bar. Afterward I foraged through back issues at libraries. Once I knew the school-board president, "fat-cat executives," "snout-in-the-trough bureaucrats," and "cheese and wine-sip liberals," their doings became an entertaining weekly serial. The heart of the *AVA* was "Here and There in Mendocino," a summary of the week's political and environmental atrocities, and a Letters to the Editor column sprawling over two pages and providing Anderson with the opportunity to pour gasoline on the embers of old disputes with replies such as, "Your opinion is so stupid and full of ridiculous hyperbole it falls off the bottom of the IQ chart," and, "PS—Up Yours."

He seemed really to believe the quotation from Joseph Pulitzer running across his masthead, NEWSPAPERS SHOULD HAVE NO FRIENDS, and at his best reminded me of George Orwell, ranting about "vegetarians," "bearded sandal-wearers," and "cranks, snobs, and optimistic simpletons."

He called the local timber owners "inheritance princes and princesses who of course resent any interference in their divine right to moonscape their properties." The local gentry and business community were members of the "rural fascist league." The Ukiah Chamber of Commerce were "crewcut bulletheads who swagger into Supervisors' meetings, huge guts spilling over their belt buckles, to denounce taxation or government regulation, apparently totally unaware that they themselves hardly seem cut out for the Darwinian struggle of free enterprise." Tourists were a pain in the ass whom he begged to "do something different—read a book, plant a tree, shave your dog, swear at your mother. Do whatever it takes, but quit driving to Mendocino (quit driving, period). And quit coming to Boonville [the largest town in the valley]." The town of Mendocino was "your basic collection of Hallmark painters and New Age Dr. Feelgoods in urine-colored *Century 21* coats all hustling for a piece of our ever-dwindling dollar." The boutique wineries replacing the hops fields were an upscale cancer, turning the valley into a yuppie playground. The "Most Assholes in One Place Award" went to any meeting of the Mendocino County Vintners. The members of the school board were "low-grade authoritarians and martinets" who belonged to the "aging hippie aristocracy," and now "quickly reclaimed their middle class advantages" by hiring administrators who were "an uncanny succession of drunks, thieves, nuts, and garden-variety incompetents," including a principal Anderson called "Walking Eagle," because he was "too full of it to fly."

He reserved a special disgust for liberals and the traditional left, denouncing "the friendly fascists of the New Age," "the P.C. thought police," and "the lockstep liberals of the cheese and wine sips." Candidates of the local Green Party were "a handful of whacked-out old hippies." Mendocino County was "national headquarters of fuzzy-thinking, especially among the comfortable class of liberals." Feminists were "single-issue gender fascists," and Oliver Stone's movie *JFK* was the "biggest turd [ever] floated in the country's media punch bowl."

I always put down the *AVA* exhausted, exhilarated, and curious how one man had time for so many feuds and enemies while writing and editing a weekly publication with a word count approaching the Sunday *New York Times*. The people I met who knew him said he had served in the Peace Corps and marines, moved up here in the 1970s, and bought the *AVA* ten years later. His enemies told me he delighted in stirring it up, could not libel anyone because no one took him seriously, and "shouldn't be armed with a pen because for him it's a loaded weapon."

Anyone notorious for being "his own worst enemy" is usually great fun. When I called asking if I could stop on my way to the Ukiah convention, a rather gentle and shy voice said sure, if I wanted to visit "the site of objections to just about everything that's happening in Mendocino County," I was welcome. But if I wanted to meet any real loggers I should forget Ukiah. Mexicans did the heavy logging and the conference would be nothing but yuppie executives in lumberjack shirts.

The San Andreas and lesser faults are credited with creating not only California's legendary beauty, but also the jumble of isolated valleys and microclimates crucial to its legendary agriculture. In the North Coast, faulting has created a landscape of isolated beaches, lonely hollows, and pocket valleys like the Anderson Valley that are also perfect for nourishing a healthy crop of eccentrics. One mountain range isolates this valley from the coast, another from the interior. A local historian summarizes the period between its discovery in 1851 by a hunter named Walter Anderson, and the 1920s, when the automobile and telephone finally opened it up, by saying simply, "Travel was difficult and most people preferred to stay at home." This backwater geography led to the development of a slang called "Boontling" that was based on local characters and century-old events, and was incomprehensible to outsiders. How, for example, could anyone guess a "walter levy" was a telephone because Mr. Levy was the first valley resident to own one, or that a "jeffer" was a fire because Jeff Vestel once liked building big ones, that to "high-heel" meant to arrest someone because one of a constable's legs had been shorter than the other, that "high-pockety" meant rich because the tallest man in Boonville had once also been the wealthiest, that a "shoveltooth" was a doctor, and a "Jenny Beck" a tattletale, or that "skraje" meant to love, "harp" to talk, and "bluebirded" meant being bucked off a horse, because after once being tossed, a nineteenth-century schoolboy had said, "I got thrown so high that a bluebird could have built a nest on my ass."

Bruce Anderson called Boontling's originators "pastoral sex fiends who made up their own language in order to insult people." The most likely explanation is that nineteenth-century schoolchildren invented its vocabulary to swear in front of adults, then hops pickers embellished it, and the community adopted it as a way of ridiculing and excluding outsiders. Boonville baseball teams found it useful for signaling plays, and Second World War soldiers wrote letters home in it to confuse military censors. During the second half of the twentieth century, it followed a predictable trajectory from thriving local custom to embalmed tourist attraction, returning to its roots as a form of adolescent insult, sometimes appearing in the high-school yearbook but seldom in conversation. With obscenities and lewd jokes so common in the media and public exchanges, who needed the fig leaf of Boontling to talk dirty? If "fuck" is no longer shocking, why call it "burlappin,' " in memory of the nineteenth-century shop clerk caught in the act on a pile of burlap sacks?

I worried Anderson had changed his mind about meeting me when I found his ranch house locked and no one home. A radio played in a shuttered cottage I took for his office, but when I knocked a voice yelled, "Not here. Come back later!"

The only way to kill a few hours in the Anderson Valley is to go wine tasting. In the Napa Valley this means balloon rides, traffic jams, gift shops, and drunk sophomores. But Anderson Valley wineries were still catering to the yuppie fantasy of a perfect day in the country—expensive casual clothes, an imported car, and a wicker-basket picnic.

The Navarro Winery had a deck overlooking rows of vines rolling like corduroy over gentle hillsides and a friendly owner pouring samples himself. I was contentedly sipping my ration of gewürztraminer until I spotted his pretentious wine-club brochure. "You are invited to place your name on a waiting list. . . . When a position becomes vacant you'll be invited to become a member. . . ." The young couple next to me was eagerly filling out an application. Her eyes, cable-knit sweater, and even the ribbons in her blond hair matched their eggshell-blue Volvo sedan. His name was "Bud" and they were traveling with a golden retriever. I followed them to another winery, hoping to overhear something I could offer Bruce Anderson as a house present for next week's issue of the *AVA*. While we waited for the "wine hostess" to uncork a bottle, a large family of Mexicans burst into the tasting room. The children were loud, the adults jolly and tipsy. When the hostess asked, "Are you familiar with our gewürztraminer?" they giggled. She gave them each a mean splash and poured full glasses for Bud and his wife. The three exchanged looks saying, "Even here. They're even *here*!"

Bruce Anderson's living room was dark and musty and could have used some Day-Glo posters of Che. He was a bearded nineteenth-century anarchist dressed by L.L. Bean, probably a good thing since the prep-school-teacher wardrobe of tweed jacket, khakis, and boat shoes made his size and piercing eyes less intimidating. On paper he had sounded strident. In person, he had the typical California eccentric's talent of making the most outrageous statements in a laid-back way. The beautiful fault-haunted geography that provided a friendly climate for his idiosyncracies had also smoothed their edges. He had a completely natural and unforced manner, an effortless way of becoming intimate without seeming to try that reminded me of the poet Laurie Lee's characterization of charm as "the ultimate weapon, the supreme seduction, against which there are few defenses."

He repeated his warning that I would be wasting my time in Ukiah, the "loggers" would be fat-assed executives who had never even stepped into a demonstration forest. I could also expect to find "Mother's Watch," an organization of "repulsive protimber women" he said wore yellow ribbons instead of swastikas. Then, without missing a beat, he railed against "yuppiefication" of the Anderson Valley and "your basic whacked-out hippie in the woods" who had bought big houses and taken over the school board. He blamed some of the unsavory changes on the former New Boonville Hotel restaurant, making it sound like a typical eighties story of inflated promise, bloated consumption, and obsession with food. A Bay Area couple had offered a now clichéd menu of nouvelle pizzas, free-range chicken, and salads with edible flowers. After the *San Francisco Chronicle* praised the hotel's "quietly elegant atmosphere" and pronounced it "status-building," food fanatics began landing private planes on the strip behind the high school. He conceded its owners were good cooks but insisted their claim to grow or raise all their food on the premises was bullshit. They bought from local farmers and distributors, keeping a backyard menagerie as window dressing. They fled to Oregon after an inspector from the Division of Labor Standards Enforcement confiscated their books. A later complaint accused them of multiple violations of state labor laws, including skimming tips and failing to pay workers' compensation. "Gleeful is not too strong a word to describe how the town felt when the place collapsed," he said. But the damage was done. They had attracted the "BMW crowd" and given the valley a yuppie cachet. People built second homes and opened wineries, destroying his dream of a progressive pastoral community.

The changes had served up some tempting new targets: liberals who opened their own private schools the moment they arrived, and corporate and tax-shelter vineyards that replaced orchards and sheep, fragmenting the valley into smaller plots and attracting a flood of Mexican workers.

"I have to be *very* careful how I put this," he said, insisting he was only worrying about the effect of so many foreign students suddenly enrolling in the local elementary schools. But ten years ago there had not been a single Spanish-speaking student, now they made up 50 percent of the system. Many arrived without a word of English, and without much encouragement to learn it since parents often planned on sending them back to relatives in Mexico for later schooling. This placed a tremendous burden on the teachers and budget.

He had received so many threats he had stopped counting, and vandals had smashed his computers and pillaged his office. The valley had a tradition of violence. A vigilante group calling itself "Cold Steel" had once routinely fired shotgun blasts at hippies, sometimes wrestling them to the ground to shave their heads. More recently "The Janitors" had armed themselves with chain saws and published a warning to "brain-dead assholes thieves." One of their communiqués declared, "This valley has a new set of ground rules. Steal from one of our select group and we are going to cut off one small finger. . . ."

In the sixties and early seventies the sociopaths of the future had drifted up from San Francisco to join communes and escape the police, and the valley had become a legendary incubator for what Anderson called "our world-class psychos." He had delivered gas to the Navarro commune where Charles Manson once lived and heard that someone had decapitated and chopped up a woman. No one was ever caught. "Was it Manson?" he wondered. Did he hang out with Jim Jones, who had taught sixth grade in the valley for two years and was a "great teacher"? Then there was Luis "Tree Frog" Johnson, who had honed his child-molesting techniques in the valley by taking hippie children camping and teaching at an alternative school. The Sierra Foothills Chainsaw Killers, Leonard Lake and Charles Ng, had met while working at the New Boonville Hotel, serving gourmet dishes before heading into the hills with chain saws to torture and dismember eighteen people.

Anderson himself had been jailed for a violent act that he now admitted was "unwise, to say the least." During a heated meeting of the school board in Point Arena, he had taunted the Mendocino County school superintendent for staffing his department with political cronies. The superintendent jumped up and shouted he was a rabble-rouser and a third-rate McCarthyite.

"I thought he was coming for me, so I hit him," Anderson admitted. "Actually all I did was graze him, so he lost his balance and fell over a coffee table. Afterward he made me sound like Clint Eastwood."

A jury in Ukiah acquitted Anderson of assault and battery but convicted him of disturbing the peace. This minor infraction usually came with a suspended sentence, but a young district attorney named David Eyster demanded a one-year sentence. The judge sentenced him to sixty days, offering to suspend it if he promised to avoid school-board meetings for a year. He refused on principle and served thirty-five days in the county jail. He believed it might be the longest sentence for disturbing the peace in California's history. When he was released he ran for school board, won 40 percent of the vote, and wrote a series on Eyster, exposing him as "a real hippie hater who had the support of the whole fascistic law-and-order community, and like a lot of Republican DAs just prosecuted a bunch of lowlifes and Mexicans with broken taillights." Now Eyster was running for judge and Anderson found the prospect of his victory terrifying. "If I ever come before that little yuppie for disturbing the peace again," he said, "he'll probably have me executed."

Three hours later I was in the community room of Ukiah's Sun House Museum at the kickoff party to elect C. David Eyster municipal court judge, shoveling down his calculating Republican canapés: tortillas dipped in spicy salsa (ethnic vote), a huge fruit salad (vegetarians, New Age, and joggers), local white wine and goat cheese (yuppies), and homemade fudge (family values). I had seen the open invitation in the local newspaper at a bar where I stopped to recover from Anderson's harangues. It promised "wine, soft drinks, and hors d'oeuvres"—a classic "wine sip."

I arrived feeling like a spy. I was still under Anderson's spell, hoping to hear something he could use to slow the Eyster bandwagon, although to be realistic, an attack by Anderson would probably have increased his vote. Balloons had been tied to empty sparkling-wine bottles and the room was brightly lit. The other guests were recently rusticated New Age Babbitts from the Bay Area: a vintner, some realtors, lawyers, and entrepreneurs, all gathered to support one of their own and eager to tell me how many cultural experiences Ukiah offered, how San Francisco was "really very close," and how often they took their children there to "enrich" them, since that was plainly impossible in this redneck town.

In his campaign photograph, Eyster had the pleasant smile and shock of black hair of the boy in the Norman Rockwell barber chair. In person he proved that thirty-five is a dangerous year for the baby-faced, when a soft, smooth face can begin aging without showing signs of character, leaving behind a decayed boy. He wore a tiepin (an article of jewelry I loathe) and had mastered that unsavory handshaking technique of shoveling your hands downward as if digging for something. Presidential candidates pump both hands like pistons, shaking hands behind their backs with people unseen. In this small gathering that was unnecessary, but Eyster did it anyway, no doubt practicing for the day he would have more hands to shake than Ukiah could provide.

His campaign manager's wife told me he was "a very intelligent person and well versed in the law." His nervous mother insisted he was smart and a nice son, then squeezed her plastic wineglass so hard it split open. His other supporters praised him for being tough on crime, saying things like "Santa Rosa has a crime wave and it's moving north toward us." "We're getting drive-by shootings now, it's moving up from the Bay Area." "It all started with the Mexican laborers a few years ago."

His wife, Gail, said, "He's honest, fair and hardworking, and wants law and order."

"He looks awfully young to be a judge," I said.

"That's probably because he had such a good plastic surgeon."

She explained that eight years before, after leaving work at his San Francisco law office to meet some friends for drinks, he had seen a big guy picking on a little drunk. He intervened, and the big guy, a USC student high on drugs, punched him in the face. He chased him by cab and on foot. By the time police apprehended him, blood was gushing from Eyster's face. The blow had shattered his jaw and it had to be wired shut for months. He sent out résumés from his hospital bed, looking for jobs outside San Francisco. Violent crime had touched her family, too. Her sister and brother-in-law had been murdered in Arizona in the seventies.

After this I no longer needed to ask why Eyster wanted to jail Bruce Anderson for a year for punching the Mendocino school superintendent, and the few words we exchanged were anticlimactic. To his credit, he refused to exploit his experiences, saying only that at his assailant's sentencing he had seen a very effective judge "take care of business." When I later overheard him tell a circle of supporters, "I'm very tuned in to violent crime. I know what the effect can be; how devastating it is for the family that gets the call," I knew I was hearing more than campaign rhetoric. It sounds farfetched that a punch thrown during a San Francisco street brawl could lead to Bruce Anderson receiving the longest sentence in state history for disturbing the peace, but I think that is precisely what happened.

12

"Our Children, Our Resource, Our Future"

I n 1913, California schoolchildren were reading *Conservation of Natural Resources* by Edward Hyatt, a progressive state superintendent of public instruction, and learning that, "In no other state or country is such variety and wealth of natural resources to be found as in California. Nowhere else is it being squandered with such a careless hand."

In 1957, when resources had been squandered in quantities Hyatt could not have imagined, the standard fourth-grade social-science textbook, *Our California Today*, said, "You have read how Californians save their water, forests, fish, game, and soil. The people of California are saving the renewable resources of our land. When the children of today grow up, they will be able to use and enjoy the resources of our state." As a fourth grader in Connecticut in 1957, I was indoctrinated by the East Coast version of this social-studies propaganda. It was so effective I did not question it for a decade, so I could understand why the Redwood Region Logging Conference had chosen "Our Children, Our Resource, Our Future" as its theme, a logger in a hard hat and a child holding a sapling as its symbol, and why the Ukiah fairgrounds buzzed with schoolchildren being taught by lectures and exhibits that, according to the manager of the convention, Charles Bendow, "trees should be used as a crop." He was the kind of "logger" Anderson had predicted, smooth, tweedy, and wearing polished cowboy boots.

I searched the exhibition hall for flannel shirts, work boots, leathery faces, or wounded hands; I found shetland sweaters, razor cuts, foppish white-collar-and-blue stripe investment-banker shirts, and "mature man" khakis.

The only person looking like a lumberjack was a fast-talking sep-
tuagenarian with tricky eyes named Earl Roberge who was hawking
his *Timber Country Revisited*. He called it "the logger's bible. The first
honest book about our industry." It was a compendium of photographs
of redwoods falling to the ax and men walking across logjammed
rivers. He had hoped to sell several hundred copies of what he advertised as a *"very* proindustry book," but admitted business was slow.
When I suggested perhaps few of the conventioneers had ever cut a tree
themselves, he whispered, "Well, yes, that *could* be the problem."

The hulking star of the Broken Top Lumberjack Show of Bend,
Oregon, looked like a lumberjack but was really more of a logger
clown who had taken the name Rex Redden. He tossed axes at a bull's-
eye, then at his assistant, Yolanda. He danced on a log floating in a kiddie pool shouting "we have to get this to the sawmill" before tumbling
on purpose into the water. During the intermission he admitted being
from New York City, and had once trained as a tree surgeon. Yolanda
had graduated from the University of Sinaloa in Mexico. "My life there,
ees different," she said, picking at her checked flannel shirt as if notic-
ing it for the first time. "I never think I will become a 'Lumber Jill.' "

The children swarming through the fairgrounds in discount-store
duds did not look like the offspring of the sleek pseudo-lumberjacks.
The bad-complexioned boys were thin and sharp-featured, the girls
pale and overweight. After lunching on Ring-Dings and Yoo-Hoo,
they clambered like Lilliputians over the steam shovels, bulldozers, and
sixteen-wheel trailers that hauled unmilled logs to freighters bound for
Asia and Mexico. A karaoke machine completed the circle, enabling
children wearing Asian clothes, staring at Asian-made bulldozers and
trailers that hauled logs to Asian freighters bound for Asian lumber
mills, to use the favorite toy of whiskey-sotted Japanese company men.
A little boy crossed his eyes trying to follow the lyrics to "Satisfaction"
on the screen and, so help me, a nervous ten-year-old girl stumbled over
"Born in the USA."

A line of children snaked out the door of an exhibition hall where a
sign announced the GIFT FROM A TREE SHOPPING SPREE. Ladies from the
proindustry group Women in Timber divided the children into teams.
The object was to select products that came from a tree. When a Timber
Woman blew a whistle, the children raced down the aisles, throwing
Tide, Cheerios, Bisquick, Bounty towels, Triscuits, and Cinnamon Toast
Crunch Cereal into a shopping cart. Their team members squealed and
jumped. A Timber Woman shouted, "It's *fun* to buy things made from

trees." Losers were scolded for choosing an aluminum baking dish. Winners got a single Frito that tasted like wood pulp.

The posters Mendocino schoolchildren had entered in a "Happy Forests" contest covered the walls of another hall. The winners had drawn "Happy Forest Communities" filled with birds, deer, clean-running streams, and happy fishermen. A boy had surrounded his forest with a border of chain saws, but the irony was clearly unintended since like other entries he had titled it with the Women in Timber slogan, "Trees Are for People." Most children had drawn trucks, saws, and bulldozers in forests that were nevertheless luxuriant and crowded with redwoods. There was not a clear-cut, tree farm, or raw stump anywhere. But one little rebel had placed a spotted owl in a tree, and another had titled her drawing of a forest thick with beavers and birds *Please Be Careful with the Future*. It was unquestionably the best drawing, but had not even won an honorable mention.

I had been reading environmental screeds and glossy timber-industry pamphlets in equal measure to prepare myself for this convention, trying to decide whether to believe the industry that "young redwood forests are growing at a phenomenal rate," or the turncoat logger who claimed, "They say they plant five trees to every one they take. Well, what they don't tell you is that only 7 percent of these trees make it to full maturity." Even articles in north-coast newspapers sympathetic to timber interests indicated the timber flacks were less trustworthy than the environmental ones. Memoranda leaked from Louisiana Pacific showed internal company protests against overcutting, and the report of a congressional committee accused the companies of including "phantom forests" in reforestation statistics and concluded, "Current forest regrowth in the Northwest is only 64% of volume cut." But even after walking with Rondal Snodgrass, my prejudices made me more receptive to the industry's arguments. I still preferred meadows, working farms, and even deserts to dense forests, and would rather hike an open ridgeline than a wood any day, or look out a window and see for miles. I did not have the time to master the intricacies of the timber wars, so I decided to choose sides by seeing who had the most appealing and trustworthy followers. I had liked Snodgrass, Dunklin, and the other environmentalists I had met, and wanted to search the convention for equally appealing protimber voices.

I found Sue Snodgrass (no relation to Rondal) and Nancy Inmon behind the Women in Timber table in the main exhibition hall. Snodgrass was married to a partner in a timber mill. Inmon was an intense, sparrow-sized woman who had taught school in Southern California. She told me, "I went on a woods tour, wrote a grant, and got the money." She believed in the cause, because "98 percent of the people in the timber industry are great," and argued, "The logging process cannot pollute because wood is a natural substance. Dirt is a natural substance, too. Logging simply doesn't put silt in rivers, it can't happen because the company would be fined."

I asked if this was what she taught the schoolchildren.

"Our supporters may *appear* to be a lot of companies, but they do not ask us to deliver a biased message," she snapped. "We're seeing 100,000 youngsters a year, we wouldn't be allowed into the classrooms if we were making them unhappy. We simply remind the children how *much* they like seeing deer and rabbits—and aren't those what most people want to see? To see them you need grass, meadows, and secondary-growth forests. The old-growth redwood forests are too dark and deep, just a lot of diseased trees."

Like me, she had not particularly enjoyed her recent visit to Humboldt Redwood State Park. "Look at the tops along the Avenue of the Giants, they're all in poor health. Those poor trees are *dying*! Why, cutting them would be like . . . like . . ."

"Putting down a sick horse," said another woman.

The neighboring display belonged to Mothers' Watch, a more political and aggressive proindustry group of women whose name had a vigilante ring. When I tried engaging Nadine, a "Mother" working for the California Forestry Association, in a discussion of sustainable forestry, she snapped, "Environmentalists don't have your best interests at heart—they're evil."

A moon-faced matron named Candace Boak identified herself as a founding member of Mothers' Watch and ticked off its accomplishments. They had erected a symbolic "tent city" for homeless timber workers, printed I LOVE TREES AND LUMBER bumper stickers, and organized a boycott of any enterprise advertising in a north-coast newspaper friendly to the environmental movement. She showed me a handwritten flyer full of double exclamation marks that reminded me of the ones muttering Eastern European women used to glue on lampposts around the United Nations. It accused the Audubon and Wilderness societies of being "greedy corporations" that "used" politicians. The Wilderness Society bred "crises and fear." The National Wildlife Federation just wanted to "make us feel guilty for our consumer habits."

The Mothers' great fear was that their husbands might lose their jobs, forcing them to move to a downstate city or suburb. They had noticed middle-class refugees moving into their communities and sensibly asked themselves why they should be forced into minimum-wage service jobs in the places newcomer environmentalists were themselves abandoning. The only thing they and environmentalists seemed to agree on was that neither wanted to live anywhere else in California.

Boak pressed on me a transcript of her testimony to the House Subcommittee on National Parks and Public Land, saying it would answer my questions about timber harvests, overcutting, and the loss of jobs to Mexico. She was proud of it, and as I skimmed it her face rose like dough. It began, "Mothers' Watch is a movement of families for families," then degenerated into a temper tantrum. The Mothers were "tired of being kicked around by preservationists," "fed up with politicians and southern Californians telling us what to do," and with "constantly being terrorized—yes, terrorized—by media-manipulating obstructionists." Timber workers were like "criminals on death row."

It was the hysterical and uncompromising rhetoric common to the abortion controversy, and of course once you believed an enemy is "evil," and had threatened your life by putting you "on death row," it became easier to consider taking theirs.

The conference's gin-fizz breakfast was billed as "a Paul Bunyan-style breakfast" and the logging-equipment salesmen sharing my table did their best to prove the myth that Bunyan's gargantuan appetite could only be satisfied by a camp stove covering an acre, greased down by lumberjacks wearing sides of bacon as skates. They wolfed down towers of flapjacks, mounds of eggs, and thick rashers of bacon, but their squishy guts told you their Bunyan-sized breakfasts were usually followed by very un-Bunyan-like days behind a desk. By nine-thirty they had become a noisy, gin-fizz-soaked rabble, eager to be roused. When the president of a timber association accused "professional environmentalists" of "promoting crises to keep their jobs," and thundered, "We reach for the good life, but are thwarted by rules and regulations passed by self-proclaimed 'experts,'" they cheered and pounded the tables.

Last year's keynote speaker had been Rush Limbaugh; this year it was the (now late) Dixie Lee Ray. She resembled a bowling ball topped with a helmet of gray hair, and despite her Stanford doctorate, twenty-two honorary degrees, chairmanship of the Atomic Energy Commission, term as governor of Washington, and "Senior Scholar of

Environmental Health and Safety" position at the University of Maryland, she delivered a crude diatribe obviously pulled from her file cabinet and tricked up with some references to timber. The gist was that every environmental complaint was fraudulent, nature existed to serve man, there could never be too much growth and consumption, and "a well-tended garden is better than a neglected woodlot."

She argued, in a gravelly, snarling voice, that we should applaud the population explosion as a sign of human ingenuity and success. Fears of overpopulation were nonsense because people only occupied 15 percent of the earth's surface (although like others making this stupid argument, she did not volunteer to live in Tierra del Fuego or the Empty Quarter so the rest of us could have enough room).

She denounced the concept of an "average world temperature" as nonsense, because "an 'average' human being would be one breast and one testicle!"

She thought industry and not the environmental movement should take credit for the fact that "we no longer see black, billowing smoke coming out of smokestacks," conveniently forgetting industry organizations had fought air-quality regulations as hard as the timber industry was now opposing government interference with its harvests.

"If we allow environmental laws to ruin our economy, we will lose our liberty just as certainly as we would lose it in war!" she shouted. "Environmental groups want to deprive you of your rights. They must be resisted! Don't be afraid of fighting back!"

Everyone at my table jumped to their feet applauding. The man across from me swore environmentalists were worse than communists. When I looked at my notes I realized if I substituted *communists* for *environmentalists*, I had just heard a Red-baiting speech from the 1950s.

If you persuade people an enemy is conspiring to deprive them of their rights and liberties, you should not be surprised if they resort to violence. If you believe Judi Bari, this is what happened when a pipe bomb exploded in the Subaru station wagon she was driving through Oakland on May 24, 1990.

When you hear about someone as much as I heard about Bari, you want to meet them. Everyone I asked about timber in Mendocino County vilified or canonized her. Bruce Anderson had called her "PC Central" and her followers in the radical environmental group Earth First! "a ragtag bag of fagged old hippies and troublemakers," but he also praised her environmental stands and believed "corporate timber" had tried to assassinate her. Her telephone was unlisted, but a woman in the Ukiah environmental center agreed to pass my number along to her. By the time I persuaded her to see me, I was south of San Francisco and had to double back to Mendocino. As I drove to her house from Willits on dirt roads becoming progressively narrower and rougher, I understood why a single mother of two daughters who lived in this lonely countryside and had already been almost murdered, might want to keep her address secret. When I met her, I understood why an enemy might want to kill her.

She had a Modigliani face, long hair, and deep-socketed, dark-circled eyes—turn-of-the-century anarchist looks. The bombing had paralyzed her foot and broken her backbone. Her damaged nerves sent electric shocks down one leg, and every limping step was a reminder.

She began by showing me her "sampler of colorful death threats." They came in the mail, over her answering machine, and sometimes tacked to the door so her daughters could read them. They ranged from the basic "Get out and go back where you came from. You won't get a second warning," to a bull's-eye drawn over a photograph of her playing the violin at an environmental rally. The "Tasmanian Teens" had written, "Accidents Happen ... Have a nice summer." A photograph of an Uzi submachine gun came with "Bari get out." The "Stompers" had printed directions to her house and promised a "Case of Coors to the stud who burns her hideout." A noose had been drawn on another Stompers warning that promised, "Our justice will be swift and very real. We know who you are and where you live. If you want to be a martyr we'll be happy to oblige."

A threat she attributed to a Southern California motorcycle club said, "It has come to our attention that you are an EF [Earth First!] lesbian whose favorite pastime is eating box lunch in pajamas." Shortly after that, she began receiving newspaper clippings of little girls killed in road accidents, with her name substituted for those of the grieving mothers, and that summer a logging truck rammed her car while she was driving with her daughters to a demonstration.

She claims that when she complained, the Mendocino County sheriff said, "We don't have the manpower to investigate death threats. If you turn up dead, then we'll investigate."

She thought people wanted her dead because she was the only environmentalist who had reached the timber workers. She was working class. No college degree, just several years toiling in the Baltimore bulk-mail sorting facility where she had organized other clerks into a union and led an effective wildcat strike. She had little use for hippie environmentalists "dumb enough to blame the timber workers." They shouted, "Do you know what biodiversity means?" in their high-pitched graduate-school voices when they blocked the loggers' bulldozers. She detested the cultural apartheid of loggers versus hippies and never said "redneck." Some loggers believed her when she told them, "*We're* not taking your children's jobs. Charles Hurwitz, who makes $8 million a year, is taking them to pay off his junk bonds." After the bombing, one of the timber workers urged her to move in with his family, another sewed the slipcovers for the couch I was sitting on.

Her office, like Albert James's trailer, was overflowing with legal documents and newspaper clippings. She apologized for the mess, but explained she had just returned from lecturing to "a bunch of spoiled Ivy League brats" on the East Coast and such speeches supplemented her disability. She said she had moved to California because she had been corresponding with a postal worker organizing retail clerks in San Diego, and, when they finally met, they fell in love. She broke up with her boyfriend and he divorced his wife. She hated leaving Baltimore, where she had become a top union official, but it was easier for her to quit her job than for him to abandon his kids. They moved to Santa Rosa and settled into a home in a meadow that within three years was circled by quarter-acre tract housing. To escape it and save their marriage they moved to Mendocino and built a house together. "A good way to get divorced," she said. After they split, she advertised for a free place to live in exchange for carpentry work and found this place in Willits.

She became aware of environmental issues only when she began building yuppie vacation houses to support her family. What converted her was an opulent mansion being constructed for a Bay Area man who insisted on a clear glass shower so he could watch his babes washing. The siding was the most beautiful wood she had ever seen: smooth, tiny-grained, without a knot. When she asked the bookkeeper if it was old-growth redwood, he said, "Oh yeah, that shit is a thousand years old."

When it was completed she presented the owner with a photograph of the neighboring clear-cut that had produced his wood and joined the radical environmental organization Earth First! She demonstrated at logging sites and became a principal organizer for the 1990 Redwood Summer, a series of protests and community organizing modeled on the

1965 Mississippi Summer Project. The bomb had exploded in her car one month before thousands of environmentalists were scheduled to arrive in Humboldt and Mendocino to protest the destruction of old-growth red-woods. She had been driving through Oakland with Darryl Cheney, another Earth First! activist and her former lover, to a meeting with the pacifist organization that would train their volunteers in nonviolent techniques.

She spread out color photographs of the damaged car, stabbing them with a finger to show where the bomb was located. The first Oakland policemen on the scene told her it had been under the seat and she was the target. Ten minutes later, FBI agents were accusing her and Cheney of being terrorists carrying a bomb that had accidentally detonated. They arrested her, held her without bail, and questioned her as she was being wheeled into surgery. Court papers called them "members of a violent terrorist group involved in the manufacture and placing of explosive devices," but the evidence was thin and circumstantial, centering on nail fragments that were a common variety. Her injuries were consistent with a bomb under the seat, FBI tests proved inconclusive, police admitted the bomb might have been placed farther forward, and the Alameda County District Attorney's Office declined to press charges. Only the tiny Willits Police Department continued actively investigating the explosion, and whoever had wanted her dead remained at large.

For several hours she led me through the loose-leaf binders she had assembled for her lawsuit against the Oakland Police Department and the FBI for false arrest, illegal search and seizure, habeas corpus, and failure to investigate the bombing. She had already won two motions to dismiss and was in discovery, but expected the proceedings to continue for years. Her thesis was that in the months preceding Redwood Summer, the big timber companies, their public-relations firms, and protimber groups had encouraged violence against environmental activists, while at the same time smearing them as terrorists. This policy had encouraged her assassin. "I may not know exactly who put the bomb in my car," she said, "but I do know who set me up to be killed, which is big timber, and who covered it up, which is the FBI."

She pulled out an internal Pacific Lumber Company memorandum from a public-relations executive praising "the fine fellow" who had waded into a demonstration with a chain saw and decked an activist, and promising him a "dinner invitation" if he could be found. Then she showed me a bogus Earth First! press release saying, "We intend to spike trees, monkeywrench, and even resort to violence if necessary. We will not stand for the destruction of mother earth." It spelled Darryl Cheney's name incorrectly and had Bari living in the wrong town. Another internal Pacific Lumber Company memorandum admitted being unsure who had written the release.

"So the timber companies disseminate fake press releases to incite their workers to violence and I get real death threats," she said, "and it worked! Soon the press was saying we were both equally violent. Just look at this!" She pointed to a *Santa Rosa Press-Democrat* editorial demanding that both sides repudiate violence. "Great! This is balance! They're threatening to kill us, while we're called violent because of a faked press release."

A month before the car bomb, the Mendocino Board of Supervisors had called her to a meeting to explain why she wanted to bring violent protesters to Mendocino County during Redwood Summer. She held up the bull's-eye drawn over her face and announced, "The person who sent me this is probably in this room." A supervisor told her she had brought it on herself. A logger gave a speech comparing Redwood Summer organizers to the Nazis and the Klan. Another promised to shoot them if they trespassed on his property. The audience and supervisors smiled and nodded approval. The video of the meeting was "chilling," she said. "Their basic argument was that by bringing so many nonviolent demonstrators into the county we were forcing them to beat us up."

She admitted her mistakes had played into their hands. She should never have allowed herself to be photographed, à la Patty Hearst, wearing an Earth First! T-shirt and holding an automatic weapon, but she was set up by a man she now believes was a police informer. He had shown up one night with a friend, supplied the weapon, persuaded her to strike this pose as a joke, then disappeared. Tree spiking had been a mistake, something she always opposed and finally persuaded Earth First! to renounce publicly. A spike had injured a millworker, although she was not willing to concede it had been driven into the tree by Earth First! She thought three other spikes allegedly found in mills were plants to discredit Redwood Summer. When someone blew up power lines near Santa Cruz shortly before her car bomb, she stupidly called them heroes even though her Earth First! chapter had called for nonviolent protests. "Another example of my smart-ass mouth getting me into trouble."

I did not have time to interview everyone in Mendocino County who liked or loathed Bari. Even if I did, I would have come no closer to knowing who placed the bomb under her seat. But I do know if I lived in Mendocino County and had to choose between her and the timber executives and their supporters, I would choose her in a minute. Compare her "smart-ass mouth" with Charles Hurwitz, who after taking over Pacific Lumber announced his version of the golden rule was, "Those with the gold, rule." Or with the Sahara Club, a motorcycle club praised by protimber organizations, whose members drove to Northern California to disrupt Redwood Summer. After the Oakland car bomb, its newsletter declared, "Bari, who had her crotch blown off, will never be able to reproduce again. We're just trying to figure out who would volunteer to inseminate her if she had all her parts." Or with the man in Fort Bragg who ran for a seat on the county board of supervisors and was endorsed by the Deputy Sheriffs' Association of Mendocino County, received campaign donations from timber executives and companies, and warned Redwood Summer would mean "eighty thousand drug-crazed hippies defecating on our lawns," adding, "We know how to handle them . . . with a six-pack of beer and an ax handle."

Compare them and ask yourself, no matter how many board feet of timber you feel should or should not be harvested every year, whose side you would rather be on.

After leaving Mendocino County for the second time, I learned that Joy and Ruth Simmerley of Ukiah were great Bruff fans, and perhaps descended from a Washington Miner. I was ready to return again until I called and discovered their connection was less direct than I had hoped, although more poignant.

In the tremulous voice of the very, very old, Ruth Simmerley said, "I'm always interested in talking to anyone who's interested in history," but admitted she and her sister were not related to any of the Washington City Miners, nor unfortunately to Bruff, since he was among their heroes. They had taken an interest in him because they had been married to brothers who were relatives of Susan Ferguson, who as a girl had been injured by a giant black oak that crashed into the tents of the sleeping Ferguson and Alford families during a storm sweeping across Bruff's camp early on the morning of October 31, 1849. The tree had killed the Alford father, his two teenage sons, and his daughter's boyfriend, but had miraculously spared the Fergusons and their nine children aged one to thirteen. The incident was so dramatic and tragic it had fascinated generations of Fergusons, even gripping distant relations like the Simmerleys.

Ruth Simmerley knew of only two detailed accounts of the calamity: one written by Bruff; the other, which she no longer had, composed in 1918 for a Healdsburg newspaper by Henry Ferguson, who had been eleven at the time of the accident.

The tragedy had occurred only nine days after Bruff and his company had separated, during a period when other Lassen Trail stragglers often stopped at his camp to gather their strength for their final push into the valley. He reported in his diary being awakened by a man crying, "Hello, here! turn out and assist, a tree has fallen on a couple of tents, and wounded several persons." He lit a lantern and discovered a decayed oak had fallen only one hundred yards from his own tent. Its trunk had grazed the Ferguson family tent pitched at its base, but a limb "capable of making a couple of cords of fuel" had crashed full force into a tent where the four men of the Alford party lay sleeping.

He and the other emigrants rolled the trunk off the victims with makeshift levers. When they raised the bloodstained tent, Bruff wrote, "There lay a shocking sight! An aged, grey-headed man, and his grown son, with their hips buried in the ground and their ghastly eyes turned up in death! next another son, and beside him, a young man, his comrade, slowly dying in agony, with broken legs and mutilated bodies—groaning and uttering the name of God, in acute suffering! The screaming of the females, the grey-headed mother kissing their pallid brows while her silver hairs swept their faces, and then she would groan & scream.—and her two grown daughters stood, with clasped hands, choking sobs, and eyes upraised to Heaven, regardless of the bleak storm and rain."

When he checked the tent at the base of the tree he found the Ferguson children unharmed except for two little girls; one (presumably five-year-old Susan Ferguson) was "slightly bruised and sprained." For the rest of the night he attended to the Alfords, laying out the dead father on the fallen trunk, placing his son's corpse nearby, and pitching a small tent over the dying brother and his comrade. Throughout the following day the Alford women went about, "parting their hair, and sobbing [while] the dying son turned his head in agony,—on one side he saw his dead brother, and on the other his dying friend."

The Alfords had arrived in Bruff's camp while he slept, and he had never met them. But although he was suffering from painful

rheumatoid arthritis, he read the Presbyterian burial service at their funeral, even climbing into the grave afterward and turning over the
corpses so Mrs. Alford could gaze on the faces of her husband and sons
a last time. (She cried out, "Why did he take them all at once—and not
leave me one!") Afterward he fashioned a headstone from the tailboard
of a wagon and composed an epitaph:

> *Their journey is ended, their toils are all past,*
> *Together they slept, in this false world their last:*
> *They here sleep together, in one grave entombed—*
> *Side by side, as they slept, on the night they were doom'd!*

It is impossible to read Bruff's account of this incident and not be
moved. It had turned the Simmerley sisters into such fans that once
Ruth Simmerley discovered I was a relative, I had difficulty ending the
call. Although Bruff had not mentioned the Fergusons by name, she
recognized their story would have been lost to history had Bruff not included it in his diaries.

Although Bruff's men had abandoned him before the Alfords and
Fergusons arrived in camp, I told myself that speaking to the widow of
a relative of someone whose experiences had intersected his, however
briefly, was at least a small accomplishment. And Ruth Simmerley also
directed me to Veda Benson in Los Gatos, a cousin of her late husband,
and a direct Ferguson descendant. I took down Benson's number,
telling myself that following the Ferguson-Alford story was more than
grasping at straws. These families had stopped at Bruff's camp just as
he realized his men had abandoned him, and it was possible their recollections might help explain his betrayal.

THREE

DOWN THE
NORTH COAST

❖

13

At Home in
Mendocino

The San Andreas shadows most of the Mendocino coast without coming ashore. It begins its underwater journey at Shelter Cove, less than three miles north of the county's northern boundary, ending it on Manchester Beach, just twenty miles from the southern boundary. This fault segment is far less active than the Triple Junction, and its inhabitants are less twitchy about quakes. The only person I could find showing any interest in the fault was a long-haired clerk in the Elk general store who claimed to have sighted formations of flying saucers hovering over it offshore. The only serious damage occurred almost a century ago, when the fault broke along its entire subterranean length during the great 1906 San Francisco earthquake, toppling buildings and starting fires that destroyed the coastal city of Fort Bragg.

Because the Working Group on California Earthquake Probabilities has given this north-coast segment a less than 2-percent chance of producing another Big One of a magnitude 8.0 or higher in the next thirty years, I had planned to stay only a short time, but even that proved difficult, because although Mendocino is one of California's poorest counties, its coast has become inhospitably expensive. In part this is because it is famous for pretending to be New England in popular Hollywood films and television programs, including *Murder, She Wrote* and *Summer of '42*.

It really looks nothing like Maine, where villages are tucked into coves or estuaries and face greens and protected harbors. By contrast, its towns ramble over meadows and teeter on cliffs marked with signs warning KEEP AWAY FROM THE EDGE! They are rickety and weather-beaten, wrapped in a gauze of fog and salt. The wind is incessant. Beams are always creaking, doors banging, and conversations get sucked upwind, like embers flying up a chimney. And unlike New England, this coast has always looked inland, making its living off trees instead of fish. There are no natural harbors, and the few fishing boats huddle in river mouths. Its villages grew up next to lumber mills and coves where logs could be slid down chutes to waiting boats. They were already becoming ghost towns in the 1930s. Now cattle and sheep graze on meadows rolling to the sea, and local histories describe vanished wharves and lost saloons and begin sentences "Once . . ." and "In its heyday . . ." But a few chosen towns, the village of Mendocino being the prime example, have reinvented themselves as cute seafaring villages. The others are approaching this inevitable destiny at varying speeds, and with varying degrees of enthusiasm.

For the moment there was little middle ground between the Navarro Beach homeless encampment and a farmhouse tarted up into a two-hundred-dollar-a-night inn. Simple bed-and-breakfasts up and down the coast had become "romantic hideaways," while roadside cabins and fishermen's motels had installed hot tubs and reproduction antiques and tripled their rates. I stopped at the Mendocino Hotel—"Timeless Elegance on California's Rugged North Coast"—to find its simple facade concealed a pricey octopus of condominium additions and garden suites. Sonoma County to the south was even worse and its St. Orres Hotel, a whimsical lodge of Russian-style carved balconies, stained-glass windows, and onion domes that looked like fun, charged twenty-eight dollars for tequila-marinated quail served with wontons. A glacial young woman at the desk said her only available room had a "two-person lovers' shower."

The inns were expensive because to keep up they had to offer a Jacuzzi, fluffy terrycloth robes, and waffles swimming in fruit syrups. There had to be four-poster beds, fireplaces, hot tubs, decks, white-water views, champagne, bowls of fruit, decanters of sherry, bubble bath, afternoon tea, wildflowers, and chocolates on pillows. Discounts for single rooms were rare, and the brochure from Mendocino Coast Reservations had SHARE MENDOCINO WITH A FRIEND . . . written over its outrageous tariffs and promised "a haven for serious romantics." The "romance" being pushed was the generic kind of television soap-opera lovers and sitcom families. One boutique had a "romance nook" offering a prepackaged "Weekender"—two small Kama Sutra love oils, wild clove bathing gel, and a feather—that perfectly reflected the desperate calculation accompanying a Mendocino weekend. Couples came to nurse wounded affairs, young men to propose in a greeting-card setting of crashing waves and chiseled cliffs. Yet everywhere I found myself eavesdropping on lovers' spats. I suppose that when romance is sold like merchandise, it sometimes disappoints the customer.

I was saved by Fort Bragg, a friendly, blue-collar, rain-soaked runt of a city with reasonable motels. Its post-1906 reconstruction had been done on the cheap, buildings were low and unprepossessing, as if its sober Finns and Swedes worried the fault might slap them down again. Still, the clanging railway bells, factory whistles, and puffing smokestacks made it a good antidote to the coast's oppressive service economy.

My motel overlooked the only working harbor between Eureka and San Francisco and every morning I woke to chugging engines, barking seals, and the whoosh of high-pressure hoses chasing them off the piers. I became friendly with a Fish and Game agent who sat hidden across the river, spying with binoculars on Mexicans unloading boxes of sea urchins whose roe would be in Tokyo sushi bars within the week. I drank Red Seal Ale at the North Coast Brewing Company, surrounded by generous drinkers who ordered a pitcher and filled every glass in sight. A bore who resembled a walrus and was obsessed with the sixties shouted questions like "What was the plot of *A Hard Day's Night?*" When no one replied he would supply the answer, "Ha! Didn't have one. That was the problem with the sixties, too, no plot."

When traveling around the equator I had rarely resorted to eavesdropping. But in California, where chance encounters are more difficult, I became a snoop. I always brought a book, pretending to read, but making notes in the margins of what I overheard. I complained about background music so it would be lowered, and drafts so I could move closer to my targets. The best place in Fort Bragg for this sport was a narrow storefront restaurant with closely spaced tables and a chef who was trying. It was slightly expensive for the town and the first time I went the only diners were two fatties in their midforties wearing matching jogging outfits. They were so bored with each other they turned every encounter with their hollow-cheeked waitress into an extended conversation.

They grandly announced themselves to have been senior political appointees in the Bush and Reagan administrations, then recited little anecdotes of courage and small-town life they had bullied out of other waitresses during their transcontinental driving holiday. They concluded that "we've got a pretty nice nation here, if you stick to the small towns."

When the waitress mentioned she was raising two children alone, the woman said, "I have some important advice for you, dear, under no circumstances let them watch MTV."

He slapped the table. "We as a country *have to stop MTV.*"

They recommended taking the children on long family holidays, visiting museums and the theater. "Expose them to everything," she ordered. "Why not go to San Francisco next weekend?"

Right now they were, as he put it, "shopping for the ideal hometown. You know, like the one in that *Morning in America* commercial." Tomorrow they were seeing real-estate agents in Mendocino village. Ten years before it had been their favorite place in California.

When the waitress revealed she had grown up there, they asked about the price of houses. I missed her reply, but it made him slap his forehead and howl, "Oh my God! It's been found. When we went there it was just like that movie, the *Summer of '42.*"

She explained her childhood home and those of her schoolmates had become summer rentals or bed-and-breakfasts. No one who grew up in the village could afford living in it. "This coast is filling up fast," she said firmly, "and as it does, many people from here are moving to Oregon."

Her voice was suddenly loud and hard, and I imagined her thinking, "filling up with people like you."

Like most large Northern California towns Fort Bragg had an "environmental center," a storefront office serving as headquarters for groups trying to lay down bike paths, end old-growth logging, promote solar energy, stop a Wal-Mart, and end admission charges at state beaches. They made me miss the sixties and the office of my college civil-rights council, which had this same smell of dust, cats, and coffee, the same sprung sofas, leaflets heaped on trestle tables, and perpetual meetings. I hung around a half hour for the next one, called to organize "Operation Camelot," a "grass-roots movement" to force the release of secret Kennedy assassination files that would prove a CIA–big-business–military conspiracy. A Kennedy assassination expert named Paul Kangas had just spoken in Fort Bragg, offering conspiracy theories that must have resonated with the aging Berkeley geniuses scratching out a backwoods living.

The Camelot organizers were in their thirties and forties. Despite their 1960s intensity and paranoia, decades of Mendocino County living had left them sweetly loony. A high-strung bald man I will call Jim (I have changed everyone else's name, too) came dressed like a deckhand and suggested Camelot members should wear the 1960 KENNEDY FOR PRESIDENT 'pins that did *not* mention Lyndon Johnson, or they could put strips of tape across Johnson's name. He "shared" a letter he had sent to a local newspaper that went, "Mr. Kangas is a dynamic, well-researched investigator, far from what he has been termed elsewhere, 'a conspiracy nut.' He will always have our undying love and admiration."

No one wanted to be Camelot's chairperson.

Jim was too busy.

The motherly Darla twisted her gray pigtails and fingered the Indian earrings that swung five inches below her lobes and muttered, "I'm not really comfortable with speaking at all at this time in my life. I have to clear a lot of boundaries first. It's a growth project."

Lisa said she was not into talking to people right now, but she was certain exposing the CIA murder of Kennedy was something everyone in Fort Bragg could get behind. It would bring the community together and she would write letters to the Kiwanis, Boy Scouts, and League of Women Voters, explaining how the Bay of Pigs, Vietnam, and Watergate all figured into the conspiracy. She had prepared a sample letter ending, "Do we have a fascist republic? We are scared for our children!"

Nathan said although no one doubted Richard Nixon and George Bush killed JFK, he was worried people were overlooking Gerald Ford's role in the plot. He refused to be chairperson on principle, since some in the group wanted to make it also part of a voter registration drive. He thought voting was a cruel trick, a way of snaring people into the system. "Why do I need to vote when I'm already being heard by people in this room?" he wondered.

Barbara wondered how you registered anyway. Did you go to the county hall?

No one knew, because no one was registered.

Tom wondered if "Operation Camelot" was appropriate. Perhaps they should call themselves "People for the People." Instead of a "chairperson," should they have a facilitator?

The conversation drifted. Someone proposed timing a voter registration drive so it would disrupt the Whale Watching Festival. Someone else asked if crop circles meant UFOs, or Christ's Second Coming.

"UFO landings for sure," Darla said. "But we don't have to worry because the space people are here to help."

Jim told everyone about Benjamin Creme, a London Asian who had become a hot channeler in Los Angeles. The dead Kenyan boy who spoke through him was an environmentalist who had predicted the fall of Thatcher and Gorbachev. Perhaps Camelot should contact him.

"Well, who does Creme say shot Kennedy?" I asked, speaking up for the first time.

As Tom replied coldly that Creme had not yet chosen to unmask Kennedy's assassins, I noticed Nathan and Lisa staring at me and whispering. They exchanged glances with Tom and he abruptly closed the meeting. Addressing me, he said, "Well, you may not appreciate it, but we've already accomplished several things. Because of the Paul Kangas visit, which we sponsored, a lady in Elk has just come forward with Lee Harvey Oswald's missing death certificate."

"And don't forget our letter," someone added.

"That's right, we've written a letter to Oliver Stone, asking him to speak in Fort Bragg."

A few people raised fists and murmured, "Right on!"

Like some inner-city maid commuting to work in the suburbs, I drove every morning from my cheap Fort Bragg digs to Mendocino village, a place whose appearance in so many films and advertisements had made it familiar in ways I found unsettling, but apparently appealed to everyone else. In the guest book of the Mendocino Historical Research Center at the Kelley House, a steep-roofed, gabled, Gothic Revival cottage known as "Jessica's House" because every week its exterior is presented to viewers of *Murder, She Wrote* as the home of mystery author Jessica Fletcher, one couple had written, "For some unknown reason we feel at home here."

But at home where? In which Mendocino? In the thriving logging town that had disappeared decades before? In Jessica's cozy Maine village of Cabot's Cove? In the all-American town where a prosperous citizenry celebrated July Fourth in the Chevrolet Heartbeat of America advertisements?

For a while Mendocino village could fool you. You saw its skyline of church steeples and water towers, its wooden sidewalks, white picket fences, steep-pitched New England roofs, and false-front Western stores, all perched on a treeless headland as green as a cricket pitch and ringed by pounding surf, and you began scheming how to become a resident. And if you stayed only a few hours and left without asking too many questions, you might never learn the sweet Norman Rockwell cottages were mostly rentals, and the friendly clerks in the boutiques probably lived in Fort Bragg, or be told that although the lodges and church basements looked like venues for vigorous New England–style town meetings, Mendocino was an unincorporated village, so every important decision was rendered at the distant county seat of Ukiah.

In a bookstore with a large New Age section where I overheard the clerk telling a friend, "The whole of *Yes!* is something that's really powerful," I browsed through a photographic essay on the village titled *Mendocino—Past and Present.* It mixed black-and-white historic and contemporary photographs, and if I kept to the photographs, it appeared to be a loving tribute. But when I read one of the accompanying essays I learned that "each summer day now, Main Street resembles a city parking lot," and "only the very young, the very drugged, or the very naive still hold fast to the fantasy that was Mendocino."

It was easy to be sanctimonious about Mendocino's ruination, but what was the alternative? Unlike Ferndale, it was not built on something as substantial as agriculture but on timber, a resource that once exhausted always sets a town adrift. It had enjoyed a brief flowering as an artists' colony, but that is usually a transitional time for a quaint seaside community, when it acquires the reputation its developers cash in later. What else can an economically depressed but unrealistically pretty town peddle except itself—as a movie location, site for weekend assignations, and surrogate "home." What else to sell besides nostalgia, weekend shopping, and sex?

You could sometimes see the spending and sex interacting. I followed several visitor couples, noting how often they sealed a purchase with a sidewalk kiss, and how as their bags became heavier and made them wobble from side to side like refugees off a boat, they leaned against one another more, held hands, hurried purchases, and spent less time in stores but bought more, as if approaching some consumerist climax.

I succumbed myself, buying a belt at the Compass Rose leather shop from Ed O'Brien, who had blown into town as a hippie hitchhiker in the late 1960s and was now a pillar of the business community and raising a family here, which was the source of many of his complaints. He railed in fine sixties style against people who came "to buy a piece of small-town America," and the lack of planning that allowed someone to purchase a single-family house next door to him and turn it into a restaurant. He had little use for the production companies that "bought" the town. They made some residents greedy and treated others like props. He had been ordered off his own front step by a boy with a bullhorn and came to work one day to find a movie crew squirting fake snow over his store. It was spooky, finding his front porch in countless paintings he could not afford to buy, or having the fire chief, "Foggy" Gomes, report seeing an artistic photograph of his bicycle in an airline magazine leaning against a weather-beaten fence and surrounded by wildflowers.

Chief Gomes's clapboard firehouse was one of many Mendocino buildings that induced a feeling of déjà vu, of inhabiting a dreamworld where everything had an eerie familiarity, and you felt nostalgic for places never seen and people never known. He was the kind of hefty, red-faced man common to television commercials pushing something homemade or old-fashioned. I found him sitting out front on a folding chair, surrounded by six old-timers drinking coffee from chipped mugs. He told me he and his wife were in the Julia Roberts movie I had seen in Eureka, and his firehouse had been the sheriff's department in *The Russians Are Coming, The Russians Are Coming.* He pointed out a faint mark on the floor showing where that film crew had placed the police desk a quarter century earlier.

"Hey, guess what?" he asked. "You're standing where that guy kissed his daughter in the Stouffer commercial. He gets $250 every time they run it—you live around here, you learn about residuals pretty quick."

The firehouse is one of many Mendocino buildings that has worn several hats: the general store was nicknamed the Ex-Lax Building because it appeared in one movie with a sign advertising that laxative. Warner Bros. installed the pillars at the entrance to the library when it transformed it into a brothel for *East of Eden.* The Presbyterian church was a favorite for wedding scenes and featured in the Kodak Happy Families commercial. And so it went, with Mendocino sounding less like a community than an open-air set where false-front houses went up and down in a week, stores changed names, and vintage cars appeared and disappeared. An album at the Kelley House museum had a photograph of the high-school band wearing Cabot Cove High School uniforms and marching down Main Street for an imaginary "Founders' Day," and a few pages later, the actual Mendocino July Fourth parade, looking exactly the same, with the same bunting and band. Who had copied whom? Did anyone know or care? Which Mendocino was "home"?

The film shoots had become folklore and there were stories about Bette Davis suffering a bad cold and swearing, Jonathan Winters telling jokes and whittling wood, and George C. Scott's double making a Hollywood career of their resemblance. Residents were locally famous as doubles and extras and I heard about the town's "Alan Alda" and "Julia Roberts," and particularly about Wally Smith, the bogus Maine sea captain with the white beard and fisherman's cap who appeared four or five times a year on *Murder, She Wrote*. Smith invited me to join him and some other Mendocino retirees at a second-floor restaurant overlooking the water. During a late pancake breakfast, they described the town that had bewitched them twenty years before as if it still existed. It was still "the way we remember our childhood" and "a great laid-back town of millworkers."

No one knew more about the film business than Jack and Toni Lemos, whose company Locations and Casting linked Hollywood to Mendocino. She had been starstruck since 1943 when Paramount built a castle on her father's property for *Frenchman's Creek* and she replaced Joan Fontaine's double, who had been stricken with poison oak. Since then she and her husband had helped producers complete thirteen features, eight television specials, and twenty-eight commercials. He scouted locations, she obtained permits and recruited extras. "Stouffer's, USAir, and all the companies love us because we symbolize old-fashioned values," she said, adding that locals were equally enthusiastic. There was money to be made in residuals and people competed for parts. Did I remember the red-haired man kissing his son in the Heartbeat of America commercial? There had been a Fourth of July parade, the firehouse, flags, children dashing across the street, and a man kissing a baby. Well, that commercial ran during the World Series and he made thousands.

Former county supervisor Norman deVall once told a reporter the village was "bigger than itself . . . a dream and hope that goes far beyond its borders." But what did this mean? If you examined Mendocino's "values" and its role as the all-American hometown too closely, you could become lost in a labyrinth of ironies. Did retired political appointees want to settle here because of the films, or had Hollywood discovered and promoted what already made it so appealing? Had

Hollywood destroyed Mendocino's village as a real community by choosing it as the symbolic American one? Was there something distasteful in using it to shill for products like the automobile, which had eviscerated the real small towns it was meant to be? And how had a town without franchises or strip malls, with nothing in common with small-town life as it is now lived, come to symbolize the small town of the American dream? Unless that dream was a California one of living in a Hollywood small town? If so, you could certainly realize *that* dream better in Mendocino than anywhere.

While visiting the firehouse, I looked up from the "Stouffer spot" to see a lithe young man with matted red hair dart from the Mendocino Cookie Company ("Scrumptious Homemade Cookies and Award-Winning Coffee") and lope down the alley behind "Jessica's House." He disappeared so quickly and was so out of place I suspected a hallucination. But afterward I noticed other Mendocino street people. Had they too come looking for home? On the busy weekend they had been invisible, but perhaps like most locals they were hiding out. During the week they gathered at sunset on the grounds of "Jessica's House" to swill malt liquor from quarts and whirl like dervishes. Some had the same middle-to-upper-middle-class backgrounds as the weekenders and retirees, and I heard about "Big Al," who had been at least an army master sergeant and perhaps an officer, and "Nellie the Cat Lady," who lived in a pickup and received a dole from her parents in Carmel.

I asked the clerks at the Cookie Store about the red-haired man. They thought his name was Spencer. Children called him "Sunshine" or "Box Man," because he lived in one across the highway. It was rumored his parents were Stanford professors who sent money care of the Cookie Company. Someone had given him ski gloves for Christmas (although he never wore them), and he had been a U.S. Olympic skier, or at least tried out for the team. His ski instructor had visited, so had a young woman who left a note addressed, "To Spencer, who used to ski the highest mountains . . ."

When I crossed paths with him in front of the Kodak Happy Families church I asked if we could talk. He muttered "Hi! Hi! Hi!" but shook his head and ignored the dollar I offered as bait. He dodged and weaved like a halfback, vaulted a fence, and was gone. Later I followed him from a distance. He never begged, but still unsettled the tourists. He was the urban bogeyman they had come to escape, as unnerving as the backlot extra who has wandered onto the wrong set— the Roman centurion in Dodge City. His unusual way of walking was no help. He cruised in great circles from one sidewalk to another, weaved around pedestrians, and climbed the hill to "Jessica's House." Then he descended in great loops, then did it again. Once you knew his story, it was clear he was skiing through Mendocino, down the streets that pushed Chevrolets, frozen casseroles, and California oranges, past the trellised, picket-fenced second homes and rentals that in the off-season were shuttered and empty.

14

The Raven and the Wizard

Someone had left a pair of pink socks and sneakers under the bullet-marked interpretive sign overlooking Alder Creek where the fault first came ashore on the southern Mendocino coast. OUR RESTLESS EARTH, the sign said, explaining how the Pacific plate had jumped fifteen feet north in 1906, destroying the stagecoach bridge whose shattered supports still stood in midstream. Nearby, cows grazed in dried sag ponds created by the fault and wildflowers carpeted meadows eyewitnesses had described rippling like rugs and being "thrown up in a great ridge, as if by a gigantic plow." The quake had moved property lines north, making it possible to lose a well, chicken coop, or ancestor's grave to a neighbor.

I found another pair of abandoned sneakers on Manchester Beach, almost exactly where the fault had ruptured in 1906. The embers of a driftwood fire glowed, but the beach was empty. Perhaps a wave had carried away a lovemaking couple, or perhaps these were the leavings of a suicide pact, another addition to Point Arena's rich history of disaster. Fires had consumed and reconsumed its main street. A winter storm had swept away its fishing pier. The 1906 earthquake had broken its log flumes into kindling, swung windmills like metronomes, and cracked the brick lighthouse that was the tallest structure north of San Francisco. Like many buildings destroyed in 1906 it was quickly rebuilt, and like many, its reincarnation was a slipshod disappointment. A company noted for designing factories replaced its graceful tower with a concrete smokestack.

The town of Point Arena filled an inland gully. Without its Sign of the Whale restaurant, surf therapy store, and salty fogs, it could have been a cow town in Colorado. I stopped at the Shell station because I heard its owner, Joe Scaramella, had experienced the great San Francisco earthquake as a little boy. I found him in his overheated office studying a ledger. He had the prophet's face common to men in their nineties and was well spoken, saying things like, "Although my education is nil, I'm blessed with my fair share of ego, so I decided that since automobiles were a mystery to me, I would start a garage."

He said his family had arrived in San Francisco from northern Italy the week before the 1906 quake. They were en route to Point Arena to join his father, who had cut railway ties for six years to earn their passage. He remembered losing their clothes and heirlooms in the fire, contracting measles, and sleeping under blankets in Golden Gate Park. Afterward they traveled north by wagon, ferry, stage, and train, over the same ties his father had milled.

His mother was tormented by flashbacks and continued speaking Italian for the rest of her life, perhaps because she had lost her Italian possessions before accumulating any American ones. In Point Arena the loggers' sons stole his toys and called him a "damned dago." He later served on the city council and won appointment to the California Coastal Commission, where he took the side of environmentalists. Local businessmen attacked him and loggers and gravel diggers stormed into city-council meetings, cursing and shouting about losing their jobs. He would not deny taking pleasure from pissing off the sons and grandsons of his childhood tormentors.

Squabbles like these had made Point Arena a lively little town. It had packed more cultures, countercultures, and controversy into its foggy stretch of Pacific Coast Highway than you find in many small cities. A New Age boutique offered a special on Tibetan medicine bracelets, and a natural-food store decorated with a sunburst was promising skin creams "without cruelty—no animal testing." A small press published *Sage Woman—a Quarterly Magazine of Women's Spirituality*, a renovated movie theater showed new and classic films, and the dance studio had just produced its "4th Annual Winter Extravaganza." A computer store catered to telecommuters, skin divers satisfied the Japanese craving for sea urchins, and the Friends of the Garcia River (FROG) fought to save the watershed from a coalition of loggers and gravel diggers who naturally wanted to continue cutting and digging.

Scaramella recommended Raven B. Earlygrow as one of the best counterculture newcomers, and when I stopped at Bookends, his bookstore-café, reggae music thumped from loudspeakers as a girl with pink hair read poetry in a stage whisper. The store was based on the dubious but popular premise that new books, sticky fingers, and black coffee are a great combination (which they are if you don't buy the books). Early-grow had labeled his shelves "Physical," "Spiritual," "Emotional," and "Planetary Health." He was a sleek, dark-complexioned man with a gray-streaked ponytail who swooped between customers. His business card showed a raven in flight and asked, FEELING ADVENTUROUS? He told me he had just taken his family to Chile, "to check out the post-Pinochet life."

His background was this: New York red diaper baby, commune hippie, natural-food enthusiast, and Zen Buddhist. He had settled here in the 1970s, turning the food coop into a thriving natural food store, joining the chamber of commerce, and forming alliances with progressive old-timers like Scaramella. Like any Main Street Rotarian, he believed his hometown was a wonderful place to raise kids, and "not so quaint you crack your camera lens . . . a mixed community where all kinds of people get along."

It looked that way to me. The bar overlooking its harbor vibrated with the jittery good cheer of men who have worked all day outdoors taking risks, and would do it tomorrow. The bartender called the urchin divers the "real risk-taking pioneers of today," and one still shivering after three hours in the Pacific said, "Man, still a lot of urchins to be had out there." An apple-cheeked boy from Fort Bragg, an apprentice diver, delighted in ticking off the dangers: a storm surge that could throw you against rocks, spines capable of piercing a wet suit, and rough water that could hurl your boat into the sea stacks. You worked alone on the ocean floor in a pressurized helmet connected to the boat by eighty feet of hose. But the profession was turning nasty, with divers fighting over turf and cutting oxygen lines. Some of his friends had moved on to Oregon.

The divers and fishermen drank with their backs to the television, preferring to talk. The wild blond children of a counterculture family swung around their legs. A waitress said the 1983 winter storm had washed away the previous saloon, but six years later its owners bought this nineteenth-century mahogany bar from a San Francisco restaurant damaged by the Loma Prieta earthquake. "Some people fail to notice how nice it is," she said. "But then some people fail to notice anything."

That evening I saw *The Prince of Tides* at the theater Raven Early-grow had helped save. The screen was big and the sound system excellent. There was even a balcony. Before the film started, the audience behaved like a church congregation, whispering and turning to watch the arrival of Rip Van Winkle hippies in clean overalls, weekenders in ironed blue jeans, and Sea Ranch golfers in cardigans. Everyone had dressed up, in his way. The teenagers behaved themselves. No one talked or put their feet on the chairs. Afterward the audience stood chatting under the lighted marquee, reluctant to climb into their Lincolns, pickups, and Volvos and end this satisfying community event.

Overnight vandals spray-painted DICK and PUNK in black letters across Earlygrow's white frame house. Next morning he pretended to be nonchalant, saying he suspected the same enemies who were trying to engineer his recall from the city council. But then he suddenly revealed he was considering moving his family to Amsterdam, "a good school system and a social system where my ideas are policy," or maybe Chile, "because it looks like California a hundred years ago."

He was also suddenly willing to point out some blemishes on Point Arena I might have missed. The school was troubled, with class sizes in the midthirties, and there had been an influx of Mexican kids who did not speak English. Many single Hispanic laborers arrived penniless, slept in cars, and pissed in empty lots. They clashed with the others on Point Arena's lowest rung, the Native Americans of the Manchester rancheria, a place where the state sent rootless ex-felons. Last week this combustible combination had sparked a murder. He followed all this with a disclaimer about of course not being a racist, and I am sure he is not. But when people with names like Raven B. Earlygrow in places like Point Arena complain about illegal aliens, some kind of upheaval in immigration policy is inevitable.

Perhaps the graffiti smeared on his house was a last straw, like the robbery, traffic jam, or smoggy day that sends urban Californians to Point Arena, the moment he would someday remember from a seaside terrace in Valparaiso. Perhaps not. I only know I wished I had left a day earlier so I could have remembered Point Arena as an unblemished Brigadoon of wild seascapes and lively culture, without also recalling the graffiti on his house and the dazed immigrants squatting by the Laundromat, shivering in their flimsy T-shirts and thrown for a loop by the cold drizzle, probably wishing they, too, were somewhere like Valparaiso.

When Lawrence Kroll was known as "Redwood" and his wife as "Savitri," they founded a 170-acre counterculture community on the San

Andreas just east of Point Arena called the Village Oz. The communards occupying its domes, yurts, tents, tree houses, pyramids, and tepees were soon calling him the "Wizard," although there is no evidence they imagined the ironies involved in this nickname. L. Frank Baum, author of the *Oz* books, was a Midwesterner who fell in love with California and wrote while vacationing or living in San Diego and Hollywood. Several of his books contain descriptions of California, and in *Dorothy and the Wizard of Oz* (1908) the great San Francisco earthquake sends her back to Oz. In *Material Dreams—California Through the 1920s*, historian Kevin Starr suggests that like other Midwesterners of the period, Baum "sought and to a certain extent discovered a new life, an American Oz, in the Southland," and that, "Los Angeles, in other words, was Oz come true." The same kind of optimism animated Kroll's backwoods Oz, although with the crucial difference that in 1910 Baum had believed Southern California was becoming Oz, while Kroll's 1970s Point Arena version was an alternative to the failed downstate Oz.

I wanted to visit Oz because it straddled the fault-haunted Garcia River. East of the fault, the Garcia, like nearby creeks and tributaries, falls from east to west, delivering water from the coastal range to the ocean and behaving like any normal stream. But once it hits the fault, its water is offset by the Pacific plate. It makes a dramatic ninety-degree turn to the north, and for seven miles follows a spooky north-to-south path, paralleling the Pacific Ocean along the San Andreas. This phenomenon is best appreciated on a topographical map or aerial photograph, particularly the one included in a USGS book, *The San Andreas Fault System*. It shows the heavily wooded Garcia Valley running straight and purposefully as a ditch, and in one place, a few miles from the ocean, crossing the meadows of Oz.

I had been led to think I could stay at Oz by my vaguely counterculture Moon Publications *Northern California Handbook*. It said, "A quite different experience is a stay at Oz, an ecotopian community in the redwoods with limited electricity, hot tub and sauna, isolation tank, private cabins with kerosene lanterns (bring your own bedding), available when tai chi, polarity therapy, and filmmaking workshops aren't scheduled."

I arrived to find a NO TRESPASSING sign and a locked gate. Back in San Francisco I learned a former schoolmate, John Hooper, had recently purchased Oz. He invited me to stay, explaining he divided his time between his tree nursery in Sonoma County, a house in San Francisco, where his children attended school, and Oz. He was converting it into an organic orchard and the famous Berkeley restaurant Chez Panisse already wanted his first crop of Moon River apples.

I arrived in a downpour to find him cutting brush. At school he had been popular for all the right reasons. He was amusing but at no one else's expense, handsome without being vain, and too kind to bully the younger boys, of whom I was one. Except for a face weathered by thirty years of farming in Nova Scotia and California, he was so unchanged in appearance and manner that our reunion seemed unextraordinary, and when I remember that rain-soaked Saturday I think more about the Wizard, although it was not until weeks later that I met him.

Hooper had been too busy clearing land and espaliering apple trees to bother eliminating traces of the Wizard, even had he wanted to. So although the Krolls had decamped in the mid 1980s, the Oz rainbow arch greeted visitors, the weather vane on the wind generator said Oz, and Hooper still used the cabins' Oz names: "Rainbow Cabin," "Bluebird Dome," and "Forest Dome." He was slightly bemused, unsure how much to change, seeming to sense that Oz might someday be on the National Register.

I thought it was already a candidate. Its skyline of domes, tree houses, yurts, and pyramids, its dripping redwoods, huge ferns, overgrown paths, and wooden suspension bridge, and its abandoned compost privy, underground house, and synthetic fuel system reminded me of the jungle ruins of a great civilization—a hippie Angkor Wat. Like all ruins, they challenged you to find the fatal flaws. So when Hooper showed me a clearing with several abandoned hippie cars, I noted the foreign makes, wondering if they were a clue to its downfall. When we crossed the Garcia River, and the fault, on an elaborate suspension bridge, I wondered why the Wizard had built it at such obvious expense. Had he imagined it swinging safely above the river in the next earthquake, instead of collapsing like the Alder Creek stagecoach bridge?

The Krolls had lived in a complex of Plexiglas domes on the Pacific-plate end of the rope bridge. Rain dripped through cracks in their ceilings, and branches scratched against one like a needle at the end of a record. A thousand-piece jigsaw puzzle lay half-finished on a table and Kroll toothbrushes hung over the sink. Among the abandoned books were *Watership Down; I'm OK, You're OK; Help from Heloise; The Mensa Genius Quiz Book; Diet for a Small Planet;* and *How to Stay Young at Any Age* by a Ms. Gypsy Boots.

In the barn the Krolls converted into a combination gym and auditorium, they had left basketball hoops, ballet mirrors, and faded photographs from the late seventies when Oz had become a counterculture kids' camp. These seemed as dated as the ones of men in black homburgs and women in bustles camping in Golden Gate Park after the 1906 earthquake. Nine deeply tanned and long-haired kids shared a hot tub, mugging and sticking out tongues. Some had painted their bodies like Amazon Indians. A beautiful girl wearing a garland of white flowers stared into the lens. A peacock strutted past a geodesic dome.

I studied the Krolls. The Wizard was tall and gangly, with thinning sandy hair worn thick on the sides. Savitri had a pretty, lively face. A teenage son wore a jester's hat. One daughter was a clown. Everyone's long hair was clean and well combed, as if they were medieval pages in a Hollywood movie.

From the brochures and newspaper clippings they had left behind, I reconstructed a rough Oz chronology. They had bought the farm in 1971 and invited friends to join them. When the commune dissolved five years later they started the camp. It offered tree-house living, goat-milking, treasure hunts, moviemaking, a sensory isolation tank, inner tubing, and capture-the-flag. The Wizard wrote prospective parents, "We love to make plays, paint faces, do slapstick for our talent show where intermission includes hand-churned strawberry ice cream. Friday nights we have a boogie in the old barn." The day began with the wail of a conch shell, then consciousness raising, body awareness, driving classes in the pickup, community meetings in the sauna, and poker lessons. "We don't have bedtimes here," he told a reporter. "No one to tuck them in. Nobody to nag them. . . ."

No wonder the kids in the hot tub looked so happy; they were having more fun in five weeks than I probably had in five country-club summers.

Three years later, in 1979, Oz became the Oz Family Camp, promising a "joyful affirmation of the family with picnics, rap sessions, and game evenings." Then it was the Village of Oz Growth Center, with workshops, retreats, and seminars. Its calendar was a bouillabaisse of late-sixties Yippie merrymaking, early-seventies ecotopian idealism, late-seventies human potential movement, New Age interests, and the approaching yuppie obsessions with money, food, and exercise.

The combination of playful intellectualism, earnest self-improvement, and up-front materialism was uniquely Californian. One week the Wizard presided over "Camp Winnarainbow," a "Performing Camp and Circus Camp" directed by Wavy Gravy, the next he offered "Fleet Oz Running Camp" with Susie Breeze. One weekend Savitri led "Enjoying Ourselves," inviting participants to "take forest walks and look for spirit guides," and "learn to become more aware of our breath and movement as our bodies and our hearts open"; a month later a program titled "The Future" promised "an optimistic look into the future as we play with computers, video equipment, alternative energy, business ideas. . . ."

You could spend a weekend in the Samahdi isolation tank with its inventor, Dr. John Lilly, who declared, in a statement impossible to parody or understand, "In the province of the mind what is believed to be true is or becomes true, within limits to be found experientially and experimentally. These limits are further beliefs to be transcended. In the province of the mind there are no limits."

Two weekends after that, you could attend an "Investing Seminar" that is a fitting Oz epitaph. The brochure said, "This workshop will gather in the country a bank manager, realtor, Swiss gold-silver gnome, and a miser to try to outguess the economy and advise you how to make money and keep it."

Hooper had invited some Berkeley graduate students to spend the weekend at Oz studying the ecology of the Garcia River. Several local environmental activists who believed logging and gravel extraction had made the Garcia almost fish-dead arrived to join them for a spaghetti supper. Many of the men had beards and wore work boots, none of the women used makeup. It could have been a scene from Oz's communal days, except there was nothing whimsical about the conversation. The students were earnest, the activists serious and slightly paranoid, perhaps with good reason considering Earlygrow's experiences.

As rain bucketed down outside I imagined teenagers in hot tubs, buckets of hand-churned strawberry ice cream, and flags captured on sunny meadows, and wished the Wizard were here with his cracked smile to paint faces, organize charades, give poker lessons, and show this bunch how to walk like Charlie Chaplin.

When I asked Hooper why, when everyone else was abandoning

cities for the countryside, the Wizard had jumped this desirable ship and swum the other way, all he knew was that he now lived in San Francisco and taught computer science and mathematics. I found him in the phone book listed under Kroll and left a message on his answering machine. I feared a newly minted conservative, a Jerry Rubin, a man embarrassed by his past, or a despairing old hippie living in exile like deposed royalty. But when I collected my telephone messages, I heard a portentous voice saying, "This is the Wizard," then cracking up and, still chuckling, adding, "Sure I'd *love* to talk about Oz."

15
Living Light on the Land

I f I had just admitted to possessing Lee Harvey Oswald's death certificate and lived ten miles up a one-lane road on a remote Mendocino coastal ridge, and a stranger claiming to be "in the neighborhood" called asking if he could stop by to discuss this document, I would have called the sheriff and loaded a gun. But Sally Sutherland said, "Sure! Come right over," and gave me directions, although she added her husband would be working around the property.

She was a large dimpled woman with a musical voice. Her house was handmade, with big windows and skylights, and circled by horse barns, wildflowers, and mountains. The pines and redwoods were tall and mature, the air dry and sharp. It was Northern California at its best, the beauty of the Rockies with the Pacific just down the road.

She claimed the ambulance attendant driving Oswald's body from Parkland Hospital to a funeral home in Fort Worth had filched his death certificate. She herself had nicked the gavel belonging to the judge conducting Jack Ruby's sanity hearing, so she understood the impulse. During a recess, she had been alone in the courtroom and unable to resist owning a piece of history. She had mounted it on a polished board, like a trophy.

The ambulance driver vanished in 1977 after telling his girlfriend he was going to Louisiana for the weekend. Sutherland met her in a bar and took pity, lending her a spare room. Six months later she gave Sutherland Oswald's death certificate to settle her debts. Sutherland tried selling it to a Dallas newspaper but was scared off by the negotiations. She went to vital statistics to compare it to the copy on file, but that, too, was missing. The clerks, nervous and suspicious, told her to contact the FBI office in Austin. After that she kept it a secret until Oliver Stone made his movie and Paul Kangas came to Fort Bragg. She had entrusted it to him and he had given her a receipt. She would not be surprised if it was priceless, or if she went down in history as the woman who had solved the assassination, although it was unclear exactly how this would happen. Moving to California had changed her luck so dramatically anything was possible.

It was her "magic land," she said. She felt earthquakes all the time, and last week one had rippled the kitchen floor while she cooked. But if that was all California cost, it was cheap.

Two years ago, she and her second husband had been living in a Dallas suburb where she worked in a school cafeteria and he was an electrician. He came home early one day and said, "How about moving to California because I done quit my job?"

She said sure since she had liked it when they went on a shoestring honeymoon, sleeping in their car and becoming *The Price Is Right* contestants. Besides, someone had just stolen the kids' bikes from the front yard, her elder brother had worked himself into a stroke, and a huge subdivision without sidewalks or parks was rising on the empty lot where her children played. Better to be homeless in California than poor or dead in Texas, so they cleared the kitchen table of dishes and designed a trailer good for hauling stuff and camping. They knew nobody in California and their friends warned everyone was so unfriendly they would be right back. But they sounded to me like perfect California material: restless and optimistic.

They piled their trailer with mattresses, cooking pans, and Lee Harvey Oswald's death certificate, hitched it to their high-mileage blue-and-white Suburban, and drove west. At first they camped at nearby Navarro Beach and her husband found work on a salmon boat. But as winter approached, the camp changed complexion, tripling in population. The new crowd was rougher. There was petty thievery, even a murder. But their children counted a hundred seals in a day, they gathered seafood, burned driftwood, laughed about the yuppies paying two hundred dollars a night for the same view at the inn above the beach, and waited for some California good luck.

The same day her husband complained about being too broke to buy coffee he found an unopened can of it washed ashore on the beach. She took it as an omen, proof this was their land of plenty. That afternoon she befriended a woman walking down the beach who was dressed like the other transients but turned out to be the wife of a millionaire who had inherited the Navarro Inn. They became friends and she invited Sutherland and her husband to move in as housekeepers. One day they were broke, the next they were living in a mansion. "Now do you see why we call this our magic land?" she asked. "Sometimes I just imagine what I want, and it happens!"

One housekeeping job led to another, then to another on this idyllic ranch. They had a swimming pool, a baseball field, and pet ducks named Daryll and Daryll. They were the happiest Californians I had met, but they still kept their trailer parked behind the barn. It looked like the one the Judds used to move West in *The Grapes of Wrath*. She showed it to me and said, "We could hitch it up and be gone tomorrow."

Once I saw Navarro Beach, their reversal of fortune seemed even more miraculous. Lines of people slogged slow-motion through sand and mud, battling the wind. Smoke from driftwood fires blew across the dunes and turkey-necked men picked at methamphetamine scabs. Mongrels bared their teeth like vampires. Three blond urchins in muddy pajamas spat wads of phlegm and made the hand-to-mouth motion of third-world beggars. The elite lived in rusting campers; the poor slept under canvas or cardboard, or in their cars. People complained of being dirty because their clothes never dried properly. They all wanted to escape California. A man living in a 1984 Subaru was hoping for Oregon, "where the Fish and Game is more tolerant and the beaches are free!" A man in a bread delivery van dreamed of Mexico. He collected shells there during the winter that he arranged in straw baskets covered with plastic. When I bought one he said, "Be happy *you* don't have to shrink-wrap conch shells over a barbecue."

Homeless was a dirty word. "What do you see on this beach?" boomed an Australian with so many booze blossoms his face resembled a fireworks finale. "You see *homes*! Get it? So what if we only have cars? What's a car? A mobile home!"

The Sutherlands were typical of the people I met on the forested ridges a few miles back from the ocean in Mendocino and Sonoma counties. All were blissfully happy to have found this uncrowded and sunny alpine backwater. Although the fault ran across the landscape for forty-three miles from Point Arena to Bodega Bay, it was largely invisible except for the straight valley it had created and followed. The 1906 earthquake had toppled redwoods and caused landslides, but logging and natural regrowth had since erased evidence of the destruction except for a split redwood near Plantation Road and a dammed sag pond that had become the Plantation Farm Camp's swimming hole.

When I drove through this camp it was deserted except for a handyman who said the owners had gone to Los Angeles to meet prospective campers. Having a kids' camp over the main trace of the San Andreas Fault—and I reckoned it ran underneath a trough in the meadow where the belled livestock made a tinkling alpine sound as they grazed—sounds more dangerous than it is. Although 1906 had carved fissures and toppled trees, the wood-frame buildings composing the former stagecoach stop and farm had all survived.

The hotel had burned in the twenties, but the 1869 vintage Druids' Hall that served as a camp library and rainy-day playhouse was stuffed with memorabilia: a 1919 teacher's register for the Plantation School, gutted typewriters, half-century-old editions of *Life*, and an advertising brochure for the Plantation House promising "no fog or extreme weather" and a place that "cannot be excelled for a quiet vacation." The camp's current brochure carried a color photograph of owners David and Suzanne Brown. They sat on a brick wall in front of the house with their young twin daughters and son. Every family member held a golden-retriever puppy, everyone was smiling, tanned, and wholesome. Their marriage sounded like a miracle of lifelong compatibility. They had met here as nine-year-old campers, fallen in love as counselors, married in 1971 by the pond, and bought the camp in 1984. Even though we never met, I still sometimes think of them milking their cows and goats in that beautiful place, giving campers a great summer, and raising sensible children. I could not imagine finding a more attractive, happy family along the fault, and I suppose I never came back and met them because if they were not, I did not want to know it.

A few miles north on what appeared to be the same ridge, I met another couple easy to envy. In fact Barbara Scalabrini, who owned the Annapolis Winery with her husband, Basil, used the phrase *our dream* so often that, nice as she was, it was almost enough to turn you against her.

They were not making much of a living, she admitted, but so what? The winery had been an excuse to escape Marin County, where they had tired of reading the same books, seeing the same art movies, and trying the same New Age therapies as their friends. So they sold out, moved their kids from a school with 2,500 students to one with 100, and bought these forty acres on a sunny southern slope a few ridges back from the foggy Pacific. Neighbors and the farm bureau insisted the soil was all wrong for wine, but they bought a tractor and an instructional book, planted sixteen acres of grapes, and twelve years later shipped their first bottles. They were now selling several thousand cases a year to visitors, local restaurants, and a supermarket in Petaluma. They were not wine fanatics, simply people who wanted to live in a lovely place like Annapolis. She was a determined proselytizer for her new lifestyle, and had chosen "A Joyful Experience" as the vineyard's motto. Her son made pottery to sell in the tasting room, another child made bookmarks. The harvest was always a "grand party." They never felt tired. Running a vineyard was not *really* work because there was no stress involved. It was actually more like meditating. The tourists who visited her tasting room were all wonderful and "wide-open." She said she had never loved people so much.

This was the cue for the Voskamps from Kansas to appear in their luxury rented car and sing the praises of the region. They had just bought property on the coast at Sea Ranch, where in three years they would retire and play golf year-round. "No one cares who you are, where you come from, or how much money you have," he said, making the timeless case for California's appeal.

"It's like a little bit of heaven here," his wife offered, taking a deep breath of mountain air and releasing a satisfied sigh.

"Because it's not like the rest of California," he added.

The Sea Ranch development where the Voskamps planned golfing out their days is a 5,200-acre former ranch purchased by Castle and Cook in 1963 and developed into a high-minded residential and recreational community.

The original utopian plan, known as the *Intent*, called for its houses and residents to have a minimum impact on the sweeping oceanside meadows. Overgrazed lands were to be rested, indigenous grasses and shrubs planted, hunting forbidden, and game corridors left so wildlife could migrate between headlands and ridges. Utilities would be buried, population density low, and grading and earth moving kept to a minimum. External paint would be prohibited, conventional gardens hidden, and even the nineteenth-century redwood stumps remaining from the timber boom that had cleared this land left in their natural state. Homes would be clustered and designed so they blended into the jointly owned open land. When the Sea Ranch concept was summarized it was usually said residents would "live lightly on the land."

In the beginning, they did just that. Among the first houses built were eighteen celebrated "walk-in cabins." Other early houses were tucked into folds or appeared to be extensions of hedgerows, and could scarcely be seen until you were at their front doors. Some of the finest architects in the state designed them, and architectural journals carried laudatory articles and pictures. When Sea Ranch's own publicity called it "the very paradigm of sensitive ecological planning," no one could accuse the company of hyperbole. It became the great California architectural monument of the 1960s, evidence the California dream of living in harmony with nature could be realized.

A San Francisco landscape architect and environmental planner named Lawrence Halprin had been the creative genius behind Sea Ranch. Just before going there I came upon a rueful interview he had given to a resident named Bill Platt in a 1983 edition of the *Ridge Review*. He said he had intended to establish a nonelitist utopian community in which people would be linked to each other as well as the landscape. He had hoped home sites would be available for as little as $2,000, enabling young people to buy land and throw up a tent or cabin. "A key part of the *Intent* was to establish a sense of community," he told Platt. "There would be a quality of aesthetics in the sense that the community would share an attitude about design. The attitude would be lacking in ego; it would be natural in the sense it would try to blend with, rather than go against, the environment; it would be modest."

Two decades later, he thought an "unfortunate economic elitism" had corrupted the *Intent*. The houses and land had become too expensive for middle-class families, and the ethnic and class and age mix was nonexistent. Most owners were retirees and absentee owners who had purchased or built houses as investments and rented them by the weekend. He had not foreseen it would become a hybrid of retirement community and resort, and thought the resortism had damaged its sense of community, preventing the healthy links with neighbors he had imagined. It had also failed to fulfill its early architectural promise. He was embarrassed by the lavish praise, because "what people believe the Sea Ranch stands for far exceeds what the Sea Ranch is." Although it had disseminated an important message about building a community in which people could be nurtured by landscape, it had also departed too much from various forms of clustering. Some of the architecture was "undistinguished," some looked suburban.

I called on Bill Platt to see if he agreed with Halprin, and because I needed somewhere to park. There were no gates at Sea Ranch, but signs on every access road off the coast highway warned against trespassing and promised fines and prosecution. I was forewarned that an energetic security service booted cars parked in the road, and copies of the monthly *Bulletins of the Sea Ranch Association* showed an unhealthy preoccupation with security for what was purportedly a nonelitist utopian community. The big news this month was an anti-abalone-diver volunteer security patrol of twenty residents who spent weekends checking identification on roads leading into the community to prevent the "unauthorized use of the association roads by drivers bent on gaining access to the ocean."

Platt was one of those retirees who give the appearance of becoming more energetic with age. He wrote for local publications, served on the Sea Ranch Association, and formed a group lobbying for a new county along the Sonoma and Mendocino coasts to be known as "Coast County." When I arrived his computer was humming, and as we spoke, messages about community affairs came into his answering machine. He was as handsome as a person his age can be, with a halo of white hair and intelligent eyes, and he let me know he was the Sea Ranch tennis champion in the over-eighty-five category.

He believed Sea Ranch's failure to become a nonelitist utopian community was even more apparent than when Halprin voiced his disappointments in 1983. Prices had risen to over $100,000 for the smallest lot, and despite the utopian blather about keeping the bluffs open and building houses in clusters, oceanfront lots had been sold. About 400 of Sea Ranch's 1,100 houses were rented out for short periods, even a weekend. Residents of the environmentally sensitive cluster houses found themselves living in something resembling a resort, at close quarters with a different holiday-making couple every weekend, or sometimes with a dozen abalone divers who treated their short-term rental like a bunkhouse.

Year-round residents like himself who wanted hiking trails, more tennis courts, and an activities center for a theater group and other community-building cultural events were at odds with the weekenders and absentee landlords who considered these unnecessary frills. It was a case of those wanting Sea Ranch to become the community Halprin imagined against those considering it an investment or tax shelter. Because the association was governed on a "one-lot, one-vote" basis, the absentee landlords usually won.

I passed the time waiting for Obie Bowman to arrive at his office on a hillside overlooking Sea Ranch by reading some of the two dozen

framed articles and awards praising the innovative Sea Ranch houses
he had designed. They personified, one said, the community's unique
spirit of "environmental harmony." He was a trim and elegant middle-
aged man with a face as handsome and weathered as one of his houses,
what you would expect from someone *San Francisco* magazine had included in its list of Best Dressed Men. Before moving here in the 1960s,
he had designed shopping centers for a Los Angeles architectural firm,
"a guy participating in the destruction of the California landscape," he
said. At Sea Ranch he found a spirit of pioneering, experiment, and adventure among architects who believed their houses reflected a spiritual
response to geography.

The walk-in cabins had been his first project. Each was a 610-
square-foot cube with a skylit sleeping loft, redwood siding, and a wall
of windows providing a diffuse and soft forest light. To spare the remaining trees he insisted owners hike in. They sold for $18,000 and
were what Sea Ranch was supposed to be, "architecture responding to
the spirit of the environment." Because they were modest and unusual,
they attracted people with the pioneering, antielitist attitude Halprin
had wanted.

Bowman worried Sea Ranch was becoming a "subdivision by the
sea," its new houses "spiritless clones" that any developer could have
laid out. More than the builders and real-estate people, he blamed the
design committee of Sea Ranch residents who let them get away with it,
and the buyers who insisted on such houses. The design committee had
been more sensitive when the developer controlled it. But under the association it had become conservative, wanting the appearance of the
original Sea Ranch, but not its ideals. Its members looked at his daring
buildings and saw the "look" of untreated wood siding, minimal over-
hangs, shed roofs, large windows, and a wind-protected outdoor area,
but missed the architectural spirit behind them, one that could easily be
expressed in a different "look." So they approved houses that mimicked
the look, but ruined the viewshed and were at odds with living lightly
on the land.

After paying a huge price for a Sea Ranch lot, people insisted on
filling it with a big house. The typical buyers were Bay Area professional couples with college-aged kids who wanted a vacation place that
could become a retirement home. They demanded a hot tub, wall-to-
wall carpeting, easy-to-clean surfaces, three bedrooms, and huge windows facing the ocean. The result, Bowman said, was "larger and larger
houses, filled with larger and larger possessions."

But what explained Sea Ranch's appeal? I asked.

"Two reasons," he said, pausing. "Los Angeles, and San Jose."

He believed Sea Ranch was not completely ruined, not yet, and conditions were becoming so bad downstate the next Sea Ranch generation might believe they really were living in a utopian paradise.

The next day I wandered through Sea Ranch. The sky was gunmetal gray and windblown drizzle pricked my face. It was a winter weekday, so most houses were empty and the only sound came from carpenters banging nails and sawing boards for identical roofs. I am not a prude about second homes, but seeing these meadows filled with empty, recently constructed, three-bedroom, fully equipped and furnished houses was enough to make anyone wish for a busload of Navarro Beach squatters.

I visited some of Bowman's houses. One end of the Brugler house was at ground level and appeared to grow organically from the meadow. The Smith cabin used redwood trunks to mimic the columns of a Southern plantation. The low-slung Brunell house had a sod roof making it difficult to recognize until you were on top of it.

But I found my eye skipping over his restrained architecture, settling instead on the high walls and vast picture windows of neighboring redwood palaces. "The lessons of Sea Ranch" was a phrase you often read in articles extolling it, but comparing the earlier houses that conformed to Halprin's original dream with the elephantine ones that did not made it seem the only lesson Sea Ranch taught was how difficult Californians were finding it to live lightly on the land.

16

"Wildlife Observation Area"

Alfred Hitchcock made two movies on the San Andreas Fault: *Vertigo,* whose most troubling and climactic scenes unfold at the Mission of San Juan Bautista, and *The Birds,* which depicts increasingly vicious attacks by birds on residents of the idyllic fishing village of Bodega Bay and ended without offering any explanation, except that nature is unpredictable and unmanageable. When asked the point, Hitchcock said, "I think people are too complacent."

Fellini called *The Birds* "one of the greatest films of all time, a poem." "A tragic, lyric poem," said Hitchcock's biographer Daniel Spoto. When I saw *The Birds* and *Vertigo* for the first time, I was too young to appreciate Hitchcock's art, but old enough to be seduced by his California. I imagined myself living in a house halfway up Telegraph Hill, like Jimmy Stewart in *Vertigo,* or like Rod Taylor, driving out the Pacific Coast Highway in a convertible for a weekend in Bodega Bay.

When Hitchcock filmed Bodega Bay in 1962, it was as blank a canvas as you could find so close to San Francisco, just sheep grazing on roller-coaster hills and nowhere for birds to hide, or to hide from them. When I saw it in 1979, it was still a place you could imagine nature making a quick U-turn.

Hitchcock's Bodega Bay had been a cozy village with a one-room school, wooden sidewalks, a friendly café, and eccentric old-timers. The real village was even smaller—just a restaurant and some cottages teetering on a bluff. I imagined building a weekend house overlooking the harbor, frequenting the café, and becoming buddies with fishermen. I had no idea it had been embalmed for the moment because of the Coastal Commission building moratorium, nor any idea that in 1906 the Pacific plate had opened a two-hundred-yard fissure across the dunes. Even if I had, I would still have wanted a house on those empty meadows.

I stopped on the way to Bodega Bay at the Potter School, a gloomy two-story Victorian Hitchcock used for the scene where Tippi Hedren sits in the playground, listening to children singing inside and oblivious to crows gathering on a jungle gym behind her. First one crow, then a dozen, then hundreds, until they perch on every bar and post.

The school had educated 125 children at a time when the interior town of Bodega was a thriving logging center. But as more trees were cut, first to rebuild San Francisco after the 1906 earthquake, then to build Southern California after the war, ranchers began grazing herds on the cleared land and their less numerous children replaced those of loggers. When the school closed in 1960 it had eight pupils. Now it traded on its *Birds* fame and had become the Schoolhouse Inn. It offered a "fruit and croissant breakfast" and "workshops," a creepy word coming to mean rooms without tools where people are encouraged to speak without restraint.

A sign on its locked door said WORKSHOP IN PROGRESS—DO NOT DISTURB. I walked across the highway to a general store selling T-shirts with the distinctive *Birds* logo of crows in flight. The clerk said thousands had been sold in 1987 to celebrate the quarter centenary of the filming. They had become "collectors' items."

I brought a sandwich back to the schoolhouse lawn. Instead of birds, people were circling the building with cameras and video recorders. A smartly dressed suburban mother with twin sons told me, "I want them to know our country's history."

Like other fault-haunted places (and like other Hitchcock locations) Bodega Bay can give you the shivers on the sunniest day. Its most dramatic and sinister feature is Bodega Head, a granite headland that has slid hundreds of miles north on the Pacific plate. It is attached to the mainland by a narrow spit of land intersected by the fault, but appears to float offshore like a whale.

I drove out to see the Hole in the Head, an eighty-foot hole that were it not for the San Andreas Fault would be anchoring the foundations of a 325,000-kilowatt Pacific Gas and Electric (PG&E) nuclear power plant. In 1962, Sonoma County and the Atomic Energy Commission (AEC) had both approved the project, and when Interior Secretary Morris Udall expressed "grave concern for potential earthquake hazards" and urged the AEC to reconsider, PG&E hurried to begin construction. Its work crews laid a road across the sandspit to Bodega Head and drilled the first of many holes for the foundation. Its geological consultants took rock samples and announced it "extremely unlikely" the fault was active. Two days later, a USGS (United States Geological Survey) team examined the walls of the hole, found evidence of an earlier earthquake, and concluded the reactor would sit over an active fault. The AEC withdrew its approval and PG&E charged environmental activists had faked the geological tests.

It is tempting to consider this incident a case study in corporate greed. But if you consider that California had experienced a half-century seismic drought, then the company's actions become simply a reflection of a pervasive denial. Since then, the fault has saved Bodega Bay from offshore oil drilling and strip mining, and some residents call it their "patron saint." I was happy to see the hole had filled with springwater and become a vest-pocket bird sanctuary, fringed with reeds and protected by a fence, probably the most expensive duck pond in the world.

During the 1906 quake, the loose sediment under what later became the fishing village of Bodega Bay moved eighteen inches. According to my usually restrained *Roadside Geology of Northern California,* it was a community "clearly destined from the day the first house was built to be destroyed every time the northern part of the San Andreas Fault releases a major earthquake." Since my visit in 1979, it had become a booming community for Bay Area weekenders. There were hundreds of new hotel rooms and a rash of second homes and resorts had spread across oceanfront meadows. One promised "luxuriously-appointed guest lodges that appear a part of these rumpled hills and tawny headlands," and an article in *Vogue* praised an inn for its "tiny Sonoma lambchops and colorful vegetable terrines," saying it was where "Vivaldi and Mozart are the composers of choice for background music, and wine is the topic of many conversations." The Sonoma County coast had become, it concluded, "the newest frontier of the American Dream."

Some things had not changed. The highway was still narrow and treacherous, and the town unincorporated, so its fate was decided by the county. There were still no sidewalks, and despite all the growth, no library.

As the number of tourists eager to visit a fishing village had increased, the population of fishermen had fallen. Salmon need free-flowing clear water, but logging, dams, and developments of the kind covering the hills behind Bodega Bay were one reason why Northern Californian rivers had become cloudy, stagnant, and silted. Every wharf had empty berths, and shortly before I arrived, government agencies canceled the commercial salmon season, turning Bodega Bay's traditional Blessing of the Fleet into a dark affair with only half the usual boats. Their crews flew black pennants and dressed in black. One hung a plastic salmon from a noose.

Since the Inn at the Tides promised "guest quarters" keeping "watch" over the "busy harbor," and the restaurant at the Tides Wharf proclaimed itself "a favorite location for watching fishing boats unload their catch," it seemed possible fishermen might soon become paid scenery, rewarded for chugging across the bay at sunset or unloading a token catch to entertain waterfront diners eating farmed salmon from New Zealand. If this sounds off-the-wall, consider that a resort on Maui keeps money-losing cane fields in cultivation as a "scenic backdrop."

In 1979 the Tides Wharf had been a relaxed fishermen's café. Now it was Bodega Bay's busiest attraction. There was a long wait for tables, so the hostess directed me to an adjoining fast-food snack bar built to handle the weekend overflow. This was a crude shed filled with picnic tables, stinking of grease, and decorated with stern signs like DO NOT BLOCK THE COUNTER! The teenage clerks were clumsy and rude, the Mexican cooks exhausted. Little boys stood on the cylindrical ashtrays, playing video games with their fathers, their backs to the water.

I gave up and bought an egg sandwich wrapped in cellophane at a gas station and drove out a sandspit that curves around the bay to the south and falls within the fault zone. Here a former wetland had become the Bodega Head Golf Course and a small Wildlife Observation Area, although I could not stop because the cars of weekend joggers filled the area's small lot. In the last scene of *The Birds,* Rod Taylor and Tippi Hedren flee Bodega Bay during a lull in the bird attacks, abandoning it to nature. But in the real Bodega Bay, people were pecking nature to death. The fish had vanished, resorts had replaced cows, and the birds had lost out to a golf course.

Despite all the new resorts, I could not find a place to stay. The young woman at the desk at the chamber of commerce was not surprised. It was a typical spring Saturday and she was already sending tourists to motels in Santa Rosa.

I mooched around the office and met Kathie Morgan, who had

been a deckhand on several commercial fishing boats before retiring to edit *The Signal*, one of Bodega Bay's two weekly newspapers. When she overheard me mention the fault she proudly said her house sat smack over it. She led me outside and pointed it out—a fisherman's shack balanced on pilings and sandwiched between the highway and bay. "I don't give a goddamn. I have termites in my pilings and the whole place will probably come tumbling down in the next quake and kill me," she said. "I like to say that like everything in Bodega Bay, it's 'Andrea's fault'!"

She explained Andrea Granahan was publisher and editor of the rival *Bodega Bay Navigator*. "We're the same age, both bleached blondes married to men named David, but that's where it ends. Her tabloid is radical, I'm a reactionary. She has a whole staff, I have one man. I live here, she doesn't."

I spread copies of the rival newspapers side by side on the floor. *The Signal* was cheerful and optimistic, aimed at the small fishing village that was disappearing. The *Navigator* was pitched to the town of retirees, tourists, and urban refugees replacing it. *The Signal's* Bodega Bay was a maritime Shangri-la where children grew prizewinning vegetables and disputes revolved around raising money for an ambulance and dividing proceeds from the Fish Fest. In its photographs, everyone smiled. Granahan's Bodega Bay was more cosmopolitan, but troubled. Her front page reported on the trials of a man who had murdered a popular high-school student, and a teenager accused of slaying a local ranch couple. There was a tribute to a student who had committed suicide. In an earlier issue, the only photograph of a child showed the winner of the Sierra Club's "Youngest Grassroots Activist Award." He held up a placard saying NO GUNS ON OUR BEACHES.

After Granahan exposed the rape and torture of female deckhands and advocated a "Rights At Sea Law," Morgan's column accused her of slandering Bodega Bay fishermen. She admitted male shipmates had beaten and threatened her, but women on commercial boats should be tough enough to fend for themselves. "What I remember about my fishing jobs," she concluded, "is the gleaming fish and the rainbows."

When I met Granahan, the gulf between them seemed even wider. She wore ethnic clothes and lived inland, away from the fog; Morgan wore stained sweatshirts and still crewed on commercial boats. Granahan was cool and intelligent; Morgan was hot-tempered and funny. Granahan found discussing Morgan distasteful; Morgan delighted in having an enemy. They could agree only that Bodega Bay had attracted them because it had been a genuine fishing village, and that the Reverend Earl Nevins of the Union Church was a saint.

I collected these comments about Nevins: "He's married and buried half the town." "He and his wife live in a trailer and have never taken a dime for all his good works." "He's put more shoes on little kids' feet than anyone." "He takes in every down-and-outer, even the ones with emotional problems." "He's the soul of this town, the Mother Teresa of the coast."

His church sat on a bluff overlooking the harbor and was surrounded by fishermen's cottages. He arrived to meet me wearing stained khakis and a baseball cap and driving a dirt-splattered truck advertising NEVINS AND FREEMAN—EXCAVATING AND SEPTIC SYSTEMS. He had thick eyebrows and a white halo of hair. His face was lined and sun-blackened, his hands rough as cinder blocks. His first words were, "I'm eighty-five but I still do dirt work."

He weather-vaned his arms, gesturing toward all the new houses perched on his foundations, and wondering if he was building himself out of a parish. The newcomers were not big churchgoers, and some fishermen in his congregation were leaving. When he described his giveaway programs for Mexican immigrants and distressed fishermen, who he said came to services in their rubber boots and suspenders "stinking of fish," I saw the problem. What Bay Area weekender wanted to spend a prime Sunday morning hour in this ramshackle church, surrounded by stinking fishermen and Mexican workers? Who living in a three-thousand-square-foot house that stayed empty all week wanted to hear a Bible-thumping sermon about the homeless from the same man who had dug his septic tank, lived in a battered trailer next to the church, refused to accept a salary, and was, if you had to summarize his life, a Bible-thumping reformed alcoholic and Alcatraz jailbird?

In the 1920s, when Alcatraz was a maximum-security military prison, he had been sentenced to twenty years for punching a superior officer. He still remembered his prison number had been 16787 and his "nickname" 787. He could close his eyes and see an inmate pick up a boy by his trouser legs and hurl him over the third-tier rail to his death, or hear band music floating over the water from San Francisco.

His early release had been a small miracle. Someone must have decided twenty years was too much for one punch. His conversion came when he joined a logging camp in Idaho populated by Christians who traveled by sled through heavy snows to church. He accompanied them one Sunday and that night accepted Jesus. I wanted him to expand on this, but he would only say it happened. He was too honest to turn it into a miracle play. Afterward he attended Bible school, married, and ministered on three California skid rows. He had stumbled on Bodega Bay when the chartered fishing boat he was on became lost in fog and followed a commercial boat into its harbor. A fire blazed next to the pier and the volunteer firemen were weeping because it had already killed a widow's dog and mynah birds. He thought, "Just imagine, crying because a widow lost her pets." He became a Bodega Bay believer on the spot, another quick conversion.

Because he had suffered in prison, or because he appreciated the powerful consequences of a single mistake, he recalled a local history punctuated by tragedy. When a capsized fishing boat drowned nine men, he had comforted the sheriff who had dropped a man to his death from a helicopter. When a bulldozer pushed a hill of sand over two boys, burying them alive, people came running, digging with their bare hands. One family moved away, the other mother killed herself.

Bodega Bay's recent tragedies had assumed a more violent cast. A local teenager had stolen a car in San Francisco and led the police on a high-speed chase back to Bodega Bay, then shoved a revolver into his mouth and pulled the trigger. Nevins thought "divine intervention" had sent him to the Kelly house, where he found Mrs. Kelly sitting outside in the rain hugging the corpse of her fourteen-year-old daughter. Being pretty and popular had not stopped her from shooting herself in the gut. And last year a Santa Rosa teenager had murdered an elderly couple named Oscar and Betty Mann on a ranch in nearby Jenner.

The more I read about this murder, the less it seemed like a burglary gone wrong and the more it seemed welded to Sonoma's peculiar geography and sociology. The county had grown fast during the 1980s, with Santa Rosa transformed from a sleepy county seat into a city of 100,000. There was talk of another Silicon Valley. Ranchers had sold out to developers, and farms bordering highways had become tracts and industrial parks. But while the interior was being transformed into a sprawling suburb, the coastline remained largely rural. Suddenly, only twenty miles separated the idyllic seascapes seen in television advertisements for new cars from the squalid commercial strips where they were sold, or middle-class ranchers who lived in modest homes on five thousand acres that had been in families for generations from office workers resigned to long commutes as the price of a big house on a quarter-acre plot. The gulf between lifestyles was as wide as that between rich and poor in Manhattan, and potentially as lethal.

The killer had been "good-looking and an athlete," "like the kid you'd trust to babysit," according to neighbors. He lived in a Santa Rosa suburb but came from a well-known coastal family that had moved inland after his grandparents sold their ranch to developers. He had taken an after-school job at a plumbing supply store where he compiled a list of the names, addresses, and credit-card numbers of its patrons. He planned murdering them and using their credit cards to finance shopping sprees at the malls. After killing the Manns, he had returned to make sure their bodies were untouched, and their credit still good.

A newspaper article described the victims as "gentle people" who had resisted subdivision and were "committed to saving their land for their descendants." The son who had found their corpses had been named Young Rancher of the Year. One friend said they had been "like the good folks of yesteryear."

With its fainting goats, wishing well, Ruritanian tollbooth, Vietnamese potbellied pigs, and mineral spring used for baptisms and hard-boiling eggs, the Old Faithful geyser of Calistoga, located east of Bodega Bay in neighboring Napa County, resembled more a roadside attraction than a promising short-term predictor of earthquakes. But according to a study by Paul Silver and Nathalie Valette-Silver, a husband-and-wife team of scientists with the Carnegie Institute, this is precisely what it is. While vacationing here in 1989, they had become intrigued by the claim of its owner, Olga Kolbek, that intervals between its eruptions lengthened dramatically in the weeks and days preceding a major earthquake. Normally it shot boiling water sixty feet into the air every forty minutes. Kolbek's hot pools gurgled, and her visitors photographed and applauded. But three times since 1973 the interval had lengthened to as much as two and a half hours. The first time, Kolbek worried her geyser had "gone kaput" and refunded admissions. Then she noticed that after each occasion an earthquake of magnitude 6.0 or greater struck within three days, at Oroville in 1975, Morgan Hill in 1984, and Loma Prieta in 1989.

After matching Kolbek's logbooks against earthquakes recorded by the U.S. Geological Survey, the Silvers concluded the eruptions changed during the three-week period surrounding a major temblor, with the greatest variation coming one to three days beforehand. When they reported their findings in 1991, the seismological establishment was skeptical and the USGS scientist heading the Bay Area Earthquake Task Force dismissed their theory as "fairly incredible." It contravened the accepted wisdom that earthquakes were local phenomena, incapable of triggering distant seismic events. Since Loma Prieta's epicenter was 120 miles from the geyser, and since instruments closer to it had not recorded changes in the earth's crust, it seemed unlikely this distant, hokey tourist attraction could be sounding an alarm.

I could see why USGS scientists sent to investigate Kolbek's claims might have seen her sign announcing MANY NOTABLE PEOPLE HAVE COME HERE TO SEE AND LEARN THE MYSTERIES OF THIS WONDER OF NATURE WHICH CAPTIVATED THE IMAGINATION, examined the time clock hooked to an infrared light on the snack-bar roof to record eruption intervals while she slept, and after hearing this pixie-sized P. T. Barnum of a woman talk nonstop about her geyser decided their trip was a wild-goose chase.

But then in 1992 the prestigious British magazine *Science* published the Carnegie Institute study, and the Ferndale and Desert Hot Springs earthquakes struck different ends of the San Andreas Fault within three days. At first most seismologists called this coincidental. But when a 7.4 rocked the desert town of Landers two months later, they did a U-turn. Minutes after Landers, the ground had trembled 750 miles away in Mount Lassen, and earthquake swarms had shaken the eastern Sierras. USGS geophysicist Paul Reasenberg told *The New York Times,* "Now we've been hit over the head with observations we cannot ignore. We are forced to look for new mechanisms to explain earthquakes."

In *Science,* thirty-one scientists said Landers challenged "a longstanding skepticism regarding the reality of triggered seismic activity at great distances." The popular and scientific press spoke about Landers and the Carnegie Institute study as "shaking up" earthquake theories. Previous earthquakes now had to be considered in a new light. It was even possible the Great Earthquake of 1906 had triggered the 6.2 that hit the Imperial Valley eleven hours later.

This was all good news for the Carnegie scientists and Olga Kolbek, but not necessarily for me. Her geyser still could not predict exactly *where* an earthquake would strike, only that it would be within a 150-mile radius within a few days.

She said I had arrived at a bad time for an earthquake. For months the eruptions had been normal. Today they were more closely spaced than usual, every twenty to twenty-five minutes. She showed me two weeks of computer printouts and led me to the geyser's pool. Craggy volcanic mountains rose behind it like the backdrop to a Chinese opera. The bamboo and pampas grass rustled in the thermal air. A full moon rose in the late-afternoon sky and hang gliders drifted overhead like butterflies. I watched a couple hugging as they stared at the smoking blowhole and felt sadly alone in this strangely romantic place.

"My geyser is *great* for love," Kolbek said as it spewed up forty feet and the couple exchanged deep kisses. They stayed on, unable to keep hands or lips off each other despite the rotten-egg stink.

In the time between eruptions she told me how she and her husband had bought the geyser on a whim in 1973. They had driven to Calistoga from Santa Rosa, where she taught home economics and had been an early advocate of natural foods and mineral spas. Suddenly they became gripped with the idea of turning the geyser into a health spa. After the sale closed, an election brought in a new board of supervisors who denied them a spa permit, sticking them with a roadside attraction. After she and her husband divorced, she had bought his share and was now working hard to increase revenues. She had built a triumphal arch over the entryway, installed a seismograph, assembled a menagerie of pigs and fainting goats and an earthquake exhibit, and was offering cooking demonstrations that entailed lowering a pail of turkey and vegetables into her natural thermal oven.

The Carnegie report had put a zing in her cash flow. A news helicopter landed in her parking lot and she appeared on twenty-seven television programs, CNN broadcast her story worldwide, and visitors from Japan and Chile suddenly appeared. She told everyone how the USGS and universities spurned her theories and how the long eruption intervals before Loma Prieta made her so uneasy she had canceled a trip to San Francisco. She liked saying, "I'm just a little old retired schoolteacher, so of course they all pooh-poohed me," then flashing a sweet, triumphant smile.

I willed the eruptions to sputter and diminish in front of my eyes. I sat for an hour at the picnic table, checking my watch, watching the honeymooners replaced by a large family of Hispanics in church clothes, then by a couple so passionate that with a tremor in her voice Kolbek exclaimed, "Look! They're hugging!" She wiped her eyes. "Everybody just loves everybody here."

She apologized her geyser had disappointed me and said I could return for free tomorrow. It would be colder early in the morning, so the water would rise twice as high. I gave her my card, and she promised to call if the eruptions became suddenly erratic.

I told myself waiting for an earthquake on the San Andreas was not unlike waiting for her geyser. The interval between earthquakes was longer and less predictable, but both were inevitable. It was just as her sign said: REMEMBER YOU ARE NOT WAITING, YOU ARE WATCHING FOR A PHENOMENON TO TAKE PLACE AT ANY MOMENT. I hoped it would. I liked the idea of California earthquakes predicted by a typical California eccentric brought to Calistoga by the traditional California obsessions with healthy food and healing waters.

17

Earthquake Bay

Back on the Sonoma coast I paid five dollars at the Lawson's Landing tollhouse where a sign promised, THIS IS WHERE THE FUN BEGINS! and drove through a meadow scattered with Portosans, Dumpsters, and grazing cows onto a spit of land almost closing the mouth of Tomales Bay. Here the 1906 earthquake had cut a fissure so deep it survived months of heavy rain, and created craters too deep to be bottomed by fishing lines.

Tomales Bay, also known as "Earthquake Bay," is a fourteen-mile-long finger of water that narrows like an icicle to stab the San Andreas rift valley. It is as beautiful and lonely as any loch or fjord. On its western shore the forested ridges of the Point Reyes Peninsula rise as steeply as a high island in Polynesia. Their rock is granite, a piece of Southern California that has slid north on the Pacific plate. This land is national seashore, while the rolling hills of the eastern shore, equally empty, are saved from sprawl by Marin County zoning ordinances allowing only one house per sixty acres. Lawson's Landing sits in the middle of this rigorously protected landscape, a stick in the eye of every conservationist, preservationist, and environmentalist, and the kind of jolly eyesore that, thanks to the Coastal Commission, will never again be built on the California coast.

It reminded me of a sleepy Caribbean island. Dogs lay sprawled in the road. A workman slowly banged a wrench around the guts of an old tractor. A boy chased a squealing piglet under the keels of stored boats. Two Vietnamese tended crab pots while a man with prison tattoos baited his son's hook. The beetle-backed, sun-faded trailers had rusty awnings and television aerials that whirled like weather vanes in the wind.

You expect unshaven men in broken-backed slippers to be managing such places. But Nancy Vogler was a sharp woman with the pleasant face and easy charm of a high-school class president. Her great-grandfather Sylvester Lawson had been a rancher who summered with his family at the hotel in neighboring Dillon Beach. He bought it in the 1920s, promoting it with jingles such as "Our bathtub is the ocean,/Our lawn—the beach so gray,/Our children dance with kelpies/To wile the hours away." Her grandfather Merle Lawson decided he preferred fishing to cows and built a road to it in 1957. He constructed a pier and boathouse, and opened a fishermen's retreat. Her father added the campground, trailer park, and a barge to take clammers to the mudflats. He hired teenage boys to handle the summer crowds and Nancy Vogler married one. When he returned from Vietnam they took over the landing.

"We run this place on the theory of 'it's not broke, don't fix it.' It probably explains why we're stuck in the fifties," she said. Her low prices helped, too. She charged $10 for overnight camping and $2.50 for a trip on the clam clipper. Her customers watched birds, pitched horseshoes, caught crabs, and dug clams. Nothing required lessons or expensive equipment.

Her husband was hooded-eyed and handsome, relaxed enough to fall asleep on his feet. His T-shirt said CLAM-DIGGING—THE GOOD LIFE. She introduced him saying, "I was just explaining how I wouldn't marry you unless you liked the landing."

"She means it, too," he said.

She could have tripled her rates or sold to developers. Some Arab investors had proposed leveling nearby Dillon Beach's two-hundred-foot dunes for an underground parking garage, restaurants, and boutiques. "They called a community meeting and showed us a scale model so beautiful that, Lordy, it just took your breath away," she remembered. "They tried buying everyone off. The only problem was water. We're the only people who have it and"—she paused for a pleasurable memory—"we said no, no, no. No water. None. Ever. So they packed their tents and left."

She rode out the stormy winters in a double-wide trailer, writing a historical novel set in a stately home. She refused to sell because living surrounded by such beauty had spoiled her for anywhere else, and because she liked her guests. She got a kick out of the families who circled their cars and campers like wagon trains for a yearly reunion, the Asian immigrants so gripped by clam digging they sent out their toddlers and grandmothers with shovels, and even the San Francisco yuppies. "They 'discover' us while they're staying in $120 rooms at Tomales and think we're their great secret. They're a hoot."

The landing was a responsibility, and her sons had already decided it would be their lifework, too. It was the only seaside resort many of her customers could afford. They returned every year, watching their children grow up together, and creating the kind of summer colony the wealthy enjoy in places like Martha's Vineyard. "Generations have been bringing their families back to Lawson's Landing," she wrote in a master plan submitted to comply with the regulations environmentalists and county officials had probably hoped would close her down. "It is this continuity of tradition that the Lawson family feels good that they can maintain. In this day of change and flux, a place that doesn't change very much from when one was young is a precious thing to hang on to."

She knew all about the fault. A state seismic study placed her mobile home directly over its main trace and she had her superstitions. While growing up, she thought about earthquakes whenever her sister made a chocolate mint cake her family called the "Quake Cake" because its baking preceded temblors and tidal waves.

She worried on the warm and still April days considered traditional earthquake weather, or whenever she noticed excessive roadkill, or when her secretary, Pam George, complained of headaches. A subduction-zone quake posed the greatest threat. Waves from the Alaskan earthquake had destroyed some of the landing's pier and covered its clam beds with sand. Even a small offshore earthquake in 1977 had turned the ocean into an undulating serpent.

She promised to call me if George had more headaches. Several weeks later she left a message on my answering machine I received a day too late. On April 24, 1992, a warm and windless Friday, George had complained of "killer headaches." They worsened the next day, then stopped, "as if someone had thrown a switch," at almost the same moment Jerry Hurley's 6.9 struck Ferndale and Petrolia.

I drove back through Dillon Beach, where some prewar bungalows were built so close you could almost walk between them with a hand on each wall. A few hundred yards above, the sprawling homes of the Ocean Marin development lay scattered like children's blocks across bluffs and dunes. Like Shelter Cove, they were all decks and windows.

The streets twisted like small intestines and had Hawaiian names. When I asked a Tomales rancher what the Ocean Marin people did all day, he said, "We call them sea sniffers."

I returned on a windy Saturday to find the decks and yards still empty, but driveways filled with cars. People were not so much sniffing the sea as staring at it through their tinted picture windows, watching waves roll in from Siberia and fishing boats bob like corks, perhaps cursing Lawson's Landing as a damned eyesore every time they saw THIS IS WHERE THE FUN BEGINS! in the circle of their whale-watching telescopes.

At a nearby real-estate office a poker-faced agent with a helmet of styled gray hair said Ocean Marin had become "a three-ring circus." Retirees and investors from Southern California and the Bay Area were bidding up prices and lots had doubled in three years. His young side-kick had a tricky smile and a Woody Woodpecker laugh. He boasted that this "community" was quiet and peaceful because so many houses were bought as investments and rarely occupied.

When I asked about the fault they made their faces register surprise.

The sidekick claimed the ground was bedrock, so no one at Ocean Marin gave the fault a moment's thought. Lawson's Landing was a different matter. "I'd sure hate to be there when the next Big One strikes and it liquefies," he said, laughing his woodpecker laugh, delighted at the thought.

"You know something?" the older agent asked. "They could have made that place into a goddamned Riviera if they'd wanted. Instead they've done shit."

The rain lifted as I arrived in Tomales, the inland town nearest Lawson's Landing. A double rainbow arched over its main street, spider-webs glistened in fence posts, and spotlights of sun swept across pastures. The highest praise pessimistic Californians could bestow on a picture-perfect village like this was to call it "un-Californian." The county newspaper spoke of "the simple look of middle America," and a third-generation resident told me, "We have what people have back east, homes that are 140 years old and farms in the same families for five generations."

But I thought Tomales was so appealing precisely because it had a distinctly Californian fizz.

Deikmann's General Store sold guns, fishing tackle, and rubber boots, and had the kind of wide aisles and high ceilings that reminded you how cramped most stores have become. There was a potbellied stove and photographs of Bill Deikmann's parents in green aprons. He had continued their practice of accepting IOUs, but also played Miles Davis and Coltrane over the sound system, and rented his second floor to Shoreline Financial Services. Across the street, the U.S. Hotel was a faithful reproduction of a nineteenth-century structure consumed by the great Tomales fire of 1920. The owner was a lifelong resident who had named each room after an original settler. But the deli in back sold gourmet sandwiches on grainy bread popular with men driving muddy pickups. The only bar in Tomales had twinkling lights, hunting trophies, and "My Blue Heaven" on the jukebox. But the leathery woman matching shots of tequila with the ranchers had a finishing-school accent and was on her second or third life. "I need a nice recipe for salmon," I heard her say. "Got to have it for my son in New York. I'm flying the salmon to New York tomorrow to show him his mom can cook."

I bought a poppyseed scone at the new bakery from a young woman with a musical voice. She and her husband had recently moved here so their children could grow up in a "real community." The last suburban straw had been an expensive preschool program that simply parked the kids in front of a big-screen television. Now she planned home-schooling her children rather than send them to the Tomales Elementary School, a curious decision for someone wanting to become part of a "real community."

I climbed the hill to see why it was not good enough for them and found a well-equipped and maintained building where the children of commuters, ranchers, and immigrant farmhands seemed healthy and cheerful. A teacher's aide named Georgia Marino who was supervising recess told me her grandfather, the brother of the famed horticulturalist Luther Burbank, had arrived in Tomales in 1854 and become its assemblyman and leading citizen. She had founded the Tomales History Center. In a town of only 282, it boasted 250 members, among them the descendants of early residents who had never seen Tomales, and visitors who had "adopted" it. They claimed it felt like the hometown they never had. She thought this said a lot for Tomales. I thought it might say more about where they lived.

After recess she led me to a storage room off the library and showed off her archives. "When people die, their relatives throw this stuff out the back door," she said, piling a table in the school library with yearbooks, scrapbooks, albums, and more primary source material than you find in most county libraries, "and I'm here to catch it."

She ran her fingers across photographs of winning baseball teams, weddings of the long dead, and men with hermits' beards on a rabbit shoot. The Great Earthquake had left Tomales resembling a blast zone. Every downtown store and brick building had collapsed. Early-rising farmers had hung on to their picket fences as the earth rocked, trees brushed the ground, and houses expanded like bellows. Tombstones pitched over and fissures plowed the land. Black smoke billowed on the horizon as San Francisco burned. The night sky glowed red and people slept outside, screaming with every aftershock.

Marino knew that all-girl pallbearers had carried the corpse of a girl crushed in an adobe house during the quake. She could identify the Uncle Sams in the old Fourth of July parades, and half the children in the 1910 school photograph, then find them in wedding pictures twenty years later. I looked up from a 1920 portrait of the Poncia family to see a ten-year-old Poncia boy who could have stepped out of the photograph. Many of the kids sitting in the library were related to her through marriage and birth. She said it showed how "solid" Tomales was; how generations stayed put, keeping their ranches and filling these classrooms.

An outsider comparing Tomales with these photographs would say it was unchanged. But she thought the same strict zoning codes that preserved its appearance were altering its character. If a rancher had three children and groomed one to take over the ranch, he could no longer subdivide to provide houses for the other two. When he died, the descendant who wanted to continue ranching sometimes could not afford to buy out the others and the land was subdivided into sixty-acre "ranchettes" for weekenders. She herself no longer lived in the house where she was raised.

She was torn. She wanted Tomales to continue looking the same and knew looser zoning would put houses on its rolling hills, but meanwhile it was becoming a dried gourd, rattling with wealthy weekenders and commuters. If there was a middle ground, a way of preserving both landscape and community, it had yet to be found.

According to one of my guidebooks, the Station House Café in nearby Point Reyes Station was supposed to be "a cheerful country café." Perhaps it was on foggy weekdays, or had been before its owners displayed a framed review from *Gourmet*. But on the Sunday morning I stopped there, I sat among overdressed city couples picking at brunch while their bored children swung their legs like metronomes. One travel writer suggested people avoid this scene by visiting Point Reyes on fall weekends, when it was less crowded and "locals are in a better mood."

But I thought rubbing weekenders and commuters against a Western cow town less than an hour from the Golden Gate Bridge had produced some interesting sparks. Pickups carrying hay bales and Range Rovers filled with suburban children shared a main street wide enough to allow double-teamed wagons to make U-turns. There was a feed store and an art gallery. The air smelled of manure and perfume. Ranchers drove cattle past the offices of a weekly newspaper that had won a Pulitzer Prize, and twice a day the town clock preserved the cow-town image by mooing instead of chiming, thanks to a device installed by technicians from George Lucas's neighboring Skywalker Studios.

Point Reyes Station's ranches still put butter on San Francisco tables, but its Old Creamery housed the studios of Art Rogers, a photographer who was famous this week for winning a copyright lawsuit against artist Jeff Koons. The appeals-court justices who upheld the district court's decision in Rogers's favor declared that by modeling four sculptures on a Rogers photograph of a Point Reyes couple holding eight German-shepherd puppies, Koons had exhibited "arrogance and greed," "willful and egregious" behavior, and "sailed under the flag of piracy." If copyright infringement had been a capital offense, I thought these judges would have volunteered for the firing squad.

Koons, a symbolic confection of the Manhattan art and media world, admitted buying a card bearing Rogers's photograph at an airport gift shop, tearing off its copyright symbol, mailing it to Italian artisans with instructions to make four sculpture copies, and selling three for a total of $367,000. He argued they were a "parody" of what had been "only a postcard photo," and congratulated himself for giving Rogers's work "spirituality" and "animation."

He was a spectacular villain for a town like Point Reyes Station that somewhat self-consciously celebrated community values, honest work, and front-porch America. He had become wealthy by hiring craftsmen to encase vacuum cleaners in Plexiglas, and cast stainless-steel replicas of inflatable rabbits. He told *60 Minutes* his three basketballs in a fish tank represented "a definition of love and death—aspects of the eternal." One exhibit featured paintings based on photographs of him engaged in explicit sexual acts with his now estranged wife, Italian parliamentarian and pornography star Ilona Staller, who had kept her own publicity ball in the air by volunteering to fuck Saddam Hussein.

A photograph of Koons I found in a back-issue magazine showed a film noir villain—dark and saturnine, with an oily, pockmarked complexion and a widow's peak. He had been shot from above, so he resembled a cobra slithering headfirst out of a snake charmer's basket. The caption said, "Plenty of artists hope to reveal themselves through their work, but nobody pulls it off quite like Jeff Koons."

I met Art Rogers in his studio. He was a short, energetic man with a droopy Pancho Villa mustache and curly black hair who had moved to California from North Carolina, and to Point Reyes in 1972 because he believed San Francisco was making him "unable to trust anyone." He had become as fervent a believer in small-town life as Georgia Marino, and was particularly proud of his photograph of the audience gathered at the community center for the premiere of a horror film shot in Point Reyes. He had persuaded everyone to light a match at once, producing a spooky picture perfectly matched to the event. Afterward he placed second behind the local pharmacist in a contest to name the most people in the picture.

His photographs reflected his own gently humorous optimism, and had the cumulative effect of persuading you Point Reyes was California's capital of the unique, eccentric, and wonderful. A farmer showed off triplet calves, triplets! Mr. and Mrs. Collins held hands over their "World Champ" 354-pound pumpkin. Wolfgang Puck cradled a glistening salmon while behind him twenty-three chefs raised fists into the air like Olympic champions. One of his favorites showed the Nelson family sitting on a wood deck at their beach house, hands raised to shade their eyes against the sun while they waited for him to snap a family portrait. They loved it because it symbolized their unity, all six Nelsons unconsciously doing the same thing at once.

His Point Reyes was filled with cows, puppies, handsome oldsters, and cheerful teenagers. If he could find room for a child, pet, or baby animal, he did. But they were never treacly, and you sensed the essential decency of photographer and subject meeting as the shutter clicked.

"But I love Norman Rockwell!" he thundered when I asked him if the comparison had ever been made. "I'm a cornball, just like him!"

He knew what made a successful community, and while I leafed through photographs of cheerful farmers and baby calves, he slapped his desk with each point. "Work ethic? ... Yes! Farming? ... Yes! Gardening? ... Yes! Most of all, children!" He had two under five. "You know people for twenty years; you have kids, they do, too. Your children become friends and it enriches the town."

He had photographed seven-year-old Stephen Henderson standing in front of his family's backyard redwood tree in 1976, then took him back to the same spot five years later. When he compared the photographs he had the idea of bringing other townspeople back to the same place every five or ten years, having them strike the same pose, and shooting them in the same light and at the same distance. He called this series of photographs *Yesterday and Today,* and they told you more about families and the passage of time than many short stories. For a state symbolizing transience, they were a small miracle.

While he replied to calls congratulating him on his victory over Koons I studied his photographs, searching the faces of the young for what they would become, and the old for what they had been.

Here was a smiling Connie Morse leaning against the railing of her deck while cradling her infant daughter in 1976, and here she was twelve years later with the same smile, but hugging a pretty teenager.

Here were four generations of Poncia men, infant to great-grandfather, on a front porch in 1975. The two oldest were seated, held canes, and had identical stick-out ears. Here were the Poncia men in 1991: a father and teenage son stood behind two empty chairs, preparing to sit in them for the next photograph, and leave the standing to the next generation.

Here was the Minor family in 1975, a mother with braids surrounded by four beautiful children, and here they were twelve years later, four young adults surrounding a shrunken gray-haired lady who had given her features to a daughter who could be mistaken for the twin of her younger self.

Here were four cowboy tomboys in 1980 wearing T-shirts and vests, their short blond hair put up in pin curlers, and here they were as teenagers in long hair and jewelry. Here was "Dani," striking a sultry pose in a black leotard in 1975, and here she was sixteen years later, the same pose, but wearing jeans and work shirt and flanked by her boys, Justin and Jeremiah. And here, finally, was Stephen Henderson, standing in front of the same redwood, hands behind his back as in the earlier photograph, but now tall and handsome in a marine-corps dress uniform, ready for the Persian Gulf.

The pictures said, "Look, here are your neighbors, having children, aging, rooted to this house, this tree, this cabin, this town." By catching the elusive concepts of "community" and "family values" on film, Rogers had photographed ghosts.

His triumph over Koons was so fresh that as we walked from his studio to a Mexican restaurant, a rancher, the postmistress, and two schoolgirls congratulated him. He became uneasy. "I *had* to sue," he said. "I couldn't let that fucker get away with it. Now I'm afraid it's all I'll be known for—not my Guggenheim or my photographs hanging in museums, but for being the guy who beat Jeff Koons."

Some of the changes occurring in Point Reyes Station seemed to echo Koons's crude piracy. As we crossed the street a sports car accelerated, forcing us to jump back. "I moved to escape all this fashion and trash, and now it's following me," he complained, adding you could once stop in the middle of the road and cars drove around you. Once there had been a hundred small ranches, now there were a handful. Once Point Reyes had been cheap and quiet, now it was expensive and had a video store. Coming next was an all-night convenience store, for the convenience of commuters. The problem was too many newcomers who did not really want to live in a genuine community, just one that resembled one and could meet their big-city needs. He was suspicious of the elitism of the no-growth movement, but if people wanted this kind of life, then, "Great! Live it! But get hip, create it somewhere else instead of overwhelming Point Reyes."

As we walked into the Mexican café for lunch he said, "A perfect example of what's happened: until last month it was a sit-down restaurant where you could talk to a waitress; now none of the employees are locals and you have to fetch your tacos from that damned take-out counter so they can sell more food to tourists."

When he made a jokey complaint that the burrito had gone up 20 percent since yesterday, the bored counter clerk said, "Yeah, but now you get real silverware and plates instead of plastic."

When he complained again she snapped, "Go eat elsewhere if you don't like it."

"There *are* no other Mexican restaurants. None within a forty-minute drive. Don't you know that? You would if you lived here. What a bullshit answer!"

Our food came in a plastic basket, with plastic forks.

"Where's the silverware? Where are the real plates?" he shouted.

(I thought of Jack Nicholson in *Five Easy Pieces* and wondered if he would tell her to hold that burrito between her legs.)

"They come with the combination platter, not the burrito." Her smile was triumphant.

"See what I mean? The lies! The greed! They'll ruin this town."

He had said he considered moving farther north, and if he found another Point Reyes Station he would keep his mouth shut. He had told his wife that the day they had to lock their door was the day they moved. But considering the double murder in Jenner, you might say that day had already come, and gone.

18
"Good-bye, Sea Drift"

I thought the most unusual thing about Stinson Beach was not the three miles of white sand, swarms of wintering monarch butterflies, balmy, almost Southern California beach climate, or that although it was less than an hour from San Francisco, on this spring weekday it slumbered like a Sardinian fishing village—it was the number of buildings devoted to books. There was a one-room public library painted conch-shell pink, John Fagan's Used Books, and Stinson Beach Books, where the bookmarks proclaimed ONLY BOOKSTORE LOCATED DIRECTLY ON THE SAN ANDREAS FAULT.

When I finally found Fagan's store open, he blamed his whimsical hours on his schedule as an Oakland paramedic. He was a rangy blond man who looked more suited to a rugby scrum than shelling peanuts and reading two books a day in his cluttered cubbyhole. Stacks of books covered tables and rose from the floor like stalagmites. He admitted being a book addict, unable to stop buying more. "I've thought of expanding, but if I had more room I'd just fill it with more books in a heartbeat," he said. Most of his stock came from library deaccessions and yard sales, and he appreciated the poignancy of trading in books chosen as birthday and Christmas presents, inscribed for the deceased by the deceased. When beach bums offered the underlined college reading that was their last link to a more promising past, it broke his heart to say, "Twenty-five cents for this, a dime for that." He worried a quake might topple his shelves, playing havoc with his eccentric cataloging system, but worried more about a former "client" seeking revenge. Psychotics he once transported to hospitals had tracked him down. When he drove a gang member to an emergency room, they sometimes threat-ened to kill him. Right now living over the fault in Stinson Beach seemed safer than saving lives in Oakland.

He thought I would enjoy meeting Nancy Sullivan and directed me up a hill to her cottage. Her sandals, baggy jeans, and a loose black T-shirt made her look more like the widow of a beat poet than of an air-force officer. She had the rosy cheeks of a Russian grandmother, and her home was paneled in dark wood and had the rustic, musty feel of a dacha. It owed its existence to the 1906 earthquake. Afterward her grandfather had bought hundreds of yards of ruptured San Francisco water pipe and laid down a water system. He had been a patron of the arts and to honor his memory she had created a downstairs "writer's room" for visiting authors who came from around the world and stayed for however long it took them to finish their work and be renewed by Stinson Beach. She seemed unconcerned her current tenant had been in residence six months and showed no sign of leaving.

Although her lot was tiny and her house close to its neighbors, it was worth $400,000, enough to buy a small farm. She stayed because she was hooked on this heady mix of climate, beach, and eccentrics. If an earthquake struck, she could not imagine a more marvelous place to die. The only problem was that Stinson had become "everybody's fa-vorite place." Young couples from the East who were heirs to consider-able fortunes had bought nearby houses, replacing creative people of moderate means and simple tastes. They raised perfect children, dab-bled in writing and New Age enterprises, and sometimes worked for nonprofit organizations in the city, buying into an artistic lifestyle rather than creating it themselves. But she tried to be tolerant and wel-come them. Anything less would put her in the camp of the weekend-ing executives, physicians, and attorneys living in gated Sea Drift, a development occupying a sandy extension of Stinson Beach between the Pacific and the Bolinas Lagoon.

For over a decade the Sea Drifters had campaigned to prevent the public using the beach fronting their houses, even posting guards and erecting fences the state finally ordered removed. The California Coastal Commission had proposed a compromise: the public could have "low-intensity passive use" of the beach, but bonfires, large orga-nized groups, and motor vehicles would be prohibited. The Sea Drift Property Owners' Association rejected this, claiming to be concerned about environmental threats to the lagoon from large crowds and dogs (although the greatest threat was that their septic tanks would rupture during an earthquake, spilling sewage into the lagoon). They would agree to allow people to walk along their beach, but not to make "stationary" use of the sand. The dispute was heading for court again and the Sea Drifters were threatening more fences.

Sullivan believed a great earthquake would render the dispute moot. Sea Drift's houses lay within the fault zone. Some northern ones sat over the 1906 break, some rested on pilings driven into the kind of loose fill that does poorly in quakes. Even a modest tsunami would roll over the sandspit. A geologist friend of hers had "gone apoplectic" describing what a temblor would do. "He says, 'One big quake and we won't have to worry about *them* anymore.' Maybe a tidal wave will get them, then it'll be good-bye, Sea Drift! Ha-ha-ha."

Other Stinson Beachers felt the same. A merchant described with undisguised satisfaction how floods in the early 1980s had damaged houses "behind the gate." A German woman working in a boutique said Sea Drift had the kind of people who set up easels in their living rooms to show off their art purchases. At a party there she had made a point of calling it "one little tidy, gated world." Afterward, she said with a triumphant smile, "they stopped inviting me to their silly get-togethers." An artist named Dino Columbo who displayed a painting for the enjoyment of passing motorists had chosen one speaking to the open-beaches controversy. It showed a white picket fence surrounding a beach populated by rooting pigs.

Sullivan offered to drive me into Sea Drift, saying a couple let her swim in the lagoon off their property and we could use their name at the gate. She did her best to make the visit interesting, pointing out where Dianne Feinstein spent her weekends, and the home of the millionaire who invented coat hangers with a hole preventing their theft from hotel rooms. We drove to the end of the sandspit and, standing over the fault trace, stared across a narrow channel at Bolinas. Its people have left-wing, counterculture roots, and would be appalled by any comparisons to Sea Drift, but she considered them remarkably similar. Both made a fetish of their privacy and were unfriendly—attitudes she considered very un-Californian. "Stinson Beach and Bolinas are as different as the tectonic plates," she said. "We sit on the North American one and welcome anyone; they're on the Pacific one and don't."

In the newspaper clippings I read about Bolinas there were so many things to dislike it was difficult knowing where to start. With the recruiting of schoolchildren to hurl eggs at cars with out-of-state license plates? The smashed windows of real-estate offices? The guerrilla war

waged against highway signs residents feared would deliver day-trippers? (When the signs were put to a vote, the antisign faction won 304
to 114.) Or the president of the utility board who had said Bolinas did
not need the "superficial visitor who comes sweeping through in a Winnebago" and "sticks his head in an art gallery." After this, you had to
admire Susan Dunn, a Bolinas resident and clinical psychologist brave
enough to tell a reporter, "There is an us-against-them mentality here, a
feeling that because we were smart enough to find this place (and are
wealthy enough to live here), we are better than other people. In my
opinion Bolinas has a disproportionate number of borderline or overly
psychotic individuals."

Nancy Sullivan made Bolinas sound like Yugoslavia. "The people
there are *not* nice," she warned. "They'll let the air out of your tires or
slash them if you have a rental. If you *must* go, turn right and park near
the post office. I always park facing out of town so I can make a quick
getaway. And for goodness' sake don't drive up to the mesa. It's full of
ex-everythings: ex-nuns, ex-yippies, ex-criminals. Above all, don't ask
questions or let them see you taking notes. And your clothes are all
wrong. [I was wearing scruffy khakis and ratty sneakers.] You'll need
jeans and a T-shirt, a very old one."

I drove there without changing but managed to walk down
Wharf Road, buy bread in a bakery, and drink coffee in the café without being cursed or elbowed into the gutter. On a weekday afternoon
Bolinas had the slow-motion feel of a tropical port built to export cash
crops no one paid cash for anymore. A humid blanket of noneffort kept
even the espresso drinking at half speed. You would never have imagined it had once been home to optimistic promoters who celebrated
whatever brought them closer to San Francisco, and to generations of
energetic California Dream seekers.

The Bolinas timber boom was so furious that its frustrated gold-
miners-turned-lumberjacks silted up the lagoon in three years. When
an egg craze gripped San Francisco, they sailed to the Farallon Islands
in small boats, gathering as many as 120,000 gull eggs in a single boat
in two days and selling them for a dollar a dozen. Prospectors drilled
oil wells on the beach in 1865, and a copper boom left behind so
many shafts they became a hazard to wandering cattle, but produced
22,000 tons for Pittsburgh mills during the First World War. The
1873 coal bust left a 325-foot-high hill of tailings. The 1874 trout
boom left fishponds along the lagoon. The 1934 ambergris boom closed
Bolinas schools for a day so students could collect bucketloads of

this valuable whale secretion. (Experts later proclaimed it "sewage butter" spewed from a passing ship or the Oakland treatment plant.) The 1906 earthquake killed a fledgling tourist boom by pitching rooming houses into the lagoon. The 1920s brought a land scam in which developers divided three hundred acres into five thousand lots and the *San Francisco Bulletin* acquired hundreds, offering them for $69.50 to anyone purchasing a six-month subscription. People acquired them in twos and threes, erecting bungalows and a bathhouse open only to Caucasians.

The last boom arrived in 1971 when two tankers collided in the fogbound Golden Gate and hundreds of counterculture people rushed up from Berkeley and the Haight to save the lagoon. They dumped straw on beaches, cleaned seabirds, hauled telephone poles into the channel, lashing them together and fashioning a makeshift boom from gunnysacks and tennis nets. Afterward they stayed, squatting or buying tiny plots on the mesa and building shacks resembling garden sheds that were small enough to fall outside the building codes. They ran garden hoses to neighboring water supplies and patched into old septic tanks, so overloading the systems that when it rained, people who had been drawn to Bolinas to fight an ecological catastrophe stepped over puddles of their own bubbling shit.

Nancy Sullivan had muttered about "a foreign-legion post for wealthy heiresses," and a rich underground vein of inherited money certainly did appear to nourish Bolinas. People could not resist spending it on foreign automobiles made acceptable by a spackling of mud. Some cars carried a little oval CH (Switzerland), F (France), or S (Sweden) sticker above their plates, proof their owners could not shake this upper-middle-class affectation, or that they were secondhand gifts from suburban parents. The other clues were golden retrievers in the backs of overaccessorized pickups, little girls on horseback in expensive riding kit, braces on preadolescent teeth, expensive watches, posters advertising "firewalks" (EMPOWER YOURSELF BY WALKING ON FIRE) costing forty dollars, and a flyer offering a $305,000 half-acre, two-bedroom "cottage" resembling a miner's shack. Of course the biggest clue of all was the country-club determination to exclude anyone wearing the wrong clothes (polyester leisure wear) or coming from the wrong place (anywhere but Bolinas).

When I returned on a Sunday hoping to see tourists being egged, I met the other half of the Bolinas equation—people who posted notices like LOOKING FOR A TEPEE SITE IN OR NEAR BOLINAS—AM WORKING AND CAN

PAY $200 A MONTH. A posse of matted-haired men who were each a different version of Rasputin had turned a weedy downtown lot into their outdoor clubhouse. They drank malt liquor from quarts and squirted Velveeta into their mouths from aerosol cans, passed joints and unfiltered cigarettes to teenage acolytes, and threw sticks at the yellow-eyed curs who sprawled across the sidewalk growling at visitors.

When a sleek, hand-in-hand city couple peered into the community center at a rehearsal involving chanting, drumming, and spoon playing, a woman in a leotard yanked a curtain across the door and shouted, "Go away!"

When a family in matching red windbreakers climbed out of a minivan with Missouri plates, teenagers followed them down the street chanting "Tourists! Tourists! Tourists!" spitting out the word like a black curse.

I was not entirely unsympathetic. What was the harm in being stuck in the sixties? Why not find a decade you liked and stick with it? After seeing how the weekend trade had corrupted Mendocino, it was hard not to root for people fighting that fate. The $300,000-cottage people wanted to hide out from tourists, but at least they had not thrown up gates and walls, and the empty pints of off-brand vodkas resting against the tinfoil-decorated necks of imported beer bottles in the trash cans indicated their willingness to mingle with the $200-a-month tepee dwellers.

I had been told Ray Moritz was interested in earthquakes, but when we met on Monday morning in the café, it turned out he was safety officer for the volunteer fire department, and a professional "fire ecologist" who believed wildfires were a greater menace. He pointed out that Bolinas had suffered little from Loma Prieta. Sure, some buildings creaked, newcomers to California ran terrified into the street, shrimp flew out of mud holes, and flocks of seagulls swooped down to eat them, but that was all. His greatest worry was that an earthquake would ignite wildfires. Lightning and Indian fires had once burned out the canyons regularly, but following wildfires in 1929 and 1945, fire departments and government agencies had imposed fire-suppression programs leading to a dangerous increase in flammable material. Now the surrounding hills were a tinderbox. Most locals opposed prescribed burns. They signed petitions and demanded studies that were still unfinished a decade later. They pretended to be motivated by ecological arguments, but he thought they worried more about the burns leaving the landscape "aesthetically intolerable."

His nightmare scenario involved a major quake striking on a busy summer weekend when Stinson Beach was packed. Water pipes would break. Landslides, tidal waves, and floods would destroy highways. Wildfires would race through canyons, bearing down on fifteen thousand panicked and thirsty people in bathing suits.

When I asked about the disappearing road signs, he gave a deep sigh and asked, "Don't you think I should be able to come downtown on a Saturday morning, find a parking place and a seat in a café, and socialize with my friends without being overwhelmed by tourists?"

I did. But then again, any Sea Drifter could have made the same kind of argument. Perhaps it was this beautiful landscape that made Sea Drift and Bolinas residents appear so mean-spirited. The more time one spends surrounded by East Marin's parkland and ranches, the easier it is to forget that open space like this so close to a major American city is the exception, and that East Marin's gorgeous countryside is a great California triumph that is the fruit of considerable struggle and expense.

Had the state widened the coastal highway to six lanes as was proposed in 1961, had a 1971 plan to build a new city of fifty thousand homes directly over the fault on the east shore of Tomales Bay been implemented, had the 1967 Bolinas Harbor District Plan that would have dredged the lagoon for a 1,600-boat marina, resort, and major shopping center not been thwarted by the purchase of a crucial island by the local Audubon Society, had the California Coastal Commission not been created to regulate seaside development, had Marin County not imposed sixty-acre agricultural zoning on the surrounding ranches, had the Marin Agricultural Land Trust not bought the development rights to over twenty thousand acres of open land, and had the United States Congress not approved the purchase of Point Reyes National Seashore and the Golden Gate National Recreation Area—then East Marin would have resembled the Jersey shore, and people in Bolinas and Sea Drift would be looking at expressways, marinas, and condominiums, instead of meadows, bird sanctuaries, and cows. Because these fortunate ex-hippies and millionaires lived in this lovely setting thanks to the work of environmentalists throughout the Bay Area, and the coerced generosity of state and federal taxpayers, it seemed ungrateful to be ripping down signs and barricading beaches against the very people who might have struggled to preserve, and had certainly financed, the natural beauty enriching other lives.

FOUR

SAN FRANCISCO

❖

19
The Wizard of
Sutro Heights

I am afraid when I tell you Lawrence Kroll, the "Wizard of Oz," lived in an upper-middle-class Victorian and said he liked teaching computer science at San Francisco State because of "the good equipment, a paycheck, and the discipline of the money culture," you will imagine a Wizard like the original, a trickster behind a curtain, never believing in Oz himself. But nothing could be less true.

Had I never visited Oz, I would have thought here is a charming and energetic man, stuffed with interests, and young looking for his age. Instead, I thought, here is the Wizard running at half speed, and my eyes went to his thinning hair and gray mustache. Meeting him was like running into an old friend after many years—you expect him to look older, but are shocked when he does.

He lived in Sutro Heights, a fogbound neighborhood at the edge of the Pacific that is the closest San Francisco has to a wilderness. The city's avenues shed traffic as they near the ocean, and by the time they reach Sutro Heights have become as empty as the boulevards of Ulan Bator. The beach is so long and wide it feels deserted on even the sunniest weekends. It attracts mostly joggers, wet-suit surfers, fishermen, and the novice homeless, who try burrowing into its sand but usually head downtown once the wind turns their cardboard into kites.

I joined the Wizard for his daily walk. It was too bleak for the beach so we set out along cliffs that drop into the Pacific just west of the Golden Gate Bridge. The wind blew drizzle down my neck and swept away some of his words. I heard, "We moved to Oz to get our kids

169

away from the television world . . . one car . . . friends came and left . . . oil crises, t-groups, and composting."

The disasters punctuating its first three years sounded like episodes in a counterculture situation comedy. He recounted them in an amused but slightly detached way, as if they had happened to someone else.

Their first crop was garlic, but the summer was dry, weeds sprouted, they forgot to water, and were into no-tillage farming because the tiller made too much noise. The crop was stunted and worthless. They decided to raise sheep and bought a flock from a neighbor. "But we had big fights when it came time to castrate the males," he explained. "We did it with rubber bands, and our dogs feasted on their balls. The vegetarians stopped talking to me and refused to cut the tails. That caused resentment because it meant more work for the rest of us. Finally we sold them back."

They tried cattle next. The neighbor delivering them grinned. That night the mother called her calves and they walked home through the Oz fences. The Wizard wired the fence, but they escaped twice more. Their organic peas sprouted into a huge, healthy crop. "The first sunny morning everyone came out to pick," he remembered. "We sang 'Hare Krishna' and 'We Shall Overcome,' but by eleven the kids had drifted away, then the women. I guess they weren't into stoop labor. Soon I was alone with peas that were quickly becoming less fresh. When I couldn't persuade the natural-food coop to pick them we had another meeting. (We were *very* good at meetings.) Some people wanted to bring in migrants from Mexico. We tried ourselves once more. We began singing 'I've Been Working on the Railroad,' but soon I was singing alone. So I called our friends and told them to take them for free. They were our most successful crop. You see why I have such respect for Hopper and his apples?"

By 1976 all the original communards had left except the Krolls, who appeared to have spent three years proving the capitalist proposition that communal farms do not work. He turned Oz into a human-potential camp for kids aged from about eight to sixteen. It provided three things he loved—children, fun, and a ready-made audience—and had clearly been the Oz incarnation he enjoyed most. The only hassle was the yearly "truth lecture" when he begged the campers not to get pregnant or busted for drugs. The kids loved his camp, he said, but every year he felt himself drifting closer to a lawsuit.

We returned to his house, where he showed me slides. I saw the clown school, kids throwing the Oz "earthball," a production of *A Chorus Line,* the rope bridge, an apple press powered by a bicycle, and the Wizard, dressed in his Yellow Brick Suit, his all-leather Paul Bunyan outfit, and naked except for a cowboy hat decorated with feathers.

The commune and camp had obviously provided lots of people with large helpings of fun and I found myself wishing I could have had it with them, particularly when I later read *Growing Up Communally* in the Mendocino journal *Ridge Review,* in which author Suzanne Axtell described her life as an adolescent Oz communard in the early seventies. At first she was horrified by the "rather scruffy adults in some place out in the sticks." She "prayed feverishly at night for God to get me out of this heathen situation," but soon changed her mind. The commune was big enough so she could escape parental nagging, and she enjoyed the film nights, Sufi dances, being encouraged to try a craft and excel in school, skinny-dipping, hot tubs, "and best of all, sex and drugs." It was "the turning point" in her life, and she felt "lucky to have been a part of it, especially as a child." She later married one of her Oz friends and the wedding photograph accompanying her article showed as ordinary a young middle-class couple as you could imagine.

The same *Ridge Review* also had a piece by an adult Oz communard named Alix Levine, who gave a succinct but colorless historical summary. The founders had been adults ranging in age from twenty-one to forty-eight, most of them early thirties, "college-educated, politically liberal, highly individualistic, aesthetically inclined, and middle class in background." Each family built its own distinctive dwelling but shared a communal kitchen. There had been "constant tension between individual autonomy and communal consensus." The Krolls had purchased the land but encouraged other members to earn ownership in it, although after three years no one could agree on a formula for achieving this. After the last scheme for creating Oz shares collapsed, "the dream of a community of equals could no longer be maintained." Differences in material wealth had probably doomed the experiment. Some members had investments and inheritances and took "trips to sunny climes" during the rainy season; others could not afford to leave. Some built beautiful houses, others lived in shacks and tents. Some took jobs outside the commune, others devoted themselves to communal projects. There were conflicts between meat eaters and vegetarians, those wanting frequent visitors and those preferring solitude. But the fundamental dispute revolved around who would own the spectacular meadows and redwoods.

The Wizard's slides ended in 1984 when his family moved to San Francisco. They had all tired of the communal kitchen and bathrooms, and he no longer wanted to be janitor, yardman, secretary, and fire marshal. But it was his youngest daughter, Zooey, who precipitated the change by throwing tantrums and slipping notes under their pillows. She wanted to attend a lively big-city high school, and like many middle-class families, they finally moved for better schooling.

The Wizard lingered over slides of his handsome children. Unlike mine, unlike most, they never looked pouty or bored. When the older two reached their twenties they sometimes concealed their communal years. Now he thought they were "equally appreciative and embarrassed." The son in the jester's hat he had wanted to protect from the television world was a Hollywood producer. His oldest daughter was a computer artist. Both were "well dressed, clean, and corporate."

Zooey had discarded her Oz name, becoming Jennifer again. She had described Oz in a college application essay that probably clinched her admission to Yale, so it was not impossible that one of Oz's greatest successes had been making his daughter just the kind of offbeat applicant the Ivy League loves. It began, "After living in a commune for my first thirteen years and canoeing to school every day, I feel prepared for anything." She had "cringed when my mother, wearing a patchwork dress over the tie-dyed flare pants, picked me up from school," and wondered, "When would my parents realize the sixties were over?"

For the Krolls they ended when Jennifer persuaded the Wizard to leave Oz. But you could argue that for California they were still around. Except in remote north-coast hollows, the physical legacies of the counterculture—the clothes, communes, and VW buses—had vanished. But the intellectual legacy had proven more hardy, perhaps because it meshed so well with California's traditional predilection for experiment, individuality, and eccentricity.

This legacy explained why small towns like Point Arena had the cultural infrastructure and buzz of a small city and could support bookstores, dance troupes, and community theater, and why Humboldt County had more artists per capita than anywhere in America. It had made the environmental movement more confrontational and prone to pranks, and I thought there had been something unmistakably Oz-like in Judi Bari's sit-in at a lumber company executive's hot tub.

Kroll claimed not to miss Oz. There he had hustled for an audience, here the California educational establishment delivered a ready-made one to his classroom at San Francisco State. He turned off the projector and pulled the curtains. After the goofy clothes, rainbows, and painted faces, his dark parlor seemed even gloomier. He sensed what I was thinking. "I guess I traded 170 acres of redwood for this," he said. "Imagine, a whole forest for a house!" He clapped his brow and shook his head as if this, more than the garlic, goats, snap peas, and wandering calves, was the biggest joke of all.

20

"The Day Our World Shook"

When I lived in San Francisco in 1979 I was impressed by how many groups offered historic walking tours and lectures, and how every bar and neighborhood came with an amateur historian who creatively mined the Barbary Coast days, Chinatown, the railroad kings, and the 1906 earthquake for yet more stories.

Fifteen years later the city seemed even more history-infatuated. Consider the foghorns that once blasted and wailed as fog rolled through the Golden Gate. When the Coast Guard announced its intention to replace the last one with a safer and cheaper electronic signal, the *Chronicle* protested they were part of San Francisco tradition, and a city supervisor called them "one of the little magical things that make San Francisco what it is." A fledgling Lighthouse Society proposed Potemkin foghorns, ignoring the possibility that the romance of the original ones owed as much to knowing their blasts were preventing maritime disasters as to their actual sound.

During my absence change had also come to the cable cars, another famous San Francisco symbol. In 1979 these relics of the pre-quake city had been another form of public transportation and residents of my Russian Hill neighborhood used them to go downtown. But after a multimillion-dollar renovation the fare had risen to two dollars, several times what the bus cost, and passengers, now almost exclusively tourists traveling between Market Street and Fisherman's Wharf, waited in long lines for a crowded car.

If you believed the romance of these two potent San Francisco symbols was inseparable from functions they no longer performed, and that they had only been preserved as quaint ornaments to charm tourists and satisfy nostalgia, then you had to wonder if San Francisco's claim to being a great city did not also depend on something it no longer was. Some residents thought so and described it becoming an urban theme park, Disneyland-by-the-Bay, Boutique City. They carped about graffiti, filthy streets, and aggressive panhandlers, and its downtown did seem shabbier, and its numerous homeless more threatening than in 1979. But was not that the case everywhere? And San Francisco was still one of the most spectacularly situated cities on earth, and certainly the most fiercely loved, where people had a unique emotional interaction with a spectacular natural setting.

The fear that their city's greatest glories were in its past made San Franciscans even fiercer preservers and chroniclers of it than I remembered. No event was more celebrated than the 1906 earthquake, and none had generated more lore and memorabilia. Although the San Andreas bypassed the city, running under the Pacific just west of the Golden Gate Bridge, the seismic hoopla made San Francisco the best place in California to experience a vicarious earthquake.

I tried out the earthquake platform at the California Academy of Science in Golden Gate Park. The simulated 4.7 sent it pitching and rolling like a small ferry, but the 5.7 felt like a Tilt-a-Whirl slipping its moorings. While a screen showed collapsing buildings, a sepulchral voice intoned, "These destructive earthquakes ... this destructive ground motion *will* happen again." Some whooping boys rode it twice, but two German girls who giggled through the 4.7 grabbed hands and jumped off during the 5.7.

I spent hours at libraries and bookstores studying earthquake photographs. Because 1906 had struck before dawn, its photographs showed only the fire. The Loma Prieta ones, particularly those in *Fifteen Seconds: The Great California Earthquake of 1989,* were as good as disaster pictures can be. But the policeman pinching his nose to stay awake, the building sliced open like a dollhouse, the man broad-jumping a fissure, and the medics pulling a man from the Nimitz Freeway depicted only the aftermath. "Stunned fans in the lower deck of Candlestick Park reacted with fear, laughter, and confusion" showed a woman clapping her hands to her face while the man behind her smiled. Since it was focused, and the fans were talking and milling around, it had probably been snapped just afterward.

After reading that eight hundred people had submitted accounts of Loma Prieta experiences to the San Francisco Room at the public library, I went there hoping to find a pure nectar of earthquake. The building was a sad mess. Wine pints littered its lawn and the homeless bathed in its sinks. But the San Francisco Room was a tidy little Switzerland, with polite librarians and the atmosphere of a men's-club reading room.

The Loma Prieta narratives were filed alphabetically by name and labeled by location. Many contributors used short sentences, dashes, and exclamation marks to describe the fifteen seconds. As the space between the aftershocks lengthened, so did their sentences. Plotted on a graph, they would have echoed the nervous peaks and valleys Loma Prieta imprinted on seismographs. Only later did I understand that they amounted to more than a haphazard oral history. Instead, they were the first concrete evidence that by breaking an eighty-three-year-old seismic drought, Loma Prieta had begun the process of changing California from a people who never worried about earthquakes to one who worried about them constantly.

The computer-composed narratives were wordy; the handwritten ones pithy. Most people seemed unaccustomed to writing letters and their sentences were stilted and self-conscious. Some had submitted Christmas circulars, apparently the only time they wrote to families and friends.

They described the emotional aftershocks in ways unthinkable in 1906, admitting to waking with racing hearts, whimpering with every aftershock, and being "terrorized by the slightest movement." Many still suffered splitting headaches, insomnia, and nausea. They believed Loma Prieta had made their lives more significant ("Little did I know I would be part of history in the making") and used titles like "The Day Our World Shook." Every emotional reaction received careful examination, and statements like "The core of my being was very tender" were so common I stopped noting them.

I had the impression more singles than married couples had participated, and their accounts tended to be the most introspective and poignant. Loma Prieta had spooked even the most self-sufficient loners, even the most determined seismic-risk deniers, and they rattled on endlessly about twitchy cats and smashed Hümmel figurines.

"I knew minutes after it occurred, that it was an event of historical significance," one man wrote, "so I am happy to be able to contribute something to the documentation of it, particularly since I have no children and will never have any grandchildren to impress with fanciful stories about it."

The weather was described as eerie: a classic and balmy, Indian-summer day, with strange hot winds. During the quake this beautiful day continued without a blink, so that when people watched chandeliers touching ceilings, water splashing from pans, gas pumps jumping in the air, and pythons slithering from the East Bay Vivarium, they saw it against a perfect California afternoon.

The endless fifteen seconds had felt like instant seasickness, a commercial jetliner in a bumpy landing, a ship in a strong sea, or being in a bowl while someone was tossing the salad.

During this shaking, people suffered sudden claustrophobia and wanted somewhere flat, open, or safe. Four miles from the epicenter in Aptos, people poured out of houses, yelling, screaming, crying. A hysterical nude woman ran through a suburban neighborhood still dripping from her shower.

"No one who was not here can even vaguely imagine the terror, helplessness etc. that hit everyone," wrote one woman. Another called the earthquake "a mammoth, primeval evil venting its wickedness."

Many witnesses were as scared by what they heard as by what they saw, and described a roar like a locomotive, freight train, or jet. They remembered glass shattering, windows rattling, doors banging, floorboards creaking. Crystal chandeliers sounded like a thousand wind chimes. Rattling windows were like hands clapping. A secretary in a skyscraper heard a banging like someone dropping a bag of wrenches as the elevator cables slapped against the side of chutes. A man discovered that a collapsing building made a sharp, wooden sound, "like a home run when it's really well hit, i.e. a perfect crack."

After the 1906 earthquake, a *San Francisco Examiner* reporter wrote, "It is impossible to judge the lengths of the shocks. To me it seemed an eternity."

The 1989 narratives also suggested Loma Prieta had stretched time. This "earthquake time" was "airless," "claustrophobic," and "the longest fifteen seconds I have ever spent." It came with an "uncanny," "eerie" silence, and slowed as the shaking accelerated.

San Franciscans noticed other 1906 echoes.

When Gladys Hansen, the curator of the San Francisco Room, looked out her office window to see black clouds of dust rising from collapsed buildings, she immediately flashed to 1906 and assumed the city was burning.

A secretary named Jane Cryan who was waiting for a bus at Fifth and Market, a center of the 1906 conflagration, insisted 1906 suddenly passed before her eyes. "I *saw,* really *saw,* Market Street burning," she wrote. When I tracked her down later she told me, "I *know* I saw the past and present at the same time. It was the most memorable moment of my life."

Although 1906 was far more deadly and destructive than Loma Prieta, its eyewitness accounts are comparatively repetitive and colorless. Because it struck at 5:17 A.M. you read endless stories of people being catapulted from their beds: "The quake awakened us, of course." "I jumped out of the little cot I was sleeping on." "Our bed went clean across the wall." The most vivid narratives describe the fire: cinders falling in eyes, flames bursting like artillery explosions, and a night sky so luminous people fifty miles away could read newspapers outside.

Had Loma Prieta struck a few hours earlier I would have read repetitive accounts of people jumping under office desks; a few hours later and the stories would have unfolded in taverns, dance clubs, and bedrooms. But at 5:04 P.M. commuters filled elevators, buses, ferries, trains, and bridges. People were jogging, making love, preparing dinner, and playing with their kids. Few were asleep or even sleepy, senses were sharp.

Before reading these narratives I had imagined Loma Prieta as a series of quick snapshots. Afterward I saw it unfolding in leisurely earthquake time.

During these airless, stretched-out fifteen seconds, a student at the Cabrillo College theater department was being videotaped singing Carole King's "I Feel the Earth Move," a young woman was interrupted in midsentence while complaining to her doctor of panic attacks, a tap-dance instructor heard trophies rattling in her cases and glanced nervously at the mirrored walls, spectators in Candlestick Park saw the plastic signs advertising Marlboros and Safeway rattling in their metal frames and rippling like liquid, diners at a popular vegetarian restaurant in Fort Mason watched the Golden Gate Bridge sway like a jump rope, and a young woman felt her '72 Volkswagen bug swerve toward a concrete center divider and considered her "soon-to-be-terminated three-month-old married life [and my] ... isolation without so much as a cappuccino in hand to keep me company."

Prisoners on San Quentin's death row moaned "Ohhhh" in unison during the first shake, then "Oohhhh Oh!" as their 1930 cell block shuddered, the lights flickered, and they realized, according to one, that "we, the convicts, would be the last on the list of priorities." A woman

swam in a lap pool that became a "stormy sea" at the moment whitecaps
sprang up on the bay, sailboats heeled, and a ferry captain landing at the
Embarcadero saw waiting passengers fall to the dock like soldiers felled
by a fusillade. The Ferry Building's chimes stopped midway through
"San Francisco, Open Your Golden Gate," the anthem of post-1906 recovery, and a band at the venerable St. Francis Hotel interrupted a popular 1906 music-hall arrangement in midstanza. A secretary working
alone on the forty-seventh floor of the TransAmerica Building, in the
apex of its pyramid, the highest floor of the tallest building in town, felt
it sway from east to west and looked out one of its 3,678 shatterproof
windows to see "a lone sailboat, a dirigible hanging over Candlestick,
[a] ferry about to dock . . . drifting on still, almost airless water."

I found evidence in the narratives of earthquake love: "a rush of
joy," "universal equanimity," and faces admiring "the vastness of the
catastrophe." The death-row prisoners filled containers of water for
their neighbors. A Marina district woman reported people drinking
champagne even as smoke blew in with the fog. An admitted loner
credited the quake with teaching her, "I need people and to be part of
my community—not a separate entity living in it."

Comments like "material possessions seem a hell of a lot less significant," and "we realized that the things we lost were just 'stuff' " had
to be weighed against more numerous descriptions of a "high tide of
broken vases, picture frames, books, shattered trophies," laments about
how the "television, VCR, and two big speakers lay facedown on the
flotsam," and complaints that smashed figurines and wedding china
had left owners feeling "violated." In 1989 no possession was mourned
more frequently or fervently than the VCR. In 1906 people bemoaned
the loss of grand pianos.

While 1906 ushered in a decade of furious boosterism and reconstruction, the Loma Prieta narratives revealed a more sour mood. People already pessimistic about California saw another reason to leave.
They wrote, "I can't help wondering if we're crazy to live here."
"Maybe it's time to move back to Nebraska." "For this native-born Californian, California is definitely losing points with each month that
passes. There is no longer anything romantic about California."

Most contributors had experienced painless earthquakes. There
was nothing from the families of people crushed to death on the Nimitz
Freeway, relatives of the boy trapped in a car on the Cypress Freeway who
watched a doctor saw his dead mother in half so he could be extricated,
or from William Ray, a young stockbroker pinned with his wife in the

rubble of a building. As firemen shouted a warning that it was about to collapse, he freed himself but was unable to help his wife. He escaped seconds before the building fell and killed her. The *Chronicle* reported, "What they said to each other Bill Ray prefers to keep quiet."

Carol Dickerson, however, had submitted an account of how her infant son Scott had died in her arms in the rubble of her Marina district apartment building. After reading her precise and restrained narrative, I arranged to meet her.

I had already seen a photograph of where she lived—a rambling, three-story, wooden building that pancaked into half its size and afterward became a backdrop for news anchors, a destination for politicians, and a tourist attraction. Her Marina neighborhood had been, and still is, one of the most appealing in the city. It has streets of tile-roofed Spanish Revival houses, less fog and more sun than Pacific Heights, unobstructed views of San Francisco Bay and the Golden Gate Bridge, and a waterfront park perfect for sunbathing, jogging, and kite flying. Joe DiMaggio and other celebrities live there, so do families with young children, and the kind of outdoorsy singles who own mountain bikes and tie bandannas around the necks of dogs trained to catch Frisbees.

During the nineteenth century, it had been a watery cove fed by a brackish estuary. After 1906 it was filled in with wet sand and earthquake rubble, then graded and covered with houses and exhibit halls for the 1915 Pan-Pacific Exposition, a symbolic celebration of the city's rebirth. Houses and apartment buildings like Dickerson's arose over the reclaimed land.

Seventy-five years later, the Marina suffered more Loma Prieta damage than any Bay Area neighborhood. There were ten deaths, sixty buildings destroyed, and 1,800 left homeless. Instruments measuring ground motion recorded accelerations in the Marina almost six times greater than those in nearby Pacific Heights. Instead of absorbing the seismic waves, its loose soil amplified and slowed them, sending them upward into foundations. Buildings and soil moved in concert, and one geologist described the ground becoming a violent Jell-O. Wooden apartment buildings jumped off their foundations, three-story buildings became two-story ones, two stories pancaked into one. Miniature seismic volcanoes known as sand boils erupted on the green. Some spewed up old bricks and pieces of wood later identified as rubble from the Palace Hotel. It had been destroyed by the 1906 earthquake and used here as landfill.

Carol Dickerson now lived on the safer bedrock of Laurel Heights. We met in an empty coffee shop where she passed up several roomy booths for a table far from the plate-glass windows. She was a pretty woman with a creamy complexion and sharp green eyes that filled with tears but never overflowed. She spoke as she wrote, in an even, matter-of-fact voice, leaving the impression she had recounted the story many times, perhaps as a way of coping with the tragedy.

Her parents had been Lutheran missionaries in India who later settled in Spokane. She was proud of having moved on her own to San Francisco. "Before, nothing bothered me, nothing," she said. "I used to think earthquakes were a big joke. When we felt a small tremor we'd laugh and say, 'There goes another shaker.' When it was hot and still, like on October 17, we'd say, 'Guess it's earthquake weather.'"

She had been standing in her building's small lobby seconds before, giving her husband money to buy reprints of Scott's baby pictures. As he pedaled away on his bicycle their neighbors were coming home early to watch the World Series. She began climbing upstairs with Scott in her arms. The first jolt sent her jumping under a door frame. When the shaking continued she bolted for the front door. The floor vanished beneath her feet and the building collapsed with a roar. She fell to the garage level. A beam fell across her back, pinning her down and breaking her arm. She froze, afraid any movement might dislodge more rubble. She told me, "I felt I had the power to hold up the whole building if it would save my son." She was in such pain the firemen rescuing her assumed she had been paralyzed. Until Scott was pried from her arms she believed he had survived. A doctor said he had suffocated from breathing plaster and dust.

Had he died in a different kind of accident they might have buried him in one of the big cemeteries just outside the city limits in Colma that sits almost on the fault. Instead, they took his remains to Spokane. She knew it sounded irrational, but she could not bear having another earthquake disturb his remains. After the interment they drove north into Canada because a woman who had lost a three-year-old daughter had suggested driving as therapy. They discussed leaving San Francisco, but there had been so much love and support from friends and the community they felt bound to return.

Nightmares filled with tidal waves and fires still plagued her, and she became nauseous whenever she drove through the Marina. Sometimes she burst into tears if she thought about her son. It happened on the bus, at lunch, wherever. "And I *still* think about him all the time," she said defiantly, "not a day goes by that I don't."

She told herself it was better he died in her arms than alone. She made herself attend a yearly reunion of her former neighbors. She was writing a children's book, "alphabetical, something like Dr. Seuss." She had been trying to have another baby. The doctors could find no physical impediments. If she conceived, they would move for sure.

21

Lotta's Fountain

Ninety minutes after survivors of the Great Earthquake and Fire gathered at Lotta's Fountain in downtown San Francisco on April 18, 1990, to commemorate its eighty-fourth anniversary, fourteen tremors shook the Bay Area. I attended the ceremonies two years later hoping for a similar coincidence and some firsthand recollections of an event that has since been eclipsed by the fires it caused. Although 1906 was the strongest quake to hit a populated part of California since its settlement, the blaze destroying 490 city blocks and gutting 28,000 buildings has always supplied the most dramatic narratives. The attitude of John J. Condon, who was seven in 1906 and recalled his experiences for a book published by the San Francisco Public Library on the seventy-fifth anniversary was typical. "At 5:13 on a Wednesday morning in 1906, one era in the city's history came to an end," he said. "Thereafter, events were referred to as before or after the fire. The earthquake responsible for the fire was a secondary matter."

When the 1906 anniversary fell on a weekday, the crowd attending it could usually be numbered in the dozens. This year it was on a Saturday, so I arrived at 4:30 A.M. to find four hundred people milling around Lotta's Fountain. The fountain was a gift to the city from Carlotta Crabtree, an eccentric actress who had danced in Gold Rush saloons at age six, liked black cigars, "knew no rules of stage or society," according to one history, and was "the very quintessence of San Francisco's love of life." It was chosen for the anniversary ceremonies because it had been the venue for the famous 1919 Christmas Eve concert that attracted a quarter million and symbolized San Francisco's rebirth.

Homeless men shambled around the perimeter of the crowd, lurching into the pools of light created by video cameramen. They begged and rattled shopping carts, impatient for the free juice and (because this was San Francisco) French pastries that would be served afterward in a bank lobby. Children perched on their fathers' shoulders, rubbing eyes and wearing pajamas under their parkas. A party of young stockbrokers finishing a Friday-night pub crawl sang "San Francisco, Open Your Golden Gate" so loudly the reporters cursed and shone lights in their eyes to keep them back from the microphones meant for survivors.

Fourteen frail men and women sat in a spotlighted semicircle of directors' chairs. The men leaned on silver-handled walking sticks and wore wing collars, spats, opera capes, and derby hats. The women had rouged their cheeks, decorated their ankle-length dresses with antique brooches and pearls, and wrapped themselves in fur stoles. If time machines ever hurl people into the future, they will arrive looking as these fourteen did: radiant, pink-cheeked, wide-eyed, and startled to be where they are.

After 364 invisible days in nursing homes, granny cottages, and residential hotels, it must have been disorienting to be suddenly celebrated by people a third their age, but they patiently mined their memories for the cub reporters. Most knew one another from previous anniversaries, and once their eyes had adjusted to the lights, they gossiped, exchanged toodle-oo waves, and speculated about who was coming—in other words, who had survived another year.

"Any good-looking ones this year?" one woman asked her neighbor.

The other woman looked blank.

"You know," she shouted, "any gray-haired ones!"

The master of ceremonies encouraged them to pass the time until five-thirteen by sharing their memories with the audience. Many had been so young they could only offer, "I have only happy memories," "For children, it was fun," and "They gave us tents and a glorious big ham." Those who were infants related what had happened to their parents. Several offered laundry lists of street addresses, neighbors, pets, and family possessions lost to the fire. Their memories were mostly of the "bed flew across the room" variety and they only became animated when recalling the fire. A man named Joseph Miller said he was one of ten children who had held hands in a chain so they could be led through burning streets to the Oakland ferry by his blind mother. And a former resident of the San Francisco Nursery for Homeless Children remembered nurses dropping infants wrapped in white blankets from second-story windows into the arms of a janitor standing below. One orphan caught by those rough hands had become a celebrated attorney, another had invented the nail gun.

Next a survivor laid a wreath at the fountain while others sang a tremulous version of "San Francisco, Open Your Golden Gate." Members of various San Francisco historical associations who had dressed in period costumes dabbed their eyes with authentic lace handkerchiefs.

A master of ceremonies led cheers for the sister of ballplayer Babe Pirelli and a ninety-two-year-old man who had driven himself down from Santa Rosa. Age was a badge of honor, and anyone raising a hand to the question, "Anyone here older than ninety-six?" received loud cheers.

The president of the South of Market Boys, an organization of local businessmen dedicated to the preservation of the history and traditions of old-time San Francisco, described his grandparents climbing to Alamo Square to escape the flames. Other civic leaders delivered graceful homilies praising the survivors as "heroes," although none had boasted of anything more than beating the actuarial tables.

I was sometimes reminded of a pep rally for an underdog team. The phrase *this great city* was often hurled against the murmurings and shouts of the homeless demanding an early start to the doughnut line, and references to "the city we'll never leave" reflected a once unthinkable weakening of civic confidence.

The celebratory atmosphere changed when a late-arriving survivor named Marion Kahn described walking up Market Street to rescue her grandmother. A building had burst into flames before her eyes and she saw a mother and her infant son trapped in the wreckage. She had never forgotten the woman's screams. When the fire reached them and there was no hope, the mother dashed her son's head against the bricks to spare him the pain of immolation. It had happened, she thought, near where we were standing.

At five-thirteen a siren wailed to mark the anniversary. Like many in the audience I had not noticed the fire trucks gathering in the darkness behind us and jumped in surprise. Firebells clanged, another siren sounded, then another and another. Some survivors clapped hands over their ears. Their faces showed bewilderment and terror, then relief.

The homeless moved in as the crowd dispersed. Their panhandling was aggressive and menacing. Although 1906 had left these elderly survivors homeless, forcing them to sleep in parks and cook in the streets, they had benefited from the most generous relief program in the nation's history. As they faced another, quite different, homeless generation, their milky eyes widened and they stumbled backward, hugging their velvet purses.

The history buffs milled around Lotta's Fountain, leaving others to jostle for the free breakfast. April 18 was their feast day and they had scheduled a full program, including visits to the Golden Fireplug and the Firemen's Museum, and tours of Victorian houses and historic gravestones at Cypress Lawn Cemetery. One of the South of Market Boys recited a list of San Francisco landmarks lost to progress, "Playland, the Mabuhay Gardens, the Fifth Street Pork Store . . ."

The Corinthian Leaguers compared period costumes so elaborate they upstaged the survivors. Most were in their twenties and thirties. "We range from people who want to meet new lovers to those who really wish they were living in another century," a man in a bowler admitted. One of the organizers was a friendly woman named Cherie Morrison who worked in advertising and public relations. She presented a business card promising HISTORICAL RECREATION, VINTAGE AMBIANCE, and invited me to tomorrow's third annual *Alice in Wonderland* tea party at the Golden Gate Park polo grounds. She said her group knew all the old music-hall songs and "gave class" to corporate openings. They were "time travelers" who only wanted "to recreate a more graceful and attractive era."

I introduced myself to a Corinthian out of a Victorian photograph. She had strawberry hair piled high, porcelain skin, delicate features, and the posture of someone accustomed to tight girdles and bustles. She told me she was a third-generation San Franciscan and that in 1906 her great-grandfather had been knocked senseless by a brick.

"Who joins the Corinthians?" I asked.

"Thirty-year-olds like me who sit in front of computer screens all day." She shrugged. "It beats doing drugs."

Two days later I joined the thirteenth annual cruise for 1906 survivors sponsored by the ferry division of the Golden Gate Transit District. Ninety oldsters boarded the boat helped by canes, walkers, and wheelchairs, Red Cross nurses, and relatives. The men wore hearing aids, the women gripped furs with tattered linings. I had never seen so many elderly people in one place, or for that matter, so many of any age so determined to pack so much fun into two hours. They included a man born on the day of the quake, nine people over 95, and 106-year-old Sidney Amber, the oldest living survivor. As we slipped from the dock a senior-citizen band called the Little Gnomes and Leprechauns sang "Roll Out the Barrel, We'll Have a Barrel of . . ."

"FUN!" shouted dozens of tremulous voices.

The choral group Seniors in Retirement sang "Daisy, Daisy," "Shine On Harvest Moon," and "The Band Played On." My father, who was born in 1894, had lulled me to sleep with these songs in the 1950s and I had always imagined them extinguished by his heart attack. But here they were again, remembered by members of his generation lucky enough to live another thirty years.

The men gathered on deck. They tossed down ten A.M. scotch-and-waters and puffed their pigeon chests into the light breeze, marveling at the skyscrapers as if seeing them for the first time. So many remarked so often about it being "earthquake weather, hazy and still . . . earthquake weather for sure" I wondered if they were secretly hoping to see the skyline jiggle like a home movie.

Reporters circled and swooped like gulls, trying to snatch a 1906 tidbit. They assumed the survivors were all hard-of-hearing and shouted their questions. They tried to ingratiate themselves with lies like, "Why, you don't look old enough to be a survivor at all!" Most survivors ignored them, gathering instead in tight circles in the lounge. Names were less important than age, and introductions went, "This lady was seven, and this one was two." They traded old jokes, and when one man said, "If God spanked San Francisco for being so frisky . . ." a chorus shouted back, "then why did he burn down all the churches and spare Hotalings Whiskey?" (The distillery had been on a small downtown plot that escaped destruction.)

I hovered with the reporters, listening to conversations about incinerated San Francisco neighborhoods, and wondering if statements like "What was the name of that bakery?" "Our street had fifteen saloons," and "Do you remember the alley where they parked the wagons?" were evidence that cities like pre-1906 San Francisco and pre-1945 Hiroshima experience a final death when the last person remembering them dies.

I met a hundred-year-old man wearing a flamboyant wide tie who was proud of having taken BART (Bay Area Rapid Transit) by himself from Oakland. He did it every year, and every year emerged from the Embarcadero Station to see a city of gleaming skyscrapers, and then a city in ashes. He had thought he was seeing the present and the past at once. But this year he wondered for the first time if he was also seeing the future.

A survivor named Edward Larsen held out his hand and said, "Shake the hand that shook the hand of a man who shook Abraham Lincoln's hand." What he remembered most about pre-1906 San Francisco was living next door to someone who had met Lincoln, and made a great ceremony of awarding handshakes to little boys. When you write it down that you have "shaken the hand that shook the hand that shook the hand of Abraham Lincoln," it looks pretty silly. But when you do it, and realize you are only two handshakes away from our greatest president, dead some 127 years, it feels like a miracle.

Everyone wanted to shake 106-year-old Sidney Amber's hand. He was the oldest survivor onboard and probably the oldest in the world. A man ten years younger took me aside and said, "You know he's a great hero and source of hope to us all." He was a patient and good-natured celebrity, posing for snapshots, assuring us he had never felt better, and recounting again and again how his family had slept in a tent. His story more or less coincided with what he had told a reporter for *The New York Times* two years earlier. "You're absolutely numb, petrified. For those seconds you can't move. They say on TV what you should do—go under a door frame or a table. But you can't stand. You can't think. You can't talk. You're helpless." It was as good a description of 1906, or of Loma Prieta, as I read or heard from anyone in San Francisco.

When the ferry docked, the reporters scattered. Passengers waiting to board other boats watched blankly, perhaps imagining a nursing-home outing as survivors shuffled and wheeled down the gangplank. Outside the terminal I noticed the man one handshake away from Lincoln gripping his wife's arm as they tried to hobble across half the Embarcadero to a traffic island before the lights changed.

Loma Prieta had forced the city to dismantle the elevated freeway that had darkened the waterfront for thirty years. Now so many cars sped along this sunny street-level boulevard that signals could not afford to give pedestrians much time to cross. The man and his wife retreated to the curb, then made another run for it, shuffling double time and getting two thirds of the way before the lights turned. Some drivers braked and honked, others swerved around them, showing no mercy.

I had counted on finding out more about Bruff and the Washington Miners in history-mad San Francisco. But when I floated his name in front of the Corinthians and South of Market Street Boys at the 1906 ceremonies, I received blank stares. I could not blame them since his San Francisco experiences had been routine for the times. He had visited saloons "in full blast," seen "Chinamen, in full costume, with long queue, umbrellas, and paper fans," been roused by a lynch mob searching for a suspect in his boardinghouse, stumbled on the corpse of a man hanged by vigilantes hours before in the main plaza, and rescued his diaries and papers "at much personal hazard" from one of the city's frequent fires.

The man taking my call at the Society of California Pioneers said of course he knew about Bruff, but he had no way of checking his membership rolls for descendants of his former comrades. The Bay Area telephone books listed some of the more unusual Washington names, but my calls were fruitless. I returned to the San Francisco Room and compared the Washington roster against its card catalog without success. But in the manuscript collection of Berkeley's Bancroft Library I found the diary of Henry Austin, the company's thirty-two-year-old physician and one of the men Bruff believed had behaved honorably. He described their chance meeting in Sacramento in 1850 as a joyous occasion, and Austin as "my particular friend."

From Bruff's diary we know Austin was one of only three men to leave him provisions as the company departed from his camp on October 22. John Bates contributed some pipe tobacco, a 43-year-old lithographer named Charles Fenderich added two biscuits, but Austin offered the greatest gift of all, a double handful of rice. We also know that Austin returned to Bruff's camp on November 1, the day after the tree fell on the Alfords and Fergusons, and treated Sarah Ferguson, Ruth Simmerley's relation by marriage. He was passing through because Major Rucker, the U.S. army officer given the task of assisting emigrants along the Lassen Trail, had commissioned him to ride back along the trail and urge the stragglers to hurry. When Austin passed through Bruff's camp again on November 6 after completing this mission, Bruff noted he had suffered much and needed medicine himself.

Unfortunately his diary turned out to be no match for Bruff's. It ran for only 118 double-spaced typed pages and was mostly a recitation of meals, weather, grave markers, and distances. But it did corroborate that the reelection of company officers had returned Bruff to office, and indicated Bruff's fateful decision to take the Lassen Trail had not been opposed by his men.

After crossing the Fandango Pass, Austin's tone suddenly shifted and he offered rapturous descriptions of the landscape. The similarities with Bruff's ecstatic praise of California were so pronounced I wondered if they had arisen from campfire conversations between the men. In both diaries, the sudden change from Nevada to California reminded me of the moment Dorothy arrives in Oz and the movie shifts from black-and-white to Technicolor.

Echoing Bruff, Austin called the Fandango Pass "the dividing line between the land of toil and trouble and that of gold and plenty of provisions." Behind them was "an extensive plain of dry mudd [sic]," before them, "a magnificent valley covered with grass on both sides of which is a range of high mountains well-timbered principally with fine spruce pine trees and some cedars."

During the nineteen days separating the Fandango Pass and Bruff's camp, his descriptions became even more feverish in their praise of the landscape, reaching a climax at Bruff's camp, where he wrote, "The view before us is truly grand. The lofty mountains[,] the stupendous rocks with the deep but magnificent vale below ... one of the finest and most picturesque views I ever beheld. Here we have the grand & beautiful combined on a magnificent scale. Language fails at the description of beauties in both."

After dinner, he retired to a rock overlooking the valley, where he reported having "feasted my eyes and gratified my senses to the fullest extent." The weather was delightful, the wind "gently moving the stately timbers the music of which is pleasant to my ears." To the west, where they were going, he saw "the peaks of mountains towering into the clouds[,] their bases being enveloped in mist." He concluded with, "Oh, nature how lovely[,] how grand and stupendous thou art!"

The next day he reported the Washington Miners heading west into this spectacular countryside with "eight mules and 2 horses [one of them Bruff's mount] all of which were as well-packed as their broken-down condition would allow," adding that, "Captain Bruff and W. Willis stay with baggage & wagons till sent for."

The "W. Willis" who he said stayed with Bruff is listed on the roll as Josias C. Willis of Baltimore. Since he left no letters or diaries, we have to rely on Bruff's version of events. His name appears in Bruff's diary for the first time on October 22, when he offers to stay. Bruff accepted, "as we could assist one another, and I believed him to be a clever fellow." During the next six weeks, Willis hunted for deer, helped bury the Alford men, cooked, and washed Bruff's clothing. On December 3, a man named Petrie came up from the settlements with food for Bruff from a Colonel Davis, whose ranch was the nearest valley settlement. When Petrie announced he had enough transport to carry back one man, Willis insisted on going. Bruff agreed, but soon had misgivings when he noticed Willis locking his own possessions in trunks while surreptitiously packing Bruff's only boots and their carpentry tools. He thought it "rather singular" conduct for a man who pledged to return for him within four days with food and a team of oxen.

On December 15, Bruff began to suspect the worst, telling himself, "He will surely come out soon unless taken sick. I know that his animal propensities are strong, but I cannot think that he could abandon us, to what would appear to him, a certain fate—for me at least—I and the child [the four-year-old Lambkin boy Bruff was feeding] are doomed, perhaps, if a very severe spell ensues. . . . But W. just surely entertains a spark of gratitude towards me—I have protected him in the Company, and I have every way been his friend, and he appeared quite attached to me—or why did he volunteer to remain here with me? Unless ill, he will surely come out soon!"

When Bruff reached the settlements the following spring he learned that Willis and other members of the company had spread "false, ridiculous statements" that he had chosen to winter in the mountains, perhaps because he wanted to steal the company's property and prey on other stragglers. Even worse, they had repeated these calumnies in letters to their families in Washington. Some letters reported his death "as though it would afford them satisfaction to alarm and grieve my family, then in a state of anxiety hear from me."

Bruff tried to convince himself that only a few "miscreants" had slandered and betrayed him. This was certainly easier than asking himself why not only Willis, but others in his company who had wintered in the Sacramento Valley within sight of the mountains where he was trapped and starving, had done nothing to save him.

22

Purported
Earthquake Shacks

The 1906 survivor who saw the Embarcadero in flames while walking to the anniversary cruise reminded me of Jane Cryan, the secretary waiting for a bus who also "saw, really *saw*" 1906 while experiencing Loma Prieta. I called her when I read a newspaper article describing her crusade to save San Francisco's surviving 1906 refugee shacks from demolition. "Loma Prieta was the most memorable moment of my life," she told me over the telephone. Windows shattered as passengers ran from the MUNI station and she leaned like the Tower of Pisa. She insisted the time travel went beyond imagining or daydreaming, and had occurred in her eyes as much as her head—the past, then the present; 1906, then 1989. Perhaps her devotion to the shacks explained it. When she researched their history she often believed herself living in two eras at once. It was the magic of history.

She lived half a mile from the Pacific in the Sunset, a neighborhood sometimes called the "Queens of San Francisco" that has an undeserved reputation as boring. It had been a bleak, sandy wasteland where people lived in converted trolley cars, until developer Henry Doelger bought it during the 1930s and built so many rows of attached wood-and-stucco pastel houses it became known as the "White Cliffs of Doelger." A joke repeated by *Chronicle* columnist Herb Caen claimed the walls were so thin if a wife asked her husband, "How do you want your eggs done, dear?" another man seven houses down would shout, "Scrambled."

Doelger's houses may have seemed without character after the war, but they were positively eccentric compared with the develop-

192

ments that later sprawled down the South Bay Peninsula. The neighborhood was well served by bus and streetcar lines, and its shops and restaurants were diverse and convenient. A steady wind blew noise and pollution inland, the Pacific was close, the light sharp, the air salty and clean. When the sun bounced off the stucco houses, there was a hint of Greece.

Cryan lived in a second-floor flat she said was temporary, part of the reshuffling of her life caused by the earthquake. She had her cats, books, and grand piano, but the rest was in storage. The newspaper article described her as a "vivacious, pocket-sized Katharine Hepburn type," but I thought she resembled Bette Davis—a feisty, red-haired bantamweight. She kept cats and smoked cigarettes from a long holder surviving from her bohemian days. She had come from Oshkosh in 1961, after Jack Kerouac answered her fan letter and insisted Wisconsin was no place for a fledgling poet. "I never met him," she admitted. "He was in his final alcoholic days, stewed to the gills in Mexico, so one of his Dharma Bums welcomed me to San Francisco."

She married, divorced, worked as a secretary, wrote unpublished novels, sang in jazz clubs, and learned the piano at age thirty-seven so she could accompany herself. She was the kind of artistic optimist who once filled cities like San Francisco. "I've just turned fifty," she told me, "and I can't wait to see what happens next."

She spread photographs of the 1906 earthquake shack where she had once lived across the kitchen table and said, "I considered it a living art form, a living being. To be honest, I considered it my lover."

She had painted it fire-engine red with white trim and surrounded it with a white picket fence. Geraniums filled window boxes and the yard was fussy with flowers. I thought of an only daughter dressed for Easter Sunday.

She said, "That damned cottage spoke to me. It said, 'Do something with me!' 'Find out about me!' So I did." She spent weeks in the San Francisco Room researching its history. One day an old man leaned across her fence and said he had occupied it during the 1920s and it was composed of three connected 1906 refugee shacks. The city had erected 5,610 similar ones on parks, squares, and military property. Their exterior was green and they had fir floors, cedar shingles, and redwood walls. A small "A" shack was ten by fourteen, the "B" and "C" models slightly larger. Residents papered their walls with newspaper, hung clothes on pegs, and cooked in communal facilities. The most common article of furniture was a rocking chair.

They were the first big California housing tract and not until Doelger did anyone build so many houses so fast. They provided many San Franciscans with their only opportunity to live outside a flat, and encouraged the hunger for a freestanding house. When the relief program ended and the city ordered the parks cleared, many occupants moved them to permanent locations.

When Cryan heard rumors a developer was negotiating to purchase and demolish her shack, she founded the Society for the Preservation and Appreciation of San Francisco's 1906 Earthquake Shacks. She identified twenty-two, mounted an exhibit at the Sutro library, persuaded the city to landmark her shack, and saved two by having them moved onto the army base at the Presidio. She argued they were the last physical record of "a monumental act of charity . . . one of the largest, most generous charitable projects ever put in place here or anywhere else." Whenever she heard about a homeless person moving into an abandoned one, she was delighted.

Loma Prieta had been a setback. The shacks had come through "with flying colors," but she had not. Her unreinforced concrete building had spun like a hula hoop and was yellow-tagged ENTER AT YOUR OWN RISK. She slept there anyway because the shelter refused her cats. Three years later they were still terrified. To prove it she crumpled some Reynolds Wrap and they stiffened at the sound. "Look!" she ordered. "Sheer terror!"

She lost her job, became as twitchy as her cats, and defected to Oshkosh. She returned for the eighty-fourth anniversary of the 1906 earthquake and decided she loved San Francisco too much to leave again. Her current cause célébre was three connected shacks on Twenty-seventh Avenue recently purchased by an elderly immigrant from Taiwan named Cheng Yu Tsai. "I wrote him a letter welcoming him to his historic house," she said with a sly smile, "and he went bananas."

She believed he had trashed the shacks after receiving her letter so he could replace them with a cheaply built apartment house. She sued when he filed to demolish them and last year the Landmarks Preservation Advisory Board had voted five to one to recommend that the City Planning Commission prohibit their destruction. The Commission would vote next week, but she was pessimistic because its members had been appointed by Mayor Frank Jordan, who had won election with strong support from the Asian community. Recent Asian immigrants could not understand why anyone wanted to save a shack that could be replaced by a multistory building housing forty people, she said, lowering her voice as though we could be overheard. They simply did not *understand* historic preservation.

But why should they? I wondered. Was it reasonable to expect last year's immigrant from Taiwan or Mexico City to care about preserving some shack because it once housed Caucasians displaced by a remote disaster?

Chinese-language newspapers had been attacking Cryan, hinting she opposed Tsai's plans because she was racist. After the Landmarks Board voted to recommend preservation, she had almost come to blows with Joe O'Donohue, president of the Residential Builders' Association. She reenacted the confrontation, giving him the thick brogue of a music-hall Irishman, while her ally and sidekick Colonel E. Wyman Spaulding (Ret.), who had become interested in the shacks while stationed at the Presidio, spoke like a British brigadier.

She played a tape recording of the meeting for me. I could make out O'Donohue shouting something like "All you have here are a few boards, some studs from an original shack. . . . It's a piece of garbage; a piece of crap."

Cryan put her hand on my arm, her eyes glistening with mischief. "Listen, this is where Colonel Spaulding jumps to his feet. He was appalled by the disrespect and foul language."

A firm voice said, "I'm Colonel Wyman Spaulding from the Presidio and I'm ordering you to leave this building."

"You're a joke. Ludicrous. A Punch and Judy show," O'Donohue replied.

The chairman threatened an adjournment.

"Adjourn the meeting because you're full of shit. No wonder this city has no money, just look at the piece of shit you're trying to save."

Cryan played the tape twice more, laughing when O'Donohue lost his temper. She invited me to their rematch, saying the Tsais would pack the chamber with Chinese and she could use some support.

I agreed, but wondered how much I really wanted to sit next to this combative woman at an acrimonious meeting that would unfold on the third floor of the Beaux Arts City Hall where a deranged supervisor had murdered Mayor Frank Moscone and Supervisor Harvey Milk.

In the meantime I visited the disputed shack and understood why a childless woman fond of cats might want to mother it. Its roof was peeling, and its kicked-in front door covered with plywood and smeared with graffiti. Chinese-restaurant deliverymen had left menus anyway, and they lay in soggy clumps in the weedy front yard.

I met Cryan a week later outside the third-floor hearing room in a city hall so badly damaged by Loma Prieta scaffolding still buttressed its stairwells. She had pinned her braid of flaming red hair to the top of her head like a goddess prepared for battle. "Thank goodness you're here," she said. "We're really outnumbered today." About fifty Chinese, presumably friends and relatives of Mr. Tsai, sat patiently in circles on the corridor floor.

"No O'Donohue yet," she said, disappointed. "But look, I *do* have Colonel Spaulding." I shook the hand of a distinguished silver-haired man with a trim white mustache. He wore cowboy boots and a string tie and kept blinking hard at the Chinese, as if waking from a dream and expecting them to disappear. This scene had probably not figured in his retirement plans.

"We're outnumbered, Colonel, and they've been telling the newspapers we're racists," she said.

"I *like* a good fight," he insisted, and began counting them in a loud voice as if they were sheep, "One, two three, four . . ." They were mostly grandparents and mothers with infants. "I make it at least fifteen to one against us," he boomed, counting me as a supporter, which I suppose I was.

"My kind of odds. Let's find some seats," she said.

He took her arm with a flourish and they glided through the Taiwanese gauntlet, heads high.

"There he is," she whispered, pointing to a ruddy-faced man with a shock of gray hair. "O'Donohue, the devil himself."

The hearing room was poorly ventilated and reeked of the fruity gum being chewed by the girlfriends of construction workers who had come to support a developer wanting to replace a single-family house in the Castro with a five-town-house complex. Girlfriend Angie told the commissioners so what if the complex would be an eyesore, it would be a "beautiful eyesore." A spokeswoman for a yuppie homeowner group laid her Gucci bag on the table and said it would be great for young professionals because it would increase property values. When the meticulously assembled multicultural panel ruled against them, Cryan took heart and whispered, "We could be a real cliffhanger."

But I realized her cause was hopeless the moment a planning-commission employee explained that although the Landmarks Board had declared this amalgam of three type "B" 1906 refugee shacks "historically significant," it had not made them an official landmark and only recommended Tsai's demolition application be denied. The acting planning director had concluded the structure was historically unimportant and that the commission should rule for Tsai.

Cryan gave an impassioned speech. She reminded the commissioners she had won praise from the California Heritage Council and authored the first scholarly text on the shacks since 1915, and research papers "regarded as erudite models in the area of . . . vernacular architectural history." She appealed to their love of San Francisco, arguing the shacks were the only tangible legacy of its most important event. They had lessons to teach about compassion and the homeless. If Tsai razed them, only one type "B" would remain, an unimaginable historic tragedy. Finally she thundered, "Let the owner restore the property and the gardens he has allowed to be defiled, get his $280,000 dollars back, and take his offensive plans anywhere else but San Francisco."

Only Colonel Spaulding applauded.

Tsai's Chinese supporters talked loudly throughout, making an elaborate show of ignoring her. They glared as she returned to her seat and I felt the unpleasant impulse to side with Cryan and Spaulding not just because they were outnumbered, or because I believed in their crusade, but because we were three Caucasians facing a block of Chinese mindlessly supporting a member of *their* race.

Mr. Tsai's daughter Rose represented him. She was a polished young attorney with excellent English, a walking advertisement for liberal immigration policy and the California Dream. She immediately played the race card, saying the Chinese community was *angry* about the Landmarks Board's decision and the story had been front-page news in the *World Journal and Chinese Times.* The landmarking process was prejudiced when the owner happened to be an immigrant who spoke little English.

She asked everyone who supported demolition of the "purported shacks" to raise their hands. About forty Chinese ones went up, at first slowly as the audience translated her request. When she invited those opposed to vote, only Cryan and Spaulding raised their hands. They looked at me, and after a moment's hesitation I did, too.

"Who is Jane Cryan?" Rose Tsai's prepared statement asked, belittling her for having "no formal training as an architectural historian." Ms. Tsai certainly had none, but that did not stop her from declaring the building without historic or architectural value. If it had been once a genuine shack, she said, "there's nothing left of it because it has undergone so many changes." Even so, her father "tried to correct problems after he moved in, now he can't live in it, all it's good for is the land value."

"Lies! Lies!" Cryan muttered. The Chinese turned and glared. "He never moved into it! It's a mess because he trashed it!"

The commissioners voted unanimously to approve demolition. As we filed out, an elderly Chinese man stepped on Cryan's ankle, on purpose I thought. She cried in pain and shouted, "Stop pushing me." He did it again.

Out in the hallway she exploded. "We were creamed. This was a sham! The cards were stacked against us. The city is antipreservationist. Asians who have just arrived have a bigger voice than people who've lived here for a generation or more. They simply have no appreciation for these buildings and our history." She stamped her foot. "The Tsais *killed* those shacks."

Spaulding looked confused. "I just wanted to save those poor little things," he said.

The Chinese scattered but O'Donohue stayed, smiling and delighting in her rage. She marched over, hands on hips, and craned her neck so she could meet his eye. She lingered over each word. "Joe O'Donohue, you're nothing but a shanty Irishman with no regard for the earth, and I hope you rot in hell!"

He laughed and patted her shoulder. She sighed and said, not without some affection, "You're the biggest jerk I've ever known." She turned to the colonel. "Get me out of here, I need a cigarette. As far as I'm concerned the historic preservation of shacks is over. I quit! I'll never get involved again. Well, there's one more shack in Richmond. . . ."

It is tempting to end on this quixotic note; to imagine Cryan continuing her crusade and cluck about Chinese immigrants showing insufficient respect for their adopted city's history. But the more you know about the 1906 earthquake, the trickier it becomes to scold Chinese-Americans of any generation for showing an insufficient passion for preserving the shacks.

I doubt Mr. Tsai's supporters knew that one month after the quake a Red Cross relief survey could find only 186 Chinese out of a pre-earthquake population of 60,000 living in San Francisco, that authorities shipped Chinese survivors to segregated camps in Oakland, that there is no record of any Chinese person receiving treatment at any emergency hospital after the earthquake, that the army herded Chinese refugees from one camp to another after complaints by white refugees that they smelled, that after shooting looters on sight elsewhere, National Guard troops themselves ransacked Chinatown, that the mayor and civic leaders seized upon the destruction of Chinatown as a pretext for proposing to resettle the Chinese on isolated Hunter's Point so the rebuilt city center could be Asian-free, or that an article appearing afterward in *Overland Monthly* said, "Fire has reclaimed to civilization and cleanliness the Chinese ghetto."

Nevertheless, these were facts that might reasonably influence any Chinese-American or Chinese immigrant who wondered how much respect should be accorded these symbols of San Francisco's "great humanitarian effort." If revenge is a dish best eaten cold, then the Tsais and their supporters had just enjoyed, without knowing it, a large frozen helping.

23

The Death Lady

I was so haunted by similarities between Carol Dickerson's tragedy and the 1906 incident described by Marion Kahn at the Lotta's Fountain ceremonies I began wondering if Dickerson's building could have been constructed over rubble from the one described by Kahn, and if versions of this tragedy would be reenacted every 50, 100, or 150 years, in the same neighborhoods, on the same blocks, and over the same rubble, as long as San Franciscans lived over uncompacted fill and reclaimed watercourses.

Dickerson had, of course, found reasons to blame herself for Scott's death. Had she not extended her maternity leave, she would have been at work in the Fairmont Hotel and he would have been at his baby-sitter's. Had she not taken him to Spokane two months before to show her family, she would have felt how dangerously her building swayed in a 5.6 foreshock and moved out, instead of dismissing the peeling walls and minor damage because, she admitted, "you never think it will happen to you."

She might have had cause to feel guilty had she left him unattended, or dashed into the street and been hit by falling masonry, or been a person who makes light of living over a fault. Instead, she had done everything right. She sought shelter under the nearest door frame, and she lived ten miles from the fault in a neighborhood that had never suffered a collapsed building or earthquake fatality.

Then who or what besides the San Andreas Fault was responsible? Considering the accusations, lawsuits, investigations, and reports following the collapse of the Nimitz Freeway and the failure of a segment of the Bay Bridge, it was not an unreasonable question to ask.

Was the fire department at fault for not extracting Scott before he suffocated? Were they stretched too thin by budget cuts? Was their emergency plan flawed? The problem with these questions was that Dickerson herself was uncertain how long she had been trapped in the rubble, or exactly when her son had died.

The builder seemed a likely villain, until you learned the structure predated modern soil compaction techniques and had satisfied codes of the time. How could he have known the next earthquake would turn its reclaimed land into soup?

There was Harris de Haven Connick, the civil engineer who had "created" the Marina for the 1913 Panama-Pacific Exposition. But he had used the most advanced Dutch reclamation technology, building a sturdy seawall and filling the seventy acres behind it with mud and earthquake rubble.

You might blame the exposition's organizers, or the civic leaders who approved Connick's reclamation, if you could prove they knew, or should have known, that made ground like the Marina's had been treacherous in 1906. But books and articles of the time blamed most of the death and destruction on the fire, not the earthquake.

I arranged to meet two former chiefs of the San Francisco Fire Department, Emmett Condon and William Murray, to see if rescue workers could be held accountable. Murray was a fifty-year veteran who had been chief for six before retiring in 1971. I found him sitting in a straight-backed chair in the common room of a Catholic nursing home in Marin County, his posture as erect as it can be in a man in his nineties. "One thing I have left is a good memory, but it may be all I have," he said, telling me he had been six in 1906, living with his parents and four sisters on the second floor of a two-story frame house at 334 Lombard Street. "My father . . ." he said, repeating himself and releasing the words slowly to give them the importance they deserved. "My father was John J. Murray—fireman!"

He did not move his head or change expression as he spoke. We sat across a coffee table, but instead of looking at me, he seemed to be looking through me to April 18, 1906, when he woke to the shake of his bed and his family saved a neighbor's house by smothering the embers with wine-soaked towels. He remembered people praying like Muslims, and the dead laid out in rows under sheets in St. Peter and St.

Paul's Church. His mother took him to the top of Telegraph Hill to see Market Street burning and said, "Will, you are now a pioneer of the new San Francisco."

"You know what?" he asked. "She was right."

He shut his eyes and recalled the wheels of his miniature fire truck click-clacking over cobblestone streets as his family fled to the ferry after being burned out. Anything on wheels was valuable and two firemen in wool undershirts requisitioned it to move mattresses. He had never forgotten that the fire department had once been stretched so thin it needed his toy. Among his accomplishments as chief he counted buying two more fireboats and extending the high-pressure gravity system out to the Sunset and Richmond. Even so, he said if San Francisco had fifty-two fires again, or anything like that number, "we'd lose the whole city."

More than water mains and fire trucks, he believed in experience. In the 1940s he was battling a fire at a bowling alley when he noticed the beams were about to break. The roof collapsed seconds after he had ordered his men to stand by the outside wall. Without his experience, they would have died. He believed fires had spread after Loma Prieta because of inadequate training and experience. One officer had been a woman with two years in the department. It had taken him eight years to make her rank. Perhaps more experienced officers might have contained the fires and rescued people sooner, but he admitted this was speculation. He was not saying women could not be good firemen, only that no one could be a good fireman in the blink of an eye.

One wants to believe that disasters teach lessons, that experts make recommendations that are embraced, and that one boy suffocated by plaster dust in 1989 means fewer dying that way in the future. But Emmett Condon, who had served as San Francisco's fire chief until 1987, told me that in the city's haste to recover from 1906, building codes had been lowered rather than raised, and the rows of charming wooden houses snaking over its hills had made San Francisco an even more dangerous firetrap. By the mid-1920s, when Dickerson's building was constructed, wind, roof, and floor-load requirements were 50 percent weaker than just after the Great Earthquake. Recently the California Seismic Commission had mandated retrofitting for pre-1948-code unreinforced masonry buildings and city engineers had identified two hundred Condon thought would collapse during the Big One. But work proceeded slowly. Modifications were expensive and the city feared owners would walk away, increasing the homeless crisis.

Condon was a third-generation San Franciscan and civil-service aristocrat. He dressed in a banker's suit and belonged to a downtown club where we met among old prints and leather armchairs. He had been a member of the California State Seismic Safety Commission, served as chairman of the governor's Earthquake Task Force, and had the firm voice of a man accustomed to having orders obeyed, so I paid attention when he said San Francisco was in some respects more vulnerable to destruction than in 1906.

Loma Prieta had ignited twenty-seven major fires and stretched the department to its limit. But Condon pointed out that according to Dr. Charles Scawthorn in his widely accepted 1987 study, *Estimates of the Conflagration Risk to Insured Property in Greater Los Angeles and San Francisco,* an 8.0 would do thirty times the damage and ignite at least eighty major fires. To fight them Scawthorn calculated the city would need 142 fire engines, four times the number available in 1987. Depending on wind velocities, he believed 22,500 to 48,000 buildings would be lost to collapse and fire.

Condon thought Scawthorn's estimates were on the low side. He worried mains would break again in the same places as they had in 1906 and 1989, and that most furniture and furnishings were now made from synthetics that burned twice as fast and hot as conventional materials, emitted five hundred times the toxic gases, and in less than five minutes could reach the "flashover stage" when an entire room simply exploded.

He worried earthquake and fire safety had not been a big issue in the last election. Mayor Agnos had gone east to reassure tourists the city was safe, while the Convention and Visitors' Bureau had launched a public-relations campaign to reassure out-of-state businessmen and investors that also succeeded in lulling San Franciscans.

He worried about flat tires on fire trucks (during the 1983 Coalinga earthquake, sharp debris punctured every tire on every fire truck), the rupture of high-pressure gas mains, and fires in the four hundred skyscrapers predating safety codes requiring sprinklers to switch on if the mains ruptured. Skyscraper fires soaked up firemen, and to control just one Los Angeles had needed more than San Francisco had on duty at once. The next disaster would find the department stretched thin. In 1906, firemen slept in their firehouses five or six nights a week. When he joined, most lived in the city. Now San Francisco had two departments: one comprised of the one third of its firemen residing in the city, the other of the two thirds in the suburbs. He did not blame these suburban firemen. Even the Sunset had become too expensive for young families. As chief, he had scheduled shifts so only a certain number of firemen could be on the wrong side of the bridges at one time. If the Big One cut bridges and highways, he had planned flying his men in on National Guard helicopters. But until they arrived, fires would spread and people trapped in buildings would wait.

He worried most about the Sunset, where Doelger's rows of houses lacked even the Sheetrock required by later codes. On some blocks, sixteen or twenty-four houses formed a horizontal wooden skyscraper that was an amazing firetrap. When a fire started in one Sunset row house, it had often spread to two on either side by the time the trucks arrived. In a strong wind, fires jumped seventy feet across a street. One in 1978 set thirty-nine row houses ablaze in the Western Addition. A year later, a fire in the Mission burned out twenty-six structures. Each had stretched the department to capacity.

"Imagine if the next big earthquake strikes during the kind of 25 mph westerly wind that often blows off the Pacific into the Sunset," he said. "You get four or five fires breaking out in different places and spreading up and down row houses, then some broken mains, an updraft carrying embers to neighboring streets, a department trying to fight the fires simultaneously. . . ." He lowered his voice to a whisper, "And then we would lose the Sunset. It would go up like an old barn."

❖

In the Museum of the City of San Francisco I saw a 1906 panorama photograph of the Great Fire that I think solves the mystery of who killed Scott Dickerson.

The museum is an idiosyncratic institution occupying a large room on the top floor of the Cannery, a Fisherman's Wharf complex of galleries, restaurants, and boutiques that was the nation's first red-brick factory to be converted into a shopping mall. Most of its exhibits concern the 1906 earthquake, reflecting the interests of its founders and curators, former city archivist Gladys Hansen and her son Richard, a former official photographer for the fire department. There is a china sugar bowl pulled from the rubble of the Spreckels mansion, a refugee tent, a milk can used to fight the 1906 fires, and one of the plastic pails volunteers used to fight the 1989 ones in the Marina, a wall of "earthquake art"—the drawings and watercolors painted on cardboard by 1906 survivors—and a stuffed canary that stares from its cage with frightened pin eyes, a replica of "one of the most extraordinary bird escapes" of the quake, according to an article from 1909 *Bird News* that explains, "The cage had been crushed . . . except at one corner in which the bird was imprisoned."

In the 1906 photograph that solves Dickerson's death, clouds of smoke rise like a fog bank and buildings blaze like torches, while in the foreground, virgin neighborhoods await destruction. As I ran my fingers across it, searching for surviving landmarks, a lazy voice behind me said, "A fraud, a complete fake, retouched to highlight the fires and erase the quake."

I looked closely. Sure enough, not a single building had lost a window or wall.

I turned to meet Richard Hansen, a soft-looking and deceptively phlegmatic young man. "Take this," he said, handing me something labeled "earthquake in a can" that began vibrating like a joy buzzer the moment I held it. He retrieved it and worked the room, pressing it on unwary Japanese who, despite their own considerable interest in earthquakes, clearly found this trick unamusing.

Gladys Hansen was at the reception desk, collecting donations and selling souvenir T-shirts saying CALIFORNIA HAS ITS FAULTS. She made no apologies for the museum's emphasis on 1906. Her former position as San Francisco archivist had turned her into a Great Earthquake buff, and led to her uncovering a conspiracy to rewrite its history. She had become suspicious of the official death toll when, after assuming her position in 1963, she immediately found herself dealing with inquiries from genealogists and relatives looking for information about 1906 casualties. In 1963, the Great Earthquake was scarcely more distant than Pearl Harbor is from us now, and its victims were still remembered and mourned. She quickly realized the number of dead mentioned by just the relatives contacting her exceeded the official figure of 498 killed. Common sense told her the actual toll had to be much higher. After all, no one had counted the Chinese, or the foreign seamen who had filled the rooming houses that collapsed south of Market Street. At Sixth and Howard, four adjacent hotels with a thousand rooms had pancaked. Eyewitnesses claimed one hundred to three hundred people had perished in the Brunswick House alone. A journal kept by Captain Cullen of Fire Station No. 6 counted fifty fatalities within a hundred feet of one intersection. The transcripts of lawsuits brought against insurance companies named scores of "unofficial" deaths.

To help establish an accurate death toll she established the San Francisco Research Project, a private volunteer organization with an advisory board of prominent engineers and historians. It mailed circulars to churches, librarians, and historians throughout the nation, requesting the San Francisco addresses of anyone believed to have died in the quake and fire. Because San Francisco had been a new city of transients, many of the dead had been missed by out-of-state relatives, but not by anyone in California. There were also cases of entire families perishing, leaving no one on the West Coast to mourn.

Her requests appeared in historical-society newsletters throughout the nation, and she was soon receiving letters addressed "To the Death Lady, San Francisco."

"It was exciting when the mail came," she remembered. "We all shouted, 'Another death! Another death!' " The research consumed vacations, weekends, and $20,000 of her own funds. Richard Hansen thought it had ended his marriage. His wife had wanted to invest in children, not documents copied from the National Archives at thirty cents a page. But the Hansens thought their research was worth the expense and sacrifice if it led to safety measures that would reduce fatalities in the next quake.

During trips to Washington, they discovered deaths from earthquake-related causes such as disease and summary execution had also been vastly underreported. People dying from injuries months later were excluded from the official toll. Mayor Schmitz had issued a proclamation on the morning of the earthquake ordering looters shot on the spot (an ironic move since the notoriously corrupt Schmitz and his cronies had looted the city for years), and the Hansens believed five hundred people were executed. A man was shot for drinking from a fire hose. Men scavenging food in ruined markets were shot as "looters." Soldiers forced civilians to empty their pockets and killed anyone carrying rings or jewelry. Fourteen were executed at one location, twenty at another. Gladys Hansen thought the word *massacred* was more appropriate.

She only added names to her death roll if they were confirmed by more than one source. Even so, she quickly doubled the official toll to one thousand. Currently her "verifiable database" showed three thousand confirmed deaths, and she continued to receive promising inquiries from genealogical societies. She predicted a final total between 5,000 and 10,000, a staggering loss for a city of only 440,000.

She had also used old city directories, insurance-company documents, and legal transcripts to construct a "death map," showing on a block-by-block, house-by-house basis where people died. (Richard Hansen believed it was never done because the authorities feared the truth.) To her initial surprise it showed deaths clustered in particular buildings and blocks. Had people perished in the blaze, her map should have shown them spread across the fire zone. Instead, the clustering suggested many died in bed when their buildings collapsed, more proof the earthquake was deadlier than the fire.

The Hansens plotted sewer, gas, and waterline breaks on their death map and discovered they occurred near blocks or buildings with a high concentration of fatalities. Since the earthquake had caused these breaks, it was more proof of people dying where the shaking was strongest. They found death clusters occurred primarily in wood-frame houses, contradicting what has been an article of faith since 1906—that wood structures survived the shaking, but brick and masonry ones collapsed. The fire had simply eradicated the evidence by consuming the wooden quake-damaged buildings.

Seismologists and engineers were suspicious at first, but soon convinced by the Hansens' research. But business and real-estate interests resisted the assertion that certain blocks were more likely to produce casualties, and that multiple-story wood-frame buildings sited on made ground, like the one in which Scott Dickerson had perished, were death traps.

Loma Prieta confirmed the accuracy of the death map. Blocks suffering the worst shaking and damage in 1906 suffered it again in 1989. Richard Hansen said, "We predicted the intersection of Seventh and Lake would be hit hard, and it was. Loma Prieta surprised people along Lake, Clement, and California. When they said, 'We weren't supposed to suffer because this area survived '06,' we had to tell them, 'Oh no, it didn't.' "

They had published their findings in *Denial of Disaster: The Untold Story and Photographs of the San Francisco Earthquake and Fire of 1906.* It was written in collaboration with Emmett Condon and published in 1989, just after Loma Prieta. It disproved or questioned almost every 1906 myth, even "earthquake love," and told of looters shot without pity, an insane soldier attempting to assassinate the chief of police, men drunk on stolen whiskey who could not outrun the flames, businessmen dynamiting their enterprises to collect fire insurance, and laborers refusing to fight fires unless paid forty cents an hour, and demanding bribes to carry the crippled to safety.

Richard Hansen had compiled the book's photographs. They included rare images of collapsed wood-frame rooming houses taken hours before the fire consumed them, and two pages of hand-tinted postcards in which the flames were an angry red. His caption under one read, "An artist had removed most of the earthquake damage from this dramatic photograph of the south of Market fires burning toward Market Street."

I ran a magnifying glass over it, and sure enough, the buildings in the foreground were undamaged.

But who had ordered the artists to repair the damaged buildings? And who had erased all traces of the quake from the Hopkins Art Institute panorama? It was no secret San Francisco's civic leaders had attempted to minimize damage from the earthquake. As Hansen put it, they said, "Hey! We had a fire—but that's something any city can have." But these doctored photographs point to a more orchestrated conspiracy.

According to the Hansens' book, geologists attempting to study the 1906 earthquake often complained of having their research hindered. Andrew Lawson, the geologist who named the San Andreas Fault, wrote, "The commercial spirit of the people fears any discussion of earthquakes. . . . It believes that such discussion will advertise California as an earthquake region and so hurt business."

A Stanford geologist on the State Earthquake Investigation Commission condemned the "general disposition that almost amounted to concerted action for the purpose of suppressing all mention" of the earthquake, and charged that when geologists tried collecting geological data, they were "advised and even urged over and over again to gather no such information, and above all not to publish it. 'Forget it,' 'the less said, the sooner mended,' and 'there hasn't been any earthquake' were the sentiments we heard on all sides."

One of the Hansens' many smoking guns was a letter sent to every California chamber of commerce by the Southern Pacific's general passenger agent, James Horsburgh, Jr., in which he outlined a strategy for rewriting the history of the catastrophe to reassure Eastern investors. "We do not believe in advertising the earthquake. The real calamity in San Francisco was undoubtedly the fire," he wrote, suggesting local chambers help prevent "California and San Francisco from being mis-represented by sensation mongers." He urged them to "reach" the eye-witness lecturers who were disseminating sensational stories about the catastrophe, convince newspaper editors that "except for a few cities which happened to lie directly in its pathway, practically no damage was done," and argue that "no city in the temperate zone has ever been twice affected in a serious way by an earthquake."

Horsburgh did not have to gather his real-estate and business co-conspirators into a smoke-filled room to persuade them to erase the quake's damage from photographs and history. Many political and business leaders had the same reflexive reaction. While the fires still smoldered, the San Francisco Real Estate Board had passed a resolution urging the term *the Great Fire* be used instead of *the Great Earthquake*.

"Clearly, real estate in San Francisco would not be worth much if subject to periodic 'Acts of God' in the form of disastrous earthquakes," Gladys Hansen argued in her book. "On the other hand, with adequate water mains, good foundations, and properly constructed buildings, the city would rise from the ashes, impervious to another catastrophe by fire."

The public was a willing accomplice. Most insurance-company claimants had a "fallen-building clause" in their policies stipulating that buildings falling for reasons other than fire were uncovered. No won-der the first two hundred claims submitted by policyholders described buildings untroubled by forty-five seconds of shaking. They were sup-ported by perjured testimony and doctored photographs that poisoned historical research for decades.

The lies Hansen had uncovered were part of a chain of falsehoods and chicanery that have sometimes combined with California's natural optimism to create fictions of extraordinary power and influence. Lesser links in the chain include a study of seismic risk ordered by the state after the Hayward earthquake of 1868 that proved so depressing the railroad companies seized and destroyed all but two copies, and the 1900 story that Chinatown's rats did not carry bubonic plague, a cover-up orchestrated by city hall to maintain investor confidence that cost 113 lives between 1900 and 1904. Unlike these smaller lies, the sup-pressed evidence, doctored photographs, and fictitious death toll de-signed to prove that the 1906 fatalities and damage had resulted from fire, and that wood-frame buildings had withstood the shaking, had lethal consequences for future generations. Because the 1906 lies were so widely accepted, San Francisco could be rebuilt quickly and cheaply, with inexpensive frame houses erected over the rubble of old ones, and over the same unstable soil that had already once failed to support them.

The 1906 lies allowed an inherently dangerous neighborhood like the Marina to rise without protest or concern, so that when some of its wood-frame buildings collapsed eighty-three years later, killing Scott Dickerson, everyone could quite honestly claim to be amazed.

At least the nineteenth-century developers who created the treacherous ground in the Mission district had been ignorant of the seismic dangers. Filling in old creeks and swamps was simply the cheapest way to satisfy the hunger for land on a peninsula where there was too little. Those rebuilding on the same made ground in the Mission, or on newly made ground in the Marina after 1906, were also unaware of the seismic risks. But had they known, one wonders if it would have made much difference.

Five years after Loma Prieta, real-estate prices in the Marina have stabilized and the word is that the neighborhood is "back." Buildings have been retrofitted, although it is debatable whether any structure on this ground can be strengthened enough to withstand a great earthquake. But young couples with children keep moving in because like so much of California, the Marina is so seductively beautiful they are willing to risk their lives for a good view.

FIVE

SOUTH BAY

24
Alive in Daly City

You have probably seen Daly City, although you may not have known it. In the sixties, my college sociology professor showed us slides of streets of boxy houses snaking over barren hills south of San Francisco. It was a symbolic suburban hell, he said, conformity and America at its worst. Photographs of it also appeared in many liberal screeds of the time. William Bronson's *How to Kill a Golden State: A Graphic Report on the Crisis of Ugly California with Over 300 Photographs*, presented them as proof California had been "polluted" with "an aggregation of shoddy construction . . . best described as schlock—flashy, shabby goods." And of course it was the inspiration for the Malvina Reynolds hit "Little Boxes," describing "Little boxes on the hillside, / Little boxes all the same . . ." The song was a minor sixties anthem, but what was never sung or said was that some of the little boxes sat over the San Andreas Fault, and on the same trace that had cracked and slipped in 1906, so that even if they had been constructed to the most exacting engineering standards, braced and reinforced every possible way (which they were not), the Big One would still crack them open like coconuts.

My *Roadside Geology Guide* said houses on active fault lines were "doomed to certain destruction," and seismic engineer Peter Yanev has warned that "heavy property damage and some loss of life are a certainty when the next big earthquake strikes this [Daly City] portion of the San Andreas." Anyone living there was "gambling the whole investment and perhaps life itself on the slim hope that a large earthquake will not strike again." His book included photographs showing

Daly City in 1956 and 1966. In the first, the 1906 trace was a dotted line superimposed over farmland, a sag pond, and cliffs marked by the landslides showing where the fault emerged from the Pacific. In the second, houses covered everything.

Using these photographs as a map, I drove down Daly City's empty Sunday-morning streets looking for the fault but finding only dead ends. A road would head for the coast only to hit an eroded cliff and turn inland. When I slowed to ask directions of a woman jogger, she waved me off and accelerated. A fog bank lay just offshore and the air was cool and damp. Few people were outside. Some teenagers picknicking in the drizzle behind the Korean Central Pacific Church said the parish hall was so packed they had to eat outside. A serious boy in a blazer said he hoped an earthquake came on Sunday, when they were praying. Two girls agreed. God would protect the church. They told me the fault was nearby, but then pointed in different directions.

I finally found it coming ashore through a landslide, then heading inland underneath houses on Westline Drive, then underneath more houses, dozens more.

The 1906 earthquake had cut a fifteen-mile-long furrow across Daly City's pastures and farms. When refugees poured down Mission Street from San Francisco, farmer John Daly gave them milk, and a lumberyard sent wood. Some built shanties, others slept on ground cracked open by the tremor and warmed themselves at outdoor fireplaces made from rocks pulled from the broken landscape. Developers bought and subdivided the quake-scarred farmland, and within weeks the refugees were buying cheap lots and building houses over the same geologic feature that had just left them homeless, an unrivaled example of the theory that earthquake survivors are afflicted by an "unrealistic optimism."

The 5.5 Daly City earthquake of 1957 was the strongest to hit this segment of the San Andreas since 1906. In San Francisco, the Golden Gate Bridge swayed and people ran into the street sobbing. In Daly City, sidewalks buckled and furrows raced across lawns. Buildings cracked and milkmen, the only men to be found in a suburban neighborhood on a weekday in the fifties, dashed inside houses with wrenches to turn off gas lines. Husbands came home early and ran fingers along fissures in their new stucco walls while their wives swept up crockery.

The epicenter was near where the fault crosses the shoreline, so the worst damage was done to the cliffs. Since no one lived on them, no one was injured. The following year, bulldozers graded the furrows to prepare the ground for the Westlake development. Its picture windows now faced the 1957 landslide. The top of the slide became a lovers' lane where condoms dangling on bushes suggested Daly City's teenagers routinely made love over the fault.

I parked and waited for someone to leave or arrive. The contrast was dramatic: suburban homes overlooking a wild shoreline; lawn ornaments facing sharks. A man pulled into a driveway. "Yeah, I know it's there," he snarled. "Big deal."

Daly City is an easy target. You can say if it were put to music it would sound like chopsticks, or that its houses seem trapped in two mirrors held against one another, a never-ending reflection of front door, picture window, garage . . . front door, picture window, garage. They are a dream come true, or a cruel joke. You want your own yard? Sure, too bad it's not big enough for both a garden and a jungle gym. A picture window? Sure, but keep the blinds drawn since it faces the picture window across the street. A panoramic view? Here it is, smothered in fog.

But the more I drove through Daly City, the more I realized this easy fun was dated. What had appeared ticky-tacky in the sixties now looked pretty good compared with what was on offer elsewhere. Perhaps its houses were not much, but it had a good infrastructure of sidewalks and parks. You could walk to elementary schools and churches, and the developers had made a stab at a Main Street of small stores. Try finding these amenities in the newer walled tracts being thrown up around freeway interchanges.

Franklin D. Roosevelt Elementary School sat closest to the fault, but its principal was cool to the idea of my watching her students observe "Earthquake Awareness Day," so I settled for the Marjorie H. Tobias School, situated about a mile away. It is an amusing and award-winning 1959 building, often described as a "doughnut" or a "flying saucer with a wiggly roof." The classrooms are in the ring while the hole serves as playground and corridor. There is no second story to collapse on the first, and because every classroom opens onto the playground, evacuation is easy.

Its principal, Burt Norall, was a gentle, owlish man in his fifties. He told me his average class size was under thirty and his students tended to be "well parented" and scored above state average. The racial makeup was 43 percent Asian, 35 percent white, 19 percent Hispanic, and 2 percent black, a slightly higher percentage of whites than the general Daly City population.

At eleven A.M. he rang a bell. Teachers pulled curtains across windows and students jumped under their desks, covering necks with hands to ward off falling glass. We circled the building, poking our heads into classrooms. The older children whispered and giggled, the younger ones looked scared. The student body reminded me of those soda-pop advertisements you see during the Olympics featuring the hand-holding children of many nations.

I returned alone to a fifth-grade class supervised by a substitute teacher. She stood with me by the door, watching as a trainee teacher led the class. "I hope I'm not here during the Big One," she said, pointing how the walls between classrooms had glass partitions at their top. There would be no time to pull curtains across both these and the front windows, and what about the exposed pipes running through classrooms above the door? They were warm and probably filled with steam or hot water.

She agreed this was one of Daly City's better schools. Substitutes elsewhere sometimes walked out before recess. She thought the best schools were those where teachers and administrators ignored multiculturalism and tried making students proud of themselves as individuals. At the worst ones, they made everyone so proud of their own race that students formed the racial cliques that became gangs when they reached junior high. They neglected their schoolwork because they thought, "Hey, if I'm already so good, why bother?" Even in this good school, eight-year-old Terminators wore gang colors and marked out playground turf. The "make my day" attitude began in second grade and cut across racial lines. Young whites were as macho as the Hispanics, little roosters with their feathers up.

The regular teacher had assigned seats to keep the races mixed, but while we talked, a girl asked the trainee if everyone could sit with their friends. When he said yes the kids dashed across the room, instantly segregating themselves.

Daly City has always stood for more than itself. In the 1960s it was the fastest-growing town in California; in the 1990s it is probably the most racially balanced. Everyone I asked thought the adult Chinese, Hispanics, Vietnamese, Filipinos, Koreans, blacks, and Caucasians got along better than anywhere in California, and certainly better than their children. The weekly newspaper had a gang story in every issue I saw. The week I arrived a car of Vietnamese youths traded shots with some Mexicans outside Denny's, sending a boy to the hospital with a head wound. Two weeks before that three Mexicans had been shot-gunned at a Jack in the Box.

Although Daly City's multicultural population of almost 100,000 puts it among California's fifty largest cities, its well-equipped library has only two books cataloged as local history, a phenomenon made more astonishing by the fact that it borders San Francisco, where local history is a religion. One of the Daly City books was published by the city in the 1970s to celebrate what its author called "the drama of the era of house-building." The more recent, *The Great Daly City Historical Trivia Book*, was a grab bag of random facts. Its authors, Ken and Bunny Gillespie, agreed to meet me at the library. While waiting for them, I skimmed both books and learned that during the late 1950s, bulldozers grading land around the clock prompted twenty-five resi-dents to file lawsuits over the noise, that the city grew 30 percent in one two-year period, and that when it marked its fiftieth anniversary in 1961 with the slogan "A Century of Progress in Half the Time," its birth rate of 707 babies per 1,000 women was double the U.S. average and the highest in the nation.

The Gillespies offered me a business card identifying them as DALY CITY HISTORIANS with the urgent formality of a Japanese executive, then explained they had the idea for their book when they were stunned into silence by a fellow cruise passenger asking, "So, what's so good or great about Daly City?"

The Great Daly City Historical Trivia Book was their answer. Ken said they had chosen the trivia format because it was "easily digestible for people who don't have any roots here." Bunny said she had been born in Daly City, but most of her school classmates had left. Many peo-ple believed if you could not escape Daly City within seven years you were a failure. The newcomer doctors, lawyers, and executives rolled over their starter houses and moved out once they could afford it. The teachers and civil servants with less elastic salaries stayed. The town fa-thers had experienced difficulty finding a king and queen for the sev-enty-fifth anniversary celebration who had roots deeper than a single generation.

The Gillespies' boosterism had a chip on its shoulder. Their fore-word declared that "looking back at Daly City's history, we find our-selves seeing positives, where others might see negatives. . . . We feel comfortable about Daly City. We find no need to apologize for her or her historic past. Perhaps some hometowns are not destined to earn greatness in the estimation of others. . . . Perhaps some hometowns have a splendid destiny but have not yet achieved even a modicum of acknowledged greatness."

They had also assembled an historical exhibit they took to nearby shopping malls. Former Daly City residents who stopped to chat said they had left town after their first raise, or after tiring of the damp. Bunny Gillespie considered these comments a triumph because at least no one had said, "Wow! Daly City, I really hated that place."

When they asked what I thought about their hometown, I mumbled something about affordable housing and clean air, but I did not say I thought a Daly City historian had been dealt an impossible hand because a rich local history is the fruit of people putting down roots that last generations, while Daly City had simply not been constructed to sustain this kind of community. It was a budget motel of a town, inexpensive but comfortable, built for transients, with few houses suitable for families who became larger, richer, or poorer. Like a budget motel, its most interesting history concerned its construction. After that, the narrative was one of transients checking in and out of identical rooms. Given this design, what history could it have *but* a trivial one? And why should anyone care about sleeping over the San Andreas Fault if they planned to be gone in the morning?

"The Daly City attitude to earthquakes is 'so what?' " Ken Gillespie said. "But we do hope you get to experience one while you're here." I studied his face. He was sincere, he really did not want anyone to leave disappointed.

Although Daly City's only museum was the Gillespies' portable one, the town had its historical sites, and as we parted they recommended the Mission Bell Motel, Vern's Café, the Globe Tavern, and Molloy's Bar in neighboring Colma.

The Mission Bell and Vern's were next door on Mission Street, once the main highway from Los Angeles to San Francisco. Vern's was a 1950s diner filled with Caucasian retirees eating poached eggs for lunch. The Mission Bell had become a flophouse. During the 1930s it was "the Stopping Place of the Stars" and celebrities like Bette Davis had considered it glamorous to spend the night in one of its pink stucco units before driving thirty minutes more into San Francisco. Perhaps she liked the novelty of staying in one of California's first motels, or simply preferred sleeping in the country, surrounded by marigolds and artichokes, with the lights of San Francisco glowing over the last dark hill. Now its stucco was chipped and cardboard panels had replaced windowpanes. Women with needle-bruised arms hung around the porte cochere.

A slippery young man from Bombay admitted to being the manager. When I described the motel's Hollywood clientele he giggled and shook his head. The idea was too fantastic. "Please understand, sir," he said in a confidential voice, "this is no longer a classy place, you would not be happy here, and our suites are fully booked by monthly clients."

I asked if a scrapbook remained from the glory days. He shook his head. He only knew the place had once belonged to a Mr. Smith whose family had owned the whole city. The present owner did not wish to be identified. Finally, to get rid of me, he produced a scratched brass plaque from under the counter. It had been presented by Daly City to Mayor Smith in 1968 for his services to the city. "This is our historical exhibit," he said. "But if you like it . . ."

He pushed it halfway across the desk. For the right price, it could be mine.

The dank little Globe Tavern had become the principal repository for six decades of Daly City history as experienced by its white civil servants. The jukebox had Irish ballads marked with shamrocks and the patrons were over sixty, mostly smokers with hacking coughs who ordered midmorning doubles. The bartender spoke through a voice box and gave me a flashlight so I could study the exhibits that were the stuff of any small-town museum: photographs of legendary baseball teams and collections of foreign banknotes brought home by seamen.

I learned from the framed newspaper articles that until 1972 no Daly City policeman had been killed in the line of duty, that a Cadillac had driven through the Globe's front door in 1955, and that on August 16, 1942, an antisubmarine blimp had crashed on the 400 block of Bellevue Avenue without its two-man crew. The newer clippings concerned deaths, retirements, and the closing of Duffy's, a similar establishment down the street. Once the Globe followed it, and from all appearances that would happen soon, these exhibits would be dispersed or junked. Certainly the children of first-generation Asian and Hispanic immigrants educated to take pride in their own cultures would not care much for the memorabilia of Daly City's working-class whites, even if it was the only history Daly City had.

❖

The San Mateo Convention and Visitors' Bureau identified Molloy's Bar in the neighboring town of Colma as one of only seven sites of "great historical interest" in this large, wealthy county. It was a rambling barn of a nineteenth-century building built as a hotel, which had become a saloon, speakeasy, and finally, after Lanty Molloy took it over from his father and restored an interior decorated with sports trophies, fight cards, and wartime headlines, Historical Old Molloy's.

Molloy had shrewd eyes and an educated voice that clashed with his classic barkeep name, and he knew more Daly City and Colma history than anyone. He had witnessed the 1942 crash of the navy dirigible, arriving in time to see its door was open and its rope ladder down, and if I cared he could show me the former homesite of "Mother" Minerva Hartman, the last surviving Civil War nurse. A 1907 act of Congress had made her the official "Mother of the United States Army and Navy," and when El Camino Real had to be widened, the county raised her historic house on stilts and built around it, an act of historical reverence inconceivable today.

His bar was as soothing as a church at twilight: no food, karaoke nights, video games, wide-screen televisions, or Lucite boxes filled with stuffed toys you tried to grab with a miniature steam shovel. Some of the credit for this went to its location. When I lifted a slat on a venetian blind I could see the raised mausoleums of Holy Cross Cemetery across the street. There were another thirteen cemeteries within a mile, and the underground population of 1.5 million guaranteed a steady clientele of mourners, stonemasons, and gravediggers.

Colma's corpses had blessed it with handsome landscaping and buildings, open space, a stable community of cemetery workers, and a reverence for history. Ever since we buried my grandfather in a splendid cemetery in Connecticut, I have liked cemeteries, perhaps because our suburb had no public parks. A trip to his grave was a treat, and we brought sandwiches and hunted frogs with butterfly nets. When I drove through Colma's cemeteries I was happy to see family groups picnicking and feeding bread to the ducks.

I called Colma's largest cemetery, Cypress Lawn, to ask if Loma Prieta had caused any earthquake damage. A woman named Christel Paul, whom I instantly liked, said it had pushed around headstones, damaged a columbarium, and cracked some angels' wings, but that was all. When we met she turned out to be a handsome and capable woman who was sliding gracefully into middle age and had the same breezy attitude toward death common to other Colmans. She was no ghoul, but genuinely seemed to like cemeteries, and was happy to have an excuse to fill a galvanized bucket with keys to the columbaria, catacombs, and mausoleums, and show me the sights.

Cemetery guides have to be name-droppers, since what else really distinguishes one burial ground from another except the renown of its corpses? Paul said Cypress Lawn had wealthier, more famous people than nearby cemeteries and true to her word delivered the remains of the tycoons who had built California. We drove slowly, as if on safari, scanning the ground for famous graves. "Look, a DeYoung!" she exclaimed. "Marked by that bronze statue. He's the *Chronicle* and the art museum. Now let's turn up this hill to the Crockers." We found the Matsons of the Matson lines, and Jackling the Copper King lying in a sarcophagus of rainbow granite. The Hearst family had ordered its name removed from its faux-Grecian temple when vandals defaced it after Patty's kidnapping.

"This is wonderful!" she said. "All this history. Honestly, I could go on for days."

We searched for the first American consul to Monterey, California's first Episcopal bishop, the builder of San Francisco's first wharf and the inventor of its cable cars, a Civil War hero whose funeral drew fifty thousand, and the actress who played Aunt Pittypatt in *Gone With the Wind*. Despite its Hearsts, DeYoungs, and Crockers, Cypress Lawn was tolerant and egalitarian, a bastion of these traditional California values. No one minded if Orientals set their plots aflame with red flowers and ribbons, or if Samoans barbecued pork on hibachis and decorated graves with plastic flamingos.

Had Bruff's stay in California been less disastrous, I might have been searching for his headstone here, too, although he would more likely have been among the 35,000 pioneers disinterred in 1939 from San Fransciso's Laurel Hill Cemetery. Their headstones had been broken down to line the gutters of Buena Vista Park and build a breakwater for the St. Francis Yacht Club, and their remains were moved here to a five-acre vault.

Carol Dickerson's fear that her son might be troubled twice by an earthquake was not unfounded. The 1957 Daly City quake had damaged California's first crematorium, a classic Greek temple where tiles spelled DO NOT DISTURB THE ASHES OF THE DEAD. Loma Prieta had pitched urns to the floor of Columbarium No. 1 and cracked the glass in niches, releasing nineteenth-century air from their displays of dried flowers, photographs, and family Bibles.

Paul thought overpopulation and crime were a greater danger than earthquakes. Vandals had smashed Tiffany windows and defaced statues. California's exploding population meant huge price increases for underground burials. She said yuppies from San Francisco liked her free weekend historical tours of Cypress Lawn. They did not come planning to buy, and there was no sales pitch, but many returned anyway to purchase a plot. They seemed keen to be buried among San Francisco's finest. She showed me an artist's rendition of a proposed addition to handle the overflow. Its identical markers were closely spaced, and recessed below the sod to make mowing easier, a Daly City kind of cemetery.

Frankly, I would not mind being interred in Cypress Lawn. I liked it that it made its chapel available for weddings, and always kept its flag at half-mast because, Paul said, "All the blessed dead should be honored, not just politicians and soldiers." I even liked the Orientals' gaudy flowers and plastic toys, and "the acceptance of a variety of deathstyles." And if someone had to feed my corpse to the fire, I could do worse than Fabio at the crematorium. When we found him mothering a distressed houseplant in the anteroom and Paul said, "You don't seem very busy today, Fabio," he smiled and turned up his palms in a "what can you do about it?" gesture. Then, with great respect and ceremony, he showed us the morning's meager output, one Ziploc bag of white ash.

I stopped at Molloy's afterward for a drink. At the bar two mourning families of Irish and Koreans were discovering that grief is a natural icebreaker. Molloy told me his motto was "Everyone Gets to Molloy's Someday, or to Somewhere Nearby," and Colma's official motto was "It's Great to Be Alive in Colma!"

"Know what the unofficial one is?" he asked with a sly smile. " 'Better to Be Dead in Colma Than Alive in Daly City.' "

25

Dream House

After 1906 many of the San Francisco tycoons now resting in Cypress Lawn believed they could escape the next earthquake by moving to the South Bay Peninsula where, without realizing it, they built mansions over the fault. Filoli is the most famous and visited of these, and because the 1906 trace runs underneath one wall of its formal garden, also the closest to the San Andreas. It is a stolid 36,000-square-foot Georgian Revival mansion adapted by the noted San Francisco architect Willis Polk. Its thick walls, multiple fireplaces, and thirsty formal gardens were originally intended for the clammy British countryside and make as much sense here as a Japanese tea garden in the Sahara. It is a big deal for California, but the kind of white elephant you find by the handful in Virginia and Maryland, where they have become boarding schools, conference centers, and asylums for Social Register embarrassments.

It was completed in 1917 for William Bourn, who inherited a mining fortune. On his death it was purchased by William Roth, who married a shipping fortune. Nothing of cultural, economic, or historical importance ever unfolded in its forty-three rooms. No one famous ever lived in them or even stayed as a weekend guest, except for the Polish pianist and statesman Paderewski. Yet hundreds of visitors come every day, paying six dollars to tour its gloomy rooms and spectacular gardens. They book places a month in advance and schedule trips to San Francisco around their reservations. Some belong to garden clubs, but most come because the credits for the discontinued television soap opera *Dynasty* rolled across its exterior, identifying it as the home of the high-living Carringtons.

Filoli has also become a major shrine in California's Cult of the Big House. When a mysterious explosion leveled the one-year-old Napa Valley faux-French château of developer Joaquin de Monet, destroying its turrets, six fireplaces, ten marble bathrooms, nine crystal chandeliers, media room, fur vault, and dog shower, some accounts played its loss as tragedy rather than farce, and a neighbor told *People* that de Monet had simply "wanted to outdo the other mansions."

According to Young and Rubicam's *California Dream Report*, 44 percent of household heads identify a house as the most important component of their dream. The most popular answer to, "If you won the California Lottery, how would you spend your winnings?" was a "bigger [and] better house." Despite all the environmental chatter, the average square footage of new houses being built in California has been increasing. Houses replacing the 2,500 lost in the Oakland hills wildfire were on average 21 percent larger. A Berkeley architectural historian told *The New York Times* they were "giant boxes, strangely unimaginative and ugly."

The same month that wildfires incinerated these Oakland houses, the *San Francisco Examiner* invited readers to describe their "California Dream House." Local architects competed to design a house matching their specifications. A jury of prominent architects chose the best plans, and the house was built and opened to public tours—an instant Filoli.

The Dream House of a population priding itself on its environmental sensitivity was a sprawling two-story three-thousand-square-foot estate facing a golf course and located inside the gated and guarded suburban development of Rancho Solano, at least an hour commute from San Francisco over busy freeways traversing several major faults. Photographs showed a cold fortress of overhanging beams and balconies resembling a Tibetan monastery on the Maginot Line. It had a butler's pantry and spa, a garage with room for three cars, four places to hang out—a living room, two-story "great room," study, and "media center," and three places to eat—a breakfast room, dining room, and dining porch. A few months before, I had visited President Truman's Winter White House in Key West. It was a white clapboard navy officer's bungalow with small rooms, louvered windows, and a deep porch. Truman's only indulgence was a card table with built-in holders for poker chips. His wife and daughter shared a room and bath, and the only guest room had two narrow beds and a tiny bathroom. Our guide said it was often shared by visiting Supreme Court justices and cabinet members. I tried imagining James Baker and William Rehnquist sleeping side by side and taking turns in the toilet, and of course I could not. At the time I mistakenly thought this inflation of what people thought they needed and deserved was a phenomenon of the eighties, and confined to the elite.

The *Examiner*'s distinguished jury called the Dream House a "skillful blend of flexibility and formality." Only its art critic had the courage to say that the only dreams behind it had been "inspired by such TV shows as *Dynasty* and *Dallas*."

The security guard at Filoli's gate complained it was often his sad duty to turn away people who arrived without reservations. Some had flown thousands of miles to see the *Dynasty* house and there were often tears. It annoyed him they did not appreciate there was more to Filoli than *Dynasty*. It had also appeared in *Heaven Can Wait*, *Dying Young*, and *The Joy Luck Club*.

My tour group included three matrons wearing white gloves and carrying handbags, as if the Carringtons had invited them to tea. A Swiss woman and her daughter who had seen every episode hugged and squealed at their first view of the house. Our docent, "Harriet," had Katharine Hepburn's charming way of being testy and looked something like her, too, forcing a brittle smile while warning us not to step here or touch that. As we walked through the front door she said, "Try to imagine you have been invited to a party here. We arrive, a servant takes our coats, and—"

"What *kind* of a party?" a matron asked.

"Why do *you* care?" she snapped.

The parquet floors, marble fireplaces, and carved moldings clashed with the ragtag furniture assembled by donation and purchase. The trophy room displayed faded ribbons and tarnished cups won by horses dead before World War II. The study was a wood-paneled coffin smelling of cigars, leather, and dust. Gloomy murals of the Bourns' Irish estate decorated the seldom-used ballroom. Harriet drew our attention to where Bourn had ordered the family's nanny painted out as revenge for some long-forgotten crime. When she said, "The Bourns were really not happy here most of the time," no one in my group seemed surprised.

She told us the story of Filoli's two families piecemeal. William Bourn, Sr, was the son of a Boston merchant who had come during the Gold Rush and bought shares in the Empire Mine just before it became the richest in California. His son invested the inheritance in wine and water, building the Greystone Winery in St. Helena and buying the Spring Valley Water Company that supplied water to San Francisco from reservoirs filling the fault zone a few miles north of Filoli. He lived a typical turn-of-the-century tycoon's life—the presidency of the Pacific Union Club and the San Francisco Symphony, a portrait by John Singer Sargent, and mansions in San Francisco, Grass Valley, and Ireland. The only surprises in his life were bad ones: a father who had shot himself on his twenty-fifth wedding anniversary, a brother who fell from a wall and died at age eleven, and a daughter who died of pneumonia contracted while crossing the Atlantic, a particularly cruel tragedy since she was returning from the Irish estate Bourn had purchased to persuade her husband to abandon his career as a British colonial magistrate in the East African countries he considered too unhealthy for the newlyweds.

Bourn suffered a crippling stroke three years after moving into Filoli, even before workmen had finished his gardens and tennis court. He spent his next fifteen years in a wheelchair watching from the second-floor winter garden as employees tended his fabulous gardens. His wife fell ill and joined him, perhaps explaining why Filoli still had the feel of an expensive nursing home.

Harriet had less to say about William and Lurline Roth, who had bought Filoli from the Bourn estate. She had been the daughter of Captain William Matson, founder of Matson Navigation, and he had become chairman and president after his fortunate marriage. She bred horses and gardened. Anyone looking for a high point in her life would pick 1975, when she donated Filoli to the National Trust for Historic Preservation after learning a prospective buyer planned subdividing it for golf condominiums.

Harriet struggled bravely to turn the thin gruel of these privileged lives into a forty-five-minute narrative worthy of the house. So we learned Mrs. Bourn founded the Hillsborough Garden Club and held a tea party for her friends every afternoon. We heard about the theft of two chess pieces during a debutante party, and the Roth twins being chauffeured every day to a private school in San Francisco. The Roths had converted a safe in the study into a wine cellar, and been photographed by Fabian Bachrach. Mrs. Roth had won a trophy for Best Horse in Show at the 1933 San Francisco horse show. In 1926 a tennis tournament was rained out, forcing everyone to play Ping-Pong in the ballroom. In their final years the Bourns had thrown parties they never attended, staying upstairs throughout the evening and never greeting their puzzled guests.

Several elderly volunteers stood at counters in the vast kitchen surrounded by herbs and dried flowers, making potpourri to be sold at a Christmas bazaar. One ingredient was a "secret oil" handed down from the Roth family. None would reveal the contents. "Why, we could never tell," a lady said. "It was Lurline Roth's secret."

The lights on the servants' call box were still labeled "Mr. Roth," "Twins' Sitting Room," and "Trophy Room," and the docents discussed the Bourns and Roths as if they were relatives. There was a pecking order. A retired teacher who had once tutored the five children of a Roth chauffeur was the expert.

Four hundred of these volunteers led tours, served teas, sold books, and worked in the gardens, fussing over the house as if it was a spoiled child. Many were retirees living in nearby suburbs, and some must have been paying yardmen to weed their own gardens while they tended Filoli's flower beds. They agreed it was a "privilege" to work in these beautiful surroundings, and performed their chores with the good cheer of Hollywood nuns. They said they volunteered because they met so many nice people, but it seemed to me they were also starved for some kind of community life, for what novelist Wallace Stegner has identified as California's greatest failing, its lack of "deeply lived-in" places.

I had assumed "Filoli" was one of Mrs. Roth's exotic flowers or shrubs, but it turned out to be a combination of the first two letters of a motto concocted by the anglophile Bourn: "To Fight—to Love—to Live." The words were so banal and inappropriate, even to his descendants, that the stonemason carving FILOLI at the base of the Celtic cross overlooking their grave had mistakenly engraved TO FIGHT—TO LIVE—TO LIVE, and no one bothered to have it corrected.

26

The Ghost of
Toys "Я" Us

The great-granddaughter of Susan Ferguson, the girl injured by the falling oak tree in Bruff's camp, is a woman named Vida Benson who lives just south of Filoli in Los Gatos, a pleasant town a few miles east of the fault in the foothills of the Santa Cruz Mountains. The Simmerley sisters believed Benson knew a great deal about the tree incident, and owned diaries or articles written by her family mentioning Bruff.

When I met her and her husband in their retirement home, I was encouraged by the thick stack of articles and photographs she had assembled. She was a fine-looking woman in her late seventies who had acquired the bearing and diction of a stage actress while teaching English at Los Gatos High. She remembered her great-grandmother Susan as a sparrowlike lady who wore a shawl and liked tatting lace for handkerchiefs, and often exclaimed, "Oh pshaw!" Her family had started across the continent in a train of thirty wagons, but hardship, cholera, and a fear of Indian raids had shrunk it to just the Fergusons and Alfords by the time they reached Bruff's camp. And that, she apologized, was the only reference to Bruff she could recall Susan Ferguson making, simply that they had stopped in his camp.

Her great-uncles had frequently spoken about the crossing when she was a girl, but also without naming Bruff. They had settled around Yuba City and Healdsburg, and in 1918 Henry and John Ferguson had written an article titled "A Trip to California." Four years later his younger brother Paris, five at the time of the crossing, published his account in the *Healdsburg Tribune*.

She had made copies for me. Neither narrative mentioned Bruff

228

except to refer to his camp, but the account by Henry and John, who had been eleven and thirteen at the time, confirmed the accuracy of Bruff's account of the falling oak, reinforcing his reputation for scrupulous reporting, and making his version of his betrayal more credible.

The Ferguson brothers had not set their account to paper until sixty-nine years afterward, but it had the easy immediacy that comes from decades of retelling. They explained how the slope of the ground and the shape of the tree had spared them, while killing the Alford men. They recounted the "frantic wailing and mourning" and "heart-rending sighs" of the Alford women, adding that, "during the remainder of the night a heavy snow fell, making a white winding-sheet that covered the dead bodies to a depth of six or eight inches, thus adding sadness to the awful scene."

Their article also made Bruff's description of his sufferings that winter even more believable and compelling. After staying several days in Bruff's camp so their sisters could recover from their injuries, their family traveled eight miles to a place below the snowbelt called Steep Hollow. There they met an emigrant returning from the settlements with a wagon and oxen to retrieve his belongings. He agreed to transport the Fergusons to the valley, and everyone left with him except John and Henry, who stayed behind on their father's orders to guard the wagon and remaining possessions until he could return with fresh animals. Although the Ferguson boys were younger, stronger, and in better health than Bruff, had camped in a milder climate below the snowbelt, and were on their own three weeks instead of five months, they remembered those weeks as the greatest trial of the crossing. They were afraid to hunt because the country was infested with grizzly bears who left tracks around their wagon every morning. They became so desperate that, like Bruff, they resorted to woodpecker soup. But unlike him they were rescued at the end of November. Their father honored his pledge to return with a fresh team of oxen and rescued them before the worst of the winter. It was more proof Bruff's comrades could have honored their promise to him.

My interest in Bruff's sufferings led me to study the more notorious Donner Party, which had been snowbound in the Sierra Nevada pass now bearing their name in 1846. The Donners led me to Martin Murphy, Jr., who with his father had brought fifty relatives and friends across the same pass in 1844, becoming the first white men ever to use it and trailblazing a route later used by the transcontinental railway and Interstate 80.

The Murphys could lay claim to a number of firsts. They were the first emigrant party to arrive via the Sierras in covered wagons, winter in the Sierras, bring oxen across the plains, and lay eyes on Lake Tahoe. Martin Murphy, Jr.'s daughter was the first child of American emigrants born in California, and the Bear Flag rebellion from Mexico was planned at his ranchero.

The Donners were rewarded for their notorious botch of the crossing by having Donner Pass, Donner State Park, Donner ski ranch, Donner Road, and Donner Lake named in their honor.

I could not find a single Sierra Nevada acre or tree celebrating the skillful Murphys.

I suspected they had been shortchanged because of their Irish name, so I was pleased when I came across them in my *WPA Guide to California*. This was published in 1939 by the Federal Writers' Project, a New Deal program that put unemployed writers to work. Its seven-hundred pages of fine print describe the history and landscape of virtually every California small town and crossroads in still-unequaled detail. Some of its physical descriptions may be obsolete (lettuce and artichokes no longer cover Daly City's hills), but those of mountain lakes "guarded by granite cliffs surrounded by tier upon tier of dark green pine," remain accurate, as does its identification of historical sites. Without the *WPA Guide* I would never have known that the town fathers of upper-middle-class Saratoga had abandoned its original name, McCarthysville, apparently preferring the name of an upper-class New York resort to that of the Irishman who laid out the streets. Nor known that in the nearby thriving little Silicon Valley city of Sunnyvale, "among fig trees grown from mission cuttings stands the two-story white Martin Murphy Jr. house, framed in Boston and shipped round the Horn when the Murphy family settled here in 1849."

This house, Bayview Ranch, was either the first frame house in Santa Clara County or in California, depending upon who you believed. It had been made in Bangor, Maine, shipped around Cape Horn, and erected in 1851. Photographs show a rambling farmhouse with a gable roof and an unusually deep veranda enclosed by wings, an attempt by Bangor's snowbound carpenters to adapt a New England design to a hotter climate. It quickly became a hub of early California life and was where the state supreme court held its first session, San Francisco's first archbishop conducted services, and the Murphys celebrated their golden wedding anniversary in 1884. This was "the most fabulous social event ever held in California," according to one histo-

The Ghost of Toys "Я" Us   231

rian, and a symbolic culmination of a life of legendary generosity. The Murphys published an open invitation in the San Jose newspaper and chartered trains. Ten thousand guests waltzed on dance floors erected under the oaks and sat at barbecue tables built to accommodate a thousand at a time. Smoked hams and roast chicken were counted by the wagon load and salads came in bushel baskets. The champagne filled a Union Pacific freight car.

Murphy died three years later. His obituary in the *San Jose Mercury* said, "Seldom has an event transpired within the city's history that has caused so general a feeling of sadness and regret." It recalled how unlike other large landholders he had offered squatters food and clothing instead of expelling them. Anyone with a sad story received a low-interest loan recorded on scraps of paper he often "mislaid." Mourners had attended his services, it reported, to glimpse "a face they had learned to love."

His Bayview Ranch remained in the family, occupied by a daughter, then a granddaughter. In 1941, the *Mercury* praised the "genuine simplicity of its architecture and the strength of materials." It was one of the county's "historic showplaces," a "forerunner of modern prefabricated homes," that stood "serenely in the tranquil atmosphere of its park-like ground." It had come "the long way 'round to California, and it means to stay a long, long time."

My 1992 edition of the *H. M. Gousha Street Map of San Jose* showed Murphy Park as a small green square just off North Murphy Avenue, at the end of the Saratoga-Sunnyvale Road. A red "26" marked the middle of the park and a box titled "Places of Interest" identified it as the Murphy home.

I drove there through a Sunnyvale that was no longer the "quiet ranchers' trade center" of three thousand described by the *WPA Guide*. During the Second World War and early days of the Cold War, it had become a booming industrial center and the incubator for Silicon Valley's high-tech companies. Now it was a thriving city of 120,000 boasting a median family income of $53,000, fine parks, a first-class library, and handsome civic center. A recent *New York Times* article praised its government as a marvel of efficiency that processed building permits in twenty-four hours and removed graffiti in forty-eight, avoided layoffs during the recession, and had declared a $30 million tax surplus. President Clinton and Vice President Gore had both declared it a model for their plan to reinvent government. "Here the mantras are performance-based budgeting and results oriented management," the *Times* said, "with a network of computers humming watchfully in the background."

On the way to Murphy Park I stopped for a bowl of Vietnamese soup on Murphy Avenue. It had once been Sunnyvale's main street, where veterans marched in parades and families walked to the cinema. Now every block except this one had been leveled for a shopping mall, and it had become the only thing worse than a skid row—a failed skid-row renovation. Sunnyvale had tried all the usual tricks: concrete planters, park benches, antique street lamps, and a cute name, "Murphy Station District." Nothing had worked. The entrepreneur who had failed to convert a pornography house into a family theater told the *Sunnyvale Scribe*, "If Martin Murphy were alive I'd bet he'd be irate over what happened to his fine ranch."

Murphy Park was across the tracks and surrounded by World War II era tract housing. A marker on a boulder said, HOME OF MARTIN MURPHY, JR. CALIFORNIA REGISTERED HISTORIC LANDMARK NO. 644. It was more forthcoming than the Indian Island marker, and described the Murphy overland expedition before concluding, "Members of the Murphy family lived here continuously until 1953, when the property was acquired by the city of Sunnyvale."

But lived where? There was no house, only a one-story concrete building resembling two copulating service stations. The marker was dated 1960 and certainly made it sound as if Murphy's house had survived until then. Nothing was said about it being lost to a fire or earthquake, nor had it been razed for a freeway or factory since its grounds, including Murphy's famous trees, had survived.

The building was locked. A sign said SUNNYVALE HISTORICAL MUSEUM, but all I could see through a window were trestle tables in an empty room.

A woman who was throwing a ball to her grandson, two elderly men playing checkers, and a workman drinking a Colt .45 all claimed to frequent the park. None had the slightest idea who Murphy was, or what had happened to his house.

A file in the Sunnyvale Library solved the mystery by revealing that on September 28, 1961, the city had demolished Murphy's Bayview Ranch. At the time a spokesman for the Sunnyvale Historical Society said, "Before plans . . . to restore the historic home could be realized the house fell to the bulldozer's blade." The city had acquired it in 1953 after the death of Murphy's granddaughter ended a century of Murphy residence. It was left empty, a policy almost guaranteeing the vandalism and suspicious small fires that followed. Some citizens formed an historical society, hired a caretaker, and lobbied to have it made a state historic landmark. California agreed to pay for restoration if Sunnyvale assumed yearly maintenance, estimated at about $22,000. The city council refused, voting in 1961 to follow the recommendation of its parks department to replace the ranch with a "beautiful city park." An article describing this meeting said, "No one came forward to address the council in favor of saving the Murphy home."

Sunnyvale later erected the "multi-use community building" I had seen without bothering to replace the marker. The historical society was given a six-hundred-square-foot room to exhibit Murphy family portraits and other artifacts from Sunnyvale's past. It was open ten hours a week and mostly visited by local school groups. When the historical society asked for more space, the city answered it would be too expensive, particularly considering the lack of interest in Sunnyvale's history and the Murphy family. One councilman opposing it said spending any of the town's huge surplus on a museum was "just out of line." There was, he argued, "just no audience for this."

If I were Martin Murphy, Jr., I would have haunted the city-council chambers instead of the Sunnyvale Toys "Я" Us at 130 East El Camino Real. But lacking a house to haunt, so the story went, his ghost had taken up residence in a store built over his horse stables and riding oval.

I have children, so of course I have been in a Toys "Я" Us. Except for Murphy's ghost this one was like all the rest, with Walkmen and Nintendos locked in cases like the crown jewels, aisles of pink, heart-shaped girl toys, transparent public-relations gimmicks like banishing poker chips while selling violent video games, gigantic shopping carts that made parents who failed to fill them feel like pikers, and board games like "Electronic Mall Madness—the talking Shopping Spree Game (Press the button. Insert your credit card. You never know what the voice of the mall has 'in store' for you!") designed to train the next generation of consumers.

It was an improbable place for a haunting, and more likely to terrify a nineteenth-century ghost than vice versa. The clattering carts, hurdy-gurdy computer music, and rattling trolleys serving up jumbo cartons of Huggies would have drowned the loudest *Boo!* And how could a few ghostly tricks compete with a Gameboy?

Lillian O'Brien had lived with the Toys "Я" Us ghost longer than any other clerk. She had a tough-sounding nickname, "Putt-Putt," and the leathery face and gravelly voice of a truck-stop waitress. But she obviously loved children and described her Toys "Я" Us career as "Eighteen Christmases." She believed the ghost had a mischievous Irish sense of humor, and told me most employees were more amused than frightened.

The haunting started in the early seventies when a doll with no movable parts cried "Mama" whenever clerks tried closing her box. Some mornings they found roller skates arranged in bizarre patterns on the floor, or a teddy bear sitting five aisles from where he was sold, yet the store's alarm system was undisturbed. The ghost played with faucets and lights. He caressed one clerk's long blond hair. He whispered to another, "I hate crowds."

Putt-Putt had seen a Care Bear fly off a shelf and encountered Murphy in the stockroom, wearing a white shirt and calling her name. He was a friendly ghost, a real Casper, and local teenagers often begged to spend the night. "To be honest," she said, "he's been good for business." After the television series *That's Incredible!* interviewed her for a 1980 segment about the haunting, people from foreign countries showed up, asking directions to the cold spots.

She took me to the game wall to see if I could feel one. "See how the temperature changes!" she declared. "Some customers complain about puffs of cold air, like he's breathing on you."

I thought it was as stuffy as the rest of the store.

We crept down aisle four. It sat over the former horse oval and was Murphy's favorite place for moving toys and whispering. Its fluorescent lamps sometimes announced his arrival with revolving spiral lights.

We poked around gift wrapping where, when psychic Sylvia Brown had held a séance for the *That's Incredible!* crew, a beanbag had tumbled to the floor and a cameraman filmed dancing blobs of light. Putt-Putt pointed out the stockroom and said, "Whenever I have to go in, I bless myself and I tell him, 'It's just me, going to work.' Although of course I'm Catholic, so I don't believe in ghosts."

She left me with a department head named Margie Hainzle, who believed Murphy's ghost was a practical joker. She had seen piñatas crash to the floor and a plastic lunch box fall on a customer who was busy arguing the ghost was a hoax. He played with the computer when she was using it, and punched the total key while she was adding the day's receipts. He particularly liked caressing her blond hair. She tossed it and smiled. It was her best feature. When she was a girl growing up in Miami she had seen the famous *That's Incredible!* segment. Now that she was working in the same store with the same famous ghost, she felt an eerie circle had been closed.

I spent an hour circling the aisles, waiting for Murphy to loft a Day-Glo Frisbee or send a Barbie dancing off its shelf. Until *That's Incredible!* it had always been assumed the ghost was Murphy. They both had the same gentle sense of humor, and at the Sunnyvale archives a clerk had found a note reading, "It is said that the ghost of Martin Murphy is seen on the nights of the full moon." But then a psychic suggested the ghost was not Murphy at all but "Johnnie Johnson," an itinerant preacher and ranch hand who had fallen for Murphy's daughter Elizabeth. On the very night he planned to declare his love, she had announced her engagement to another man. The next day he killed himself with an ax in the orchard that became the Toys "Я" Us parking lot.

The *Cupertino Courier* remarked that "the credibility of this remarkable tale is debatable." A former president of the Sunnyvale Historical Society had never heard of Johnson and could not imagine the genesis of the story. But the wire services circulated it and soon Murphy's name began disappearing from articles about the Toys "Я" Us ghost. Haunting a discount toy store was not much for the man who had blazed the California Trail, but it was something. At least while he was the official ghost, employees and journalists had to learn something about him. Once the more lurid Johnson replaced him, he returned to the oblivion reserved for pioneers whose houses were too modest to warrant preservation.

If Murphy *was* haunting Toys "Я" Us, I wondered if he regretted not listening to the friends who had urged him to replace his ranch with a grand California estate. He certainly could have afforded it. Instead, he had preferred remaining in the more modest home where he had raised his children. Perhaps he should have demolished Bayview Ranch, eliminated the free champagne, called in his generous loans, and built a Filoli.

27

The Fast-Food Flasher

I stopped in Saratoga because it is about five miles east of the fault, closer than any other Silicon Valley suburb. Its $7 million in damage during Loma Prieta sounded like a lot until I saw a brochure listing a "prime acre" for $750,000 and an "affordable" family home on a third of an acre for $495,000. It was the kind of town where damage gets repaired quickly and I drove down its manicured streets looking in vain for a cracked wall so I could have an excuse to ring a doorbell and defy the octagonal signs promising trespassers an "armed response."

One real-estate advertisement called Saratoga an "accessible dream" and it did seem a pleasant trophy for success in the office parks below. Most Californians would probably say it was as close to the Dream, accessible or not, as you could hope to get. The weather was a delightful succession of spring days. Houses looked up to the Santa Cruz Mountains or down onto the tight grid of less fortunate valley suburbs. Its quaint main street smelled of coffee and fresh bread. On weekends, children wore karate robes, leotards, and soccer uniforms, and teenagers cruised around in their parents' discarded imports. It had the lowest crime rate in Santa Clara County, and the highest percentage of high-school students bound for college. It was illegal to put a FOR SALE sign in a parked car and you could be jailed for cutting down an oak.

This week the front page of the *Saratoga News* had a photograph of the National Charity League Mothers and Daughters showing two handsome women helping four beautiful teenagers fill paper sandwich bags with "rice and beans for farmworker families in need." The girls had decorated them with stickers and happy cartoon faces. One had written, "Enjoy!"

The midmorning conversations at the International Coffee Exchange concerned food and exercise. I overheard some young mothers planning Thanksgiving dinner a month ahead. Men my age in fancy biking duds sprawled at the outdoor tables, eyes closed, racing caps turned backward, faces to the sun. A man with a thick mustache who had shaved his legs to increase his racing speed told me he was "retired." But his newspaper lay open to the classifieds and his naked legs jiggled like tickertape keys.

To disguise my eavesdropping I opened the *Saratoga News* and read, "Students Arrested For Gang-Related Violence." The gang called itself the "Insane Hoods" and strike teams from the sheriff's office had arrested sixteen last week, removing them from area high schools in handcuffs. Eight came from Saratoga and warrants charged them with attempting to incite riot, making threats, and felony battery that included sending one boy to the hospital with a ruptured eardrum and shattered jaw. A gang intelligence officer said they had over one hundred active members, most from middle- to upper-income families. They copied the "values" of ghetto gangs, beating up kids because gangs on television did. It was violence as an attitude.

Saratoga contracted with the county for police services, so Captain Bob Wilson, who commanded the Westside substation in Saratoga, was the de facto police chief of Saratoga and four neighboring communities. Had he been elected or appointed by the town, I wondered if he would have dragged the sixteen-year-old sons of upper-class taxpayers from school in handcuffs, or speculated so freely as to why some Saratoga teenagers preferred terrorizing classmates to filling bags with rice and beans for campesinos.

He was an articulate, intellectual man, and it was easy to imagine him in a blazer, working as a corporate chief of security. He brought certain handicaps to the task of sympathizing with the Insane Hoods. He had himself escaped a gang-plagued neighborhood in Indianapolis, and spent many of his twenty-five years in the department policing the east San Jose barrios. There the gang problem was easily understood. Families were poor and unstable, and boys joined for friendship, a family structure, and to make money. When he said, "One fight with a real barrio gang and the Insane Hoods would be dog meat," I suspected I was hearing a satisfying daydream.

Saratoga had known about its Hoods and only two sets of parents seemed surprised by their sons' arrest. Besides the charges listed in the newspapers, they had trashed homes and intimidated kids with guns. In jail they had attempted to lynch a prisoner they suspected of being gay. Some students had thanked the deputies afterward, claiming they had been too afraid to complain to parents or teachers.

The problem went beyond the Hoods, Wilson said. There was gang activity at the junior high, and last Halloween a riot had started at an unsupervised private party attended by two hundred teenagers. The parents owning the house were in Lake Tahoe or Palm Springs, he had forgotten which. There had been a keg, live band, and an admission fee. When his deputies responded, kids threw pumpkins through squad-car windows. The police handled it like a ghetto riot and formed a skirmish line. The kids scattered. One roving gang destroyed an empty house, another broke into a school and dumped gallons of motor oil on expensive hardwood floors. These were upper-middle-class to upper-class kids, destroying their own comfortable houses and schools.

He wondered if the recession was to blame. Some executives had suddenly gone from six figures to nothing and his deputies were finding themselves intervening in barrio-type family conflicts. There was also not much for kids to do. After-school jobs were scarce because many yards were too small to require much maintenance, and most of the restaurants were too serious to employ teenagers. Some neighborhoods had no sidewalks, and kids living in the hills were isolated if both parents worked and they were too young to drive. The problem was less working mothers than Saratoga's suburban geography: rural kids had open space, urban kids had mobility, but many of these kids had neither. Some were into after-school activities, but some went home to empty half-million-dollar houses filled with expensive toys. He had seen latchkey kids in San Jose. In Saratoga, the locks were nicer.

He was too diplomatic to blame the parents, but he did think Saratoga's ordinance prohibiting the high-school football team from playing home games had caused resentment. It had succeeded in eliminating noise, bright lights, and crowds of unruly out-of-town fans, but gave students a sense of grievance. Incidents involving the Hoods had often occurred at these away games.

He offered me a "ride-along," an opportunity to spend a busy Friday or Saturday swing shift on patrol with a deputy. If I was lucky we might intervene in a domestic dispute in a mansion, or be called to break up an Insane Hood party at the home of weekending parents.

My first inclination was to pass. It would mean staying another four days in Silicon Valley and I was eager to reach Parkfield, where the USGS had invested $20 million in experiments based on its prediction of a 95-percent chance of a strong earthquake striking that segment of the San Andreas during a five-year window that would soon be closing. But after spending the afternoon driving around Redwood City, Cupertino, Sunnyvale, and San Jose, I changed my mind and decided to accept, mainly because his offer amounted to ten hours of a free car and driver.

It was difficult to see much of these towns otherwise. The malls and shopping centers were set far back from the road behind parking lots, and it was hard to check them out and negotiate the heavy traffic. Since one freeway interchange, office park, and strip mall looked like the next, getting lost was easy. Walking was impossible, riding a bike impractical, and it was hard having casual exchanges with strangers who drove locked cars and parked in guarded lots. Along the north coast, gas stations had been good places for meeting people, but here they were designed to protect employees from customers and you paid a cashier in an upright Plexiglas coffin before you pumped, a double reminder of how little you were trusted. It was no good trying to talk to people at the Kmarts or Long's Drugs either. They were not places to linger, and the clerks were busy and bored. Most towns no longer had thriving downtowns because, despite the advertising nostalgia for Norman Rockwell Main Street America, Californians were like most Americans: cold-blooded community killers, ready to administer the coup de grâce to merchants who had sponsored decades of Little League teams and high-school yearbooks in order to shave some pennies off a tube of Colgate.

The shopping malls were the zebra mussels of community life, killing other species and leaving the water as suspiciously clear as an acid-rain-plagued Adirondack pond. They eliminated the two great rewards of travel, diversity and surprise, and because they were virtually identical, they defied description. Forty-five minutes from home I could find the same chain stores, bad air, piped-in music, fast-food court, multiplex, and shoe-box stores built without angles to discourage shoplifters, walk similar corridors twisting just enough to conceal the distance to the next anchor store, and experience the same feeling of being a participant in one's own con that is the principal feature of any casino. So I called Captain Wilson back and gratefully accepted his ride-along, telling myself the best way to see a place that is hard on the single traveler, and to meet people fearful of strangers, is from the front seat of a squad car.

The sergeant I will call "Grief" who was assigned to take me on the ride-along was a muscular young man with a drill-instructor posture, a G.I. Joe doll come to life. He said more Insane Hoods had been arrested since Monday and the Gang Intelligence Unit believed the others were lying low. We would be patrolling Cupertino. It was more middle class and had more crime than Saratoga, but if that town's rich teenagers caused trouble, we would certainly be called to assist. Meanwhile he had been told to watch for an overweight white male in his early twenties with shoulder-length dirty-blond hair driving a battered white compact with a black right front fender that was filled with trash. The suspect liked exposing himself to junior-high girls. Sometimes he chased them with a club.

Grief admitted being suspicious of rattletraps. In a suburb without skid rows or Main Streets, cars were all you saw, and he tended to run the shabbiest through the computer. Otherwise policing Cupertino was a geometric exercise, up and down and back and forth the same grid of streets and boulevards, again and again. We began his four P.M. to two A.M. shift by circling a fast-food strip and the Apple Computer campus. He knew the shopping center parking lots like a bobby knows the East End's alleys and could drive through interconnected ones without joining the traffic.

When I mentioned that the newer subdivisions had the highest walls, he smiled and said, "You've noticed." Then he pointed to some red tile roofs circled by walls flying pennants like some medieval city-state and said, "Ten years ago I jogged through that orchard."

Ever since graduating from his Pennsylvania high school, he had dreamed of living in California. He joined the air force and specialized in law enforcement so he could become a California policeman. When he joined the sheriff's department in 1979, Santa Clara County had seemed a golden place of open land and safe streets. Since then he had moved to a cabin in the mountains. "Redwoods, blue jays, and squirrels, that's for me," he said, making it clear Cupertino was not. He spoke about these valley suburbs with the detachment and disdain you expect from an officer policing the inner city. He had grown up in a row-house neighborhood where several generations of one family lived together and neighbors knew each other's birthdays and raised each other's children. He was amazed by people living in tract mansions separated by a few yards, and neighbors meeting for the first time in court while suing one another.

The kids shocked him most. He answered 911 calls about out-of-control teenagers and arrived to find thirteen-year-olds screaming "fuck you!" at their parents. A mother telephoned saying her sons had ordered her to drive them to a nearby school so they could join a gang fight. What should she do? She hated to say no. The Saratoga teenagers rioting last Halloween had been "rich kids, kids who have all the advantages," he said in a voice making it clear he had not. "Kids from poorer neighborhoods have more respect for nice things. They understand how much work it takes to buy them."

Cops working a ghetto usually have a cop bar near the station house that is an oasis from the street life. Grief's equivalent was Cupertino's last farm. The clapboard house sat high on an empty ridge, but underneath a tangle of high-tension wires. We arrived at dusk, just as streetlights and headlights were clicking on below. A woman in a Dale Evans shirt brought us coffee. She thought she lived closer to the fault than anyone in Cupertino and pointed out its path along the crest of the Santa Cruz Mountains. Loma Prieta had set her truck dancing and her power lines singing. Moments before, her horses had torn around the corral bucking and snorting, crazy with fear. She rented the farm from the Catholic church that had inherited it and would someday plow it up for a cemetery. Her boys had driven tractors, milked cows, and turned out well. Most Cupertino teenagers were starved for space and physical labor. She said, "I can tell you I raised a lot more than my own kids up here."

Fifteen minutes later we were checking the rush-hour traffic on Stevens Creek Boulevard for speeders and battered white cars. At 7:30 P.M. Grief said, "Now the nervous calls begin," and sure enough, Cupertino was suddenly alive with nosey parkers. The complaints came mostly from women whom I imagined raising the slat of a blind, then dashing for the phone to report a slow-moving car or strange man on foot. An Asian salesman was reported to be "acting funny" and "out too late." A brown Buick had been cruising back streets before parking in a remote corner of the T.J. Maxx lot. We staked it out for an hour, watching as sprinklers watered concrete islets of weeds and stunted trees, and sent rivulets sluicing into gutters.

A liquor-store clerk tripped a silent alarm and made a hysterical call to 911. Grief swerved onto the sidewalk to pass stalled traffic, almost hitting a boy on an unlighted bicycle. The clerk was a Pakistani who was furious we had taken so long. He had become frightened when a gang of Hispanics was "disrespectful." He was unapologetic and said, "All the time I am alone here, so I am scared."

A block away we stopped a dented white Toyota with a black right front fender being driven by a young man with long blond hair. Trash and dirty clothes filled the backseat. Grief whispered, "Bingo," and summoned another patrol car.

The boy had an obsequious smile and pretended to be delighted to pose for a Polaroid snapshot. When we released him because he had no prior record or outstanding warrant, he said, "Sure hope you catch him, sir."

"I think we already have," a deputy muttered.

Grief shook his head. "Not the guy, too skinny."

Ten minutes later we turned onto a dark residential street and almost rear-ended a battered white Nissan driven without headlights or license plates. It had a black right fender and another boy with blond hair at the wheel. This time when Grief demanded license and registration the boy threw the car into gear. Grief grabbed his filthy hair and shouted, "Turn off the engine! Right now, sir, or I'll have to shoot you."

When the boy hesitated he yanked him out of the door by his hair, threw him on the pavement, and handcuffed him. The boy arched his back and flopped like a fish. He was a generic deviate—dirty, overweight, unshaven, and pimply—the effeminate, soft-bodied fat boy everyone teases. His belt was loose and his zipper open. I could see the reddish-brown hairs covering his egg-shaped stomach thickening into a pubic triangle.

"We've caught him at work," Grief said.

An avalanche of dirty pictures and fast-food wrappings tumbled from the front seat onto the pavement. One look inside the car and I would never again argue that pornography and sexual violence were unrelated. Hard-core photographs wallpapered the dashboard and door panels. A loaded crossbow was angled so the tip of its arrow pierced a woman's clitoris. A farrago of filthy towels, jockey shorts, Taco Bell wrappings, and old Whopper boxes filled the backseat, the remains of weeks of flashing, masturbating, and fast-food feasting. The trunk contained clubs and bamboo poles wrapped in duct tape, and what appeared to be a bloodstained black cloak.

A tow truck arrived. When its driver saw the martial-arts clubs and defaced pornographic pictures, he whispered, "One sick puppy."

Grief was so elated he forgave the boy his attempted escape. "It's a normal human reaction, and I certainly don't hold it against him."

The dispatcher ran his name and reported he had just served eighteen months for molesting a child. After his release he had burrowed into the suburban service economy, becoming a bank teller and Pizza Hut deliveryman.

More deputies appeared. One praised Grief for "saving some kid from a nasty experience," another said he had only postponed the inevitable. The suspect would be jailed again, perhaps for three years. He would receive more "treatment," then be released.

The longer the boy remained facedown on the asphalt in the drizzle, unbuckled, shivering, and whimpering, the more I began to pity him. But the moment he was seated upright in the back of a squad car I saw a surly and unrepentant giant, a bogeyman who could give any little girl a lifetime of nightmares.

For over an hour the headlights and bubble lights of four squad cars and a tow truck had illuminated this tidy middle-class street like a movie set. I knew its residents were home because of the blue television glow visible behind shutters and curtains. During all this time not one person had stepped outside, or even opened a front door, although we could just as easily have been arresting a neighbor, or someone who had raped or murdered one. I noticed a woman, a man, and then a couple park in nearby driveways and hurry inside, showing no interest in what had happened just yards from their homes, a reaction in certain respects as disturbing and unsavory as the mutilated pornography and bloodstained cloak.

28

Lost Cats and "Smashed" Pigeons

The first thing I noticed about the United States Geological Survey office in Menlo Park was the absence of the checkpoints, security guards, briefcase searches, and paranoia common to most federal offices (although in the aftermath of the Oklahoma bomb, I imagine this has changed). The USGS employees were an informal and likable bunch who worked with their doors open, caucused in hallways, and huddled around seismographs like elephants at a water hole. The charts, maps, and graphs lining their corridors depicted "landslide susceptibility," "potential for debris flows," "potential for liquefaction," and "where quaking will be the most severe where the 1906 earthquake is repeated based on water saturation"—in short, who living where was most likely to live or die in the next great earthquake.

The high-school students on a tour could not have cared less. The girls blew purple gum bubbles and studied their manicures. The boys looked hungover but, believing they should be interested in things scientific, made a better attempt to conceal their boredom. If they could not be interested in the odds of being crushed to death by the roof of their school gym, they were probably lost to science.

The USGS public-affairs officer, Pat Jorgenson, was as breezy and honest as everyone I met at Menlo Park. She cheerfully admitted that although for years USGS had been lecturing Californians about preparing for earthquakes, it had failed to back up its instruments with emergency power sources, so its telephones and computers went down during Loma Prieta. She had been in her office and, as she jumped under her desk, thought, "Damn! There goes my evening."

244

Loma Prieta had disappointed her. The floors only *seemed* to wave. She hoped the Big One would catch her outdoors so she could see the earth undulate like a snake. The Menlo Park scientists attending an East Coast conference had cursed their bad luck. And why not? Imagine a brain surgeon missing his one chance in a lifetime to operate. They wanted to experience a great earthquake, but dreaded the casualties. When their beepers signaled a 4.0 or 5.0 they said, "Hey, we got a good one going—" then stopped in embarrassment.

She did not dismiss the claims of people like Jerry Hurley out of hand, but the USGS was responsible to the public and had to be sensitive to the consequences of a failed prediction. A panicky evacuation could kill people, and if they cried wolf too often, who would listen to a warning based on scientific principles? She sometimes heard from numerologists whose forecasts depended on the number of Apostles and the letters in Christ's name, from a woman in Woodside who based her predictions on house pets, and from someone who called whenever her teeth ached. Jim Berkland, the official geologist for Santa Clara County, used tide tables and classified advertisements for lost pets. Jack Coles of San Jose monitored radio waves and claimed to have predicted Loma Prieta. But I might do better walking down the hall and speaking to Bill Bakun about Parkfield.

Bakun told me, "The USGS makes geological-hazards warnings. The word *prediction* is taboo." He had been involved with Parkfield for much of his career, doing graduate research there and studying the historical pattern of its earthquakes. He and Alan Lindh, director of Menlo Park, concluded that a quake struck the Parkfield segment of the San Andreas an average of once every twenty-two years. If they were right, there was a 95-percent chance of a greater-than-magnitude-6.0 striking it between 1987 and January 1, 1993. Based on this research, the USGS had invested $20 million installing, monitoring, and maintaining a network of seismographs, creep meters, and laster Geodimeters in Parkfield to record the stresses and strains preceding the anticipated earthquake. If the devices picked up changes in groundwater levels, magnetic fields, electric currents, strain, and creep, scientists could decide if short-term predictions based on these factors were practical. If they recorded nothing, short-term earthquake predictions would appear less feasible. Even if an earthquake failed to strike Parkfield, the experiment would still produce useful data.

When we met, the end of his prediction window was six weeks away and he already appeared to have abandoned hope, saying he would not consider it "a big deal" if there was no earthquake in his time frame, but would be upset if an experiment already producing such useful data was abandoned. He was one of the scientists who according to Olga Kolbek had "pooh-poohed" the theory that fluctuations in her Old Faithful were linked to distant earthquakes. No matter how much you believed Parkfield had yielded valuable data, the Carnegie Institute's report did make it seem that to date Kolbek's geyser had done a better job of predicting earthquakes, and that it was more likely quakes triggered seismic events hundreds of miles away than that they were localized events following independent schedules on each segment of the fault.

To Bakun's credit, he was more rueful than defensive, even good-natured about "waiting for that dumb earthquake to happen." The 1980s and early 1990s had delivered such a full menu of seismological surprises that Parkfield's failure to perform on schedule seemed like small potatoes. He could even laugh about how Loma Prieta had caught him at the urinal. The lights failed but there was no panic because everyone was too busy and excited to be afraid. "We love a big earthquake because it's what our careers are all about," he said. "You realize it's a tragedy, but you're delighted by the wonderful data."

I came back a few days later to meet Robert Wallace, the Grand Old Man of the San Andreas Fault. His 1946 Caltech thesis had been the first detailed geological study of a fault segment, and he was one of the pioneers who had mapped the fault and made it a household word. He had held senior USGS positions in Menlo and Washington, and accompanied Dan Rather on a helicopter tour of the fault after Loma Prieta. He was silver-haired, courtly, and confident, perfect for television. Like many grand old men, he was offhand about his accomplishments, and more fascinated by how little he knew than by how much he had discovered. He remembered how in the early 1950s the San Andreas had not been properly charted and geological wall maps showed vast areas as "unmapped." Even now scientists disagreed on basic questions such as what stresses and factors produced a quake, whether one precluded another one occurring in quick succession on the same fault segment, or if it was a good idea to predict them at all, considering the social and economic costs of a failed prediction. A forty-member panel of scientists had recently split down the middle on whether a general forecast such as "a 60-percent chance of a major earthquake on a southern segment of the San Andreas in the next thirty years" was too optimistic or pessimistic. Earthquakes were mystifying, frustrating, and elusive. Studying them was almost as humbling as experiencing them.

He believed reliable short-term earthquake forecasting was achievable, and during his acceptance speech for the Medal of the Seismological Society in America had called it "the most fundamental ingredient in any rational approach to earthquake hazard mitigation." He likened it to weather forecasting and hoped people would eventually watch a strain in a fault move across a region, just as they did a weather front, knowing with a high degree of certainty when and where a flurry of seismic activity would occur. Earthquake prediction had to start with the fundamental principle that before something broke, it had to bend. The Parkfield experiment made sense because it was trying to determine how to measure this bending. The "more fun things"—abnormal animal behavior, earthquake lights, sensitives, geysers, and radio waves—were worth study, but there was not enough money available to pursue them at the expense of more essential research.

He was more gentle than most scientists about Jim Berkland, the Santa Clara County geologist claiming an ability to predict earthquakes using lunar and tidal tables and newspaper advertisements for lost pets. He thought him articulate and smart, but cursed by a lifelong need for attention. While working for the USGS, he had eaten a poisonous mushroom and almost died. The next day he ate a smaller sample, and almost died again. That was Jim Berkland.

Before I left he gave me a reprint of an article he had published in 1980 titled "Prediction of the Sungpan-Pinwu Earthquakes, August 1976." It described the "impressive achievement" of the Chinese government in predicting three large earthquakes within a day of their occurrence, and substantially reducing potential casualties through evacuation and other precautions. Chinese scientists had based their forecast on a combination of physical, chemical, and biological phenomena, including falling groundwater and well levels, changes in the taste, color, and odor of well water, outbursts of natural gas from rock fissures, a marked increase in seismicity, and unusual noises known in China for centuries as the "sounds of the mountains." Several months before the earthquake, these sounds were heard as a low rumbling; several hours before, they reached a higher frequency, came in short bursts, and could be likened to the sound of frogs. The final noises reminded observers of torrents of water or ripping cloth. People reported earthquake lights resembling meteors or UFOs. Nausea plagued peasants living near faults, and there was an abnormal growth and withering of plant life. Fruit trees bloomed a second time, and a drop in groundwater withered bamboo along fault lines, confusing the pandas.

Wallace had reprinted photographs from China illustrating abnormal animal behavior. One look at these grainy snapshots of a domestic rabbit who had climbed onto a roof, pigs fighting to escape a pen, and rats running down power lines, and I knew I could not leave Santa Clara County without asking Jim Berkland how many cats had gone missing in San Jose last week.

Much as I liked the USGS scientists, they were too cautious to predict an earthquake for me. But Jim Berkland would, gladly. The only question was whether his prediction was worth anything. A USGS scientist named Jerry Eaton had told *The Wall Street Journal*, "We've known this guy throughout his professional life, and he's distinguished himself by being a clown the entire time." He thought Berkland's theories were "*Reader's Digest* science . . . pure hokum." Senior geologist Ed Bortugno at the California Office of Emergency Services conceded he was a "very good geologist," but thought his predictions were "bull."

Berkland replied to the criticism by claiming 80 percent of the 270 predictions he had made since 1974 had proven accurate. But although he had a degree in geology from Berkeley, a doctorate from Davis, and had taught college-level geology before Santa Clara County made him its first official geologist, and although he had worked ten years for various government agencies including the USGS, discovering a shrew fossil in Oregon afterward named *Adeloblarina berklandi*, an unmistakable carnival hoopla did surround his predictions.

Dial 900-226-JOLT (two dollars for the first minute and one dollar each additional) and you reached *Quakeline*, his earthquake warning service that offered a psychic among its menu of options.

Subscribe to his *SYZYGY . . . An Earthquake Newsletter*, and you received four chatty pages beginning "Hello Folks," offering warnings like, "Get ready for a shaky summer," and featuring the Pet of the Month. Recent ones had included Humphrey the Humpbacked Whale, a calico aranda (goldfish) belonging to Jean Simpson of Salinas named Rootbeer, who floated upside down before earthquakes, and Michael Bennette's hamster, "Dribbles," who had spun squeaking in circles four minutes before Loma Prieta.

A Berkland prediction might depend on springs, geysers, and disappointing pigeon races coinciding with certain alignments of the sun, earth, and moon. On Sunday October 21, 1990, his *Quakeline* had predicted a 3.0-to-5.5 within seventy miles of San Jose by October 26 based upon, "(1) a disoriented whale spotted in the South Bay, (2) the above average tides accompanying the New Moon of October 18, and (3) highest level for 1990 of missing cat ads in the *San Jose Mercury* on October 19, when the count reached 23 (compared with the 27 ads before the Loma Prieta quake)."

Two days later, the strongest California earthquake in a year struck near Mono Lake and was felt 170 miles west in the Bay Area.

On October 13, 1989, a short article headlined IS "WORLD SERIES" QUAKE COMING? in the *Gilroy Dispatch* said, "While the Bay Area is rumbling with excitement over the first-ever Bay Bridge World Series, the earth may be putting on its own show. A county geologist is predicting an earthquake to hit the Bay Area anytime from tomorrow [October 14] to the 21st of October. It will be the 'World Series Quake,' according to Santa Clara County geologist Jim Berkland. The temblor, he predicts, could be anywhere from 3.5 to 6.0 on the Richter scale. Berkland is basing his prediction on the unusual gravitational pulls of the moon and earth."

After Loma Prieta struck on October 17, the *Hollister Freelance* proclaimed, "If predicting earthquakes was a game, Jim Berkland would be the Babe Ruth of shakers."

Despite all this, what Berkland called "High Science" still dismissed him as a crank. Conventional seismologists argued that using tide tables and lunar schedules was a discredited technique and world seismicity catalogs showed the alignment of planets had not predicted periods of great seismicity. They claimed he had made more failed predictions than he admitted and seriously underestimated the magnitude of Loma Prieta; that just like people, animals sometimes behaved strangely for no specific reason; and that because California was so seismically active, any prediction relying on a "seismic window" of several weeks hedged with a "probability" of 70 to 80 percent was a reasonable gamble.

But even if you conceded High Science all these points, you could not escape the fact that Berkland had been an early advocate of some far-out theories that had recently become less so. He had believed in the forecasting possibilities of the Calistoga geyser since the late 1970s, often calling Kolbek and basing his forecast of the November 1980 Eureka earthquake on her geyser's behavior. He had suggested for years that seismic events hundreds of miles apart might be related, even arguing that 1906 had transmitted stress five hundred miles south along the fault, triggering a 6.5 striking Brawley the same afternoon. His May 1992 *SYZYGY* ridiculed High Science for arguing there was no connection between the Desert Hot Springs 6.1 of April 22, 1992, and the swarm of six-plus-magnitude earthquakes in Ferndale and Scotia three and four days later. "What arrogance!" he wrote. "The only honest answer would be 'We are not sure.'"

Two months later, High Science admitted earthquakes might indeed be triggering distant seismic events.

His house was a monument to his obsession. Charts, ledgers, and boxes of files swamped his kitchen and dining room. Everywhere I saw bookshelves without space for another book and files without room for another piece of paper. Graphs even covered his refrigerator door.

He had a flat, Scandinavian face and a sweet, triumphant smile I saw whenever he pulled another fistful of proof from a cabinet in his packrat kitchen. He had acquired the salesman's and politician's skill of communicating at breakneck speed, compacting his pitch into the fifteen minutes or less I imagined he was allowed, if he was lucky, at whatever scientific conferences tolerated him.

He said he believed in tides and moons before pets. Then in 1979 a Xerox physicist had called his office saying, "The cats are disappearing again." He had been tracking them in classified advertisements since spring. Large numbers had vanished before the 4.4 in Pacifica because "the animals get the message and run away."

He was skeptical but soon was peeking at lost-pet ads in the furtive way one consults a horoscope. When his own cat, Rocky, went missing six days before a moderate earthquake, he began clipping classifieds from newspapers in Los Angeles, San Francisco, San Jose, and Oakland. Six months later Rocky came home, sleek and well fed. He wondered why he had deserted what had obviously been a comfortable second home. The answer came four days later when an earthquake shook Livermore.

Since then he had become a clearinghouse for seismically sensitive pet stories and had persuaded animal-control workers to report their weekly tallies. On a normal week they received four hundred calls, but the week before the 1980 Eureka earthquake they fielded 853 complaints of dogs wandering on highways and cows on the wrong side of a field. A Dr. Deshpande in India, who had documented abnormal animal behavior before subcontinent earthquakes, sent him a paper by Soviet scientists mentioning how an hour before the 1988 Armenian earthquake, "a very tame pet hamster bit his owner for the first and only time." A veterinarian reported crystals forming in the urinary tracts of cats just before an earthquake. This was a common cat complaint when a family added a dog or moved, but the vet noticed it happening at five times the usual rate just before earthquakes. A pigeon fancier in Danville called to report a "smash race" from Nevada occurring the same day as an earthquake. Some birds had taken twice as long to finish, others had not returned for days. Berkland had raised pigeons in high school and knew they circled when released, waiting for the deposit of magnetite behind their eyeballs to identify due north. It seemed obvious the magnetic energy preceding an earthquake was disturbing their sense of direction. So he went through a pigeon period, frequently calling the pigeon master at Morgan Hill to ask about smash races. One of the worst occurred during the Bishop–to–Los Angeles race of November 23, 1978, the same day as a 5.8 hit Mammoth Lakes just north of Bishop, two days after the eclipse of the sun, and a period when Southern California cats went missing in great numbers.

"Did you know that the most disastrous smash race in Santa Clara County, one in which only 10 percent of the birds found their way home, occurred on March 24, 1964?" he asked.

When I looked blank he exclaimed, "My God! Three days before the Good Friday earthquake in Alaska."

He was astonished I had not known that three weeks before Loma Prieta, two rare beaked whales had washed up on San Francisco's Ocean Beach, that the Japanese used catfish as seismic sensors, and earthquake predictions in Japan always prompted a run on fish suppliers, or that before the 1976 earthquake in northern Italy, every cat in one village vanished at the same time that herds of deer came down from the mountains.

There seemed to be no pet fancier with a story he would not hear out, no theory he would not entertain, except the one of a 95-percent chance of an earthquake occurring in Parkfield before the end of the year. His samples were too small to be scientifically reliable, but it was possible he had stumbled on some seismic precursors, and even if his theories reflected only coincidence, you had to admire his determination to push them.

He refined his methods during the 1980s, dropping San Francisco because it was a "tight" city where pets were usually found before owners had time to advertise. He was presently paying more attention to Las Vegas, a "loose," growing city where animals wandered, and more attention to cats. Dogs were less reliable because they took fright and disappeared during thunderstorms and Fourth of July fireworks. His missing dogs had shot up from thirty-six to eighty-five after Independence Day 1982, and the numbers had gone "through the roof" during the Bicentennial.

He registered his predictions with the media and pasted press clippings in scrapbooks. He showed me some to prove his accuracy. Here was Berkland announcing "Chance Good for Moderate Quake," on January 28, 1987, and there was a report of a moderate quake in the Bay Area three days later. "Up to 47 missing dogs on 1/29/87 and my cocker spaniel ran away on this date for the first time," he had noted on the margin in his spidery hand.

Everything had come together for Loma Prieta. Earlier that year the missing cats rarely hit double digits and the September average was usually ten. But by September 27, 1989 he had recorded twenty-seven. Missing dogs went up in the Bay Area, too. This, combined with the closest approach of the moon to the earth since 1974, convinced him to make his famous Loma Prieta forecast. It received attention because of his official position as Santa Clara County geologist. He had warned journalists off-camera to expect a 6.5-to-7.0, explaining he was only predicting a 3.5-to-6.0 to avoid panicking the public. He put rubber bands around his files, filled empty milk containers with water, and bought earthquake insurance for the first time in his life. When it struck, he was in his office at the county building, calling the seismic station at Berkeley to see if any quakes had been reported. As he screamed, "I got my quake!" his bookcases crashed and a microfilm reader slammed into him. The headline in next morning's Gilroy newspaper said GEOLOGIST IS ON THE MONEY.

His reward was to be fired. It happened after the *Oakland Tribune* ran a story misquoting him as predicting a 7-plus for the following month. He demanded and received a retraction, but the damage was done. The lie snowballed and he was condemned as an alarmist and suspended. He sued the county, won on appeal, and was reinstated after agreeing to stop making predictions on office time.

He blamed his troubles on real-estate interests opposed to having a county geologist, and on the intrigues of his eternal enemies, the USGS scientists in Menlo Park. They were "variously hubristic, patronizing, ridiculing, disbelieving, and rarely open-minded." Calling him a "clown" was the least of it, he said. They belittled him at conferences and treated his theories with contempt. They detested him because his theories predicted earthquakes, and theirs did not. His most implacable opponents were "the same ones whose own predictions have been most glaringly futile."

He delighted in rubbing salt in the Parkfield wound. He had criticized the experiment from the beginning, arguing its 1934 earthquake had been an anomaly and there was no reason to expect another before the end of 1992 with a 95-percent certainty. His newsletter said the USGS had put all its prediction eggs in one basket and would end up with egg on its face. He accused it of "giving the rest of us predictors a bad name."

When I asked traditional seismologists if they suspected an earthquake next week, they usually thought I was joking. But Berkland immediately pulled out his lunar tables, consulted tides, and ran a finger down his recent tallies of wandering San Jose pets. He had entered their numbers in a ledger labeled "My CATalogue." The cover said, "It's 10 p.m. Do you know where your cat is?"

He kept dogs and cats separate, plotting their disappearances on graphs and charts. The peaks and valleys sometimes echoed the rising and falling of seismic activity. "Just look!" he said in the dreamy voice of any collector exhibiting his life's passion. "A record number of eighty-three dogs missing on the fourth of April 1992, just eighteen days before Yucca Valley. Look at the numbers around the earthquake. Fifty lost, then fifty again, eighty-three, seventy-nine, forty-three. What a beautiful normal curve!"

Right now his lost pets were stable and he foresaw no unusual seismic activity. His next seismic window would not come until the spring tides, but he urged me to keep in touch and I did, sometimes calling *Quakeline* to hear him rattle on about tides, moons, and lost pets at a machine-gun pace. On one occasion he alerted callers to his appearance on *You Bet Your Life*, a syndicated quiz show hosted by Bill Cosby. He was on it because he had happened to see an advertisement for contestants next to lost-pet notices in the *Los Angeles Times*. I was in Palm Springs when the program aired. When Cosby asked him, "What do you do?" he replied firmly, "I predict earthquakes," and spoke of full moons, wandering cats, and two hundred correct predictions including Loma Prieta. "I was *on* the money," he concluded. "Now I want to be *in* the money."

Cosby asked if he had ever predicted any earthquakes for Philadelphia, where the program was being taped.

"Well, it's the 'Quaker State,' " he answered with a big grin.

He was relaxed and funny, a natural showman. His partner was a gorgeous six-foot black model who wisely let him answer everything. They split $13,400 after beating a country-and-western singer teamed with a female Hispanic chimney sweep.

If any of his USGS detractors caught the show, I imagine they took it as more evidence that he was a buffoon. But you might just as easily consider it an act of desperation by a man convinced he had discovered a way to predict earthquakes and save lives. If High Science ever decides the magnetite in a cat's ear can pick up electromagnetic signals from the grinding plates weeks before a quake, and that this is useful in forecasting earthquakes, then a tape of the Cosby program showing Berkland standing next to the gigantic model and talking a mile a minute will seem less comic than tragic.

Even if Berkland had not recommended Jack Coles as a young electronic whiz and "hands down ... the best quake predictor we have," Coles's dark and cluttered rooms, stale air, exploding files, and all the other evidence of a life consumed by their common obsession would have reminded me of him. Because Coles was younger and more determined, his monomania had swallowed more of his time and living space, and as I arrived I noticed furniture and boxes stacked in his carport and covered with tarps. Inside, venetian blinds were pulled and monitors and dials glowed green and orange in a perpetual twilight. A video camera was pointed at the spectrum analyzer measuring the disturbances in radio signals he believed indicated an impending earthquake. A World War II–vintage army radio receiver, police scanner, computer, and several answering machines covered kitchen countertops. A broken computer lay in the sink, gutted like a fish.

He looked pallid and haggard, like a submariner after a long cruise, and kept running his fingers through his tangled beard and hair and rubbing bloodshot eyes. He was so afraid of missing a signal he rarely left the house or slept more than two hours at a time. "I become nervous away from my equipment," he said, his eyes flicking to a screen. He had rigged alarms to wake him when the telltale radio waves appeared. He could not afford the fully automated system that would unchain him from the equipment. His wife worked to support the family while he watched the youngest child, a serious girl who sat on the rug playing video games on a giant television. While waiting for signals, he kept busy writing children's stories he said would reintroduce the concept of Happily Ever After.

He admitted enjoying the adrenaline rush accompanying an earthquake signal, and felt more quickened than scared, but insisted he was not doing this for thrills or to become famous. He reasoned that if he missed a signal and failed to predict an earthquake, then he was partly responsible for whatever casualties ensued. "I wasn't looking for this," he said plaintively, "but once I knew I could predict quakes, it captured me. I'd love to hand this over to someone else and get a life."

As a boy he had enjoyed messing around with radios and stumbled on his discovery while taking apart a radio receiver. He picked up some unusual ambient noises and klitches when he turned the volume to just below audible, and heard a four-and-a-half second signal he likened to a "bump." An earthquake struck four hours later. Six months later he received another strong pulse while working on a receiver with its volume turned low; it was again followed by an earthquake.

He believed these pulses were long-wave, low-frequency radio waves produced by the grinding of tectonic plates preceding an earthquake. He reasoned the increased pressure on the quartz rock was creating a rudimentary transmitter that oscillated and vibrated, sending signals detectible on the low end of an AM radio band, and perhaps detectible by animals and people like Jerry Hurley whose higher-than-normal quantities of magnetite in their brains made them more sensitive receivers. He noticed a pattern to the signals: nine days before a quake there was a bump; four days before, a series of pulses; then more frequent and noisy signals during the final twenty-four hours.

During the early 1980s, he picked up signals before the Mount St. Helens eruption, and more before a string of small-to-moderate California earthquakes. In 1982 he moved to Alaska because it was seismically lively. He enrolled in the state university, taking courses in music to develop his skill at recognizing radio tones, and in public speaking so he could handle the press interviews ensuing when he began predicting earthquakes. He later moved to Arizona hoping to pick up signals from Mexico, then back to San Jose, where a month before Loma Prieta he found a day job as a salesman at The Good Guys, a San Jose electronics store where two hundred audio and video units played constantly in the showroom.

Nine days before Loma Prieta, he received a strong signal and alerted the three hundred individuals, corporations, and journalists on his early-warning list to expect a maximum 6.5.

Sixteen hours before, he received a "significant main signal," called them again, then packed his monitors and equipment and told his children to place their belongings in footlockers he had bought for the occasion. Because he anticipated only a 6.5, he did not evacuate. He reported for work at The Good Guys and told his coworkers to select the desks and doorways they would use for shelter once the shaking began.

Although Loma Prieta was stronger than he predicted, it made him a local celebrity. His fame increased after he called ten more earthquakes in the next two years. They ranged from a 4.0 in Livermore to a 6.9 off Eureka on August 17, 1991. Major newspapers took notice and local television stations profiled him. He quit The Good Guys to stay home with his equipment. Hewlett-Packard loaned him a more sophisticated spectrum analyzer and other Silicon Valley companies donated surplus equipment. He spoke at school earthquake-safety fairs, met with the Santa Clara County Emergency Managers Association, and created a phone tree so volunteers could alert the thousands of people joining his early-warning list. High-tech companies, school districts, hospitals, and the Red Cross asked to be on it. He offered free earthquake updates and ran up huge telephone bills returning calls. After he predicted a series of strong earthquakes off Humboldt County on August 16 and 17, 1991, the *San Jose Mercury News* said, "When Jack Coles predicts quakes people listen."

He realized his fame had raised the stakes, and a mistaken forecast would destroy his reputation. On the other hand, he said, "If I kept a forecast to myself and anyone died, I couldn't have lived with myself."

When he announced at least a 72-percent probability of an earthquake greater than 7.0 striking the Bay Area during a four-day window beginning September 10, 1991, police in some towns went on alert and fire departments pulled vehicles from garages. The media sensationalized his warning, making it appear a "killer quake" was a certainty instead of a 72-percent probability. Stores ran out of flashlights, duct tape, and water containers. People skipped work, made impulse purchases, and refused to sign real-estate contracts.

This time Coles evacuated, taking some equipment with him. On September 11 he noticed the signals shifting farther south and revised his forecast, calling for a weaker earthquake and saying it might occur farther south and a week later. On September 17 a 5.1 hit San Simeon. Two days later San Juan Bautista experienced a small earthquake in line with his revised prediction.

They were too late. The press and scientific establishment ignored these events and criticized him as an alarmist. He had learned an important lesson: a weatherman could say clouds had moved and a storm changed course, but an earthquake forecaster could not. A computer company that once offered surplus equipment as a gift now demanded payment. Grants promised by the state were no longer available. Half the scientists at the USGS were publicly critical, while the other half slipped him their home telephone numbers, asking him to call when he received another main signal.

He was not bitter. He understood the USGS and the Office of Emergency Services operated under political constraints and had to be cautious about forecasts. There was naturally a rivalry, he said, "Because if I can predict earthquakes out of my garage with a couple of donated computers and some old radios and they can't, even after spending $20 million plus on Parkfield, well, it's hard times for them."

He added me to his early-warning list, but offered little hope for a big California earthquake in the immediate future. He had called a 4.1 in Utah last week, but California had recently been quiet. When the USGS announced a "B" level alert last month for an earthquake on the San Andreas Fault at Parkfield that never occurred, he had announced a 98-percent chance there would *not* be an earthquake there of that size.

Afterward I telephoned his answering machine from gas stations, bars, and motel rooms along the fault and heard warnings of moderate earthquakes in Mexico, Asia, and Nevada, and of insignificant ones in California.

The following year my phone rang at two A.M. in upstate New York. It was Coles, calling long distance on his own nickel and talking a streak about a main signal from Mexico, a twenty-four-hour window for Southern California, and a possible major earthquake. Before I was completely awake he was gone. Thirty-six hours later I heard a radio report of a moderate earthquake rattling the eastern Sierra Nevadas. I was happy for Coles, but spooked he had done it, and curiously unsettled that for more than a day I had known about this potentially lethal event.

Nine months later I heard his name mentioned again on the morning news. On January 16, 1994, he had faxed a warning to the Associated Press predicting a strong Southern California earthquake. The following day the Northridge temblor shook West Los Angeles for forty seconds, causing over $30 billion in damage, and killing more than the official death toll of sixty-one if you included fatal heart attacks suffered by those who, had they known of Coles's prediction, might not have been scared to death when the ground began shaking.

SIX

SANTA CRUZ
TO PARKFIELD

❖

29
Holy City

Tom Stanton thought I had come to sell Holy City out from under him because who but a real-estate agent would wander through the weedy ground behind his stained-glass workshop, taking notes and photographing Loma Prieta mountain? He was a wiry terrier of a man with curly black hair, who crackled with so much energy I expected a shock when I shook his hand. He explained that his landlord was an elderly Italian immigrant in Los Angeles who had charged the same rent for eighteen years, but suddenly his children were demanding he sell. Last week he had appeared with an agent, and Stanton recognized this for the bad news it was.

When I explained I was looking for Holy City and the San Andreas Fault, he relaxed and said, "Well, you've found them both." We were standing not far from the fissure Loma Prieta had carved in John and Freda Tarnbarger's front yard, attracting gawkers in the thousands. And as for Holy City, well, his ramshackle workshop was it.

I had expected more from a place calling itself a city. It had caught my eye because on most road maps it and the Redwood Estates subdivision sat alone at the crest of the Santa Cruz Mountains, the only towns for miles. My fault map also made it seem an important landmark. The San Andreas ran for a hundred miles along the crest of the Santa Cruz from Filoli to San Juan Bautista. The only major highway crossing it was Route 17, a four-lane road connecting Silicon Valley and the city of Santa Cruz. Holy City and Redwood Estates both straddled the intersection between fault and highway.

I was not the first to be fooled by Holy City. After Loma Prieta's

5.2 foreshock, Stanton had received calls from journalists whose maps showed it being the nearest town to the epicenter. They had called information, asking for the Holy City Town Hall, Police Department, and finally for *anyone* living there. They got Stanton, who had the only listed number.

He tried sounding casual about his appearance on thirty-three national and international television programs, but he had bothered to count and seemed miffed that when Loma Prieta struck, everyone but Dan Rather had ignored him.

The Bay Area's spectacular fires and collapsing freeways had hogged the Loma Prieta spotlight, but people in these mountains had suffered more proportional damage. Over three hundred hermits' cabins, summer camps, and commuter palaces had pancaked, burned, and fallen into ravines. Stanton's stained-glass windows had shattered and his drawing board crashed to the floor. But even more than the quake itself, he remembered the pounding headaches that had preceded it for twenty-four hours, then vanished seconds before the first tremor.

When he began rubbing his forehead I asked, perhaps too hopefully, if he was having another earthquake headache. He said no, but since quakes came in clusters he expected another soon. One more and he was moving to Arizona. He believed Edgar Cayce's prophecy that a big earthquake hitting Mammoth Lakes would precede a series of Big Ones. It was all part of a bigger cosmic picture. "Something's going on in the universe big time, it's filtering down psychologically and geologically, a new program, and earthquakes are only part of it," he said. "So I watch my headaches, Cayce's prophecies, Mammoth Lakes, and Fiji— and I watch them *very carefully*."

When he explained that he had avoided applying for a Federal Emergency Management Agency (FEMA) loan because he distrusted the federal government because it suppressed evidence of UFO landings and alien abductions, I thought, "My God, another UFO enthusiast." There had been Jerry Hurley, the Operation Camelot people, and the owner of the store in Elk. Jim Berkland had also talked about UFOs. Stanton was the most serious believer of the lot. He was treasurer of the Mutual UFO Network (MUFON), taught the first adult-education class in UFOlogy accredited by the California Department of Education, and when he was not repairing stained glass or driving a son to soccer games, he deprogrammed alien abductees using hypnotic regression therapy.

Several days later I read about earthquake lights and saw the beginnings of an explanation for why the fault might be home to so many flying-saucer enthusiasts.

These lights are most likely the result of static electricity created when quartz-bearing rock is stressed and scraped. They have been variously described as flashing, glowing, being the size of a basketball, and hovering over the epicenter of an impending quake. Witnesses to the 1952 Kern County earthquake reported balls of light and streaks of lightning. In 1961, a poultry rancher near Hollister named Reese Douley reported a number of small, sequential flashes lighting up the sky during a small earthquake.

In 1993 USGS geophysicist John Derr presented a paper to a Seismological Society of America conference suggesting earthquake precursors such as changes in groundwater flow and the crushing of underground rock could account for the lights, and arguing for a connection between seismic activity, earthquake lights, and UFO sightings in New Mexico during the early 1950s. He had found eighty UFO sightings between 1951 and 1952 clustered around the epicenters of three moderate earthquakes. In many instances the description of the spacecraft as an orange ball of light could as easily have applied to ball lightning.

Derr and Michael Persinger, a psychologist at Laurentian University, had also published a series of articles in the journal *Perceptual and Motor Skills* proposing connections between UFO sightings, alien abduction reports, seismic activity, and earthquake lights, and suggesting that since UFO sightings preceded earthquakes by as much as four months, they might help predict them.

They claimed similar lights, or "luminosities," could be produced in a laboratory by fracturing a rock sample in a hydraulic press. When this was done, fast-frame photographs recorded small, spherical luminosities resembling miniature flying saucers that lasted about a second. The ball lightning created by tectonic strain would be much larger, and last several minutes. It might appear to be a number of red lights rotating around an object or a rotating object with red lights. Their studies of Washington State UFO sightings between 1970 and 1976, and of the 1967 UFO hysteria in Utah's Uinta Basin, indicated a strong correlation between earthquakes and "spherical luminous displays, metallic-looking phenomena, multi-colored lights and close encounters."

Persinger argued seismic luminosities might also explain reports of alien abductions. He believed earthquake lights could alter consciousness, perception, and memory, and create vivid dreamlike se-

quences, terror, vertigo, and a sensation of floating, all affecting the
temporal-lobe structure of the brain of anyone standing too close. Similar reactions were common symptoms of temporal-lobe epilepsy and
had been produced in a clinical setting. He speculated a close encounter
with earthquake lights could even be lethal (an autopsy would show
heart failure or electrocution), or result in an intensification of religios-
ity and the compulsion to proselytize. In another article he and Derr
pointed out that in 1968 and 1969, thousands of Egyptians had witnessed luminous apparitions of the Virgin Mary over a Coptic church
in Zeitoun that coincided with an unprecedented tenfold increase in
nearby seismic activity.

If you thought Derr and Persinger's theories had merit, you had
to entertain the possibility of earthquake lights being mistaken for flying saucers, and of people too near them imagining themselves kid-
napped by aliens or meeting the Virgin Mary, suffering heart attacks,
or becoming messianic figures. And then you had to wonder if California has more cults, fanatics, and UFO believers than anywhere else, not
because of its climate, geography, and unusual history, but because it
simply has more people living near active faults.

Holy City's founder, "Father" William Riker, certainly sounded
like someone whose brain had been scrambled by earthquake lights.
Among the UFO clippings on the wall of Stanton's office I saw a copy
of a February 5, 1961, press release typed on letterhead proclaiming
Holy City "a friend to every man and religion on earth—headquarters
for perfect system of government" and advertising its "Service Station,
Garage, Lecture Hall, Auditorium, Picnic Ground, Amusements,
Restaurant, General Store, Butcher Shop, Printing Shop, and Barber
Shop." The release, headed "For Immediate Revelation," announced
Holy City's board of directors had removed Riker as patriarch of the
Perfect Christian Divine Way Inc., expressing unhappiness with his in-
tention of running for governor of California, yet again, and with his
dealings with a Hollywood promoter claiming to be the New Jewish
Messiah.

Stanton said someone had recently slipped it under his door.
When he arrived in the seventies Riker had been dead for a decade, his
disciples scattered, and his buildings demolished. If I wanted to know
about Holy City I should speak to Bruce Franks, who lived nearby and
had met him. Before calling him, I spent the afternoon in the Los Gatos
Library reading about Riker. One disciple remembered "a fat man . . .
with a little beanie on his head," a "lecherous old guy" who slept with

the female disciples. Photographs showed a whale-shaped man resembling W. C. Fields. He was called "certifiably insane," and "one of the greatest promoters of all time." He referred to himself as the Comforter, the Wise Man of the West, and the Great Emancipator—more evidence, if any is needed, that someone calling himself "the" anything is usually mad.

He launched Holy City in 1919 after thirty years of hotel bellhopping and street-corner preaching in San Francisco had brought him enough capital and followers to buy thirty acres along the summit of the San Jose–to–Santa Cruz highway. He used bricks, lumber, and other detritus from the 1906 earthquake to build a string of ramshackle roadside attractions over the San Andreas Fault, at the same time preaching that the next earthquake would kill everyone except Christians and Jews.

At first glance Holy City may seem like a typical California enterprise of the 1920s, dependent on advertising and the automobile, and tricked up with a pseudo-religion, but there was also an endearing eccentricity and self-mockery to it. Riker's "Ten Commandments for Women" began, "Marry for a bank account," and one billboard proclaimed, OUR FAITH IS FOUNDED ON THIS PRINCIPLE—MIND YOUR OWN BUSINESS. He added to the traditional roadside attractions a Fountain of Health and eighteen life-size wooden Santas holding up signs with advice like IF YOU ARE CONTEMPLATING MARRIAGE, SUICIDE, OR CRIME, SEE US FIRST. He subdivided the moon and sold souvenir plots. He persuaded his disciples to live in segregated barracks, while he shared a bed with his wife. There was a Museum of Philosophy, a dance hall ("agreeable dancing is as near heaven as any mortal will ever get"), two telescopes so patrons could inspect their moon lots, and the Sunshine Soda Bottling Works, where his disciples concocted the original recipe for Hawaiian Punch.

He had plans for a seventeen-thousand-seat amphitheater and a statue of a woman large enough to accommodate twelve elevators. The only thing missing from the world's only Holy City besides the Vatican was a church, unless you counted the small steepled buildings housing peep shows with titles like "Temptations of the Flesh . . . look at the legs of naked ladies and decide if they're saints or sinners."

During the 1920s and 1930s he remained an appealing minor-league charlatan, and his Holy City became a praiseworthy roadside attraction. It cheered up carsick children and provided services on a highway badly needing them. He made hundreds of hobos his "disciples," giving them food, shelter, and a stake in Holy City in exchange for work. He rehearsed his followers to mimic the crippled and blind so they could be miraculously healed, and designed a system of wires and mirrors for staging resurrections. He had a weakness for Cadillacs and jewelry, but also served forty thousand free meals to the hobos and charged reasonable prices. He did not flimflam widows out of their nest eggs, indoctrinate gullible college kids, encourage mass suicides, or make the mistake of thinking he could heal or help anyone but himself.

He emerged victorious from investigations by the police and state charity board, a grand-jury indictment on charges of corrupting public morals, and a lawsuit lodged by a disgruntled disciple—the kind of skirmishes coming with the crackpot-religion territory. But when a new four-lane highway bypassed Holy City in 1939, his typical California hokum turned suddenly nasty, in a typical California fashion.

He ran for governor in 1940, perhaps hoping the publicity would attract visitors. Although Holy City proclaimed itself "a friend to every man and religion on earth," he courted the racist vote with a Perfect Government Plan that would prohibit blacks and Orientals from owning commercial property. "No longer will the white man tolerate your undermining and polluting facts," he warned. He was arrested in 1942 for writing admiring letters to Hitler, but acquitted when attorney Melvin Belli persuaded the jury he was a "poor, senile, duped fool." He repaid Belli by suing him for defamation.

His flock shrank to twenty after the war. One disciple hanged himself in his front yard, and a reporter described the others as "tottering, vacant-eyed and cane-supported through the deserted village." Arsonists torched some Holy City attractions, others collapsed. Riker was swindled by a former partner, deposed, and converted to Catholicism before dying at age ninety-three in a state hospital because he had been expelled by a private institution for being a cranky pain in the ass.

While waiting for Bruce Franks in front of Holy City Art Glass, I watched dozens of bicyclists pedal into Holy City, their front wheels wobbling and legs slow-motioning after the climb. They high-fived, hugged, and milled around Riker's empty lots in their lurid polypropylene shirts and Lycra shorts, resembling a convention of parrots. When they removed their helmets I saw a field of fuzzy white dandelions and realized they were all over sixty. The young couple who were their guides delivered florid speeches praising their stamina, saying each one was special, with "special abilities."

Bruce Franks resembled Colonel Sanders in a gimme cap. As we sat in his truck leafing through his Holy City scrapbook, I glanced up from photographs of a Riker billboard proclaiming, LOOK IN THE MIRROR AND FOR SURE YOU WILL SEE GOD DREAMING to see the senior-citizen bikers lapping up the New Age version of the old heresy that we are all splendid little Gods.

Franks said he owned the local water company and enjoyed living in these mountains year-round. He had spent his boyhood summers near Holy City in his father's 1886 cabin, and could recall peering through Riker's telescope at his subdivided moon and hearing loud-speakers blast his sermons to distant ridges. He remembered him as "Just a big bald guy who walked with two canes because of a car accident."

As we drove down the bypassed highway he pointed out the former locations of the opera house, service station, bottling works, and neon HOLY CITY sign that lit up the night sky for miles. "It was a thriving metropolis," he said, as if he could still see it, "a *real* community."

We crisscrossed the fault, dipping to hollows packed with former summer cabins converted to year-round use by commuters. They looked dank and depressing. A fern-shaded creek is great in summer, but when the winter sun sets behind the mountains and rain turns the mossy ground to sponge, you might as well be in a cave or flooded basement. I saw NEIGHBORHOOD WATCH signs nailed to utility poles, and new houses surrounded by gates and walls, evidence it was becoming a fortified mountain suburbia. Franks said there were more year-round residents than before, but less community spirit. Winter residents had once gathered for potluck suppers and whist; now they worked, commuted, and watched television.

He knew the history of every house. "Just a summer cabin on 2,500 square feet and it sold for $260,000," he said, pointing to one. "Would you pay that to be jammed up against your neighbors and live in darkness for three months every year? I call it high-cost tract living without the convenience of a tract." He showed me quake-damaged houses being rebuilt in landslide zones, and new houses set on slender pilings. After the next earthquake their owners would probably curse the government for being slow with the disaster aid and low-cost loans. We visited a construction site where workmen were laying decks for a motel-shaped house perched on a narrow ridge. He shook his head and said the next big earthquake would send it sliding into the valley. "None of these houses belong here. I call them transplants. But I'd build here again, too, rather than live in that valley."

After he dropped me back in Holy City, Tom Stanton walked me down an overgrown path to a fairy ring of thirty redwoods, his favorite meditation spot. Riker had wired the trees with loudspeakers and lights and delivered speeches to his followers here. Stanton had nailed a crucifix to a redwood in hopes of scaring off the satanists who were attracted by the prospect of defiling a Holy City. He had already found burned torches, Latin words scrawled on trees, and splattered blood. The police warned him to expect animal sacrifices. The Gulf War had brought rumors of Islamic suicide squads. Nothing had happened yet, but he worried that Holy City, built by a gentler eccentric in gentler times, would continue attracting fanatics who now came armed and dangerous.

The eccentrics gravitating to the Santa Cruz Mountains have usually been ambivalent hermits who want to leave civilization behind, but not too far.

The pattern was established by a penniless Irish teenager who drifted in from the goldfields, settled into the trunk of a burned-out redwood, and on the strength of a famous bear fight that left him with a metal plate fashioned from Mexican dollars built up a colorful reputation as "Mountain Man Charley McKiernan." In the beginning he led a hermit's life and collected tolls at the pass, and if his story had unfolded in the Rockies, it would have ended with a bearded and disfigured eccentric dying alone in a remote cabin. But in the nineteenth century the Santa Cruz Mountains were already a shrinking wilderness and his life had a surprising second act. He married, fathered seven children, and prospered by selling refreshments to passengers on his stage line. He moved into a farmhouse surrounded by orchards and vineyards, then into San Jose so his children could attend a better school. He became an active Mason, owner of a grain warehouse, major shareholder in San Jose Power and Light, and President of the Pacific Coast Wine Company, transforming himself in less than two decades from bear fighter to Babbitt.

Consider Charley Parkhurst, a stagecoach driver legendary for drinking, swearing, and taking risks. Tobacco had turned his lips and teeth black, and he supplemented the usual driver's costume of muffler, gloves, and buffalo-skin coat with a black patch covering an eyeball lost to a stallion's hoof. He sounded like a good candidate for a potter's field, but in the Santa Cruz Mountains his story had a quite different ending. When he died, the undertaker discovered he was really Charlotte Parkhurst, who had escaped from a Boston orphanage disguised as a boy.

Or consider Erskine Scott Wood, a West Point graduate and the first white man to descend the Yukon River. He was a remorseful Indian fighter, successful Portland attorney, political radical, and a friend to John Reed, Clarence Darrow, and Chief Joseph of the Nez Percé. He left Oregon after falling in love with Sara Field, a suffragette thirty years his junior. They moved to San Francisco, where he earned the first million-dollar fee in the history of American jurisprudence. They moved again to Los Gatos in 1919 to protest and circumvent Prohibition. He cleared thirty-four acres, planting a vineyard and building an estate he called Poet's Canyon. In another state, even in another part of California, an aging radical with a beautiful young consort might have clipped his vines and enjoyed retirement. But Wood would enjoy his most prolific and energetic years in the Santa Cruz, hosting a salon where Yehudi Menuhin played and Carl Sandburg recited, and publishing a well-received poetic tribute to the Nez Percé and a widely read diatribe against fundamentalist ministers and the Ku Klux Klan.

I worried bohemians like Wood and Field were becoming extinct as the mountains filled with commuters, but I finally met one in a Los Gatos bistro where we both sat struggling to read our books by candlelight. She was operatic-sized and wore the traditional hippie outfit of Birkenstocks, woolly socks, turtleneck, and subcontinent skirt. "My *real* name is just Annie," she said, "like 'Cher,' a single word. But the damned phone company wouldn't list me that way, so I added 'V' as a last name."

Today was her seventieth birthday and she had stuck a pink feather into her nest of gray hair and come down from the mountains to celebrate. She flirted with the teenage busboy and sent him away blushing. After asking the waitress the price of lemon cake and another glass of wine, she sighed and said, "Well, I guess I'm pretty full anyway, dear." While I forked up the cake she had rejected as too expensive, she said she had come to California from the East as a child bride, divorced, remarried, became a Los Angeles teacher, and bought a Victorian cottage in the mountain town of Boulder Creek as a vacation home. When her husband died she became a year-round resident after the police told her any widow living in her Los Angeles neighborhood should buy a gun. But Boulder Creek was no perfect paradise. It was damp in winter and neighborhood kids had vandalized her house and called her a witch. She worried about the rednecks who "smelled out" long-haired peaceniks like herself but said she was "too poor to move, and the air smells like champagne."

She had a guardian angel who had pulled her back from a precipice at the Grand Canyon and saved her life during Loma Prieta. "Go outside and read," a voice in her head told her just before the first tremor. She rode her front porch like a surfboard and flashed back to the San Fernando earthquake of 1971 when she covered her daughter's body with her own. A heating pipe crashed through the ceiling inside, hitting the floor where she had been standing moments before. Loma Prieta damaged sixty houses in Boulder Creek, but most people had insurance and credit lines and rebuilt. She refused the FEMA money because, she said, she did not want government computers knowing the color of her panties. So she warmed herself in winter with earmuffs and a space heater, and covered the hole with canvas.

When I called later to accept her invitation to inspect the last remaining Loma Prieta damage in Boulder Creek, she said "Bring me a little surprise. My recovery group is teaching me to say 'I want.' "

Boulder Creek was becoming a bedroom community for Santa Cruz. Its main street had an unfinished frontier feel, but for every mud-splattered Chevy, there was a Range Rover or Grand Cherokee. Some false-front stores had become boutiques, and at the health-food supermarket I noticed a white teenager with filthy dreadlocks shoplifting a carob brownie.

Annie V lived a block off Main Street in a Victorian cottage in the woods. Snowdrifts of old magazines and children's books lay against walls, mismatched china and chipped figurines covered bureaus, tables, and chairs. Dust immediately plugged my ears and sinuses. She whirled through her overstuffed rooms, explaining the provenance of a rusty popcorn popper and a dartboard with half its numbers, asking, "Don't you think I have exquisite taste? Isn't this marvelous?" Her urgent, small-time materialism had a crazy charm.

She insisted I finger her sand-washed red kimono. "Cost me every last penny of my birthday money. It's so small I wear it as a shawl, but I *had* to own it!"

She collapsed into a tattered armchair. "Okay, I know this room is too busy, but I like a Zen-like space, so I'm always recycling things." It was her living. A Social Security widow could only survive in this gentrified mountain suburb by taking up the time-honored eccentric's profession of junk trader, so she bought flea-market and yard-sale leftovers by the boxload and resold them from tables unfolded in friends' front yards.

"I *knew* I'd have a good time with you, Thurston," she said, putting on a kettle for tea. "I'm going to trust you to drink from my favorite mug. Sixteen dollars, and I almost died to ask for it. A present from my husband just before he died. You'll be the first man since him to use it."

I protested, but she insisted. While I cradled it in my hand like a Fabergé egg, she described her attempts to befriend the children who had uprooted her trees and thrown the red dye that stained her porch. She had tried bribing them with odd jobs and leftovers from her yard sales. Nothing worked. "I'm a good target," she said matter-of-factly, "an old fat lady no one loves."

Her emotional life was as crowded as her parlor, crammed with revelations and passions. She told me her "soul mates" were Austin and Sally, friends who had picked her up hitchhiking to Santa Cruz and thrown a fifth birthday party for her because her parents had sold her train set for ready cash on her real one. Whenever I moved to leave she offered another story or snatched another treasure off a side table. Finally I headed for the door and never stopped. I liked her, she was amusing and had style, but being around her was as exhausting as spending the afternoon with a five-year-old who had lived seventy years.

30
Eye of the Beast

Santa Cruz said to me, "Live in this balmy pleasure dome and you'll never age, at least not much," and the head shops, students sharing joints, troubadours singing "Blowing in the Wind," Volkswagens plastered with college parking permits, radical broadsheets covering utility poles, and women in granny glasses walking with that sixties sidewalk-scraping shuffle did make it easy for a middle-aged man to imagine himself a quarter century younger. Certainly the middle-aged Peter Pans skateboarding down Pacific Avenue with their baseball caps turned fashionably backward so the plastic straps left lines imprinted on their receding hairlines did. So did the surfers floating beyond the break on "Steamers' Lane," who came ashore and peeled off wet suits to reveal gray hair cut into trendy wedges.

I finally stopped feeling twenty-one when the prettiest waitress I saw in California served me breakfast. I gave my order and she looked through me. Twenty minutes later she wordlessly slid my eggs across the Formica table. When the elderly couple in the next booth asked if the fruit cocktail was fresh, she sighed. "No one's ever asked me *that* before. 'Fresh'? Well, fresh from somewhere, I suppose. Want it or not?" Then three beautiful surfer boys sat down across the aisle and she poured on the charm and easy California banter.

I suppose I paid so much attention to how people looked in Santa Cruz because the city itself had made such a big deal of it by becoming the first in the nation to fight "lookism." With great fanfare and squabbling, the city council had added "height, weight, or physical appearance" to the customary antidiscrimination ordinance. Progressives who had long controlled city hall expressed astonishment that the testimony of outraged local fatties and lachrymose "transgendered individuals" should intrigue the national media. But what journalist could resist the man claiming discrimination after he had driven a peg through his tongue and lost his job as a psychiatric aide, or the woman who, after shaving herself bald except for a lock of fuchsia hair and tattooing her pate, complained of being "treated like a cretin"? I know I can't. Angry Santa Cruz merchants fretted about "unsavory, unclean, and obscene" workers repelling their customers, frivolous lawsuits, and the "lookism police," and sure enough, the progressives soon demonstrated their Big Brother tendencies, although not in the way the merchants expected, by drafting an ordinance restricting the right of appalling street musicians ("people of very limited talent and repertoire") to repeat endlessly the same execrable versions of ballads like "Mr. Tambourine Man."

The Lookism Law struck me as a brilliant although unintended act of cultural and historic preservation, a way for Santa Cruz to husband its human attractions after Loma Prieta had inflicted more per capita damage and deaths on it than anywhere else, destroying most of the stores in its main shopping area, sending wrecking balls smashing into the remains of its venerable stucco palaces, and endangering its position on the National Register of Historic Places. Nostalgia sells, and as retired baby boomers begin hitting the road in recreational vehicles, a 1960s version of colonial Williamsburg could become a big draw. The *Bay Area Backroads* guidebook was already praising its "funky remnants of the 1960s." In an article titled "Santa Cruz—the Land That Time Forgot" in the Dream Weekends column of *Los Angeles Magazine*, author Ben Stein celebrated it for being where "Bob Dylan is always hip, Nixon is always President, the revolution is in your mind."

I assumed Mayor Don Lane would also be hip. The photograph accompanying an article about his retirement in the *Sentinel* showed a bearded man in his thirties with a sweet, flaky grin. It began, "He hasn't been your average mayor," and made him sound like great fun. He owned a student hangout called the Saturn Café, wore blue jeans to meetings, and grew his beard "with the seasons." He had attempted to proclaim a "Madonna Day" and once sent an obscene valentine to a political enemy.

I found him at his café, where the cheap soups, honest breads, and counterculture bulletin board clashed with signs forbidding various kinds of behavior, evidence even his legendary tolerance could be abused. He had the trusting, liquid eyes of a Walt Disney deer, always close to tears, and was treating his teeth to some extensive orthodontics. The retainer made his cracked smile even more boyish and endearing. He was a painfully honest but naive man who had spent most of his adult life in Santa Cruz, the kind of straight arrow who administers small Midwestern cities or rises to colonel. He should probably never have been mayor, and to his credit he knew it.

He blamed his forthcoming retirement on Loma Prieta. Before, the progressives had been united in a policy falling somewhere between no growth and slow growth. But by destroying so many commercial structures, the quake had reduced the revenue flow to the city's generous social welfare programs. Because he wanted to rebuild quickly and generate sales tax, he supported construction of an outlet mall. Suddenly he found himself allied with probusiness people and vilified by former supporters. I had been told that criticism from his friends had caused him to burst into tears at city-council meetings. When I mentioned this he said, "Listen, I can't imagine *ever* running for *anything* again," and disappeared into his kitchen.

I suppose I listened to talk radio in California so much because I had never spent so much time alone in a car. At worst, it was like sharing the front seat with an entertaining enemy; at best, I learned more than from a local newspaper homogenized by a chain. In Santa Cruz I listened to Harry Lee Curtis, a conservative who began every program with, "Join me as we examine the politically correct theater of the absurd," and introduced his farewell program for Mayor Lane with, "We the audience bid you a fond farewell knowing that when you send in the clowns, everything else is just a circus."

His callers did the predictable bitching about "welfare queens," illegal immigrants, and the homeless, but in laid-back California voices I had always associated with a lazy tolerance of almost anything.

In a mellow surfer's drawl, Dave protested the progressives' policy of forbidding the police to cooperate with the Border Patrol. "Yeah, it's like those illegals drive without a license or insurance. They run over our kids and go back to Mexico and laugh at us." A Hispanic grandmother with a lovely musical voice said, "They're hurting our country! They don't contribute. They take their money back to Mexico and build houses. I'm embarrassed to say it, but 85 percent of the people in the county prison are Hispanic." A shy housewife whispered, "Harry, this town is becoming a national joke." When one caller attacked the progres-

sives for mismanaging the Loma Prieta reconstruction and Curtis replied
he had the earthquake to thank for his job, I had my excuse to meet him.

His fans and enemies so often compared him to Rush Limbaugh
that I expected another bug-eyed fatty with a well-lubricated ego.
Instead I found myself sitting across a table in the studio from a free-
spirited vagabond with a gray goatee and wind-blasted red face. He introduced the motherly woman in a helmet of gray hair as his producer
and wife, "Sha-na-na the Queen," and the animal at his feet as "Bradley
the Wonder Dog," your average hippie commune names.

Loma Prieta hit just after Curtis and Sha-na-na had taken delivery
of their prefabricated Mailboxes Etc. franchise in Watsonville. He was
watching the delivery truck leave as the shaking began. Their ceiling collapsed and windows shattered, but they opened anyway. When the aftershocks became too much for Sha-na-na they bought a trailer and hit the
road. After a friend in Washington State suggested his loud mouth might
make him an ideal radio talk-show host, he canvassed stations in Washington, then in his former hometown of Santa Cruz. He offered to work
for free but scared off Public Radio by promising to "climb your audience's tree and blow their minds." He found a job at this commercial AM
station when it advertised for volunteers to replace a vacationing host.

He was a reformed red-diaper baby. His father had been a socialist
and his mother a communist, "one step from throwing bombs." Vietnam, Watergate, and the military-industrial complex had infuriated
him. He had thought people who owned guns were lunatics and Marx-
ists were great. He began his show as a skeptical liberal who no longer
bought the liberal act. Within months he was a self-described "lonely
voice crying in the damned wilderness" against the Santa Cruz progressives. For twenty years conservatives in town had been, he said, "run
over, intimidated, and told to shut up." They felt isolated; he had provided them with a community. They were the underdogs, desperate for
a champion; he was it.

His conversion had been more visceral than ideological. He had
been antichurch, but when he heard the progressives heckle conservative Christians, he realized groups he once considered his political allies
were filled with "a whole bunch of awful, bigoted people, acting just
like brownshirts." They were a "nasty bunch" who did not play fair,
taking the high moral ground but funneling jobs to left-wing architects
and contractors.

He ticked off their crimes at a machine-gun pace. They had advocated homelessness as an alternative lifestyle, turned the Women's

Studies department at UCSC into a "snakepit of lesbians," and wasted Loma Prieta reconstruction money by constructing low-cost housing, an instant ghetto.

He was the kind of instinctive rebel who aims his guns at whoever is in power, and I suspected he might alter course again, although probably not so dramatically, if conservatives became entrenched at city hall. Meanwhile, he was the most genuinely counterculture outlaw in town.

From Santa Cruz I drove south to what the rangers at Nisene Marks State Park call the Loma Prieta "epicenter." They have rounded off its longitude and latitude in order to place it near a hiking trail and a landslide that was aggravated by the earthquake, but created by the torrential winter rains of 1982. New Agers meditated, and schoolchildren, more willing than their parents or teachers to admit to the primal earthquake fear of being swallowed by the earth, came expecting dinosaurs and science-fiction fissures.

A Mill Valley attorney told me his wife had come here on a pilgrimage "to stare into the eye of the beast." Like many others, she left disappointed not to have seen the ground zero of a nuclear explosion, or redwood groves resembling cornfields after a tornado. And like many others, she did not understand that an epicenter is simply the ground above the subterranean point, the hydrocenter, where a rupture begins, not necessarily where the damage is the worst. That distinction depends on soil, landscape, and paths taken by seismic waves. Because Loma Prieta's hydrocenter was unusually deep, eleven and a half miles underground, and because the rock above it in Nisene Marks State Park was sandstone bedrock, there had been less shaking here than in Santa Cruz.

By the time I hiked to the bogus epicenter on a muddy path, the trip had become less fashionable. Instead of passing society ladies in high heels and suburban shamans, I was almost flattened by kamikaze mountain bikers. Some parks have cut new trails to separate them from hikers, but here everyone shared. What was called the "epicenter area" faced a wide landslide. While I stared at the stumps and fallen firs, trying to imagine the ridge rippling like a flying carpet, a biker almost cut down a jogger who had also stopped to read the sign. "God, I hate those bastards," he shouted, his face twisted in fury. As I walked down, more came at me from behind, whistling and hooting warnings so I could jump to safety, their clacking pedals sounding like an approaching subway, or the beginning of one of Mr. Steinbrugge's tape-recorded earthquakes.

31
Greywolf

San Juan Bautista was a chameleon.

On Saturday nights with its saloons running full tilt, it was a rowdy outpost of cowboy charm. Muddy trucks parked in front of Mom and Pop's Saloon, where a sign begged, CITIZENS OF SJB — PLEASE CHECK YOUR GUNS BEFORE IMBIBING, and you could almost imagine yourself in the nineteenth-century town of four newspapers, seventeen saloons, and streets busy with stagecoach passengers and cattle traders.

On Sunday mornings it became a devout Spanish outpost, where families in white flickered like ghosts back and forth behind the columns of the mission cloister. By day it was dry and sunny, unmistakably Western. After dark, Pacific fogs hung on the peaks of the Gabilans, and willows and bougainvillea smothered the lights in cottages, giving them an underwater glow and turning it into a tropical village of moonlit alleys and secret gardens. On spring weekends, day-trippers filled its galleries and boutiques, but on this November weekday it felt like a moldering rural village bypassed by an interstate.

The fault ran underneath a small, well-preserved stretch of the centuries-old Camino Real, the stands of an abandoned rodeo ground built on a forty-foot scarp thrown up by centuries of quakes, and the corpses of 4,300 Indians interred in mass graves in the mission's cemetery. The seismograph above it in the Plaza provoked jokes. "Did the earth move for you, Barbara?" a man asked his wife. "It's all your 'fault.' Ha-ha," another said.

But the sudden swarm of earthquakes striking California in 1992 had given this seismic bravado a nervous edge. When some Germans giggled about standing on the famous San Andreas, a local woman in a jogging outfit shouted, "Ha! Earthquakes never bother *us*." A man walking a dog snapped at some tourists, "If you out-of-staters are so nervous why don't you stay home? This mission has been here two hundred years. *We* don't worry." (In fact, an earthquake leveled the first mission in 1800, and in 1906 its replacement was so extensively damaged repairs were not completed until seventy years later.)

The mission's thick walls and red tiled roofs are so romantic and typically Californian that Alfred Hitchcock chose it for scenes in *Vertigo*. In that film, Kim Novak played a character pretending to be bewitched by a nineteenth-century California pioneer named Carlotta. In the end, the real San Juan Bautista so bewitched the cast that for twenty years Hitchcock and James Stewart returned to eat in La Casa Rosa, and like Carlotta, Novak could'be seen wandering alone through the plaza.

The mission's church was a fragrant cavern, as smoke-blackened and incense-perfumed as any provincial South American cathedral. The first American to settle in California, a carpenter named Thomas Doak, had painted its handsome frescoes. Indian laborers had bound its rough beams with redwood thongs. Spanish priests had immersed thousands of Indian children into its limestone font, baptizing them Alexander, Plato, and Cicero, and teaching them to sing Gregorian chants. The floor tiles carried the paw prints of mountain lions, coyotes, and bears who had wandered down the aisle while the fathers slept.

The other buildings surrounding the small plaza were almost as old. The Castro-Breen adobe had been purchased in 1848 by Patrick Donner, who thanks to his meticulous diary was the most celebrated survivor of the Donner Party. It was now a museum where curators had threaded Isabella Breen's sewing machine and laid out her slippers. The Plaza Hotel had seen the plotting of two California revolutions and been home to Helen Hunt Jackson when she began writing *Ramona*, the nineteenth-century novel responsible for the romantic myth of the California mission.

The landscape was also unmistakably Californian. East and north of the plaza giant sprinklers rolled across a checkerboard of crops. The soil was a dark chocolate, almost good enough to eat, and the richest farmland in the western hemisphere with the possible exception of a remote valley in Chile. To the south and west, cattle grazed on the lower slopes of the Gabilans that had been the setting for Frank Norris's celebration of ranching life, *The Octopus: A Story of California*.

San Juan was such a crowded intersection of California history, symbols, and myths that although it had little in common with what the state had become (its wood-and-adobe cottages would be "tear-downs" elsewhere), it was still a place Californians brought out-of-state visitors. "Look! Here it is," they seemed to be saying, "the *real* California."

I followed a couple from Menlo Park who were showing off the plaza to some English friends. When they proudly pointed to a sign declaring THIS IS A HOUSE OF PRAYER SINCE 1797. DO NOT DISTURB, the Englishman said, "Why, we just celebrated the millennium of our local church—but at least this is a change from those ghastly office blocks you showed us yesterday." In the cloister garden the American asked, "Isn't it just like an English garden?" The Englishwoman said, "A dead British garden."

I stopped at city hall to ask about Loma Prieta damage and met Russ Carlsen, an interim city manager recently hired to save San Juan from bankruptcy. He was as jumpy and hollow-eyed as a student after a week of amphetamine-driven cram sessions, but delighted to talk to an outsider. He rattled on about the lawsuits, indictments, and recall petitions marking San Juan's political life while raking his thinning black hair and plucking imaginary lint from his socks. "My God, this town has taken a toll on me," he said. "All the problems and conflicts of a medium-sized city, and the anger is incredible. There's a real saloon culture, with lots of drinking." He dropped his voice and shot his eyes around the room. "You know, these people are not well."

There were feuds layered on feuds, a muck of hatred so thick it swallowed most newcomers. The main one pitted old-timers who wanted modest growth against newcomers who wanted none. The modest-growth faction was headed by a real-estate agent and former mayor named Leonard Caetano. His most active and controversial opponent was Becky McGovern. Each side had enjoyed some victories. The antigrowth people had defeated an industrial park; the progrowth ones had backed the shopping center being constructed on the highway. It was tempting to see the feuds as part of San Juan's picturesque history, until you learned someone had set McGovern's house on fire, and the county district attorney had investigated sixty-eight allegations of public misconduct in a single year. In 1990 a San Juan merchant told the *Los Angeles Times*, "You can cut your own throat if you say the wrong thing."

Carlsen had laid off all seventeen city employees, including the police force, and replaced them with part-timers and volunteers. He had skirmished with every faction and now understood why an old-timer had welcomed him with, "Anyone who knew anything about this place wouldn't come within a hundred miles of it." He was sick of the "mudslinging," and when his contract ended he planned on getting married and changing careers.

Many of the conflicts swirled around former Police Chief Lonnie Hurlbut, who had come from Ohio and charmed the town by wearing a Wild West sheriff's outfit and patrolling on horseback. He ordered his two officers to introduce themselves to a new person every day, resisted issuing tickets to locals, and suspended himself for falling asleep on duty. He became so famous *People* magazine profiled him. He was "steely-eyed," tipped his hat to ladies, and offered "a macho-quick nod to the hombres and wide-eyed kids." There was talk of an acting career and a Movie of the Week. He told one reporter, "If enforcing the law means sticking a gun down some dirtbag's throat, hell, I'll do it!"

This unbuttoned style had ended the careers of councilmen who both supported and opposed him. He was fired after being found guilty of a misdemeanor for pulling a gun on some men in Monterey, then rehired when his conviction was overturned on appeal. After the antidevelopment Cultural Resources Board ruled merchants had violated the ordinance against large public advertisements by flying their American flags too low, he was fired again for not ordering the flags raised to face level. Then he was reinstated, then the councilmen who had reinstated him were recalled. I looked for him, but like a real Western lawman, he had ridden off into the sunset. "He just disappeared, and I don't think anyone knows where," Carlsen said, sounding relieved.

Leonard Caetano, who had been mayor between 1962 and 1978, told me he liked Lonnie Hurlbut but conceded, "He got a fat head and paid more attention to publicity work than police work." He had no idea where he was. "Vanished, just vanished, and no one knows where."

Caetano was a bald and cheerful bantamweight who was proud his father had been born in San Juan and his mother had been the first Portuguese child born in Santa Cruz. His poky office was decorated by photographs of the San Juan rodeo. It made him sad to discuss it. The crowds had turned ugly in the early 1980s, causing vandalism, a riot, and rising insurance premiums, the usual scenario. It was canceled and its fault-straddling stands were now scheduled for demolition. He had been one of its principal organizers, and profits from it had repaired the 1906 quake damage to the mission church. Workmen had reinforced the building outer walls with steel bars, replaced its tile roof with red asphalt, and pumped epoxy into its arches to make it earthquake-proof. If it survived, he could take credit for helping to preserve one of California's most historic buildings. It sounded to me like he had performed other good works as mayor—burying utility lines, ordering advertising removed from street corners, banning new neon signs, proclaiming the commercial area an historical zone, and advocating an ordinance to limit growth at 3 percent a year. Anywhere else he would have been embraced by preservationists.

He wanted San Juan to remain affordable for old-timers like himself, and when the local cement plant closed in the early 1970s, he advocated replacing it with an industrial park. Since a factory had occupied the site since 1917, he could not understand the newcomers' determined opposition. When the antigrowth faction on the City Council killed the plan 3–2, he never forgave them. Like most old-timers he understood how a single event could shape a town's destiny for a century. When San Juan had been a hub for several stage lines, its leaders had refused to pay the Southern Pacific an eight-thousand-dollar subsidy to run a rail line through town. Instead it went through Hollister, making that town the county seat while San Juan became a backwater, preserved or ruined, depending on your point of view, by one nineteenth-century decision.

When I mentioned Becky McGovern, he shot up from his swivel chair like a missile. "She's anti*everything*," he snarled. "She wants *nothing* for this town. No more houses; no more businesses. She rents and doesn't pay taxes, of course. Poor thing had a brain tumor several years ago and they say she's looking *real* bad. I say, 'BULLSHIT! She's looking disgustingly healthy.' "

She turned out to be a small, middle-aged woman with a leprechaun's face and close-cropped hair who lived in a shabby red farmhouse hidden behind a wall of vines and trees. She told me that although she and Lonnie Hurlbut had been on opposite sides of the American flag controversy, she disapproved of his being fired, and worried Carlsen's cost-cutting measures were part of a sinister conspiracy to unincorporate the town so the county could deed its water rights to developers. Her first thought on arriving in San Juan after leaving her job as an editor in Boston had been, "My God! What a perfect place for an artists' colony." She imagined "the Williamsburg of the West Coast," "the Aspen of California," and started a classical-music association, lobbied for the purchase of a "world-class organ," and promoted theater groups and a music festival. They were all sidetracked, she said, "because the jerks and rednecks screamed we were trying to take over their town." Her gourmet restaurant had folded "because the food was far too sophisticated for San Juan."

Her plans for San Juan meant preserving its physical appearance but changing its human community. Caetano wanted to preserve the human community and make some changes to its physical appearance. The only way to choose sides was to ask yourself which was more rare and endangered: an eccentric town of cowboys, saloons, artists, and fifth-generation ranchers, or an artists' colony for day-trippers?

One of Sonne Reyna's enemies (and in San Juan most people had many) claimed he was "no more Indian than George Bush." I dropped into his store, Reyna's Gallerias, because both it and his house were close to the fault, and because he was said to know Lonnie Hurlbut's whereabouts. I found him perched on a stool surrounded by baskets, turquoise amulets, and cassette tapes of Native American music. He was reading a paperback Western. The cover showed bare-chested Indians and square-jawed cavalrymen and said, "Captain Morgan Nance was an unusual officer. He did not believe that the only good Indian was a dead Indian."

He wore wraparound sunglasses and had a jack-o'-lantern smile. "How ya' doing, buddy?" he asked, gripping my hand hard, but releasing it gently. One look at his shaman's eyes and the frizzy, black hair pulled back into a braid and I knew the "fake Indian" stories were nonsense, the fruit of another poisonous San Juan feud.

He was an appealing mixture of the convivial and mystical. "Make yourself at home," he urged me in his Texas twang as he sold jewelry to some Japanese tourists. He called his store a "living expression of our philosophy of one earth, one people," and his 10-percent Vietnam-veteran disability payments "untouchable spirit money." The spirits bringing him to San Juan had urged him to awaken its Native American soul. He believed earthquakes unleashed powerful forces for good, and Loma Prieta had brought "a new cycle of hope, peace, joy, and happiness." Quakes were a sacred language, warnings from Mother Nature. "Unless we can get along, faults all over the earth will open," he said. "Nature needs to purify herself of the poisons we've created. Remember, buddy, anytime she can take us—extinguish us! We're simply insects walking on her skin." The intersection of the fault, Indian graves, and ancient Indian ceremonial grounds made San Juan the most powerful sacred ground in the country. Some visitors to the mission experienced miraculous revelations, bursting into tears afterward at his boutique.

Like Reyna, the store was a hybrid: a commercial enterprise grafted onto an Indian community center. While we talked he received calls from Indians in the Midwest wanting to reserve stalls at the Monterey Holiday Gifts Festival, and welcomed a family of Pomo who had made a long detour to meet him. Although he was Comanche from south Texas and the few surviving Indians around San Juan were Matsun, he had adopted their grievances. He asked a honeymooning couple from Sacramento, "Hey, you guys know that during the colonial period the Spanish fathers promised the Indians a million acres around the mission when they were civilized? So now all we're saying is, 'Hey, we wear the white man's clothes, speak his language, and pay his sales tax, so how's about that land?' "

Sometimes he burned sage and cedar to the Great Spirit and prayed for a sale during the slower winter weekends. When Indian hunters prayed for a kill, the Great Spirit communicated with the herd until finally one deer would volunteer, stepping forward and saying, "I will sacrifice myself and feed that man." The hunter loosed an arrow at random into the nighttime woods and hit it. This was sacred stuff, powerful stuff, he said, "It's where the Indian still is. So I tell the Spirit, 'Hey, you know who we are; you know we have to pay the rent tomorrow.' When a customer comes in afterward saying, 'Hey, wow, it's my wife's birthday next week and I like this piece.' Well, he's my deer."

He believed as many as ten thousand Indians lay in the fault-intersected mass grave behind the mission. Many were victims of Spanish atrocities, and when he walked home along the Alameda he imagined them hanging from its trees. The violence had cursed San Juan, and until whites admitted their guilt it would remain a troubled place. The political feuds and Lonnie Hurlbut's misfortunes were different manifestations of the curse. He had persuaded Hurlbut to become an adopted member of the Reyna-wolf clan and take the name "Greywolf" (thereby performing the neat trick of being a sheriff who was both cowboy and Indian).

Reyna and other Indians stuck by Greywolf after his arrest, using the American Indian Spiritual Freedom Law to force the county sheriff to allow them to visit the prison to hold prayer sessions on the roof. Right now Greywolf was making a spiritual pilgrimage to Micmac Indian territory in Nova Scotia, getting in touch with his mother's tribal roots.

Had I not met earthquake sensitives, or read that the grinding of tectonic plates could perhaps produce radio signals and lights, and that before a quake streams had been observed to run hotter, water pressure might drop, and animals became twitchy, I might have dismissed Reyna's claims for the fault. Instead, when he called it a place of miracles characterized by electricity, power, and supernatural stuff happening, where Indians sought visions and talked to ancestors, I wondered if these were not simply the logical conclusions of a people who had been experiencing these seismic phenomena longer than anyone in California. And when he argued that if the white settlers had asked Indians about earthquakes, they would have learned the Matsun never built permanent dwellings over the fault, and that Mother Earth opened her jaws once every hundred years in San Juan, I thought of the Wiyot, and agreed.

He believed omens had preceded Loma Prieta. Mother Earth had appeared to a local medicine woman in a dream, warning the earth would shake in seven days. A local man had swerved off the road into Reyna's yard, killing his dog Wolf Dreamer at a spot directly over the fault one year to the day before the earthquake. The tremor had caught him stepping out of his car. The earth revolved and telephone wires cracked like whips. His house seemed to take a deep breath and he saw daylight through cracks in its boards. His wife ran outside, her hair standing on end. A pillow of dust floated overhead and birds seemed frozen in the sky, their embrace occurring in a timeless, windless, noiseless bubble. They spent the evening in their sweat lodge thanking Mother Earth for sparing them. Afterward they were extraordinarily productive, as if the quake had supercharged their brains.

Was he sensing any earthquake omens right now? I asked.

"Nothing, buddy," he said. "Mother Earth's real quiet."

He drove me to his house in a rattletrap truck protected by a collage of dashboard charms that included a turtle shell, garlic bulb, and feathers. His bumper sticker said ONE EARTH—ONE PEOPLE. He lived across the highway from San Juan, in a farm worker's cottage backed against a creek once lined with Indian villages. His backyard spiritual camp was an uncanny reflection of the condition of Native Americans, making it all the more convincing. The sacred lodge was a circle of warped plywood and tin panels built over the fault to connect with its power. The remains of Wolf Dreamer lay beneath a dead tree with twisted branches he called his altar tree. He offered tobacco, prayers, and songs to the ancestors from a ring of blackened boulders—the sacred fireplace.

He peeled some bark from the altar tree and presented it to me as a souvenir. Then he gripped my arm and said urgently, "Right here we began our sacred 'One Earth, One People' peace mission. Right here we are in Indian country! The spirit is here; the fault is here. Hey, buddy, this is *very* powerful stuff."

I thought, "So what if he is one quarter, or one sixty-fourth Indian? Or if his Indian beliefs are seasoned with loopy New Age platitudes?" Without his Indian market, sweat house, or store, I could have easily visited San Juan and never known it had been an important Indian settlement. I did not care that much for his curios, and their prices were more hopeful than realistic, but I bought a necklace anyway, paying eighty dollars without haggling for the honor of being his next deer.

32

Quake City

South of Gilroy I smelled garlic, not the bitter stink of a cheap ethnic restaurant, but a gentle garlic perfume. I opened the windows and filled my lungs.

At the Christopher Garlic Ranch, Don Christopher said, "I could be an overnight multimillionaire if I plowed up my garlic and subdivided." But instead of adding to the sprawl from San Jose lapping against his holdings, he preferred the challenge of satisfying the national craze for garlic, and preserving Gilroy's open spaces. He was the largest grower in the nation, with 28 percent of the market, and right now the demand seemed insatiable. It was the fastest-growing agricultural product in California, driven by immigrants (the Koreans averaged a bulb a day), health faddists, and thousands of new Asian and Mexican restaurants. When his father planted ten acres in 1955 garlic had been a joke, eaten by foreigners and somehow un-American. In 1950 the average American family did not even eat a bulb a year. Now it was so chic he sold garlic salsas, pesto, and barbecue sauces to gourmet stores. It was shaken over food instead of salt, taken for colds and a feeble heart, and rubbed on sores to make them vanish. He swallowed a clove with a glass of milk at bedtime.

He was a good advertisement for garlic—a trim man in his late fifties with the unlined and untroubled face of an Ivy League diplomat. He had just been sampling new salsas but his breath was spicy, not sour. Worrying about garlic breath was passé, he said, its new connoisseurs demanded strong flavor.

Gilroy was the mother lode of the garlic gold rush, the self-proclaimed "Garlic Capital of the World," and when he wore his garlic pin to New York City, people shouted, "Hey! You must be from Gilroy!" Its garlic festival attracted 140,000 tourists, who washed down garlic slivers pressed into bananas with four-clove vodka cocktails. "I think garlic just plain makes people happy," he said, trying to explain it. "Mention garlic and anyone smiles. It puts everyone in such a good mood I think they should serve it to prisoners." It had certainly made him one of the happiest Californians I met. Photographs of garlic covered his walls, and everywhere jars of open garlic condiments were surrounded by crackers, ready for snacking.

His sheds were wonderful, several stories high and reeking of garlic. Cloves overflowed wooden crates, boiled away in kettles, and rolled down conveyor belts to women in masks for sorting and cleaning. Even their names made me smile. There was Flor, Giant, Jumbo, Extra Jumbo, Super Jumbo, Colossal, and Super Colossal. I chewed on a Colossal and felt as if my sinuses, closed for weeks by pollen and pollutants, had been irrigated by high-pressure hoses. I was suddenly light-headed, drunk on garlic.

He had painted his cross-country garlic trucks with wonderful murals. Their colors were exaggerated, almost psychedelic. They showed a sun setting over fuzzy green fields of garlic stretching to the Santa Cruz Mountains, just the kind of panorama of agricultural bounty and mountains that once decorated California orange crates. Every week these murals sped across the continent, a rolling advertisement for the California Dream. What they did not show, and what Midwestern farmers looking up from tractors to see them racing down interstates could not have known, was that they omitted the guards and police cars needed to protect Christopher's crop. Like other things in rural California not bolted down, fenced in, electrified, or guarded, garlic was being stolen in record quantities. A caravan of cars would screech to a halt, and the garlic rustlers would dash into fields with burlap sacks. Christopher had hired guards and the sheriff's department had assigned a full-time deputy, but the thefts, like the demand for garlic, only increased.

Hollister was a seismic Times Square, where the main trace of the San Andreas and the Calaveras Faults drew closer, narrowing like a V to merge just south of the city. Its own canny publicity proclaimed it "the Earthquake Capital of the World," and "epicenter of California earthquake country . . . sitting uneasily on top of the notorious San Andreas Fault system." It was also an agricultural crossroads, where rich limestone soil met drought-stricken rangeland, and billboards north of town screamed HOUSES FROM $159,000, while to the south a sign warned, NO SERVICES FOR 65 MILES. Lettuce, broccoli, onions, walnuts, and grapes filled its fault-created valleys, benefiting from the microclimates left by millions of years of Loma Prietas. But they might not fill them for long since sprawl from San Jose had leapfrogged some prime agricultural land and was beginning to strangle Hollister from the south. A developer was proposing a gated golf course and senior citizens' condominium for the rich valley I had admired from the mission of San Juan Bautista, and there was talk of expanding the airport for cargo planes and corporate jets, and of a self-contained "village" of ten-thousand houses. Developers were burrowing cicadalike into local society, buying ranches, turquoise jewelry, and cowboy boots, learning to ride, and elbowing their way onto the boards of whatever local institutions would have them.

But even the suburban sprawl and Loma Prieta damage did not entirely account for all the empty downtown stores and lots ringed by Cyclone fences. A determined arsonist had been at work. He took a souvenir from each conflagration and was only apprehended when a fireman saw him escaping on a bicycle clutching a stuffed rabbit snatched from the flames engulfing a florist's shop. The clerk in one of the last downtown stores who related this story said, "It seems real funny now, but he killed Hollister faster than any shopping center or earthquake."

Thanks to him and Loma Prieta, downtown remained the calm eye in the hurricane of concrete, earth movers, and flapping GRAND OPENING flags swirling around its outskirts. Its main street was a prize-fighter's grin—every other tooth knocked out. It was the kind of California downtown that is almost as predictable as the shopping centers and malls replacing it. There were storefront social welfare offices, secondhand stores, a courthouse lawyers' café, and a martial-arts center where nine-year-olds pulled menacing scowls behind the dusty windows of a defunct shoe store.

Like many of these downtowns, Hollister could pull a surprise. One was Bob's Videos, whose signs announced it rented tapes for THE PRICE OF A POLITICIAN and only closed on Richard Nixon's birthday. Another was the San Andreas Brewery, which had preserved the tile floor and swiveling stools from its incarnations as a creamery and luncheonette and decorated the labels on its "Earthquake Pale," "Survivor Stout," "Seismic Ale," and "Oktoberquake" with a seismograph's squiggly line. It was more proof that after decades of denial, Hollister's boosters had come to their senses and turned their earthquakes into a tourist attraction, selling QUAKE CITY T-shirts, and offering guided tours of buckled sidewalks and cracked foundations.

I ordered a beer and hoped for an ironic earthquake, imagining the story I would tell: "Would you believe, I was raising a glass of Seismic Ale when ... " Since the grid of faults underlying Hollister produces about 21,000 tremors a year, it was not impossible the earth was slipping right now. Instead, the brewery's front door banged open and boys in white karate robes swarmed into the front room, kicking and chopping the air, still jazzed from their lesson. When the smallest one tilted the pinball game, an older one, blond and angelic, screamed, "Fuck you!" and slapped him hard, bringing tears. Another pointed at an upright piano and, so help me, asked his parents, "Hey, what's that?"

Hollister is geologically notorious for the slow sliding of a fault known as "creep." It was such a new concept in the 1950s that the winery plagued by it had no idea why one side of its warehouse was separating itself from the other. Now it was so sick of gawkers it posted NO TRESPASSING signs. During the seventies, Hollister's faults became the most studied in California. Scientists wired them with tiltmeters to measure vertical displacement, magnometers to detect changes in the magnetic field, and creepmeters to measure horizontal movement. They argued whether visible creep relieved strain, making a serious earthquake less likely, or if it indicated an impending rupture. The ultimate goal was the usual seismological Holy Grail, forecasting earthquakes.

I picked up a fault map at the chamber of commerce and, looking for creep, followed the main trace of the Calaveras through a leafy residential neighborhood and busy park. The fault ran under first base of a softball field, the front porches of some restored Victorians, and bungalows top-heavy with the monster aerials of hostile embassies. The children riding bikes over humps in the sidewalk, and the men repairing cars on cracked driveways made me think of those 1950s horror films showing insects increasing in size and number while small-town Americans get on with their lives.

As I looked for wavy sidewalks, offset hedges, and rectangular garages becoming triangles, I was also reminded of Daly City, another town where people became uneasy at the approach of a stranger. A woman watching her children in a playground near an offset sidewalk said, "Are you trying to scare me? I don't like to talk about earthquakes, it's ghoulish." When I approached a porcelain-skinned grandmother who was standing on a cracked sidewalk in front of her house, she retreated behind her front gate and said a gentleman friend would soon be arriving. A Hispanic laborer whose house overlooked the softball field said he was building a Kmart extension designed to withstand any earthquake. Even if the rest of Hollister collapsed, it would survive. "I spit on the fault," he said, sending a gob of saliva toward the baseball field.

The proprietor of the video store closing on Nixon's birthday was a sweet, mountainous man named Bob Valenzuela whose scraggly beard and fringe of shoulder-brushing gray hair made him look like Santa Claus gone to seed. After several minutes of watching him throw customers the peace sign, I figured him for an old yippie stuck in the sixties. Instead, he wrote a weekly column in the *Hollister Free Lance* and was the most influential journalist in San Benito County, courted by politicians and called by informants, he claimed, "whenever anyone in this town so much as farts."

One of the many developers he had vilified had sent an attorney to check the voting rolls, betting he would be a registered socialist or communist. Valenzuela liked imagining his expression when he discovered he was a Republican who never missed an election. He delighted in these contradictions. He had been raised in a family of Catholic Democrats, so naturally, he said, he became a Protestant Republican. He had organized the first antiwar march in Hollister's history to protest Desert Storm, but was also leading a campaign to have a street named after a Hollister boy killed at Pearl Harbor. While serving as high-school junior-class president, he had met Nixon twice during his 1962 campaign for governor, admiring the "really sharp" way Nixon remembered his name the second time.

Celebrating his birthday was a typical Valenzuela stunt. The photographs of the secondhand bookstore he once owned in San Francisco's rough Tenderloin district showed signs saying B.O.B.'S USED BOOKS—BOOKS FOR THE PRICE OF A POLITICIAN, and JOAN CRAWFORD MEMORIAL DAY CENTER COMING HERE SOON! The reformed dopers and alcoholics who became addicted to reading raced through three used paperbacks a night, then hung around all day rehashing the plots. "They drove us nuts, so we shifted to videos," he said. "But it was the same thing. They'd rent five and watch them all night." His policy of fostering a community store by renting only to people living within four blocks had created problems with Mayor Feinstein when he rejected her as a member of his video club for being geographically incorrect, and with yuppies from outside the neighborhood who were so upset to be denied access to his unique collection of vintage films they sued for discrimination.

When bureaucrats dumped addicts onto his San Francisco block, it changed overnight into a drug market. He and his wife and partner decided to move and spent months driving across California looking for a rural town with good tap water and a vintage movie theater. They narrowed the choice to Hollister and Hanford, the county seats of two small agricultural counties. He preferred Hanford for its Fox Theater, but his wife and partner outvoted him, so they returned to his boyhood home. When he was growing up in Hollister, it had been 30 percent Hispanic; when he moved back, it was almost twice that. Otherwise he thought race relations were about the same. "When I walked downtown in the 1950s people muttered, 'Here come those lazy, fucking Mexicans,'" he said. "When I moved into this store the Republican campaign headquarters was next door. The man in charge had known my father and he said, 'Hey, Bob. Why the fuck did you come back to Hollister? The goddamned Mexicans have ruined the place.'"

He settled in happily, adjusting his video library to satisfy the local appetite for Westerns, World War II, and anything starring John Wayne. He got a kick out of the politicians who courted the liberal vote by being photographed shaking hands with Hollister's bearded hippie, then took him to lunch and said, "I hate what you write, and I don't think you're the least bit funny, but did you know that . . . "

He had pasted some of his press clippings on windows and kept others close at hand in a manila envelope. His Nixon's birthday celebration had landed a mention by *Paul Harvey*, an appearance on the *Today Show*, and a Rona Barrett interview. Announcing a free rice-and-condom giveaway after the Gary Hart–Donna Rice scandal had put him on the wire services. Editing the diet Pepsi commercials out of his *Top Gun* videos was worthy of mention in *Variety* and the *Village Voice*.

All this notoriety struck me as more evidence California eccentrics were becoming an endangered species. *People* had lionized Lonnie Hurlbut, *Oprah* had found Jerry Hurley, and every eccentric seemed to come with a thick media scrapbook. Had the national appetite for California's eccentrics expanded, or was there a local shortage? If California could lose its eccentric main streets, and if formerly eccentric towns like Monterey and Mendocino could be turned into commuter dormitories and tourist destinations, perhaps it was only logical the eccentrics they once nurtured should become more scarce, and I am sure some Californians reading about Valenzuela must be thinking, "Not *him* again!"

The same issue of the *Hollister Free Lance* inviting the public to an open house at the new $7.8 million county jail also announced that San Benito County's supervisors had decided to save $100,000 a year by closing the library. This library already had few frills, and toilets so graffiti-plagued you had to trade your telephone number and signature for the key. Still, it was busy with the senior citizens and schoolchildren who have also become the principal constituents of most churches.

While jails were essential and mandated by the state, parks and the library were discretionary, "at the end of the county food chain," one functionary explained. No explanation was given why this rather paltry sum, the cost of one low-end tract house, had not been offered by the developers surrounding Hollister with Exclusive Residential Communities and promising "all the comforts of a modern California community," and a town "well known for quality education in all grades." Or why a county enjoying the increased tax revenues and prosperity from this development could not support a library. Politics were, of course, involved. Even so, a free public library is symbolic of a healthy community. To threaten it so cavalierly indicated a community unraveling at the same time as it was growing, one where lives unfolded more in private than public, and that was perhaps coming to resemble that suburban street in Cupertino where Sergeant Grief ran the fast-food flasher to ground.

Numerous financial and accounting excuses had been offered for banishing the library to the bottom of the county food chain. But you were still left with the fact that the officials making this decision had been elected, and it probably reflected the will of many constituents. One woman I asked to weigh the jail against the library told me, "I'd rather be alive and dumb."

Sheriff Harvey Niland had wanted to celebrate the opening of his new jail by offering dinner and overnight accommodations, but the county's perilous finances had shrunk this to an open house where, he told the *Free Lance*, taxpayers would have a chance to see what they are getting for their money. What they were getting was a concrete blockhouse that without its fences could have been a Wal-Mart or Costco. Niland was at the door, dressed in full cowboy sheriff regalia, pumping hands, embracing friends, and shouting. "Thanks for coming!" When a giggling matron said, "It's my first time in jail," he boomed, "A likely story!"

He was a courtly and rangy man with the confidence and charm you find in many people whose families have lived in the same place for generations and can trace their ancestors back to the first arrivals. His great-grandparents were Patrick and Margaret Breen, the only Donner Party survivors not to lose a single family member, although according to the definitive history of the affair they had resorted to cannibalism.

His open house had attracted schoolteachers, Boy Scouts, ranchers, a brace of widows, a nurse in hospital whites, and a farmer smelling of the barn. They all called him "Harvey." For some reason, anyone with a uniform had worn it.

Like any good politician he anticipated their complaints. This was no Taj Mahal, he declared. The old jail was seventy-seven years old and rated for only twenty-nine inmates. At its most crowded it held 102. This new one could accommodate twice that. The county was "looking to the future."

He led us inside to a control room resembling the command center of a submarine. Red lights indicated locked doors; yellow switches activated the intercom. The televisions could be blackened by remote control, a much-feared punishment. Reinforcing the submarine atmosphere was a ladder to a hatch in the roof so a guard could lock down and escape during a riot. It was smoke-free, wheelchair friendly, and politically correct, a state-of-the-art jail with unarmed guards and facilities for separating the child molesters, murderers, and youth gangs increasingly common in even this sparsely populated rural county. Noise sensors tripped alarms and fluorescent lights were unbreakable. Windows were narrow slits, stools were fastened to tables, and walls resistant to graffiti. One man wielding a high-pressure hose could wash it down in minutes. Eliminate the bars, and this hard-edged, brightly lit, easily cleaned interior could almost have been a state-of-the-art school, and why not, since the design of both is now determined by similar concerns with vandalism, supervision, and easy maintenance?

When Niland boasted of his guards being unarmed, a distinguished-looking gentleman I took for a retired teacher said, "I dunno, if I was a guard, I'd want to shoot to kill."

A rancher laughed, "No smoking! Ha-ha-ha, that's good. I bet they're smoking up a storm right now."

Another rancher disagreed. Better they got cancer and died.

But the policy was cost-effective, Niland argued; it stretched out the time between paint jobs.

"How about those skylights?" an elderly cowgirl asked. "Couldn't they open those bolts and escape?"

Niland seemed to understand his taxpayers had come hoping for a generous helping of advanced revenge, but he refused to pander, at least that much. He was the kind of straight shooter who would have stopped a lynch mob at the jailhouse door, and when a woman complained the sink for taking blood and urine samples could be broken and used as a weapon, he shook his head and said softly, "I doubt it."

When a rancher asked, "Why do you need such a big kitchen for bread and water?" Niland defiantly pointed out boxes of Uncle Ben's rice pilaf, Sierra sliced peaches, and buttermilk-pancake mix and said, "This kitchen is our pride and joy. Our inmates will eat better than they do at home."

The rancher looked disgusted. "That's for sure. *I* never get buttermilk pancakes."

Later he threw them some scraps. When a woman wondered about fires, he said, "Don't worry, nothing would burn except inmates and beds." When a man complained about the expense of making everything "wheelchair friendly," he replied, "Before, we had to let the handicapped go, but with these facilities I expect we'll be locking a lot more up."

We examined a vending machine while a Boy Scout read off the treats an inmate could buy: "Doritos, Grandma's Cookies, Cheetos . . ." There were also prestamped envelopes, dandruff shampoo, and playing cards.

Niland interrupted him. "Every time a prisoner buys a Three Musketeers we get a 25-percent markup. It goes into the inmate welfare fund to buy the television sets."

Orange punch and homemade cookies had been set out on a trestle table in the multipurpose room. "Used as a classroom and for AA meetings," Niland reminded us, "and don't worry, it's visible from the control room."

When the deputy ladling out punch said, "The inmates are just as excited as we are about this new facility," he got cold stares. The cookies were appalling, pure sugar. Niland announced the inmates had made them, and I thought I saw a smile cross his face as several hands jerked back from the plate.

By the time he led us outside, it was dusk and the setting sun had left an artillery-flash glow on the horizon. I saw it through a concertina of jagged wire that made me think of trench warfare. A man spat in the direction of the jail and said, "First thing Monday it'll be chock-full of goddamned Mexicans," a prospect he found equally disgusting and satisfying.

A rancher wondered if one coil of wire was enough. "Why not put in a high-voltage fence and electrocute them?" he suggested. "That'd be the best way."

When I asked about earthquakes Niland said that although Loma Prieta had damaged many buildings in Hollister, the old jail had suffered only a tiny crack. This one was even sturdier. Its power system was on springs and there were no sharp edges or big windows to shatter. He paused, then lowered his voice and said, "This is probably the safest place in the county to ride out a quake."

After the jail I was so desperate for fun I went to the high school for a student talent show. The newspaper said a panel of teachers would judge the acts, banging a gong to silence the worst. I hoped for a talented garage band, Asians playing violins, some singers and rappers, perhaps some tasteless but sharp teenage humor.

I found five-hundred students filling the movie-palace auditorium in a venerable Mission-style building. The teachers on the panel and an Hispanic family in church clothes sitting across the aisle were the only adults in evidence. Music videos played across a giant screen, and teenagers around me shouted back obscenities. Some girls passed a joint, a boy behind me looked at his program and shouted, "He sucks, she sucks, too. What fucking idiots!"

The program promised twelve acts. The crowd rewarded the student master of ceremonies who announced the first one with whistles and shouts of "fucking asshole!"

"Fallon" was four boys who pounded electric guitars, struck poses, and shouted "Do it! Do it!" for about a minute. "Bubbles" was three out-of-step girls lip-synching a rock song. "Disco Fever" was eight kids in bell-bottoms pretending to dance. Then a Chicano girl recited a poem unintelligible except for its final scream, "Fuck the police!" The "Funky Divas" were so pretty and scared and trying so hard that the judges, who were pathetically eager to be liked by their students, gave them high marks. Next, a boy dressed as "Waldo" ran onstage with a Super Squirter, pretending to masturbate and shooting streams of water into the audience.

So it went. No one could sing or dance. No one had rehearsed. Most lip-synched, imitating music videos. The audience screamed obscenities. Performers answered back with the finger.

The Hispanic man across the aisle from me whispered to his wife and she gathered their children and left. He stayed to videotape his son, who performed the only polished act, a break dance that brought the crowd to its feet. During the intermission, a jolly, bearded, good-guy teacher stood up and shouted, "Hey, guys, thanks for being the best-behaved crowd we've had in years!" While his back was turned "Waldo" ran back onstage, masturbating furiously with his Super Squirter, and spraying us with geysers of imaginary sperm.

33

Vehicular Recreation

For the moment, the southernmost outpost of the 150-mile-long Bay Area sprawl that begins in Sonoma County is Hollister's Stonegate subdivision. It sits on the edge of the southward-moving frontier separating ranchers from cellular-phone commuters, and is the last huddle of houses before the sign warning of sixty-five miles before the next food and services.

It was a pretty scary place for anyone nervous about earthquakes, or the health risks of high-tension wires and electromagnetic fields. A line of electric pylons marched across it, casting shadows and creating a death strip of unbuildable ground and somewhat undermining its promise of "truly unspoiled natural beauty." Meanwhile the Paicenes Fault, an extension of the Calaveras, was just across the road, and the San Andreas another mile beyond a low scarp. The two merged just south of the spiked James Bond–villain gates that gave Stonegate its name and cachet.

Anyone buying one of the three-to-four-acre lots had to promise to erect an "estate" (a "Residence of Distinction") of at least 2,500 square feet. The faux-Tudor, Georgian, French Provincial, Norman, and Italianate mansions looked good from the highway, but seen closer up they were puffed-up bullfrogs on small lily pads, just tract houses tricked up with columns, porte cocheres, gas lamps, and three-gar garages, half-breeds mixing Mission roofs with Tudor beams, or hunting-lodge stone facing with *Gone With the Wind* columns, but lacking the hedges and trees that conceal ego in an established suburb.

The agent at the sales office had the glacial manners of a veteran flight attendant. She said forty-four of seventy-three lots had been sold but prices were negotiable. The Hollister schools were great and crime was low.

But how about the library?

No one ever asked about *that*.

And the fault?

She gestured the wrong way. Over there, somewhere, but *real* Californians never worried. Was I from out of state?

Our conversation moved to the more comfortable ground of security and Stonegate's gates. She handed me a fact sheet promising, "When lots are sold out, gates will be open 6:30 to 6:30 during the week, closed Sat. and Sun. At close of escrow buyers receive two gate remotes, two keys to gate, acess (sic) code and two keys to tennis courts/restrooms."

"But if Hollister is so safe, why the gates? And why lock the toilets?"

"For the convenience of people."

"Which people?"

"The people who live here, of course. Anyone who can afford Stonegate doesn't want strange people driving around. Don't you think it's *convenient* to be safe?"

The Stonegate brochure made a big deal of Hollister's ranching heritage, cowboy neighbors, and "friendly, slower-paced quality of life." The recent issue of a magazine published by a developer was also devoted to San Benito's ranching heritage. Its cover showed a photograph of a freckled ranch girl in chaps holding a fiddle. In its articles I read "Our roots are in ranching," and "We are proud to honor some of the families who are continuing the tradition of ranching in San Benito county." A Stonegate advertisement in the same issue said, "You won't believe what you will find behind our private gates."

But just where would a Stonegate resident meet these cowboys? In their guarded streets? At the padlocked park?

A mile down the Paicenes fault from Stonegate I found three real ranchers in their late sixties named Dick, Jack, and Fred working at the San Benito County Historical Park to reassemble the nineteenth-century buildings they had saved from the bulldozer. Their faces and hands were cracked and sun-peeled, but their soft white upper arms showed short-sleeve construction work was new to them. They teased in the relaxed way of men whose parents had grown up together, and I was not surprised to learn that Jack's and Dick's ancestors had come "in the fifties—the 1850s," while Fred's had arrived in the 1880s. He was

black and the most passionate about local history. Dick was the organizer and spokesperson and exclaimed, "Aw shoot!" when he wanted
to swear. He said a carpenter or lumberjack sometimes gave them a
hand, otherwise they had the men in orange jumpsuits I could see nailing a roof. They were minimum-security Soledad inmates, mostly
drunk drivers from Los Angeles.

Fred, Dick, and Jack had not planned spending their retirement
building an open-air museum on this three-acre park, but after losing
the Paicenes store and stable, sites of the famous murderous rampage
of Tiburcio Vasquez, they felt compelled to do something. Already
they had saved the 1875 Willow Creek schoolhouse and the Sullivan
House, a homestead predating Hollister. A nearby heap of boards had
been the Tres Piñas jail, and the Four Corners Community Hall had
arrived yesterday and waited on pilings for its new foundation. The
history of the buildings they were reconstructing was sketchy, but they
were interviewing old-timers. Meanwhile, they tried staying a step
ahead of wind, fire, and the wrecking crew. "They're not the prettiest
buildings in the world," Dick admitted, "but they're all that's left from
the early days."

When the sun fell behind the steep San Andreas scarp shadowing
their park, they rubbed their arms but hesitated to leave. They admitted being too old to finish this job alone, and wondered if they should
furnish the buildings and open them to the public, sponsor community
dances in the hall, or throw a picnic and beg everyone to weed and
clear. So far no one had helped much—not the newcomers, the
younger ranchers, or the county. "In fact, San Benito County has
washed its hands of the whole thing," Dick said. "They gave us three
acres, and as long as we don't cost them anything, they're happy. The
modern power people say, 'We like what you're doing but don't ask us
to help.' The newcomers are up at five or six, coming or going in their
two cars. We'd like to meet them, but I don't think they have the time
for us."

My map identified a butterfly-shaped piece of land on the San Andreas
Fault just east of the historical park as "H.H.S.V.R.A." The initials remained a mystery until I saw a boy wearing a HOLLISTER HILLS—RIDING
ON THE FAULT LINE T-shirt and read an article beginning, "They come
from as far away as San Francisco, rising with the sun, lining up at the
gate before it opens." The letters stood for Hollister Hills State Vehicular

Recreation Area, which according to its literature was "The Mecca of Moto-Cross," and "the premier mountain for off-road vehicles (ORVs) in the state," where riders were "modern knights, their standards bearing the colors of their clan—yellow of Suzuki, red of Honda. . . . "

Hollister Hills was directly over the San Andreas and the state parks department advertised it as an added attraction, promising the only known moto-cross with an earthquake fault, and publishing a guidebook titled *Riding the Fault Line on THE EARTHQUAKE TOUR—a Self-Guided Vehicle Trail*. On the cover a cyclist jumped a fissure, maps inside directed riders to slumping hills, a scarp, and other fault-related features. Before I saw H.H.S.V.R.A. my attitude was so what if driving a truck, motorcycle, or dirt bike down bumpy dirt tracks was not exactly recreation; if some taxpayers preferred ORVs to bird-watching, why not give them some sacrificial public land.

A motorcycle recreation park at the birthplace of the legend of the outlaw biker also made historical sense. On July 4, 1947, four-thousand motorcyclists had gathered in downtown Hollister for a convention that became a riot. They held drag races, lobbed beer bottles at the police, and roared through the lobby of the historic Hartman Hotel. Police cordoned off streets and arrested hundreds for indecent exposure and inebriation. A press corps of ex–war correspondents called it an "invasion." A picture in *Life* (which its photographer later admitted posing) showed a grizzly-bear-sized biker sprawled across a Harley, a beer in each fist. "Cyclist's Holiday—He and friends terrorize a town," the caption said, launching the Hell's Angel myth even before they were founded.

When I asked about the riot in Hollister I heard exaggerated stories about blizzards of beer bottles, public fornication, topless girl bikers taking on men behind a jukebox, and a local girl rescued by heroic high-school boys. "The most exciting day of my young life," Bob Valenzuela had told me. "Motorcycles racing down sidewalks. Fights, people sleeping on lawns. The first time I saw a woman smoke in public."

It would later be said that Hollister was postwar America's dead canary in the mine shaft. *Harper's* published a short story about it that Stanley Kramer turned into *The Wild One*, starring Marlon Brando. *Life* mixed photographs of the actual event with stills from the movie and soon even Hollister residents had trouble distinguishing fact and fiction. The film attracted more biker clubs and rallies to town, and the demand for off-road riding helped persuade the Harris family to make some of its rangeland available to private moto-cross clubs. In 1970 they opened it to the public as the "Hollister Hills Motorcycle Playground." Five years later they sold it to the state.

Before the motorcycles, their land had been a private hunting club; before that, a legendary producer of garlic, melons, cattle, and grain that set a state record for growing walnuts; before that, a provider of wild oat hay to Wells Fargo teams; and before that, its beauty had bewitched Jesse Whitton, who had been John C. Frémont's surveyor and map-maker, and the man who drew the early maps of California that seduced Goldsborough Bruff as he copied them in Washington.

In March 1846, California's Mexican rulers had denounced Frémont's men as bandits, prompting him to build a log fort on Gabilan Peak and raise the Stars and Stripes. When a Mexican general dispatched soldiers to arrest him, he began retreating to Sutter's Fort. That first night his men camped along Soto Creek, the one now flowing through the H.H.S.V.R.A. The author of a history of San Benito County, Marjorie Pierce, writes of this first night, "The streams were flowing, the wild azaleas were in bloom and the birds were singing, and surveyor Whitton was enchanted."

He renamed Soto stream "Bird Creek" and vowed to make it his home. He returned after the Civil War to find a homestead association had just sold the property to another settler for fifteen dollars an acre. He immediately liquidated his Virginia farms and Arizona mines so he could pay fifty dollars an acre to make it his own. A few years before it became a motorcycle park, Pierce had written, "The scenic beauty of the ranch today is everything Whitton remembered it to be on his first visit." She described wild ferns, azaleas, twenty-seven varieties of oak, and a waterfall surrounded by six-foot tiger lilies.

I arrived on a Saturday morning to find the H.H.S.V.R.A. parking lot filling fast. Many riders had woken before dawn, driven several hours, and were impatient to hit the trail. It was a bad time to be asking about the Hollister riot, or how they felt about jumping the fault.

A computer technician who had started his son at age five said it was a great outdoor sport—"You know, nature and fresh air." A dentist from Walnut Creek whose six-year-old boy's hands shook as he adjusted his boots said it was a good way for fathers to spend time with their sons. Mike from Fremont said sure, riding the fault was an attraction because it created fun "washouts." His companion thought the fault had made it the most scenic off-road vehicle park in California.

I saw evidence of faulting where Whitton's Bird Creek made a ninety-degree turn when it hit the San Andreas near the ranger station. From an overlook near the Radio Range minibike track I could see it knifing through a saddle in a distant ridge. Just below, motorcycles scooted across it like mosquitoes. I leaned on a fence with a line of mothers whose sons rode dirt bikes around a track. The boys were all ten to fourteen. "They look like little warriors," a mother said, "and I like that." They praised the sport as good clean family fun. It kept their kids busy and off the street, and was more exercise than Nintendo. The boys stopped for lunch and took off their helmets and jackets. Most were little fatties with buttery faces.

Whitton's beloved Bird Creek Canyon magnified the jackhammer motorcycle engines. Its air was gritty and thick and it smelled and sounded like the Lincoln Tunnel, although it was worse since you could not roll up your windows and tell yourself it would be over in five minutes.

I stopped at a track in an oak grove where little kids drove dirt bikes in merry-go-round circles. Their parents had plugged boom boxes into trucks, setting the volume high so they could hear it over the racket.

The Pit-Stop was a windowless shed next to the creek. It sold full-face helmets, knee, shin, and shoulder guards, chest protectors, hip pads, kidney pads, over-the-calf boots, and color-coordinated riding pants. The manager insisted the press had sensationalized the Hollister riot. This was a family sport, and most of his customers were professional people who did not welcome low-grade bikers. Besides, Hell's Angels had not visited Hollister Hills in years and even they were into a clean-cut image, "out of black and into real cheerylike colors." The cranky environmentalists' complaints about ORVs eroding land, tearing up mountains, and filling the air with exhaust and dust (to which you could add a waste of medical resources since an inset in the trail map showed the fastest route to Hazel Hawkins Hospital) were all slanders on a great sport.

He used words to describe Bird Creek Canyon that could have come from Whitton's mouth. It was "a beautiful wooded canyon . . . filled with ancient oaks, ferns, and songbirds," and the only ORV park in the state with "canyons and other pretty stuff, and hot-water showers."

When he saw my canvas boots he pointed to a shaded triangle on the map marked "Restricted Use Area—Closed to Vehicles." It was set aside for hikers, he said. "We like to highlight this when the conservationists accuse us of not taking care of the land."

It was as lovely as Whitton claimed—a cool, narrow canyon filled with azaleas. A sign on the Bird Creek fire road marked the turn to the San Andreas Geological Observatory, a seismological station operated by the University of California, but declared it off-limits. Later I learned this "Restricted Use Area" was not closed to motorcyclists because of the off-roaders' environmental sensibilities but to avoid disturbing observatory's sensitive equipment. You could argue I suppose, that the fault was responsible for preserving this small wedge of Jesse Whitton's California Dream.

34

"Be Here When It Happens"

After the 65 MILES BEFORE NEXT SERVICES sign, the San Andreas ran through a string of valleys where red swirls of rock ground into powder by the colliding plates had painted scarps steep as railroad cuttings. At the northern end of this fault segment, ranchers sold their land for housing tracts, at the southern end, for vineyards. In the dry-ranching, drought-scorched middle they were selling their cattle.

At a restaurant I overheard a rancher tell his daughter, "Honey, don't you wish for anything but money, because then you can buy any ranch you want." When she asked, "But suppose I find a nice, rich, ninety-year-old guy?" his laugh was scratchy as tumbleweed. "Good luck, he'll have willed it to his children."

In a café, four ranchers drinking iced tea from mason jars gossiped about neighbors selling out to wineries and weekenders building houses with lookout towers, while they ate noodles and chili beans. Replacing cattle with grapes was a reversal of some fundamental natural law. An older man asked, "If I sell out for grapes, then what? Where do I go?"

I stopped in Coalinga to look up Fred Fredrickson, a friend of Richard Hansen's who had been fire chief during the 1982 earthquake that destroyed one fifth of its residential housing and leveled its sixteen-block downtown. The epicenter had been twenty miles off the San Andreas on an unmapped thrust fault, and provided the first evidence California was more seismically hazardous than anyone imagined. This danger registered on seismologists, but not on the public until the Northridge earthquake of 1994 struck another unknown thrust fault. Perhaps it had been easy to dismiss Coalinga's quake as an anomaly because the town was so isolated and unlike the rest of California. Its oil rigs, cows, unbroken horizons, and workmen in suspenders connoted Texas in the 1950s. The masthead motto of the *Coalinga Record* was, "The Only Newspaper in the World That Gives a Damn About Coalinga."

When I met Fredrickson at the nondescript fire station replacing the fine art-deco one destroyed in 1982, he said that when the world finally did give a damn about Coalinga, the attention was unwelcome. The newsmen were "a bunch of honks" who ran down hospital corridors shouting, "Where are the blood and guts?" The only looters were security guards from Los Angeles, stealing what they were hired to protect.

He darkened a room and showed slides from the earthquake. Other firemen drifted in to see Coalinga's lost treasures: the shattered stained-glass windows of the Masonic Hall, the State Theater, Coalinga Inn, and Morgadery's, whose mahogany bar had come around the Horn and had been the longest one in continuous use in the state. He explained that restoring commercial activity after the quake had been the biggest priority. How Coalinga looked (it now resembled a string of adobe strip malls) was less important than having it look like something quickly. Businessmen who argued for saving the least damaged structures, or salvaging bricks and cornices and reincorporating them into the new buildings had been easily outvoted.

"We had the best collection of unreinforced masonry buildings in California," Fredrickson said. "Now the tallest thing in town is the McDonald's arches."

The youngest fireman was a softhearted boy whose eyes watered when he related how the earthquake had devastated patients at the convalescent home where he had been working. Their memories had been buried in the rubble of the stores. They were bewildered, and he sometimes noticed them wandering like sleepwalkers through the hastily rebuilt downtown.

Before leaving, I stopped at the one-room Baker Museum, where the only other visitors were two elderly women flipping through photographs of elementary-school classes and downtown buildings. Had I not joined them, I might have left Coalinga grieving for its quake-destroyed history and disoriented senior citizens. Instead, I saw newspaper clippings describing the "Whiskey Row" fire of June 13, 1930, in which arsonists destroyed the town's most historic buildings.

The *Record* said the fires had "removed from the community its fountain head." Their ground floors had been speakeasies, their upper ones cathouses with extravagant names like the "Louvre". Coalinga's leading citizens had finally lost patience with this minor center of vice and torched it.

Once I knew Coalinga was willing to incinerate its history just to eradicate a little drinking, gambling, and whoring, I saw the earthquake damage in a new light, and left the museum wondering if the descendants of the arsonists, or the arsonists themselves, were among the dazed senior citizens bemoaning the loss of their favorite landmarks to the quake.

From Donalee Thomason's couch I could stare into the lens of a video camera mounted near the ceiling by the National Geographic Society, one of four in Parkfield calibrated to start filming at the first tremor of an earthquake. I reckoned it would catch her Hümmel figurines tumbling off tables, the collapse of her stone fireplace, and if she was unlucky, Thomason herself being crushed to death, and me, too, if it struck during the next hour.

She was a senior-citizen tomboy who wore flaming red cowboy boots and reminded me of Ethel Merman in *Annie Get Your Gun*. "If I'm going to die and my house is going to be destroyed and they want to film it, well that's okay with me, I guess," she said. In this "Earthquake Capital of the World," where ranchers raised cattle in California's empty quarter, one did not worry about the fault. "But I *do* think about that fireplace sometimes," she admitted. Because her househad been constructed after 1966 and never tested by a strong quake, she could only hope her fireplace's steel reinforcing bars would hold.

"All the *National Geographic* said was to be careful what I wore in front of that camera, because you never know when it might hit," she said. She had taken this suggestion as a joke, but perhaps it had occurred to someone that if she was caught running naked from the shower, the footage could never appear on public television.

Had there been a camera in the frame house across the road where she experienced the 1966 earthquake, it would have filmed her feverishly wrapping her Hümmels in bath towels after the foreshock, then jumping under a door frame during the main shock. You would have seen two fireplaces collapsing, the floor spinning like a roulette wheel, and glassware shooting from a china cabinet before hanging suspended in midair for the time it took her to count "one and two and three and four . . . "

Had there been a camera in the Parkfield school in 1934, it would have filmed the entire town gathered for an end-of-the-year program. Onstage nine-year-old Donalee Thomason and other students lined up behind a large white window frame. Before each child had a chance to step through it and recite a passage, the quake extinguished the gas lanterns and slammed them against the walls. When the shaking stopped, their teacher relit the lamps and they continued. When an aftershock threw little Neva Durham into the arms of the audience, she climbed back up and continued. Thomason said it was a typical Parkfield earthquake story, just like the family rebuilding a chimney toppled in 1901, oak trees slapping the ground during the moonlit 1922 quake, the hobo vanishing when a quake shook the barn where he was sleeping, and the cowboys lowering two lariats sixty feet into the 1934 fissure without hitting bottom. All were remembered and discussed.

A new Parkfield earthquake narrative began in 1985 when the USGS wired it with more earthquake sensors than anywhere on earth because of what appeared to be its predictable earthquake history. Suddenly cattle grazed among green seismometer boxes and ranchers watched boreholes being drilled for tiltmeters. A shed was erected to house a two-color laser Geodimeter, and creepmeter posts sprouted in the shallow gully over the main trace.

Journalists poured into the valley in helicopters, satellite trucks, and rental cars whenever the California Office of Emergency Services issued Parkfield earthquake alerts. Instead of a terrified population, they found a collective shrug. Why be afraid, Parkfield asked, when the main danger is a falling oak? When 150 years of earthquakes have produced no injury graver than a broken toe in 1966 and another in 1922 when a man kicked his fallen fireplace in frustration?

Some people hoped for a quake to strike soon, ending the press visits. Even Jack Varian, the rancher who had built a café and inn to cater to visiting journalists and scientists, had told a reporter, "We're hoping for a good ol' ripper to get some people out here to look around for a week. And then they'll go home and we'll go back to feeding cattle."

"It'd be all right with me if it happened," Donalee Thomason said. "We know it's coming, so why not get it over with?"

She gave me a tour that included the former elementary school where she had experienced the 1934 earthquake, the bridge offset twenty-eight inches by the fault since its construction in 1932, and some cracks where the fault crossed the road to Cholame. The county had thrown some blacktop on them last week, but she thought they would reappear soon. "I just *know* it's coming soon. It has to. It *always* has. There's just no reason for it to stop now," she said, with an equal measure of fear and longing.

Although she praised the fault for bringing the world to Parkfield's doorstep, her son refused to talk to reporters. A school-bus driver joked about running them over, the schoolteacher's wife was appalled at the waste of money on helicopters, and someone had spread a tall tale about a famous cow suffering convulsions before every earthquake that sent reporters dashing into pastures with flashlights. I heard stories about fifty journalists descending on the Parkfield Café and throwing fits when its two waitresses did not produce dinner at once, and New York reporters becoming nervous upon finding themselves sleeping in ground-floor rooms without security bars. The more reporters searched for fear, the more uncooperative people became. They would say, "Sure we're scared," raising hopes, before admitting to fearing drought, drunk drivers, falling beef prices, and their children being bitten by backyard rattlesnakes—anything but earthquakes. In Shandon, twenty miles to the south, a lizardy ranch widow told me, "We're nervous down *here* all right, but Parkfield people, they make it their business *not* to be afraid."

The clippings Thomason produced made me feel even sorrier for a reporter sent to Parkfield. They had filed stories headlined RESIDENTS AND MEDIA FIND NOT MUCH IS SHAKING IN PARKFIELD, and photographs of the road sign announcing, PARKFIELD, POPULATION 34, ELEVATION 1530' and the one painted on the café water tower declaring, PARKFIELD CAFÉ. EARTHQUAKE CAPITAL OF THE WORLD. BE HERE WHEN IT HAPPENS! (Since the café had partly been built to cater to the press, this amounted to a war correspondent returning from the front with photographs of his barracks.) Someone had even painted a red line across the Cholame road to show the path of the fault, then photographed that. Television cameramen had shot a display of earlier newspaper articles tacked to the café's walls. So many journalists had asked students at the one-room school to stage an earthquake drill that their teacher had posted a NO MORE NEWSPEOPLE sign. Anyone willing to be interviewed, was, again and again, particularly the café's owner, Jack Varian, who believed the San Andreas Fault had presented Parkfield with a great opportunity. "I'll make advantage of anything," he said. "If people want to make a big deal out of earthquakes, I'll go along with them. You got to take your liabilities and make advantages out of them."

Sometimes the stories described cowboys mending fences, cattle grazing under huge oaks, the one-room school, the library housed in a trailer, dogs asleep in the highway, and the "Old West" atmosphere—a small town that was clearly everything the rest of California was not.

After hearing from so many outsiders how lucky she was to live in Parkfield, and how awful their own hometowns were, the prospect of losing the two-thousand-acre ranch that had been in the family since 1915 worried Thomason more than any earthquake. Some ranchers had survived drought and falling prices by leasing land to hunting clubs or having a family member work in Paso Robles. But cattle and hay were her only source of income, and after five years of drought, she worried about making it through the year. Perhaps they could survive by renting property to hunters, perhaps they would fall victim to the epidemic of heart attacks striking ranchers quite literally scared to death by the prospect of losing their land. Her eyes watered and her voice broke when she told me, "We really don't know what's going to happen, and maybe that's a good thing."

I stopped at the Parkfield school to meet Duane Hamann, whom Thomason had described as the nicest man in the Cholame Valley. I hoped that since he monitored the Geodimeters for the USGS, he might know if I should stick around for an earthquake. When I arrived, school had just ended and his students were in the playground. There were twelve boys and four girls ranging from kindergarten through sixth grade. Six were the dark-haired children of Hispanic ranch hands, the others corn-silk blonds. The school was a concrete rectangle resembling a highway comfort station, a disappointment for anyone connecting *one-room school* with a cozy white clapboard building topped by a cupola. But inside I saw eight computer terminals, a piano, long bookshelves, and well-equipped science tables. Hamann said the state had given him $11,000 for new furniture, but he had repaired the old wooden desks himself and bought computers instead.

He was a strapping, sandy-haired six-footer. But twenty-three years of figuring how to get along with the same child through seven grades, handle siblings who fought at home, make good students out of those arriving without a word of English, and teach kids who were never on the same page of the same book at once had resulted in a soft-spoken, gentle man at odds with his imposing appearance.

He said running a one-room school was like flying a kite. You had to know when to pull the string tight so a kid wouldn't crash, when to let it loose so he could soar.

Like most Parkfield people he was an instinctive optimist, looking for ways to turn disadvantages into advantages. He had turned the earthquake alerts into advantages for his students by requiring reporters to lecture them about their home states in return for an interview, and he had turned the USGS experiment into a hobby and second career for himself. Several times a week he checked the Geodimeters that measured movement along the fault and reported back to scientists in Menlo Park. He worried that if the USGS prediction window closed without an earthquake, and the government cut back the budget and his equipment wore out, then when the inevitable Parkfield quake did strike, he would never know if his instruments might have predicted it. But there were six weeks left, and if the earthquake came soon afterward, his devices would still be functioning. Even last month's false alarm had the positive effect of reminding people to take precautions, and the experiment had already produced a wealth of useful scientific data. The USGS had always argued its main purpose was to gather information to help predict future earthquakes, not predict the next Parkfield one. It was the state of California that insisted on these embarrassing alerts as the price of its cooperation.

Like me, like the scientists in Menlo Park, and like most people in Parkfield sick of the waiting, he was rooting for an earthquake. But he saw no hopeful signs. The Geodimeters he checked were incredibly sensitive, capable of measuring a fraction of a millimeter. Over the eight years of the experiment they had shown the Pacific plate to be moving north at about its customary speed of a growing human fingernail. Recent weeks had seen no change in this pattern. He said if I had come to Parkfield for an earthquake, I was probably, like the USGS, out of luck.

Whenever I debated how long I should stay in a place like Parkfield in hopes of encountering an earthquake, I felt Bruff peering over my shoulder, reminding me he would have stayed longer.

The more I compared us, the more I came up short. He had been "the most skilled and consistent artist" of the Gold Rush; I am a sloppy photographer and have trouble managing even a simple line drawing. He had mapped, named, and traveled regions never explored by whites; I sometimes felt my trip was a succession of Taco Bells and Best Westerns. He had adopted the abused Lambkin boy and shared his meager rations with starving emigrants passing through his mountain camp; I had passed up the chance to give some pocket change to the homeless haunting the Lotta's Fountain ceremonies.

He was even better looking. In 1837, his wife had described him as a man of medium height, about thirty-seven years old, with a military bearing, a fine aquiline nose, and yellow-hazel eyes under long lashes that twinkled with merriment. "Laughter and merry jokes, pretty speeches to the fair sex, and a general light-hearted view of life, made him good company with all," she claimed. "He did not look his age by ten or more years. His hair was black as jet and fell coarse as [an] indian[']s to his shoulders." I am balding and fondly remember the journalist who described me as "pleasant-faced."

A saintly ancestor can be a burden, and after so far failing to find either an earthquake or a descendant of a Washington Miner, I was in the mood to comb through his published diaries again, this time looking for flaws. I reread them while staying in a motel near Parkfield, but the only moral failing I could find in almost one thousand pages was an admission that although he loved his wife, six-year-old daughter, and three-year-old son "as much as any husband and father can," he had been "compelled to leave [them] on credit."

Perhaps the praise heaped on him by the chroniclers of the Gold Rush provided clues to his shortcomings. Did not "careful to a fault" mean just that? *Too* careful? Had his insistence on keeping a careful journal resulted in him crossing the continent at slightly too leisurely a pace? (But you could just as easily argue that had he pushed his men more, they might have become *more* mutinous.) The historian describing him as "a soft touch for anyone in need" also noted he was "strict and correct in dealing with the men of his company." Too strict? His editors conceded his insistence on posting nightly guards against Indian raids caused grumbling. But although they listed twelve instances where Bruff mentioned problems with the company related to guard duty, they also noted that other companies of forty-niners experienced similar disputes. That Bruff was reelected in mid-August, and that unlike the Michigan Wolverines and most organized companies, his did not dissolve its constitution and divide its property, still argued for the friction being confined to a few malcontents, until the company reached California.

❖

Despite Hamann's gloomy prognosis, I hung around Parkfield a few more days, in part to live up to Bruff's reputation for patience and meticulousness, in part because I still believed the USGS scientists that it presented my best chance for an earthquake.

Because the inn was full, I stayed almost an hour away in Paso Robles, where the week before, Lynwood Drake III had gone on a thirty-five-mile, six-person killing spree that included a stop at the Oaks Card Parlour two blocks from my hotel. His suicide note said, "Damn the American family to hell," but his choice of victims reflected more specific complaints. In Morro Bay he murdered his former landlord and the man testifying against him at an eviction hearing. He shot up the Oaks because it once expelled him for being a nuisance. Two of his three victims had been dealers there, but the incident had left almost no footprints. When I stopped by, an animated bar crowd was placing bets on a football pool, and I drank surrounded by inebriated soldiers and tattooed lowlifes who looked capable of mass murder themselves. A plant decorated with yellow ribbons sat on a plastic box filled with stuffed animals you scooped with a toy steam shovel. It was already withering from smoke and lack of attention. The bartender said in a flat voice, "Yeah, it's for the guys who got shot," and kept pouring shots of tequila without missing a beat.

But seven miles up the road at the Mission San Miguel a 150-year-old mass murder was as fresh as yesterday, recounted in the guidebook published by the fathers, and by ladies in the gift shop. In 1844, Mexican Governor Pio Pico had sold the deconsecrated mission to an Englishman named John Reed, who converted it to an inn. Four years later Reed entertained five British sailors who had deserted their man-of-war in Monterey. They pretended to leave, hid in a canyon until darkness, then crept back hoping to steal a hidden stash of gold. When they found nothing they murdered the entire household of eleven, including servants, children, and an infant whose head was bashed against the cloister's stone pillars. Two of Reed's friends found the bodies heaped in the parlor. They buried them behind the sacristy and organized a posse that tracked down the sailors.

Inside the mission, nothing appeared repainted or retouched. The light was dim and the murder room meat-locker cold. The original chandelier swung overhead and the uneven bricks that soaked up the Reeds' blood still paved the floor. The fathers had added only a spinning wheel, antique organ, and a painting so time-blackened its subject was a mystery. Even if you knew nothing about Reed, or the clairvoyant who later claimed to have seen the massacre and woke from a trance with a mysterious bleeding wound on her back, you would have still sensed the room was haunted.

The third death spot within an easy drive of Parkfield is sometimes capitalized as The Death Spot or The Deathscape. It is where state highways 41 and 46 intersect, and where at twilight on September 30, 1955, the actor James Dean slammed his Porsche Spyder into a Ford driven by young Donald Turnupseed, who had the bad luck to be turning left from highway 46 (then 446) onto 41 at a T-junction that is directly over the San Andreas Fault. Anyone believing the 1950s were a kinder, gentler decade might consider that immediately afterward attendants rolled Dean's corpse for pocket money, a caravan of horn-honking teenagers circled the funeral home preparing him for burial, and burglars ransacked his Los Angeles house and made off with his bongo drums. Turnupseed received death threats (after the accident, police and ambulance attendants ignored him and he hitchhiked to Tulare, where his injuries were treated five hours later), and the friend of Dean's who inherited his scrapbooks locked them in a steel strongbox and slept with loaded pistols.

The "Deathscape" is so forlorn Hitchcock used it for his crop-duster scene in *North by Northwest*, and so monotonous it seems to say, "If you can't do 100 mph here, well, where can you?" Even though Cal-trans has moved the fatal intersection a hundred yards and installed a stop sign, flashing yellow lights, and a safety lane, fatal accidents are common. In one four-year period in the seventies, forty-seven people died along ninety-two miles of Highway 46, including two teenagers who collided head-on three miles from the Death Spot on the twenty-ninth anniversary of the Death Day, forcing participants in the annual James Dean Death Day Memorial Car Rally to detour around the wreckage.

I pulled onto the shoulder and walked back to the new James Dean intersection. The Death Spot and the fault were now beyond a fence on private land, its crumbling asphalt disappearing into the carpet of brush. Oncoming cars shot out of the dusty horizon like rockets, but traffic was so heavy the speed that killed Dean was more difficult.

Cholame was a half mile east of the Death Spot. It had a café, one-room post office, and stainless-steel memorial resembling a decapitated swastika that a Japanese businessman named Seita Ohnishi had erected in 1977. It was set in a rock garden around an oleander tree, and situated so it provided a distant reflection of the Death Spot. Plaques around its base carried quotations from Gide and Saint-Exupéry, and one from Mr. Ohnishi I hope suffered in the translation. It said, "Every day we find reminders that the drama of James Dean is the theme that we live," and offered a kamikaze glorification of his youthful early death: "The petals of the early spring always fall at the height of their ephemeral brilliance. Death in youth is life that grows eternal."

Given the mad Japanese crush on American pop culture, I thought Ohnishi's tribute was less remarkable than the fact that during the two decades of necrophilic hoopla preceding it, no one else had bothered to erect anything.

After Dean's death, fans continued writing him at the rate of eight-thousand letters a week. Journalists interviewed waiters at his favorite restaurant and reported what his cat had eaten the day he died. Fan magazines published photographs of his mangled corpse, and the Hollywood store where he bought the red leather jacket he wore in *Rebel Without a Cause* sold hundreds of copies at $22.95 each. Los Angeles spiritualists offered to put clients in touch with his ectoplasm, and an actress who had dated him built a speaking tour on the claim he spoke to her through the radio. His likeness appeared on hats, greeting cards, and windbreakers. A sculptor created life-size copies of his head covered with a fleshlike plastic. His wrecked Porsche was stolen during its nationwide tour by thieves hoping to sell its pieces, or perhaps by members of his own family appalled by the sordid sideshow.

Once you knew all this, it was obvious no one else had put a Dean memorial on the Death Spot because there was no profit in it. Weepy fans might decorate it with flowers, ticket stubs, and playing cards, but until Mr. Ohnishi, nobody had left anything worth a damn. Compared with the flesh-textured Dean heads and commemorative dishrags, his memorial was an exemplar of restraint and good taste.

A waitress at the Cholame café said if I was interested in Dean I should speak to Lily Grant, the retired postmistress and unofficial Dean historian.

Grant's ranch was the sort of homestead the Okies abandoned: tumbledown sheds, sagging fences, a tangle of gutted tractors, and livestock (who turned out to belong to her neighbor) grazing on sand. Only a satellite dish told you it was not 1932. She explained its downfall in the matter-of-fact voice of a guide covering familiar ground. It had been in her husband's family since 1880. They had spent the last fifty-two years ranching cattle and growing wheat and barley. When their last tractor died, they sold their last animals. The land was so eroded the government paid them not to farm, but when it recovered and the subsidy stopped, they would probably abandon it. Earthquakes were the least of her worries. The fault ran along a ridge a hundred yards to the east and her house was over a dry lake bed. Standard Oil had laid a pipeline across the property in the thirties to monitor it and reported tremors every thirty-six hours. She sometimes felt a shudder.

Since every possible circumstance of Dean's death had been examined by his fans, I asked if the fact he died on the San Andreas had merited any attention.

She led me into a parlor smelling of low tide and produced her scrapbooks. Like many houses on hard times there was at least one pleasant surprise, in this case a bookshelf lined with the *Encyclopedia Britannica* and bound editions of the *National Geographic* back to 1934. As I sank into a sprung sofa she said, "We got electricity in 1949, but when the power goes off it's a treat for me and I say, 'Hey! Don't go for that generator. Leave it alone.' Reminds me of my early days as a bride."

The older newspaper clippings turned to yellow confetti at my touch. She seemed stunned to have collected so much. "Understand, I was never really a *fan*," she said, explaining that Dean's death had not moved her and she only became interested later because of people like Mr. Ohnishi. Her duties as Cholame's postmistress included monitoring the seismograph outside the post office and answering questions from tourists. Almost every day brought a new Dean fan. One man displayed a portrait of Dean tattooed on his back, another arrived in a replica of his Porsche and stood leaning against it for hours. On the Death Day impersonators lounged against telephone poles up and down the highway, imitating his sultry pose. She had stumbled on the truth that obsessive fans are often more interesting than the object of their desire.

She put his fans in touch with one another, and invited them to visit and pore over her scrapbooks, making herself the center of an international community of his admirers. Sometimes she drew the line, and she had refused a written request to share her private Dean fantasy with a writer.

After two decades of Death Day fans she was not surprised when Mr. Ohnishi appeared with an interpreter and cameraman, announcing grandiose plans for a memorial in the parking lot and writing to her afterward, "Understand I am thinking about James Dean memory-establishing in your town." She imagined pagodas and geishas, but his architects submitted a tasteful design that even pleased the Hearst ranch, owners of the land. I sensed he had been a welcome change from run-of-the-mill Dean fanatics. "We communicate through gestures and interpreters and I find him *very* homespun," she said, showing me a snapshot of a heavyset businessman. They became buddies and lunched together on his yearly Death Date visit.

Building the memorial had only inflamed his passion. He published a Dean biography in Japanese, converted a floor of a Tokyo motel into a Dean museum, and commissioned a French sculptor to create a second memorial, a 120-ton, thirty-six-foot-high limestone monolith containing a three-times-life-size bust of Dean titled the *Wall of Hope*. The sculptor promised "a living piece of art" designed to encourage graffiti. When the Hearst ranch rejected it, he bought 350 acres in neighboring Shandon. Now everyone was holding their breath, waiting for his next move.

She was disappointed he had missed the last three Death Dates, sending instead letters postmarked September 30. One began, "Greetings on the 37th anniversary of the day we lost the rising star James Dean who is still influencing so many people today." His American attorney also wrote, apologizing for his client's absence and explaining that construction workers had struck a hot spring with medicinal properties while working on an Ohnishi property in Kobe. It was being developed as a spa and, "In regard to the above blessed, mysterious phenomena some people who know Mr. Ohnishi say this has happened because of what he has done for James Dean."

I wondered why Mr. Ohnishi had not done something for his friend Lily Grant, say a small loan so she could feed her cattle and repair her tractor. Had it occurred to her to ask? Or to him to offer? Had he seen this desperate ranch? The contrast between its condition and his eagerness to squander money on Dean drained some of the charm from their friendship.

Her notebooks were thick with newspaper articles and letters from fans, but contained no mention of the San Andreas Fault. A law student had sent a copy of Dean's favorite book, *The Little Prince*. Don Henderson of Santa Monica had drawn a map showing the exact spot on his roof he had stood while watching the film *Rebel Without a Cause* across the street. The persistent Sharon Hauser, a frequent visitor to Cholame, begged for postcards of Ohnishi's memorial.

"Don't let me hurry you," Grant said when I began flipping fast through material that was mostly interesting for the fact it existed in such quantity. She had saved everything: customs slips accompanying

Ohnishi's shipment of polished pebbles to replace ones stolen by souvenir hunters, an appalling drawing of Dean in angel's wings, even the brittle petals of a rose left at the memorial by Ms. Hauser.

"Take your time," she begged as I skimmed police photographs of the accident, an obituary of the highway-patrol officer who issued Dean a speeding ticket, and an article describing how Dean enthusiasts had built pieces of the Death Car into Porsches that suffered horrible accidents of their own.

The articles and correspondents described Dean's death as a "tragedy," but I thought the real tragedy was Donald Turnupseed's. He received death threats from one generation of Dean fans, and creepy attention from the next. "Reclusive Donald Turnupseed still dodges questions," said a 1992 clipping, implying he had something to hide. He was a "mystery man," "terrified of being branded as the man who killed the big Hollywood legend." The cofounder of "We Remember Dean International" declared, "We don't hate him. We don't want to get even," as if this were a generous concession. Mr. Ohnishi was frantic to correspond with him, meet him, persuade him to attend a Death Date ceremony, anything. He enlisted Grant in the crusade, asking her to inform Turnupseed he would travel to Fresno "at his convenience."

"I'm *still* not a Dean fan," she said when I closed the last scrapbook. "But I *am* interested in history, and my scrapbooks *are* history."

Well, a kind of history, I thought, the kind you find in Mendocino, Filoli, Bodega Bay, Cholame, and anywhere else once the setting for a popular film or television series, and a history certain to thrive in a state with so many famous film locations. The Colma graves of California's nineteenth-century pioneers and magnates were largely ignored, Martin Murphy's house in Sunnyvale had been leveled, no one was helping Fred, Jack, and Dick save San Benito County's historic homes from the wrecking ball, and Bruff's name appeared on a single, inaccessible marker, but like Filoli, the Potter School in Bodega, and "Jessica's House" in Mendocino, Mr. Ohnishi's memorial to Dean received thousands of pilgrims a year, and Lily Grant's scrapbooks will someday command a good price from whatever library is assembling the primary source material for this flourishing new discipline.

SEVEN

TO THE
SALTON SEA

❖

35

"Master-Planned Community"

I arrived in Taft at night, which was probably the best time to see it. Lights twinkled on its oil rigs and storage tanks, and its main drag was so wide and empty I could have made a U-turn blindfolded. Interstate 5 was eighteen miles away and AAA and Mobil had not approved a single motel. The cinderblock taverns were out of the fifties, a good decade for bars, with timeworn leather banquettes and small televisions perched in high corners. The waitresses had no interest in revealing their Christian names.

The next morning it was a bleak, blue-collar town of deep porches, rusty air conditioners, and small windows, a place built for scorching summers. Pumps pulled oil from one of the richest fields in North America and the air smelled of asphalt. It was so unlike anywhere else in California that I declared a vacation, staying another night in my twenty-five-dollar motel, lunching on perhaps the cheapest and best nonfranchised burritos in California, and reading that in 1926 a "mouse army" of thirty million had swarmed into town, terrorizing the oil-field roustabouts and devouring sheep. State officials had dispatched an exterminator named Piper.

The fault ran about ten miles to the west across the barren Carizzo plain and I drove there through slumping, dunelike brown hills. In photographs, the Carizzo resembles Morocco, West Texas, Nebraska, or North Dakota, almost anywhere but California. But once I saw its sag ponds and scarps, I knew I was on the San Andreas. What appeared in aerial photographs to be a fissure cut by a giant plow turned out to be a narrow valley running through scarps created by earlier earthquakes.

The strongest San Andreas quake in written history struck just south of the Carizzo at Fort Tejon in 1857. Every building cracked or fell. A circular corral became an S, and a miner watched the earth swallow his camping gear. Although the shaking probably continued longer than in 1906, the only fatality was a man buried in his adobe house. Eyewitnesses were few and the quake had no effect on California's settlement. Fort Tejon is more likely to be remembered for what happened the following year when it hosted the U.S. Army's first and only camel corps. The animals' tender feet were unsuited to the rocky ground, so they were sold to carnivals or released into the desert where they sometimes trotted out of the heat haze like a mirage to terrify prospectors.

The fort sits on the saddle of the Tejon Pass along Interstate 5 and the exhaust fumes and rumbling trucks straining to make the grade make a visit no joy. It is a state historic park, but budget cuts have eliminated full-time rangers, so there was no one to tell me where the damage had occurred, and I wandered across the parade grounds and up a gully without finding a marker or ancient landslide.

Across the interstate, the former stagecoach stop of Gorman had become a two-café rest area. An exhausted woman behind the mini-mart cash register said, "The fault? You're standing on it. We feel every tremor over five." A few years before the Bulgarian artist Christo had erected thousands of gigantic yellow umbrellas across Gorman, I-5, the fault, and this parking lot, attracting sightseers in the tens of thousands. "It was the biggest fun thing that ever happened in Gorman," she said with a sigh, conveniently forgetting the fun had been cut short when wind hurled a Christo umbrella into a young woman and crushed her to death, and ignoring that "the biggest thing" happening here had been the Fort Tejon earthquake. If another struck right now, and if she was right about an active trace running directly underneath the counter, then she could have watched me jerked twenty feet to the north on the Pacific plate as the fault ripped her store in two.

I drove southeast down the fault on deserted roads to Nancy's Up the Road Café in Three Points. It was decorated with rattlesnake skins and served pickled eggs from a jar. The waitress balanced a Kool on her lower lip as she spoke. "The fault? You're sitting on it," she said. After the Landers 7.4 threw her neon beer signs askew, she left them that way as a conversation piece. She liked the fault. "Makes the country interesting and pretty. Besides, living over it must be safe because we haven't had much damage from the last few quakes."

From Three Points I followed Pine Canyon Road through a narrow valley broken by sag ponds. The smaller ones had attracted ducks, the larger were called "lakes" and ringed with houses for retirees, weekenders, and long-distance commuters. A real-estate flyer I picked up in Lake Elizabeth asked, "Can you picture an easier, calmer lifestyle in a pristine setting?" It promised an escape from Los Angeles traffic, smog, and crime, but this pristine setting had a golf course and housing tract, and at the public campground vandals had covered toilets and signs with graffiti and hurled a picnic table into the water. A sign said I had just crossed into Los Angeles County.

Like Loch Ness, Lake Champlain, and other deep, mountain-bound lakes, Lake Elizabeth has its monster—a creature with batlike wings, six legs, and a bullfrog's head. It terrified Spanish settlers into abandoning their homesteads, and American squatters later fled swearing the lake was haunted. One paranormal researcher has speculated that if earthquake lights can explode across night skies during tremors, "then perhaps the same forces can create fantastic mirages and illusions like flying monsters."

Ten miles down the road in Leona Valley, mysterious springs had been erupting along the fault. They had started last year when ponds dry for decades suddenly filled with water and attracted families of mallards. Torrents swept through horse barns, a spring erupted in a living room, a pond swarming with tadpoles appeared overnight at the community center, and rivulets flowed down driveways, collecting in puddles that refused to shrink. USGS geologists took photographs and water samples, but lacked funds to map the springs and determine their source. They speculated the eruptions might be part of the natural recharge pattern caused by a sudden shift from drought to heavy rainfall, or somehow connected to the Landers earthquake, or the movement of plates along the fault.

Mary Ann Floyd, who lived over the San Andreas Fault in Leona Valley, told me she blamed it for the springs erupting under her horse barn. If this was simply a case of runoff or recharging springs, then why had water also filled sag ponds at high elevations? Why would springs on the North American plate dry up while those on the Pacific plate were still erupting?

When I met her she was digging up her front yard in a hunt for the gophers that had attacked her fruit trees. She had an outdoor face and a rancher's rough hands, and did not look like someone a development company owned in part by Barbara Walters's ex-husband Merv

Adelson would sue for $3 million for defamation, but that was what was happening. She had no money to mount a defense and no clue how to find it, unless she sold her property. "The wealth and power these people have is terrifying," she said, hugging herself and clenching her teeth as if caught in an arctic wind. "If they want to bury me, they can."

She and her family had first visited the valley during a weekend excursion in 1975. As they left the U-pick cherry orchard they saw a 4-H Club girl herding her sheep down a country road lined with cottonwoods. "The peace and tranquillity of that image implanted itself upon us," she said. "Then we returned to the San Fernando Valley to find someone had stolen the kids' bikes and that burglars hit my parents in San Diego for the third time." Her father had dreamed of a ranch, now they all dreamed of Leona Valley. They saved for seven years, sold both homes, and moved in 1982, sharing this house. During the first winter the roads iced up and the electricity went out. They felt like pioneers. Her husband found work nearby, but until recently she had risen every morning at four A.M. to commute sixty miles to an administrative job at Lockheed. It was exhausting, but she never considered moving back "down below," the term Leona Valley residents use for Los Angeles, as if it were hell.

She invited me inside for coffee. The view from her picture window of mobile homes, homesteaders' shacks, and ranch houses scattered among oaks and cottonwood showed Leona Valley was no unspoiled wilderness. "We're not the best-developed place, and many of our houses are pretty shabby," she admitted, "but it's us."

The valley's 2,500 people were a lively mixture of old-time farm and ranch families, horse-loving retirees, weekenders, and middle-class shift workers like policemen, firemen, and pilots, who could stay home three days or more at a stretch. The newcomers had arrived during the last twenty years. They bought animals, enrolled their children in 4-H, and adapted to local ways instead of trying to change them. They had no illusions of suddenly becoming cowboys because they owned a horse, or farmers because they grew backyard fruit, but they participated in local customs like the Cherry Parade, where their kids decorated family horses and tied bows around pet goats. Some of their children married ranchers' children, others returned to the valley to raise their families, and three of Floyd's children lived nearby.

She was not sure how to define the valley. "We *say* we're rural, but too many of us commute; perhaps we're a sort of rural subculture.

Whatever we are, we want to stay that way." And that, to hear her tell it, was why Ritter Ranch Associates was suing her and other current and former members of the Leona Valley Town Council.

Four years before, Ritter Ranch had announced plans to construct a "master-planned community" of 7,200 houses on 11,500 acres stretching southwest along the San Andreas Fault from the valley to the western edge of the city of Palmdale. The sector nearest Leona Valley would have 1,500 houses and be three times its size. Like all of Leona Valley it was an unincorporated area governed by the Los Angeles County Board of Supervisors. Recently, the long-distance-commuter city of Palmdale had annexed this land and given Ritter permission to build on it.

Leona Valley residents complained the development was too big, dense, and different in character from the rest of the valley. They were appalled by the four-lane divided highway and flood-control project, and argued that the road leading to the proposed high school followed the main trace of the San Andreas Fault.

The valley's only democratically elected body was its town council. It lacked any official standing and could only advise the county supervisors. When its objections to Ritter Ranch were brushed aside, it filed three lawsuits seeking to reverse Palmdale's annexation and block construction until the project was scaled down so it was more in keeping with the valley. After the state supreme court ruled against the council, Ritter Ranch sued its current and past members, charging defamation and seeking redress for what its attorney characterized as unfounded lawsuits.

Mary Ann Floyd believed it was a classic SLAPP (Strategic Litigation Against Political Participation) suit, brought to frighten the council from appealing the court's ruling and, because it contained blank "John Doe" spaces that could be filled in with future members of the council and their supporters, to frighten people from running for council seats in upcoming elections. Friends had called her before the last council meeting to pledge their support, but admitted they were too frightened to attend. The meeting had been so emotional that even the men, even the ranchers, had cried. They collected $4,000 in a coffee can for a legal defense fund. Children threw in nickels, someone contributed $800. A former missionary gave an impromptu sermon of encouragement. A rancher thundered "How dare you!" at Peter Wenner, the general manager of Ritter Ranch Associates, and announced his candidacy for one of the empty council seats. They later demonstrated

at the Ritter Ranch offices in Palmdale wearing T-shirts saying I LOVE
LEONA VALLEY . . . SO SUE ME!

Floyd drove me around Leona Valley so I could understand why
she loved it. Although the houses were small, many had animals, gardens, and fruit trees. Children were outside, feeding goats, riding
horses, and doing yard work. I saw a Tudor mansion, an adobe house
once used as a drug lab, a barn where a bear had spent last winter hiber-
nating, the home of a Los Angeles attorney who raised llamas, and the
grounds of a leading authority on lilacs who sometimes opened his gardens for free tours. "We're a delicious mixture," she said, "full of real
individuals."

We drove up canyons on the Pacific plate side of the valley, where
streams of water from the mysterious springs still flowed down ditches.
She pointed out houses tucked into narrowing canyons and said, "See
how isolated these people are? No one locks doors, and all we have is a
single deputy. But once you suddenly add 1,500 houses . . ." She conceded
the upscale Ritter Ranchers would not be a threat, but they would attract
the bad guys who, when they found Ritter Ranch guarded, locked, and
patrolled, would turn their attention to houses that were not.

I returned two nights later for the Spring Time Country Dance at
the community center, a former Edwards Air Force Base barracks
moved here in the fifties and unwittingly plunked down on the fault.
Although a flyer for the event warned that "Spurs and Firearms will be
checked at the door," and asked, "Have you had it with your livestock
and kids? Do you need a hot time on the old town tonight?" it felt more
like a church social than a debauch. I smelled pot in the parking lot, but
there was no fighting or raised voices. People wore Western shirts, but-
ton-down shirts, polo shirts, work shirts, and T-shirts, leather-fringed
buckskin coats and tweed sport coats, boots, work boots, and sneakers,
white cowboy hats and baseball caps, gingham dresses, denim skirts
and leather miniskirts. Young people line-danced, square-danced, and
slow-danced to a country band under the eyes of their parents and
grandparents, and generations sat jumbled together at long tables decorated with horse-dung centerpieces.

I ate beef barbecue across from Juanita Kirkpatrick, a high-
spirited redhead who was also president of the town council and another Ritter defendant. People stopped to hug her and ask her to dance.
One whispered that she was the most beloved figure in the valley and
had taken the lawsuit hard, sobbing at the last council meeting. When I
mentioned it, her eyes teared and she changed the subject to what she

liked about Leona Valley—the four seasons, close-knit families, and people still leaving their keys in their cars. Last month the sheriff's office had received one complaint from Leona Valley, and that was only a nuisance call. Imagine, one complaint in a town of 2,500 in Los Angeles County.

I met another Ritter defendant named Mark Johnstone, who had immigrated from Australia in 1966 to build the space station at the Rockwell plant in Palmdale. He was chummy in the best Australian way and said he was not losing any sleep over the lawsuit. Without it, he would never have experienced last week's community meeting. It had been how he imagined the signing of the Declaration of Independence, easily the most emotional moment of his life, and he had Ritter to thank for it. He thought the suit a big mistake: "Because we're their neighbors, and we'll still be their neighbors if they build it." Like many Leona Valley residents he was politically conservative and supported private property rights. He was not against development on principle, nor even against more houses in Leona Valley. In fact, he thought Ritter Ranch would set a higher standard for development in the high desert. He only opposed its massive scale—putting four houses on the same amount of land where Leona Valley residents put one. If the number of its new residents was smaller, the valley could absorb them. All he wanted was for them to become part of his community rather than overwhelming it.

He also opposed the annexation by Palmdale. He had moved here six years ago after his home in Palmdale's upscale Quart Hill neighborhood was repeatedly burgled. Although Palmdale and Leona Valley were only separated by a twenty-minute drive along a highway twisting along the fault, they seemed divided by a thousand miles and twenty years. Palmdale was horrific, he said, while Leona Valley, in part because of the geographic isolation imposed by the fault, was the last good small town in Los Angeles County, perhaps in Southern California, a real community in a state with precious few.

When I asked people at the dance what lifestyle they were trying to protect, I expected to hear the usual blather about "family values." Instead, they had very specific ideas about what distinguished them from Ritter Ranch. They had moved to Leona Valley to escape playing by the suburban rules; the Ritter Ranchers would be paying a premium to live behind gates and surrender such fundamental rights such as the kind of vehicle they could park in their driveway. They lived in small houses with big yards and drove old cars; the Ritter Ranchers would live in big houses with small yards and drive new cars. Scrub oak, fruit trees, chickens, goats, and tumbleweed filled their yards; Ritter Ranch would have manicured lawns and fancy landscaping. They liked riding, hunting, and hiking; the Ranchers would play golf at their private course. They kept farm animals and horses; the Ranchers would have household pets. They ignored snakes; the Ranchers would want to exterminate them. They had a volunteer fire department and a part-time deputy; Ritter Ranch would have salaried firemen and roving security patrols. Their children wore blue jeans and boots, listened to Western music, raised animals, and played outdoors; the Ranch kids would wear gang fashions, listen to rap music, and live an indoor life of television and video games. They were the way Southern California had been; Ritter Ranch was what it was becoming.

When I called the Ritter Ranch office, its manager, Peter Wenner, shouted answers to my questions through a speakerphone. He said no one cared that the ranch would be near one of the most overdue-for-an-earthquake segments of the San Andreas Fault. People in their focus groups worried about crime and schools, not earthquakes.

His words boomed and faded like night signals from a distant AM radio station, perhaps because he was swiveling in his chair or pacing, so his polished monologue fluctuated between being earsplitting and faint, and came with a hollow echo. I heard, "We're building a sense of community . . . a sense of being . . . having a home . . . preserving the environment . . . A combination of the best of the twentieth and twenty-first centuries . . . We went back to, and focused on, old towns of the Midwest . . . It'll be a small Midwestern town with front porches . . . elements and sophistication from the twenty-first century . . . Top-of-the-line security measures . . . a roving patrol . . . You should see our video. It's wonderful."

It was. A computer had superimposed Ritter Ranch on photographs of the Leona Valley. You took an animated drive through a utopia of wide boulevards, pleasant parks, and dramatic open spaces. As Mark Johnstone admitted, Ritter Ranch really *did* seem to have incorporated many of the ideas that critics of suburban sprawl and sterile tract housing had been advocating for decades. Its video and accompanying literature portrayed it as a seamless tapestry of good deeds, community building, and environmental sensitivity. The ridgelines and 70 percent of the property would be left in their natural state. Senior citizens' housing meant the elderly would not have to move away when their children left home. There would be low-flow utilities, drought-resistant plants, bicycle, equestrian, and hiking trails, an amphitheater, farmers' market, campground, library, day-care center, and neighbor-hood parks. There would be generous setbacks between roads, side-walks, and houses, and homes ranging from single-lot luxury estates to clustered and multifamily attached houses, in order to preserve open spaces and make the community socially heterogeneous. There would be a compact commercial area to encourage bike and pedestrian traffic, and to foster community spirit.

Had I not known about Leona Valley's opposition, I would not have gagged when I read that Ritter Ranch was "designed to respond to a particular setting and to address specific issues, concerns, and desires communicated through intensive interaction with local community groups," and that "respect for the character of adjacent communities dictates special care in planning."

Had I not known about Palmdale leapfrogging over miles of open land to annex part of Leona Valley, I might not have questioned its lo-cation, or wondered if building a new city from scratch in a remote val-ley at least a two-hour commute from downtown Los Angeles over a crowded freeway that had suffered severe earthquake damage the year before, made more sense than redeveloping one of the county's fast-de-caying inner suburbs.

Any ambivalence I felt about Ritter Ranch vanished two days later when I read in a file of recent clippings in the Palmdale Library that after one of the council's lawsuits had been dismissed, Wenner sug-gested that Leona Valley residents "should give credit to the fact that this project was designed with them in mind," a statement revealing more about the soul of Ritter Ranch than any of its brochures, blue-prints, or videos.

36

Family Values

The first of many civic lies about Palmdale was its name, bestowed by Swiss and German settlers who arrived overland from Nebraska and mistook its Joshua trees for palms and called it "Palmenthal." Within thirteen years all but one of the original families had fled. Indians considered this corner of the eastern Mojave so lacking in the buttes, mesas, canyons, and oases that make a desert appealing none ever bothered to stay. Kit Carson's and John Frémont's expeditions explored it, but there is no evidence its members ever dreamed of returning, as Whitton did to Bird Creek. Its climate and landscape were considered too harsh for human settlement until the Southern Pacific laid tracks, in a stroke eliminating most of the now extinct antelope from Antelope Valley because they balked at crossing the tracks to their traditional grazing grounds. For much of the twentieth century the valley was notable for being the Siberia where John Wayne and Judy Garland endured bleak childhoods. A chronology of Palmdale history prepared by its library begins in 1772 with "Captain Pedro Fages is the first white man to cross the Antelope Valley," and ends in 1991 with "Antelope Valley Auto Mall opened."

I could see this auto mall from my fourth-floor freeway-side room in the Palmdale Holiday Inn, which I reckoned to be the nearest motel to the fault. It was also near the Antelope Valley Freeway, so I usually woke at 4 A.M. to the traffic hum and flashing headlights of the first wave of commuters heading "down below."

The first time I saw the dawn skyline of golden arches, revolving fried-chicken tubs, and Eiffel Tower–sized gas-station signs, the street-

330

lights glowing over red-roofed housing tracts corralled by stucco walls, and the spotlights illuminating the Antelope Valley Mall's vast parking lot, where a shopper had just been murdered during a carjacking, I wondered if I had not seen enough sprawling franchise cities, slouched through enough malls, eaten enough fast-food tacos, and sat in enough sticky-floored multiplexes. But skipping Palmdale was impossible. After Daly City, it was the largest town on the fault, and if you believed its boosters, the most successful in California at delivering Young and Rubicam's dream of a detached single-family home.

For several days I nibbled around its edges, procrastinating. I ate in Leona Valley's Mexican restaurant and returned to the Holiday Inn after dark. I found the wavy gray lines in a cut on the Antelope Valley Freeway that signaled the fault, the sag pond that had become Lake Palmdale and was the prettiest place in town, and the unusually spacious front lawns along Bayberry Street, mandated by state seismic regulations because the fault shot down the center of the road.

The day after the Leona Valley dance I swam laps in the hotel pool, drank too many beers, and fell asleep at nine. I woke again at four in the morning to the infernal commute and picked up the chamber-of-commerce *Civic and Business Guide*. "Always bright, sunny days, slight breeze, and mild winters," chirped the president of the chamber of commerce.

During my week here, gritty winds rarely cleared the overcast skies, and I had read of summer temperatures exceeding one hundred degrees.

"Low crimes rates," she promised.

Crime stories filled the *Antelope Valley Press* and its second page even carried a street map titled "Crime in the Antelope Valley," showing where criminals had struck the day before. One day last week three of the four local news briefs had been titled: "Man in underwear tries to attack officers," "Mall employee robbed at gunpoint, carjacked," and "Palmdale market robbed by hooded gunman."

But this booster literature was right about one thing: during the eighties Palmdale had been the fastest-growing city in California. Its 1980 population of 12,000 had increased to 68,000 by 1990. By 1994 it would probably pass 100,000. It had almost doubled its area in seven years, three times winning the "Fastest Growing City in California" title, and choosing its slogan, "The City Without Limits."

"There's more to come," promised the chamber of commerce, citing the annexation of twenty-three square miles that had "paved the way to welcome the 11,000-acre Ritter Ranch."

Palmdale was more than another sprawling suburban city. It could claim to be the Southern California dream city of the decade. It had been built virtually from scratch during that prosperous decade, a "city of the future" whose mottos had included: "Moving Forward," "The Good Life," "These are the Good Days," "A Better Way to Live," "Riches in Education," "Fun Is Always in Season," "Homes to House Your Dreams," "Family-Oriented Lifestyle Leads to Unique Community Spirit," and "Unique Blend of Space Technology and Old-Fashioned Charm."

It had been widely praised as the kind of city developers could build when government got out of the way. *California Business* magazine "top rated" it as the best small California city for business, while *Southern California Land* magazine said land-industry professionals had voted it "One of the Best Cities with which to Deal." The chamber of commerce summarized these lavish testimonials by saying, "With its location, labor pool, and land, land, land, Palmdale is a major discovery for major developers. They like what they find here, including a visionary, pro-business atmosphere at all levels of government."

After reading this, I was not surprised that Palmdale had become the Imperial City of chain stores. Fast-food signs dwarfed the plastic huts selling it, and its three-acre Wal-Mart was the largest in the nation. Their message, as everywhere, was "We know you don't give a shit how we look just as long as we can sell you a Mr. Coffee cheap," and in Palmdale they had obviously read their customers just right. Its voters had trounced a slate of slow-growth candidates in 1987, and one morning my *Antelope Valley Press* turned up with a thirty-two-page insert titled "Antelope Valley Best," listing the results of a poll of twenty thousand readers. The title Best Department Store went to Mervyn's, the Best Drugstore was any one of four Long's, the Best Toy Store was Toys "Я" Us, the Best Card/Gift Store was Hallmark, the Best Shoe Store any one of seven Payless stores in the valley, the Best Video Store Blockbuster, the Best Pizza Little Caesar's, the Best Salad Bar could be found at one of three Sizzlers, and the Best Homemade Dessert was one of the sweet confections at Marie Callender's, which had also won "Best Bakery."

I decided to judge Palmdale on its own terms. Its *Civic and Business Guide* said it continued "to cherish the small-town values of a family-oriented community." An advertisement sponsored by the city declared it was "Hometown to a Whole New Generation!", built by a baby-boom generation that "wouldn't settle for what their parents called home," and "wanted something new. Something better ... A family-oriented community." So to see what kind of family-oriented community Californians build where land was cheap and regulations nonexistent, I visited what twenty thousand Antelope Valley residents had voted Best Place to Take Kids. This was the Dimples Family Fun Center at 1050 Commerce Center Drive in Lancaster, a slightly larger city ten miles up the freeway from Palmdale that is in most respects indistinguishable from it, and will soon merge with it to form a mega-city.

The *Antelope Valley Press* had praised Dimples for its "variety and individuality." It shared a shopping center with Cloth World, Party World, and the Family Fitness Center ("Best Fitness/Health Club"), where parents went after dumping the kids at Dimples. It turned out to be a tricked-up penny arcade offering miniature golf, skeeball, video games, a change machine accepting twenty-dollar bills, and the "Fun-maze-ium," a $3.25-an-hour plastic jungle gym smelling of dirty feet and providing less exercise and fun than most playgrounds deliver for free. Hectoring, liability-conscious signs warned NO CLIMBING ON OUTSIDE OF PLAY STRUCTURE, ONLY FOUR KIDS AT A TIME IN THE BOUNCE, ABSOLUTELY NO FLIPS! KEEP AN ARM DISTANCE APART, and I heard a sour-faced man in a striped carnival shirt tell a young father who was throwing colorful plastic balls at his son, "The balls have to stay inside or we'll have to ask you to leave." Coming here was an event and some parents brought video cameras. Although the weather was finally fulfilling the chamber-of-commerce promise of gentle breezes and perpetual sunshine, Dimples was packed.

What else was there for children in this family-oriented community? For a valley of 300,000 the Yellow Pages listed two piano teachers, no art galleries, children's museums, or museums of any kind. A curfew, part of the "ongoing effort to combat graffiti and gangs," made it a criminal offense for teenagers under eighteen "to loiter, stroll or aimlessly drive or ride about in any unsupervised place during the hours of 10 p.m. to sunrise." Palmdale did not have a single hiking or biking trail. Its kids could swim at only two public pools, play in only 71 acres of parks and 260 acres of designated open space. (Ritter Ranch was offering 3,512 acres of parks, 7,628 acres of open space, and 85 miles of trails). Most backyards were scarcely large enough for a barbecue and a few lawn chairs, and like tenement kids, older children had made a playground of the street. The layout of walled tracts separated by busy avenues made it difficult to visit a library, store, playground, or friend without an adult driver. But many parents were on the road until sunset, commuting four hours a day to buy this life for their children.

Even if Palmdale's kids did get downtown, it was a dangerous place to hang out. Some older shopping centers were boarded up, or blackened by arsonists and surrounded by razor wire, or home to five-dollar haircut parlors or stores where everything cost a dollar and signs said, ONLY TWO STUDENTS ALLOWED TO ENTER AT ONE TIME. Cheap rents had turned neighborhoods into dumping grounds for paroled convicts and hard-core welfare cases from Los Angeles. Gangs staked out turf, and in a town that barely had a downtown, people avoided it.

A sign over the door of Mesa Intermediate School, the closest I could find to the fault, warned its seventh and eighth graders against "guns, vandalism, and loitering." A laminated notice on the administration office counter said, SCHOOLS WILL BE WEAPON FREE. The Mesa dress code ran for almost a thousand words and prohibited, among other things, slits or tears above the knee, sandals without backs, halter tops, leggings, heavy-metal T-shirts, flight jackets, high knee socks, creased T-shirts, frayed pant hems, initialed belt buckles, dangling earrings, bandannas, and "shirts, jackets or other clothing ... which represents athletic teams which have been determined by the L.A. County Sheriff/Probation Department to be representative of gang involvement." It concluded with a vague prohibition against clothes "determined to be representative of unacceptable groups," and those "which pose a threat to the physical and/or emotional well-being and the safety of ... others on campus." Teachers had permission to unbutton the top buttons of students' shirts (a sign of gang activity and poor attitude), and they must also have had the right to measure the distance between their navels and the tops of their trousers, which the dress code insisted could be no more than two finger widths.

The dress code had not done much for academic achievement. In 1993, average SAT scores were down from the year before at five of six Antelope Valley high schools, and verbal and math scores, with the exception of one school, were below California and national averages. At Palmdale High School, the average verbal score was 373 compared with 415 for California and 424 for the nation. Math was 413, compared with 484 for California and 478 for the nation.

The news clippings filed under "Crime" at Palmdale's public library revealed that in 1991 the number of gang-related crimes had doubled from the year before and homicides had tripled from twelve to thirty-six. The *Los Angeles Times* said downtown Palmdale was plagued with crime and rampant drug deals. High-school teachers met to plan strategies for combating gangs, satanism, and homemade bombs. A sheriff's office spokesman trying to explain the rise in juvenile crime said, "We have thousands of kids in the Antelope Valley that are unsupervised for six hours a day or longer."

The absent parents, curfew, lack of recreation facilities, walled-off tracts, and heat and wind conspired to keep Palmdale's kids indoors. Streets had a neutron-bomb feel, with bikes and toys scattered across driveways and yards.

To see what indoors was like I walked through some model homes in developments near the fault. The Fiesta ("Homes of enduring value that fulfill your dreams ... You'll never feel more at home") offered three-to-four-bedroom houses between $115,000 and $128,999. The $130,000-to-$155,000 homes at The Laurent ("Reflecting the serenity and beauty of the Riviera") were slightly larger. Every model I saw, regardless of size or price, had elaborate bathrooms called "spas," and at least two places for watching television. Even the largest models lacked a living room large enough to accommodate six people in any degree of comfort. Instead, there were many small spaces where family members could escape one another. These were called the "bonus room," "family room," "media niche," "entertainment niche," "nook," "den," or more honestly, the "retreat." They ensured that when parents returned exhausted from their two-hour commute, they did not have to share a room, television, or computer with their kids. They indicated that life in Palmdale was a dark, indoor one for many adults who left home five days a week before sunrise, returned after dark, and slept late on weekends to recover.

The more expensive houses simply provided more "retreats," and despite their colorful furniture, dried flowers, and soothing watercolors, they felt more lonely than any rambling Victorian three times the size. They were Palmdale writ small, the last Russian doll in the set, the compound within the compound, where people could pursue indoor pleasures alone.

But it was possible even these floor plans did not separate families enough, since, in 1992, the Antelope Valley sheriff's substation led Los Angeles County in the number of child-abuse reports, accounting for 15 percent although it had only 2.8 percent of the county's population. (The figures lump Palmdale, Lancaster, and several smaller Antelope Valley communities together.) Child-abuse homicides included a boy shaken to death, a newborn tossed into a trash bin, a five-year-old girl fatally drugged by her parents, and a thirteen-month-old baby raped and sodomized. The crimes that year were not an anomaly. Throughout the early 1990s, Antelope Valley children were abused at a considerably higher rate than those "down below," and county officials reported it having the worst child-abuse problem in Los Angeles County.

A child-abuse rate almost six times the county average could not simply be excused by higher reporting rates, or a larger-than-average population for children. Experts blamed heavy methamphetamine use, which made people oversensitive to crying babies, and the way Antelope Valley had been settled and developed. Sexual abuse usually happened in isolation. The valley was isolated from the rest of the county, and its tracts were isolated from one another. Parents who were isolated from family and friends returned from exhausting four-hour round-trip commutes with a low tolerance for the noisy demands of infants and toddlers.

The perpetual California debate about "limits" usually concerned how much population, logging, and water use the state could support before flirting with catastrophe. But there was one undebatable and inescapable limit: the fact that every day only contains twenty-four hours. When parents spent one sixth of these alone in a car, sacrificing years of parenting time to live in a single-family detached home in Antelope Valley, you might say an important limit had already been disregarded, and that these child-abuse statistics were the proof.

I came across another explanation for why parents who had moved here to give their children an extra bedroom might murder them in it when I came across a copy of *Movin' Out* in the Holiday Inn lobby. It described itself as "California's complete real estate guide to the OTHER 49 states." Its advertisements asked, "Thinking about leaving California?" and it contained eighty pages of listings for houses in glamorous states like Montana and Idaho, and more mundane ones like Oklahoma, Missouri, and Arkansas, where farms could be had for

$68,000. Because Antelope Valley boasted the cheapest detached single-family tract homes in Los Angeles County, it was both a geographical and financial last chance: the farthest east from Los Angeles you could go before saying, "What the hell, might as well keep 'movin' on' to Nevada, Arizona, or Oklahoma." For many newcomers it was a last desperate grab at the California Dream, and desperate parents are the kind who beat their kids.

37

Some "Doggone Individualists"

Although Tony Vacik, Jr.'s grandfather once roomed with Lenin, when we shook hands in his driveway he announced, "I'm the last white guy in Littlerock working in the orchards," as if that was the most important thing you could know about him.

He said his childhood friends had moved out when the big orchards swallowed smaller ones and housing tracts spread from Palmdale. After selling their orchard, he and his father had become seasonal residents, spending summers in Montana with an aunt and returning every winter to work. He had picked up a bowlegged cowboy walk and a Rocky Mountain twang, but maintained a California interest in his appearance and wore his graying beard neatly trimmed. He was one of those men who are so soft-spoken you wonder if they are gentle or sad, or both.

"I don't know why we come back," he said, glancing at the weathered ranch house. "I like to hunt, fish, and hike, and sure, you can still do that stuff here, but it's not the quality it once was." Littlerock had once been more rural than Leona Valley, but Palmdale was sprawling down the busy Pearblossom Highway and there was talk of annexation. He believed soon the orchards would be gone and houses would stretch from here to Victorville. When I said I liked the way the snowy San Gabriels rose in a wall from the desert, he sighed and shook his head. "You can't camp there without a permit now. There's gangs, graffiti, and crowds everywhere. God Almighty, I guess the only reason we come back is because of my old man."

I had come to see his father because he was the only member of the Llano Del Rio Cooperative Colony still living in the Antelope Valley. Llano had been founded by Job Harriman, who had run for vice-president on the Socialist ticket with Eugene Debs in 1900, and was twice nearly elected mayor of Los Angeles. He abandoned politics in 1914, bought ten thousand acres here, and asked for volunteers to build a utopian community without capitalism or competition. In just three years his colonists built a school, lumber mill, fish hatchery, tannery, soap factory, stables, workshops, and rows of tidy cabins. They kept bees, hogs, rabbits, and sheep, planted apple and pear orchards, dug canals to bring water from Big Rock Creek, and became the largest "master-planned" community in the valley until the housing boom of the 1980s.

Llano sounded like fun. The colonists assembled an airplane, won the valley baseball championships every year, and encouraged their sons and daughters to cross-dress for a "Suffragette Ball." They were culture mavens and self-improvers on a par with the Raven Earlygrow set in Point Arena, and had organized a barbershop quartet, theater group, orchestra, dance band, and debating society. A typical Sunday-night program at their landmark stone hotel went: "The Llano Orchestra in Several Selections. The Mixed Quartet. The Mandolin Trio. Speech on Life at Equality Colony by a former Member. Junior Dramatic Club in *Lovebird's Matrimonial Agency*. The Choral Society Accompanied by the Entire Orchestra in the Anvil Chorus from *Il Trovatore*." They had the first Montessori school in California because Harriman believed that "the training of children must be conducted in such manner as to induce the unfoldment of the ethical and spiritual nature. Failure to do so means destruction of the community itself."

Los Angeles Times publisher Harrison Gray Otis detested Harriman for defending union organizers charged with bombing the *Times* building in 1910. He vilified Llano in his newspaper and its collapse in 1917 was precipitated by his campaign, as well as by the colony's mismanagement of its funds, and a lawsuit filed by neighboring ranchers challenging its water rights. When Harriman launched a second community in Louisiana many colonists joined him, including Tony Vacik's family. But his mother hated the climate, so they soon returned to the Antelope Valley.

Before we went inside, Vacik warned that discussing Llano could make his father cranky. I would have a better chance of having him give me a tour of the ruins if I said, "Hey, let's go for a ride." This turned out to work, but to preserve the fiction of a casual drive we spent some time first cruising through the orchards on dirt roads.

At first his father would only say, "I'm Tony and I'm an old man." But as we bounced along he began muttering in a low voice, "Peaches, nectarines, plums, cherries ... This was a thirty-acre orchard with a farmhouse." Bigger orchards than theirs were folding now, and some farmers had turned packing sheds into farm markets selling produce trucked in from elsewhere. If one farmer surrendered to a subdivision, his neighbors soon followed, a domino effect. The newcomers complained about spraying, Mexican laborers, and the hunting of rabbits and other pests. The shotgun blasts made them think of drive-by shootings and they wrote petitions and sued for emotional distress.

Without the Vaciks I would have mistaken the ruins of the Llano hotel for a roadhouse gutted by fire. Indeed, there was so little interest in local history that less than a decade after the colony's collapse, newcomers were already describing the remains as once having belonged to a German-speaking religious group, or a reclusive millionaire.

As we circled crumbling walls and cracked foundations the old man squinted and said, "That was the post office. Its roof fell down in 1930 when a truck hit it. Those fireplaces were in the hotel. Those stone pillars supported the roof of the porch. There's the circular trough where we watered the horses, and the driveway where they parked the truck and Model-T Fords. Look at the cisterns and irrigation ditches. God, how we worked on those!"

He appeared not to notice, or care, that the ruins of the most successful socialist experiment in twentieth-century U.S. history were defaced with graffiti, filled with garbage, and had not even merited the customary plaque with which California has honored other less noteworthy sites. But his son did, shaking his head in disgust at the twisted lawn chairs, middens of beer cans, cracked toilet bowl, and exploding BarcaLounger. Only lime from the Llano kiln held the stone walls together and you could scrape it away with a fingernail. An energetic pack of vandals could make quick work of it, and no one would care.

We walked deeper into the ruins through blossoming yellow creosote, saltbush, and twenty other varieties of knee-high bush known by name to both Vaciks. The old man strode ahead, pointing out the foundations of the bakery and commissary. When we reached the blacksmith's forge he spat and said, "Meanest man in the colony; hated kids so much he buried hot horseshoes just underground so we'd step on them barefoot." Aside from this man, and the ranchers who called the colonists "Reds" and sent their kids sneaking into the compound at night with horsewhips to attack the older boys, Llano had been a children's paradise. Vacik remembered the swimming hole, twice-weekly dances, and lightning striking the Joshua trees on hot summer nights. Everyone learned an instrument and at age eight he played trumpet in the band. They chased cows, climbed silos, dived into hay, and tamed the rattlers like snake charmers.

"Were we happy? Hell! The best time in my life I ever saw!" he said.

What had he liked most?

"Hell, that we all *knew* each other! Now you hardly know anyone out here anymore."

Even as a boy he understood the conundrum of communal life that would bedevil places like Oz. "You try to get twenty little kids to do a job, only four end up doing it," he said. "And I was always one of the four." When he complained his father snapped back, "You're too much of a doggone individualist to make a good socialist."

Later I found a photograph of the Vacik family in an article about Llano. Young Tony was sticking out his tongue. Perhaps becoming a capitalist farmer on the former site of his father's failed socialist dream had been some kind of final "doggone individualist" victory.

We drove toward the foothills of the San Gabriels, slowing so the old man could point out the former Llano cookhouse, which now carried the unlikely address of 33037 165th Street East, and the barren, ass-poor, piss-poor acres where John Wayne's family had scratched out a living. Once this valley had been a kind of Southern California Alaska where actors and writers came to find adventure. In the 1920s, John Steinbeck had drifted through to pick pears. Vacik had shared a room with him, read *Tortilla Flat* in manuscript, and remembered him as "the laziest bastard I ever met."

Upton Sinclair had been "too damn dominating," while Jack London was more proof that socialist writers were all "lazy sons of bitches."

"Once he starts remembering he hates to stop," Tony Vacik, Jr., whispered in my ear.

The main trace of the San Andreas ran under a lot that was the former site of Aldous Huxley's favorite honky-tonk. He had lived here in the early 1940s, working in a studio with a view of the Llano ruins and inspired by them to write *Ape and Essence*. He and Vacik had been drinking buddies, "always shouting and bullshitting about socialism," Vacik said. They argued because Huxley was a Llano fan, while he remained a doggone individualist.

It was twilight when we pulled into the Vaciks' driveway. Tony, Jr., went inside, but even after I had climbed back into my car and turned on the ignition, the old man stood by the window shivering in his T-shirt, determined to tell me one last thing. Lowering his voice, he revealed that before emigrating to the United States, his father had been Lenin's roommate in Switzerland. "They looked so alike people mistook them for brothers," he said with pride. (I suppose no matter how you felt about communism, Lenin was still a celebrity.) After the revolution, Lenin had written several times inviting his father to join him and promising an important position. He was tempted, but his wife, imagining Moscow would be Llano writ large, refused to go. A good thing she had, too, because the Vaciks were just the kind of foreign communists Stalin had liquidated. If his father had pursued his socialist dream any further, it would have ended in Siberia.

The next morning I picked up the fault near the site of Huxley's favorite saloon and drove along it to St. Andrew's, where the Benedictine monks assured me that giving their priory the same name as the fault running underneath it (Andreas is Spanish for Andrew) was pure coincidence. Belgian fathers had founded the order in China and settled into this former ranch after the communists expelled them. They felt tremors all the time, but accepted them as God's will.

The scrubby hills resembled Palestine, but everything else was eccentrically Californian. The monks included a wizened Oriental, an owlish intellectual, an elderly man who seemed barely alive, a burly and bearded blue-collar monk, a counterculture monk with a ponytail, and a brisk executive type who gave the impression of having once enjoyed considerable financial success. They supported themselves through mail-order sales of kitschy ceramic angels with the big, woeful eyes of the Keene children, and even offered a "TV angel" watching television, a "diet angel" on a scale, and a "real-estate angel" holding a FOR SALE sign. The grounds were spacious and peaceful, the buildings unpretentious, the climate perfect, and the brothers jolly and welcoming, although their conversation revolved around in-jokes and was as incomprehensible as Latin.

After the noon mass they served a lunch of middle-class comfort food—tomato soup and egg- and tuna-salad sandwiches. Their bread, surprisingly, was terrible. I sat opposite a handsome young man wearing cutoff blue jeans and work boots who often said "oh, wow!" I assumed his sisters had dragged him off his surfboard and brought him along to visit a relative. But no, today he was beginning his observership, the first stage of monastic formation. After lunch, his bemused parents and sisters would be leaving him to six months of work and prayer.

A few miles down the fault from the priory at the U.S. Forest Service's Valyermo Station, the ranger in charge was a sundried and sparrow-sized elderly woman who looked tough enough to stare down a bear or race a teenager up one of these ten-thousand-foot peaks. But when I asked if anyone showed any interest in the location of the fault in the Angeles National Forest, or took out permits to camp over it, she said, "I wouldn't camp here on a bet. I like to go to sleep knowing I'll wake up alive."

She explained Los Angeles street gangs had made some lower canyons their turf, and when the reconstruction of a dam temporarily closed them off, they had moved deeper into the forest, camping at higher elevations and spreading through its thickly wooded 700,000 acres. They fought, vandalized toilets, sprayed graffiti on rocks, and threatened other campers. Families bumped down dirt tracks to remote campsites only to find exactly what they had come to escape, except here, miles from a telephone and the police, the gangs were more terrifying.

When the docent up the road at the Big Pines Visitor Center led me outside to show how the fault ran behind his office, he also pointed out the foundations of the original visitor structure, a historic wood lodge destroyed in 1987 by arsonists. He admitted the horror stories were true. During these slow weeks between the ski season and summer, the mountains were usually deserted, but if I came back in two months, I would see the busiest national forest in the nation, and discover that gangsters liked getting away for the weekend, too.

Crime in the Angeles had a *Clockwork Orange* quality. Vandals had flattened rest rooms with a stolen bulldozer, and three youths had executed a good Samaritan who was helping push their car from the mud. There were disemboweled coyotes, gang stabbings, paramilitary groups staging mock battles, impromptu weekend drug labs, and a campground so vandalized rangers had to rebuild it every week. A Forest Service spokesman described the forest as "the biggest dumping grounds for dead bodies and stolen vehicles I've ever seen." A Forest Service employee said crime in the Angeles was far more pointless than down below, a "psychotic eruption of anger."

The fault-created terrain did not help. Earthquakes had made these mountains unusually steep. Two thirds had a grade of over 60 percent, so the large weekend crowds were jammed together in the few level areas, a situation encouraging confrontation and violence.

When I saw a sign on the Mile High Café door announcing its toilets were for paying customers only, and that travelers wanting a glass of water could pay fifty cents, I would have driven on if my map had not shown the fault lying directly underneath. After the sign I was surprised to find a pretty teenage waitress with sharp blue eyes and a talent for convincing adults they were interesting. She introduced herself as Leann and said her parents owned the café and were responsible for preserving an interior that could have been displayed on the floor of the Smithsonian featuring vanishing American interiors. The sign would have said ROADHOUSE, CIRCA 1930, and drawn attention to its wagon-wheel chandeliers, 1916 stone fireplace, and low ceiling dating from its days as a stage stop.

"You're sitting on it," she said when I asked about the fault. They felt quakes all the time and her mother had become skilled at predicting their distance from epicenters. They took advantage of the fault, sometimes going bird-watching in the sag ponds down the road.

She said she loved living in Valyero, and particularly loved her school. They were within the Antelope Valley Unified District, so she should be attending Littlerock High, but her parents drove her to Phelan in San Bernardino County. Littlerock had too many urban problems. A student there had recently poured cleaning fluid into a teacher's open soda can, causing her permanent liver damage.

"That Littlerock school is only four years old," her father said, carrying my eggs from the kitchen, "and it's already torn up, graffiti everywhere."

He was a bear-shaped man with a faint speech impediment who had fled the San Fernando Valley seventeen years earlier. When I asked about the unfriendly sign he showed me a snapshot of his parking area taken last President's Day weekend. Parking lots at the Wrightwood ski area six miles up the road had filled early and traffic had backed up for miles. Hundreds of skiers had decided to wait around and go night skiing. They parked outside and demanded to use his toilet, drink his water, and sit by his fire, but without buying anything. These were middle-class people—skiers! They lugged in ice chests, picnicked at his tables, and cursed him out when he suggested paying for his toilet and water. He was not asking for much, only the purchase of a coffee or Coke. It was a matter of principle. He had to pay for firewood and pump his septic tank after every busy weekend. Even his paying customers were rude. They wanted inexpensive fast food and stamped out shouting, "I'm going to McDonald's!" His meals took longer to prepare and he charged slightly more, but he also gave directions, fitted chains on cars, and provided a fireplace.

"You know the only problem with the Mile High Café?" he asked. "It's in California!"

He stayed because his children liked their schools, but he was counting the days until they graduated and he could escape Los Angeles County's most idyllic corner. In the meantime he worried about fires and earthquakes because he knew he would never be permitted to rebuild so close to the fault.

Leann worried about snakes, and the graffiti that had suddenly appeared on their mailbox this summer. She thought it was the beginning of some kind of end, like the first swastika on a Jewish wall. "But even more," she said, "I worry some of the people who stop here will see how alone we are, and come back at night." Her parents thought it would reassure her to know the police would erect roadblocks, and there were only three escape routes. But how would anyone know they had been attacked? And so what if they were caught, afterward?

According to Robert Iacopi's *Earthquake Country*, a 1964 guide to the San Andreas that I often used to locate the fault, if I stopped just up the highway from the Mile High Café, I could see one of the best exposures anywhere along the San Andreas Fault, a place where a creek had cut a deep notch into the fault, exposing the powdery granite crushed by the grinding plates.

I pulled into the Appletree Campground to find a tour group gathered around a geologist for a lecture preceding their visit to this celebrated site. He was telling them they were at the heart of the fault system. Nowhere else would they see such dramatic evidence of an earlier earthquake, in this instance the Fort Tejon one of 1857. They left laughing and joking. When I passed them on their way back they were quiet. The fault here was enough to silence anyone. You looked down from a precipice to a rock wall marked by gray swirls of rock turned to powder by the grinding plates. I dug some out with a pocketknife and it crumbled in my hands. A hundred and fifty years earlier the Fort Tejon earthquake had ground granite into talcum powder.

A team of USGS scientists has recently identified this Wright-wood segment of the fault as far more likely to produce a great earth-quake than previously believed. After digging trenches along a creek to determine how 1,300 years of earthquakes had disturbed the sediment, they concluded that a significant earthquake struck here about every 100 years. They suggested to the Working Group on California Earth-quake Probabilities that it reevaluate its forecast of a 20-percent chance for a great earthquake on this segment in the next 30 years. Fort Tejon had struck 150 years earlier, and by their calculations the next Big One was already 50 years overdue.

The village of Wrightwood was a pleasant little resort of ski shops and boutiques that had recently been discovered by commuters from down below. The spring sun was warm and the breeze scented with pine. I could see why someone would drive an extra forty minutes to live here.

I watched Little Leaguers play on a diamond about a quarter mile from the fault. Their parents bitched and rode the umpires. One father shouted, "Fucking ridiculous," after a disputed call. When several mothers screamed, "Hey, how about some chatter?" the boys on the bench took up a soprano chant of "Hey . . . batter, batter, batter . . . Hey, batter, batter, batter. . ." trying to unnerve the boy at the plate. This was the first Little League game I had seen since playing myself in the 1950s, so for all I know heckling like this is common everywhere. But consid-ering how timid the little players looked, it seemed unforgivable that adults should be encouraging it, and I wondered if it had been the rule before Wrightwood became a suburb for long-distance commuters.

The San Bernardino mountain resort town of Big Bear was close enough to Los Angeles that I was not trusted to pump gas without pay-ing first. Even though I was paying with a credit card, the motel in-sisted I make a deposit on its sheets, towels, and furniture. The owner said too many guests had stripped her rooms bare.

Big Bear called itself a "four-seasons resort" but there were really only two, skiing in winter and water sports in summer, when on some weekends as many as 100,000 people drove up from the Los Angeles basin. The big news when I arrived was a gala Kmart opening and the highway being widened. But so what? It was a democratic and affordable resort, unlike nearby Lake Arrowhead, which had been purchased by local landowners and turned into a "gated" lake. Big Bear's lake was the largest in these urbanized mountains and open to everyone. Its downtown was a bustling mixture of Western fronts and alpine chalets that had a stupendous view of surrounding peaks.

I went skiing on what was almost the last day of the season. College kids and divorced fathers with children filled the deck of the lodge. The fathers called sons "buddy" and daughters "pumpkin" and began conversations about tomorrow's fun with, "Wouldn't it be great if . . ." A disc jockey offered prizes for the funniest jokes. They were good prizes, ski gloves and a sweater, and I struggled to think of a winning joke. The students tried, too, but halfway through every one, the disc jockey had to clap his hand over the microphone. "How about a semi-clean joke for the kids," he begged.

Silence.

Steven Munson of COPE (Counseling Ordinary People in Emergencies) was a local boy with a gingery beard who dressed like a lumberjack and seemed an unlikely-looking mental-health professional, until he opened his mouth and the jargon tumbled out.

COPE was funded by federal taxpayers, in this case the Federal Emergency Management Agency (FEMA), but operated by the San Bernardino County Department of Mental Health. It had branches in Yucca Valley and San Bernardino, and offices here on the second floor of a new office plaza decorated with I CAN COPE IN A QUAKE balloons. Munson said Big Bear's 6.7 earthquake of June 29, 1992, had sent the lift cables wobbling like spaghetti and carved fissures into ski slopes. Liquor stores thrived and toilet-paper sales at local supermarkets soared. People really had been scared shitless.

The chamber of commerce had been so desperate not to lose the lucrative Fourth of July business it encouraged tourists to "come on up" anyway, and over 75,000 did, enraging residents by gawking at the damage and cleaning out supermarkets. Then the Los Angeles con men descended. Out-of-town contractors hired local workers to repair damage, then absconded without paying wages. One mountebank collected big down payments to epoxy chimneys before he skipped town. Burglars slapped stolen Red Cross insignias on panel trucks so they could loot vacation houses without arousing suspicion.

So much for earthquake love.

COPE's staff of six offered walk-in counseling and clinics at senior centers. They lectured at schools and organized "community recovery groups." While I was there the office bustled with meetings, phone calls, and visitors. Big Bear residents apparently still needed advice such as, to cite some examples from COPE's many leaflets, "Try to lighten up if you can," "Validate each other," "Take time to do fun things," "Share about recent changes in your lives," "Be supportive and nonjudgmental," and "Give hugs."

Munson said children, the elderly, single mothers, Hispanics, and anyone who had actually seen fissures opening or the earth undulating needed his services most. Some children still slept in their parents' beds, and a woman in her sixties had lived for months in a backyard pup tent. The earthquake's artillery-barrage rumble and the sirens of fire trucks and ambulances had triggered flashbacks for World War II and Korean War veterans. The rescue helicopters set off Vietnam survivors. For some people the sixty-thousand aftershocks were as traumatic as the first tremor, reminding them of the quake and delaying their recovery. It was another reason why earthquakes were a uniquely terrifying natural disaster. Hurricanes and tornadoes did not leave behind months of echoes.

He thought Hispanics had been among the most traumatized because (like Joe Scaramella's mother in San Francisco in 1906) they were new arrivals and the most isolated from the community. The single mothers and elderly were also less likely to have the support of family or close friends, and were therefore the most in need of COPE, which, when you stripped away its jargon, was mostly a paid friend.

I had read of no government agency counseling the 1906 survivors in the importance of sharing feelings, rebuilding personal relationships, and hugging. But photographs of the 1906 earthquake shacks and refugee camps did show extended families gathered outside around makeshift outdoor stoves and wash stations, comforting one another.

38

The Rebus Letter

I made a detour to Pasadena to search for Bruff material in the Huntington Library and meet Henry Clifford, whom the secretary of the Society of California Pioneers in San Francisco had described as a Bruff expert. I had spoken to Clifford twice by telephone and he had sent me a copy of his *Mystery of the Rebus Letter of Joseph Goldsborough Bruff of August 1856*, a reproduction of Bruff's two-page rebus letter, and an extract from Bruff's 1869 letter to the secretary of the Pioneer Association of California. This was included so a reader could judge if its handwriting was the same as that of the rebus letter, which it mysteriously was not.

In a rebus letter, some words are replaced by phonetic pictures. In Bruff's, for example, "My Dear Friend" was represented by the word *my* followed by a drawing of a deer and a Quaker. "Safe to hand" was a safe, toe, and hand.

His letter was addressed to W. S. Burche in San Francisco, but since no Burche is listed on the roster of the Washington Miners, Bruff presumably met him after arriving in California. He must have known some of his former comrades because Bruff asked him to convey his regards, adding, "My old associates of 1849 during the times that tried men's souls are aware that I exerted every faculty for their welfare and success. How far I succeeded, eventually, let them be the judges."

Bruff admitted being "poor as a church mouse," adding he was sending by the same post a prospectus of his Gold Rush memoirs, because "the publishers will not publish it unless a sale is guaranteed—So for the want of a few hundred names it has been kept back. . . . Get me a long line of names and we'll soon give you a bril-liant book."

This was one of his many efforts to secure publication of his diaries and drawings. After returning to Washington in 1851, he had transcribed his diary entries and submitted them to Harper's in New York. The firm agreed to publish them if he would permit extensive editing and condensation. He refused, saying he "preferred being the author of what I had accomplished in the most creditable form, or not at all."

He next sent the manuscript to Dr. Richard Adam Locke, a New York City man of letters who helped him make revisions and corrections, "without interfering with my own style," Bruff said. Locke wrote a critique, calling it "a work of extraordinary merit and interest, possessing elements of emphatic popularity, at least equal to those of any book of travels that has achieved it within my recollection. Its adventures and incidents, more numerous and exciting than are usually found, even in romantic works of fiction, are irresistibly heightened by the palpable sincerity and truthfulness of their recital. . . ."

Another publisher promised to print an edition if five hundred subscribers could be found. Bruff wrote a prospectus and persuaded a civil servant leaving for San Francisco to enlist subscribers there. After a few months this man reported signing up two thousand Californians, but while returning to Washington he lost his list of names while crossing the isthmus of Panama, thus, Bruff wrote, "putting the extinguisher upon all my labors."

After this setback, Bruff made sporadic attempts to find a publisher, writing to London editors, and in 1869 mailing the last of his prospectuses to the Society of California Pioneers. I read his covering letter to this effort in its entirety in the appendix to a rare 1944 unabridged two-volume edition of his diaries and sketches kept at Pasadena's Huntington Library. In it, he extolled his manuscript as "a grand panorama of Travel!—The trains on the plains and among the hills; buffalo adventures; Indians; extraordinary Scenery; remarkable places . . ."

In its last paragraph he made a thinly disguised attempt to bribe the California Pioneers by promising a new appendix containing the location of rich gold deposits. He explained that in Washington he had befriended an indigent old Californian who had repaid his charity by revealing where these "rich deposits" could be found. He claimed to have "carefully noted down all the facts, then constructed a map of the country on a grand scale, and put all the information on it." He offered to include it with the manuscript. "Millions are in it," he promised.

His last recorded attempt to sell his manuscript came seven years later in a letter to the editor of the *Arizona Weekly Miner* of Prescott, Arizona, that I also found reproduced in the appendix to the two-volume edition. On June 2, 1876, this newspaper had published a Bruff poem titled "Address to a Seal at Baffin's Bay." Four weeks later it offered a "reminiscence" of Bruff based on the account of Gideon Brooke, who owned a Prescott ranch and was the former vice president of the Washington City Miners.

Bruff's diary portrays Brooke as a major villain, perhaps the architect of his abandonment. He was one of the six men who returned to the camp at the end of October and "avariciously" packed wagons with the company's stores and tried to claim Bruff's tent as company property. When Bruff finally stumbled into Lassen's ranch six months later, he discovered Brooke had pledged the company's actual property for his personal debts and absconded.

Brooke's account in the *Arizona Weekly Miner* was a skein of lies, at odds with everything reported by Bruff and Austin. He wrote Bruff had remained in the mountains not to guard the company's stores, but to stay near a source of fresh water. In his version, Bruff immediately built a cabin "stowed nearly full of provisions," and winter set in as soon as the miners reached Lassen's camp, "closing all possible relief." In April, a party of travelers found Bruff "healthy, rugged and apparently reconciled to his lot."

Bruff shot back an angry reply, pointing out he had *lent* his horse to a companion, and *volunteered* to stay and guard the company supplies and await the return of his men to take in the remaining wagons. Contrary to what Brooke claimed, "There was nothing in the shape of provisions left but half a bag of coffee and one-fourth of a package of salt." He admitted having an "extra inducement to remain on the heights—in obtaining notes of the stragglers, to complete my history of the great exodus," but had never imagined being abandoned for the entire winter. Instead, his men "made off with all they got—three wagons and contents, some 25 or 30 mules, and my horse. So much for my services to them." Even so, Bruff was so desperate to publish that to this bitter settling of accounts he added two paragraphs making it clear his diaries were still available, and were "an accurate account of the great immigration[,] the first settlement of California from Alpha to Omega, with all my wild travels and explorations, adventures, etc. . . ."

In the early twentieth century Bruff's descendants attempted again to interest publishers and persuaded the noted bibliographer George Henry Sargent to read the manuscript. He declared in the *Boston Evening Transcript* that, "it is probable that there has never been penned by any other California emigrant of 1849 a narrative so full of interest, so true to detail, so concise in descriptions, and yet so graphic and full of the most valuable scientific interest."

Despite this, and despite revived interest at Harper's, the manuscript was so long and its illustrations so expensive to reproduce it was not until 1944 that Columbia University Press finally published it at the urging of Bruff's granddaughter, and of Frederick Hodge, director of the Southwest Museum in Los Angeles. He had grown up in Washington, D.C., played with Bruff's grandchildren, and in his foreword remembered him as a "white-bearded patriarch" living in a brick mansion where the entire lower front room was known to friends as the Bruff Museum. It was "the holy of holies of the grandshire," filled with a heterogeneous collection of Indian and other primitive artifacts gathered during Bruff's wanderings.

Hodge's reminiscences were meant to be fond and cheerful. But I read them and saw Bruff in his eighty-fifth and final year, contemplating his unpublished manuscript and the mementos filling his dark Victorian parlor, perhaps finally accepting the judgment of essayist Bayard Taylor, who had observed that "the experience of any single man, which a few years ago would have made him a hero for life, becomes more commonplace when it is but one of many thousands."

When I had spoken to Henry Clifford two weeks before, he had sounded like a man in failing health who was nevertheless eager to assist a Bruff relative. He promised to check his files for the descendants of other members of Bruff's party, and explained he had acquired the rebus letter from a friend who had bought it from a Benjamin Tighe of Massachusetts. He had contacted his widow but she was ignorant of its provenance.

There were several "mysteries" involving this letter. First, Clifford's copy and the one in the Bancroft Library differed slightly. The Bancroft's contained some minor errors, even though like Clifford's it had been lithographed. Was it possible Bruff had made copies to entertain his friends and corrected the errors before lithographing a second batch? Yet one of the misspelled words in the Bancroft rebus was Bruff's own middle name.

But this was less of a mystery than the fact that Bruff's handwriting in every version of the rebus letter was entirely different from that in his letter to the Society of California Pioneers. If the rebus had been written by someone else, then by whom? And why? Clifford promised to share his theories with me. But I arrived in Pasadena to discover he had died the week before.

I consoled myself with a day at the Huntington Library, where the librarian came up with nothing after cross-referencing the Washington Miners' roster with his registry of diaries. At his suggestion I checked the roster against Merrill J. Mattes's *Platte River Road Narratives*, a comprehensive listing of published and unpublished overland accounts of the California and Oregon Trail. Some names were tantalizingly similar. There was a Charles M. Moxley instead of my C. G. Moxley. There was an Isaac Owen, but unlike mine he had been a Methodist missionary. Mattes had rated the narratives for historical and literary value and Bruff received his highest mark, five stars.

As I was leaving the reading room the librarian gave me the address and telephone number of the *Oregon–California Trails Association*. When I called, a secretary directed me to a woman in Tahoe City, California, named Kathy Roubal, who administered their Census of Overland Emigrant Documents (COED), an ambitious project to index every diary, letter, and narrative account of the overland migration.

Roubal told me her unpaid COED volunteers had already entered 1,600 documents and 51,000 names into their database, but because they did not list people according to mining companies, I would have to pay for a costly computer search of every name on the Washington roster. But she knew of a woman named Wendy Lucas who lived on a ranch in Lakeview, Oregon, and had some connection with the Washington City Miners.

I checked an atlas and saw Lakeview was fifteen miles north of the California border and less than thirty from the Fandango Pass, so close it was almost, as I discovered when I went there, in its shadow.

When I called the number listed for Lucas in Information, a woman with a twangy ranch voice said sure, she was the great-great-granddaughter of Washington Miner John T. Coumbs, who had been twenty-four years old when he crossed the continent. Her ranch was less than three miles from the California border and from it she could see the Warner Mountains, Fandango Pass, and route of the Lassen Trail. Although Coumbs had not left any letters, diaries, or papers about his overland journey, she could tell me about his life and descendants, and show me the overland diary of Washington Miner John Bates, the man who had given Bruff some tobacco before leaving his camp. Coumbs had Bates's diary when he died, and she assumed he had inherited it. It was too fragile to copy or mail, and she kept it in a plastic bag in her safe, but if I came to Lakeview I was welcome to sit in her parlor and read it.

39

The Integraton
Prepares for Takeoff

The 7.6 rumbling through the eastern Mojave Desert town of Landers three hours before the Big Bear earthquake was the strongest to strike California in forty years. It shook for thirty seconds, twice as long as Loma Prieta, and moved the ground twenty-two feet. Five-foot-deep craters appeared on Highway 247 and an unbroken fissure cut across the desert for forty-four miles. Sympathetic tremors occurred as far away as Montana. The California Office of Emergency Services afterward issued the strongest-worded warning in its history, declaring a 50-percent risk of a 6.0 plus aftershock and recommending Southern Californians avoid the freeways. Had a similar quake struck a more densely settled area, it would have produced more damage and casualties than Loma Prieta. But in sparsely populated Landers it killed a little boy, left 150 buildings uninhabitable, and was soon forgotten by Californians, although not by scientists and engineers who argued its wide ruptures indicated the twenty-year-old Alquist Priolo Act permitting construction within fifty feet of an active fault might be dangerously permissive.

When I read about the Landers quake I was struck by the number of eyewitnesses who admitted to being paralyzed by fear and insisting it was "different" from other tremors. Their reaction ran so counter to the usual Californian response, and to the traditional wisdom that rural people who face fewer risks from collapsing buildings and expressways handle earthquakes better, that I decided to find out what had made it so frightening.

On the way to Landers I drove through Yucca Valley, another

high-desert franchise eyesore that was only better than Palmdale because it was a third the size. Its distinguishing feature was "Desert Christ Park," a collection of larger-than-life cement statues depicting the life of Christ that was worthy of mention in my one-volume encyclopedia of the state, *Companion to California*. Sculptor Antone Martin had erected them during the 1950s, "to bring mankind together before we are obliterated completely," he said.

His park was a sad mess. Vandals had decapitated an apostle and pulled saints off pedestals, leaving them facedown in the weeds. Statues had lost noses, arms, and wings. The rusted rebars and faded graffiti showed the damage had gone unrepaired for years. Yucca Valley had been too busy opening shopping centers to bother fixing the only thing making it different from anywhere else.

I stopped at a defunct drive-in theater to check out the swap meet from which eight-year-old Sylvia Mangos had been abducted and murdered five years before. Dozens of unattended children wandered the grounds and I could have easily repeated the crime while their parents traded in Vegematics, manganese knives, Gemsonic jewelry cleaners, Dr. Scholl's footbaths, Miracle TV aerials, hot-dog steamers, popcorn poppers, and other impulse purchases laid out on trestle tables and plastic sheeting. Swap-meet junk can be as revealing as the official statistics, and these gadgets spoke of people living in small spaces on tight budgets, of a town of late-night TV viewers buying mail order. Much of the crap was displayed in original boxes and appeared unused, and never would be since every minute the wind blew more grit into its delicate gears.

There was also a desperate commerce in objects acquired for free. A woman with skin like beef jerky hawked complimentary sachets of Holiday Inn shampoo and the foil-wrapped packets of breakfast jam offered gratis at greasy spoons. The presence of her preadolescent son had not stopped her from wearing a black T-shirt announcing, I WORK FOR SEX. He was shy and sweet looking, and when I began flipping through his stack of ratty comic books he stepped around the table and said earnestly, "I've got lots more at home if you're interested."

"Hey, mister, you're walking over our stuff," his mother shouted at him. "Get your butt back in that chair."

Along the road to Landers I passed a highway-patrol officer handcuffing some lowlifes in camouflage fatigues. Five minutes later two equally ratty hitchhikers lunged from the shoulder, forcing me to swerve and so unsettling me I turned too soon into Flamingo Heights, a hardscrabble desert subdivision two miles south of Landers where the only flamingos are plastic ones and the occupant of almost every mobile home or homesteading shack seemed to be holding a yard sale.

I stopped at a bungalow where cracks shot up the discolored stucco walls like lightning bolts and plastic sheeting had replaced a window. Aside from this earthquake damage, it was a typical Flamingo Heights house: a try at a cactus garden, a cannibalized motorcycle, bed-sheets instead of curtains, and a plastic flamingo, in this case leaning against a security service sign showing a gun barrel pointed at my kneecaps.

Several hundred items covered plywood tables out back. Almost everything was rusted, bent, cracked, smashed, or afflicted by some defect rendering it essentially worthless. I could have bought an empty plastic cigar tube, a single shoe, a free Pampers sample, or a broken ski pole. There was even, so help me, an empty Coke can (five cents), one lightbulb, and a sign of interest only to another "Parish Family." Who bought this flotsam? From the looks of this crowd, dusty children with strange haircuts, scarecrow teenagers, over-the-hill biker groupies whose lank hair had marinated for decades in perspiration-stained caps, and men with sun-peeled faces resembling crocodile bellies.

This buffet of junk belonged to the pale and twitchy Sandra, who told me she was a "collector" and I was only seeing half of her original stash of "antiques." Thieves and the earthquake had wiped out the rest. The thieves were her neighbors—"the chickenshit ones who didn't lose much in the quake themselves." They broke in after she and her husband fled to Lake Havasu to escape the aftershocks, and stole food, clothes, and whatever appliances still worked. Her girlfriend had returned to find her car on blocks and her tires missing. Her husband had lost his job down below because the highway was closed. They squabbled and separated. He was still unemployed, and she was moving to a smaller house in Landers.

The good news was that she was escaping Flamingo Heights, "a world-class center for lowlifes." They had moved up from Los Angeles in the mid-1980s to raise their kids away from drugs and get them involved in something healthy, like riding motorbikes. Then Los Angeles started dumping its parolees and welfare cases here. To an outsider it might look like lower-middle-class people living in small houses, but there was a big difference between people like her who held jobs, threw block parties, got involved in the school, paid attention to their kids, and maintained their property, and the newcomers, who did drugs, ripped off their neighbors, and lived in low-income housing that was better than what she could afford.

When a customer asked to use her bathroom she paused before saying, "What the hell, but I got to follow you." To protect him from her guard dog, she claimed, but I suspected to stop him cleaning out her bureaus. Once they disappeared inside, his companion pocketed a bent fork.

Sandra's customers did not strike me as the kind to be spooked by a quake, but I circulated anyway, asking if anyone had seen the earth open. At last a pretty woman named Sue Grey who had piled her blond hair into a beehive said her husband had. As he dashed out of the front door a fissure had opened at his feet and he almost fell in. Afterward their sons insisted on sleeping on the floor of their bedroom and he had suffered three months of insomnia, waking with every aftershock and having elaborate nightmares. When he suffered a nervous breakdown and sought help, the counselor shouted, "Hey! We finally got a man in here!" He was not ashamed because he knew other men just as shaken, but too proud to admit it. Counseling and medication had helped, but he still slept with a flashlight and mumbled about the devil in his sleep.

She thought it was not his personality or a case of women being emotionally stronger, it came down to this: He had run out the front door while she had grabbed their son and headed out the back; he had seen the earth split open, she had not.

When I asked to meet him she sighed and said, "We just want to be left alone." Reporters and sightseers had overwhelmed Landers. Tour companies from Palm Springs ran excursions, parking buses across the street because their front-yard fissure was so dramatic. Tourists walked across their property looking for damage, staring in their windows, sometimes climbing into their cars, and when they thought no one was watching, stealing souvenirs.

I asked if she knew of anyone who had suffered headaches before the quake. She said no, but it was funny I should mention it since she had just seen a man on *Oprah* named Jerry Hurley who claimed his predicted earthquakes. When I said I knew him, and that we sometimes spoke by telephone, she changed her mind, saying perhaps I could stop by, and perhaps I could take their number and phone if he felt an earthquake coming.

I had trouble matching Kevin Grey to his nerves. He was lanky and dark-haired, a generically handsome young man who rode a motorcycle and worked as a carpenter. He was as honest about his seismic fears as he was about his family's modest financial condition, admitting the loss of two weeks of food they had bought the day before had been a big setback. They had accepted an emergency payment of sixty-five dollars from FEMA so they could eat until the next paycheck. "But that's *all* we took," he insisted, making it clear even this had made him uncomfortable. "We saw so many people worse off we just didn't want to take advantage of the situation." Instead, they paid for their own repairs, sought Salvation Army furniture, and ate off plates donated by friends.

As he remembered the quake he rubbed imaginary goose bumps and glanced through the venetian blinds at his front yard. When an RV rumbled down the washboarded dirt road, he jerked like a puppet.

"He does that whenever a big truck goes by," she said. "It was *real* bad when everyone was moving out after the quake and their vans kept making that earthquake rumbling noise." She stared at him intently, like a physician evaluating a patient with a perplexing ailment.

"My property moved nine feet ... nine feet! Never, *ever*, in my wildest dreams had I imagined we were living over a fault," he said. The first thing he recalled was their dog waking him up. "He was whimpering and wanted to go out. I opened the front door and he took off. Then my back was against the wall, then it wasn't; then the wall moved toward me. I screamed for Sue but the roar was deafening. Through the window I saw the earth opening and closing: opening and expelling dust, closing and sucking it back. Our neighbor's house burst into flames, another house was cut in half so cleanly it looked as if God was using a knife. I thought we'd been bombed, a nuclear bomb, the Second Coming of Christ, the end of the world. Honestly, I expected to see the devil jumping out of that crack."

He led me outside to see the fissure. Even after months of wind and rain, its outline was visible. As he walked across his yard, explaining how the land had fallen in three levels and terraced the ground, he lengthened his stride, never once stepping on the crack.

His neighborhood was a big improvement on Flamingo Heights. The houses were better maintained and surrounded by five acres. In the 1950s it had been called "Homestead Valley" because the government gave five-acre plots to anyone agreeing to build a cabin and pay taxes. Their house was a renovated homesteader's cabin on five acres he proudly called "the property." He said they never regretted leaving Orange County. Here they lived close to nature, camped in the desert, and saw mesas and mountains from their front yard. They had persuaded some friends and relatives to join them and were creating a community. But just as he was saying, "We've found our own little five acres of heaven and—" a UPS truck rumbled down the road and he stopped in midsentence to shut his eyes.

Even if Kevin and Sue Grey had not told me the Grubstake was the best restaurant around, and its owners Roger and Tina Stockman great people, and that during the earthquake a fissure had split open its parking lot, I probably would have stopped anyway when I saw its tepee and bogus boothill cemetery. Roger Stockman was a jumpy chain-smoker with sad puppy eyes. He said his decorations—the stuffed bison wearing a hat, oil paintings of lachrymose Indian chiefs, model airplanes, and fringed lampshades—resulted from years of dedicated collecting. Before moving to the desert he and his wife had spent their vacations driving back roads, searching out "Route 66–type roadhouses," and buying antiques to furnish the one they dreamed of opening. The Landers quake had destroyed most of their lamps and chandeliers, but they were already acquiring replacements.

After feeling three foreshocks preceding the earthquake he had insisted his family sleep outside in their trailers. This probably saved their lives. When the ground broke, six neighboring houses burst into flames. He dashed into the parking lot to see a fissure heading for the Grubstake, then miraculously branching in two and sparing them. Little mushroom clouds of dust exploded from the ground, "as if monsters were pushing their heads out." Like Kevin Grey, the cracking earth made him think of hell.

The Grubstake was so badly damaged friends urged him to burn it for the insurance. There had been fires everywhere and it would have been easy, but shutting off the gas was the moral thing to do. For six months he was paralyzed with fear, unable to provide for his family. The quake had scrambled his memory and he forgot customers' names. Rebuilding was hard and FEMA unhelpful. Finally the great deus ex machina of California life, a celebrity, provided the loan that saved him. This celebrity was one of many who liked driving up from Palm Springs or Los Angeles. Stockman had promised to keep his or her identity a secret, but he would say Bruce Springsteen and Nancy Wilson sometimes ate in his restaurant. Springsteen came on his motorcycle on spring weekends when the desert bloomed. Nancy Wilson's parents lived nearby and were regulars.

I could see why someone would want to save the Grubstake. The "Where Friends Meet" motto was no phony. Stockman really *had* fulfilled his dream of owning a restaurant recreating his Iowa hometown. On Thanksgiving and Christmas he filled his tables with people whose children had dumped them in cheap desert shacks. It reminded him of having the whole big family over for the holidays in Iowa. He was always adopting people into his extended family, and housing down-and-outers in tents and trailers behind the kitchen. A hobo who came begging food a year earlier had become an honorary grandfather to his children. He had found the Grubstake's young chef abandoned, dyslexic, and illiterate. Now the boy was whipping up Iowa potato salad, free with each dish.

After leaving Iowa, Stockman had worked in the food-service industry in Sunnydale, moving here in 1985 when his children reached school age because he wanted them to grow up in a place where you knew your neighbors and could leave bikes on the lawn without having them stolen. After buying the Grubstake, he lost most of his capital to the stock market and swindlers. When he reopened after the earthquake he had less than a hundred dollars to his name. He was bitter about California, saying, "I want to live a morally decent life, work hard, and raise my kids well, but in California that's hard to do." But I doubted the Grubstake could have flourished or been as interesting anywhere *but* in California. Celebrities ready to bail out failing restaurants were not thick on the ground in Iowa, nor did it have the Indians, Chicanos, blacks, movie stars, bikers, retirees, and desert hermits he had skillfully woven into a community. Perhaps he had proved, without knowing it, that the tolerant and eccentric California of the past was still possible.

I liked the Grubstake so much I stayed late into the afternoon, drinking iced tea and writing in my notebooks. I met his dyslexic cook, his Navajo wife, Tina, who had given their children her exotic looks, his strapping teenage boys, and his daughter, Roxanne, who waited tables and was determined to attend Stanford. Then he introduced me to Nancy Wilson's sweet parents and to Jack Brockway, who owned Cardinal Auto Wrecking in Adelanto and wore a gray work shirt with JACK written in script, but had an educated voice, and the smooth upper-class looks of a male model. He told me his dream was to make a tour of the world's "power centers"; in the meantime he was caretaker of the Landers "Integraton." The noted UFO enthusiast George Van Tassel had constructed it during the 1950s, and after his death in 1978 one of Brockway's friends had bought it. Brockway believed it was "built on a sacred power vortex," and combined "sacred geometry, electromagnetics, sonics, future science, and ancient wisdom."

He showed me a photograph of a large white dome resembling a flying saucer in a low-budget movie. It was a major purity focus, he said, and visiting was like going to the Vatican. He had happened to be inside with his sons during the Landers earthquake. They had felt as if they were in a tornado, heading for Oz.

As we drove there he explained he had abandoned Los Angeles because it lacked grounding and energy. His *real* home was anywhere beautiful where the energy felt good. He had to honor that. California had bad energy, but he was giving it this last chance. So far, the desert was proving to be soothing, very supportive, but he was not optimistic. The rule seemed to be that someone like him could not afford to live anywhere nice in California, except perhaps in the Integraton. It was currently rented out for workshops, conferences, and weddings. Musicians liked recording in it because the domed second floor was a unique sound chamber where music became so all-enveloping it seemed to replace the air.

From a distance the Integraton resembled the decapitated rotunda of a minor state capitol. It floated serenely over the creosote and tumbleweed, a perfect white mushroom appearing larger than its thirty-eight feet high and fifty feet in diameter. Its telescope tower, locked fence, and DEDICATED TO RESEARCH IN LIFE EXTENSION sign gave it the *gravitas* of a scientific institute. Only the ring of silver spikes surrounding its middle like a dog collar suggested something else was up. The spikes, Brockway explained, were supposed to whirl around the building, creating a powerful electromagnetic field for Van Tassel's time-travel, antigravity, and rejuvenation experiments.

Like many California cranks of his generation, Van Tassel had crossed paths with Howard Hughes, inspecting his aircraft until abruptly moving his family into a cavern under a large boulder known as Giant Rock five miles east of the Integraton. From there he became a leading figure in the 1950s UFO cult, contacting beings from Venus and the star Arcturus via energy beams emanating from his weekly meditation sessions, and in *I Rode the Flying Saucer* describing how aliens had lifted him through the bottom of their saucer with a gravity-nullifying beam. He sponsored an annual Giant Rock Space Convention that attracted eleven thousand at its zenith in 1959, and began building the Integraton. It was unfinished and lacking the motor necessary to make its dome spin when he died at what had to be, for a man claiming to be an expert in rejuvenation, the embarrassingly early age of sixty-eight.

Like Father Riker, he had never stockpiled guns or demanded people abandon their families. In many respects he was a more appealing crank. At least he believed his claims, and in this seismically active desert perhaps he had mistaken earthquake lights for flying saucers, or once stood so near to them that as Professor Persinger might argue, they had scrambled his brain and persuaded him he had met an alien. Best of all, he left behind an unusual, handsome building that is the only surviving temple of a movement attracting the attention of reputable religious scholars and historians.

The Integraton had the glistening wood interior of a well-made yacht or Adirondack lodge. Van Tassel himself had developed the laminating process making possible the gluing and doweling together of its handsome boards. It was empty except for some stacked garden chairs, Indian drums, a table of T-shirts for sale to weekending New Agers, and a multiwave oscillator with a wand that buzzed and turned pink. Brockway and I stood in the corner where he and his boys had been sleeping on the night of the Landers quake. He said the Integraton had magnified the earthquake's "woo-woo-woo," like a megaphone. Its center column whipped back and forth, and it vibrated like a plane preparing for takeoff. Had it been less well constructed, it might have collapsed on them.

His first thoughts had been, "My God, it's finally worked. Aliens have landed. I hope they're nice ones." When he recognized an earthquake he ran to the center of the building to get the full effect. He believed earthquakes were gifts and miracles, and that experiencing one at the Integraton had rearranged his molecular structure, changing his personality, making him more humble. Van Tassel had claimed it would reenergize and rejuvenate subjects who stood in its center as the dome rotated, and he wondered if the quake had not produced this result. Ever since, his friends swore he looked younger every time they saw him. He summed up his experience by saying, "Being Integrated is all a matter of focus. It's a gift, part of my great adventure on this planet. There's something to it; and there's nothing to it."

I have no idea what he meant. But I do know that until I asked his age I had assumed this thirty-nine-year-old man was in his mid-to-late twenties.

I picked up my car at the Grubstake and drove back into the desert to Giant Rock, where Van Tassel had held his festivals and built a giant UFO viewing platform. This 100,000-ton, seven-story-high, 65-to-136-million-year-old boulder is the largest in the world and sits on land owned by the Department of the Interior's Bureau of Land Management (BLM). It was defaced by graffiti, blackened by fire, pitted with bullet holes, and surrounded by mounds of beer bottles and the garbage of weekend campers who did not know or care it was sacred to UFO enthusiasts and Indians, their "Great Stone."

Several families had circled recreational vehicles like a wagon train and unfolded lawn chairs. They raced dirt bikes, took target practice, and blasted music from boom boxes. They were unfriendly, and the combination of beer and guns spooked me. I walked about a mile down a track only to stumble on another camp where a man and his son were shooting at cans while his daughter rode a dirt bike in circles. He strode up and said, "Like, we've been coming here, to this same spot for ten years. . . ." I kept walking.

The abuse of the Mojave is an old story. In the 1930s travelers crossing it at night set fire to Joshua trees to guide other motorists. Giant Rock was damaged by the first man to occupy it, a crazy miner named Frank Critzer, who lived in its four-hundred-square-foot cave before the war. After a 1942 confrontation with sheriff's deputies, he blew himself up in his cave with dynamite. Now it was a blackened hole filled with cans and disposable diapers.

I stuck around until after sunset, searching the horizon for the flashing and hovering lights people had reported seeing here. It was speculated they were artillery shells from the Twentynine Palms Marine Corps Training Center, shooting stars, flying saucers, or ball lightning from an impending earthquake.

The next morning I told rangers at the Joshua Tree National Monument visitor center I wanted to meet someone who liked the Mojave for more than its role as garbage dump, rifle range, burial ground, and motorcycle track. They recommended Willie and Barbara Robb, BLM volunteers who lived in Twentynine Palms and kept a prospector's cabin in Music Valley. When we met they were crestfallen I could only spend a day. You needed at least three or four weeks to really appreciate the Mojave, they insisted. In fact, they could drive me around for six months without showing me the same canyon or miner's cabin, or telling me the same story. The desert was that varied, its history that rich.

While we drove to Music Valley in their truck he gave me a narrative history of the area that wove together stories about a Japanese internee who hid at the El Medina Ranch throughout World War II and the two marines who had unwisely used old tires to light a fire that spread to the gas tank of their Jeep and immolated them. Corpses were always turning up in the desert. In the early days a prospector would lie down and that was it. A tourist had recently stumbled on the mummified body of a miner reduced to twenty pounds by a colony of ants, and a local sheriff liked saying that if everyone who had been murdered or had their corpse left in the Mojave stood up and screamed, the sound would be deafening.

They had befriended the previous owner of their Music Valley rock house during one of their many desert excursions. His widow had given it to them after he died. At first the BLM tried evicting them. Finally they reached a compromise whereby they kept it as a weekend retreat while becoming BLM volunteers. They distributed maps, fixed flats, gave directions, left out pans of water for coyotes, rummaged through garbage for clues to its owners, posted warnings and fences around abandoned mine shafts, asked visitors who picked up tortoises to put them down in the same direction they were traveling, and provided water to the many families who drove into the desert with a single bottle of soda pop.

I thought the rutted track to their rock house wound through some pretty third-rate desert scenery. Instead of the sweeping vistas, dazzling colors, mesas, and oases that can make a desert appealing, I saw slag heaps of rock, scrub, vandalized cabins, and fifty years of junked cars. Miners had cannibalized them to power their buckets. Then hunters shot up their chassis and pyromaniacs burned them.

"A Studebaker, Buick, Buick, Ford," Barbara Robb said, like someone pointing out wildlife. "Over that ridge there were some fine Indian petroglyphs—until the target shooters filled them full of holes."

We stopped to collect garbage from a place they had swept clean only last week, then examined a mine shaft containing the carcass of a 1950s sedan, then another that had claimed the life of a boy exploring it. Because of this incident and because their own son had suffered a concussion after falling down an abandoned shaft, the Robbs had become fanatics about fencing and posting them, even though their signs were frequently vandalized.

They claimed to love the night skies, meteor showers, wildflowers, and solitude, watching the antelope squirrels out their front door, and finding ravens rooking in abandoned cabins. Other deserts had these, but the Mojave was unique because of its history. Most desert travelers considered the abandoned miners' cabins a source of firewood; he saw them as unmined history.

"Well, I also have my eyes out for one of those fifty-pound nuggets," Barbara said.

Their rock house was just that—a blockhouse made of boulders set on a breezy hill. "Sixteen locks," he said while fumbling with keys, dead bolts, and a steel plate.

What was there to steal? I asked after seeing the rough furniture and Depression-era kitchen.

"That's the $100,000 question."

But even here, an hour from a paved road, vandals had blasted shotguns at his windows and broken in three times to spray the fire extinguisher. But they had overlooked his collection of square nails, old milk cans, and bones that were "*probably* not human."

He called the cabin his time machine and thought he might have occupied it in another life. There was no television, nothing to interrupt his daydreams, and he sometimes imagined himself as a boy growing up outside Sparta, Illinois, "playing in the old Jesse James caves, living so far in the sticks if you broke a leg you had to fix it on the spot."

He insisted I take a rock as a memento, so we walked in ever-expanding circles around the house looking for the right one, and picking our way through beer-bottle shards from the vandals' target practice. We settled on a quartz-bearing rock she liked because it would sparkle under a full moon and remind me of Music Valley.

Less than a hundred yards from their front door we came upon a mine shaft and the rusted frame of a stripped motorcycle. "People use the desert to hide their crimes, so we have to be careful, *very* careful not to get in their way," she said bitterly. They sometimes heard shots and saw smoke rising from burning cars. A half mile down the road thieves had recently cut up a Cadillac, and their guns and dogs had kept the Robbs awake.

When my photographs came back from the developer, his description of the rock house as a time machine made sense. One snapshot showed him standing on the porch in a sheepskin vest and wide-brimmed campaign hat. His face had the crevices you find on a man who has spent a lifetime outdoors. Had the picture come tinted and embossed with the name of an antique photography studio, you could have easily mistaken him for a nineteenth-century prospector, perhaps a Washington City miner who had staked a claim and prospered.

40

Cabot Yerxa's Eyesore

In a room adjoining his stock of commando knives, machine-gun tripods, and grenades labeled DON'T PULL PINS! the owner of the Trader of the Lost Surplus had displayed his sizable inventory of Nazi memorabilia with a reverence usually shown icons on a Greek Orthodox altar. While "Mockingbird Hill" played from a loudspeaker, a Korean woman ran a feather duster over flags, uniforms, weapons, and photographs of the Führer.

I took it as bad news that the store was crowded with shoppers, and its parking lot noisy with their unmuffled rattletraps, and a few miles later, in Desert Hot Springs, the large number of shopping carts abandoned on sidewalks or tipped into gutters was more bad news.

It was not what I expected from a place with such an evocative name, and I would have kept driving had scientists not agreed that the fault segment between Desert Hot Springs and Salton Sea, where the last major rupture had occurred in about 1680, is the most likely to produce at least a 7.5 during the next thirty years. A 1989 study put the odds at 60 percent, but after the Landers, Big Bear, and Desert Hot Springs earthquakes of 1992, the consensus was that these tremors on minor faults had increased the chances for a Big One.

The distinguished Caltech geologist Kerry Sieh told *Time*, "It's just a gut feeling, but I think I'll witness a great earthquake on the southern San Andreas Fault in my lifetime."

Lucille Jones of the USGS Pasadena office said, "There is nothing to suggest stress has been relieved on the San Andreas [by these earthquakes]. If anything, this is a sign of increased stress . . . the longer-run prospect for a big quake on the fault may have been fundamentally changed for the worse by recent events." Landers was "a wake-up call," she told *The New York Times*. The Big One was probably closer than thirty years, perhaps less than five.

Allan Lindh, who directed the USGS office in Menlo Park, said, "Most of us have an awful feeling that thirty years is wishful thinking. . . . There is evidence we're near the jumping-off place for a big one. . . . Anyone who thinks they can ignore this should be dissuaded now." He told the *Times* Landers was a "final warning," and advised people in Southern California to "act as if the damn thing will happen tomorrow."

But the head of the USGS office in Pasadena, Thomas Heaton, said, "You can't predict earthquakes." He believed calling Big Bear and Landers "last straws" made no sense since scientists had no idea how many smaller earthquakes you needed to advance the timetable for the Big One. Still, at a press conference three weeks after Landers, he said the fault had gained as much stress as it normally would in a ten-to-fifty-year period, adding that if there was a large earthquake on the San Andreas in the next few years, he would not be surprised.

Five months after Landers, a panel convened by the Southern California Earthquake Center at USC reported the probability of a magnitude 7.0 or greater on this segment of the San Andreas was 5 to 12 percent each year, and as high as 47 percent in the next five. So if I hung around for weeks, my chances of experiencing an earthquake were as much as 1 in 250.

At Waterman Canyon near San Bernardino, the San Andreas branched into two parallel zones that joined up again fifteen miles north of Desert Hot Springs at Biskra Palms. I decided to follow the northern branch into Desert Hot Springs, because in *Earthquake Country*, Iacopi had described it as the most visible of the two. His book contained an aerial photograph of Desert Hot Springs with a thick orange line superimposed over its grid of streets. I laid it next to a current street map and noticed the fault ran more or less underneath the library, city hall, and post office, and something called Cabot's Old Indian Pueblo Museum.

I walked through downtown along the fault's diagonal path, peering into the windows of a karate parlor and thrift store, then stopping in Roberto's barbershop for a haircut from the liver-spotted Roberto, who ended his loving description of driving across the continent in a convertible from New York to California in 1946 with, "Now I'd rather die in an earthquake in Desert Hot Springs than live another ten years in L.A."

After weeks in these desert fringe towns, I was getting tired of the Los Angeles bashing, even though I sometimes cheerfully engaged in it myself. To silence him I began reading a copy of the weekly *Desert Sentinel*. A front-page article was headlined RESIDENTS HEAP CRITICISM ON SHERIFF'S DEPARTMENT. They were complaining about criminals running wild and retirees terrified of leaving their homes. An anonymous caller to the newspaper said vigilante groups were forming, adding, "I don't mind shooting any a——— that breaks into my house. I fought overseas. I don't mind killing . . . in fact I kind of like it." A Riverside County Sheriff's Department spokesman made the customary excuses about a shrinking budget and growing population (although crime had increased 400 percent since 1979, while the year-round population had grown only 75 percent). But in this town where many of the population of twelve thousand were elderly seasonal residents who only contributed to the statistics as victims, the previous month had seen ninety-three burglaries, eleven assaults with a deadly weapon, thirteen cases of forcible entry, and seventeen instances of "tattooing a person under age eighteen."

From Roberto's I drove up the fault to Rancho Del Oro, whose literature made a big deal of it being a "completely walled community." The young salesman leaned toward me as if I was a challenging weight to be lifted and insisted I take a handsome brochure with DESERT HOT SPRINGS . . . A TERRIFIC PLACE TO LIVE splashed across it in huge letters. The copy began, "It's the dream and desire that's part of the American ideal. . . ."

I handed him the *Desert Sentinel* article describing the "frustration of residents thoroughly disgusted with escalating crime here."

He talked fast. "We have a six-foot wall, which for you means added security, and all the homes are prewired for security systems." Besides, many Rancho Del Oro buyers were retirees. Would they be moving here if it was dangerous?

A potbellied man I took for one of the contractors slapped my newspaper on the counter. "Ha! Nonsense! There's crime everywhere. I've lived here thirty years. What's a few extra homicides?"

In Rancho Del Oro's model homes, speakers automatically launched into a spiel when you stepped into a room. A soothing voice repeated the words *home, community,* and *dream* as if they were an exorcism. But signs on every coffee table warned, DECORATOR ITEMS ARE SECURITY-PROTECTED AND CAN BE ACTIVATED BY ELECTRONIC BEEPERS.

The next day, the *Palm Springs Desert Sun* had an article about a joint meeting of the Desert Hot Springs Planning Commission and City Council during which the planning commissioner had objected to using the word *small* in Goal Number Four of Desert Hot Springs' general plan that currently read, "The city shall preserve its character and small-town atmosphere." He was concerned this might "limit our horizons somewhat," and was inappropriate for a town about to approve construction of housing tracts containing thousands of new homes. The vice chairwoman suggested "quaint" instead of "small-town." The interim planning director wanted "special." The city attorney proposed "small but growing." But the mayor had the last word, and they unanimously voted to replace it with "hometown atmosphere."

A female detective at the sheriff's substation told me, "Sure we know this station is near the fault, but frankly that's the last thing we worry about." She said two deputies wearing bulletproof vests handled forty calls every twenty-four hours, and seventy-five on a weekend. The cheap rentals attracted parolees, and it sometimes seemed as if no one else lived here.

A senior police officer shut his office door and demanded anonymity before saying, "It's the kind of nasty little town where you almost feel you *ought* to be throwing your McDonald's wrapper out the window." He thought crime could only increase. The Crips and Bloods were recruiting and this month there had been an explosion of vandalism and graffiti. Last year there had been six murders, an incredible number for a small town. The elderly were outraged by crime but unwilling to pay for more police. Most assessed property was undeveloped land held by speculators and developers who only voted for the most austere budgets. The city services were impoverished and the streets a disgrace. The kids were "bored and mean," and they set fires and rammed shopping carts into parked cars for fun. Last week two boys had dug a pit, camouflaged it with branches and earth, and persuaded an elderly neighbor to walk into it, sending her to the hospital. There was a boys' and girls' club with a new swimming pool and tennis courts, mountains to hike, the best moto-cross track in the county, soccer fields, volleyball courts, and empty lots to play in, but the kids bitched because there was no shopping mall or video arcade.

He pitied the retirees who moved in and discovered a landlord had just rented to some lowlifes next door who played music all night, drained oil from their junkers into the gutter, fought, dealt drugs, and let their kids and mongrels run wild. And he pitied people working their asses off at low-paying service jobs in nearby Palm Springs who came home to get ripped off by people on welfare. Yesterday he had given a ride to a single mother who was hitchhiking to her job guarding a country-club gate because a car was too expensive.

His solution to the crime wave was this: "Bulldoze this nasty little town under and pretend it never existed. Or hope for the Big One and push what's left into the crack."

I accepted his invitation to see for myself by taking a ride-along with a boyish deputy named Mark Schmitz, who had a freckly Norman Rockwell face and was alternately distressed and disgusted by the calls we answered, every one of which somehow involved a woman being mistreated by the man she loved.

We drove to a flimsy tract house to answer a complaint of a man assaulting a woman. The young woman answering the door was red-eyed and cradled a filthy baby. Upended furniture filled the room behind her. "Just leave me the *fuck* alone," she screamed, slamming the door. Schmitz stood in the doorway for several minutes, hoping she would change her mind. He thought the guy was inside, and would resume beating her once we left.

A woman flagged us down in a shopping-center parking lot with the heavy flashlight she said she carried for defense. She waved a cashier's check made out to her boyfriend. He had warned her not to come home without cashing it, but the banks were closed and the supermarket clerks suspicious. What could she do? "I just *can't* go home without the cash," she said, her eyes wide with fear.

We were called by a chubby teenage girl who met us on the front steps of her mother's mobile home. She was fifteen, and her twenty-one-year-old boyfriend was inside, drunk, screaming, and smashing things. He staggered out the door, shirtless and cursing, a beautiful, long-lashed man who had covered his chest and arms with tattoos. Her mother returned home from work and cursed her for throwing nail polish at him to defend herself. It had stained the furniture. The girl refused to press charges. "That's 'family values' in Desert Hot Springs," Schmitz said as we left.

At the fire station an emaciated woman named "Sally" who was covered with methamphetamine scabs was moaning and rolling on the concrete floor. Her four-year-old daughter sobbed and her six-year-old boy wiped his eyes with his sleeve. A bored ambulance attendant believed she had a blocked urinary tract, but said regulations prohibited the kids from accompanying her in the ambulance. She had no relatives and had already called three sets of friends who all refused to watch her kids while she went to the emergency room.

Between gasps of pain she told us her boyfriend, Bill, had promised to collect them at the elementary school across the road five hours ago. But they had been fighting, and she was moving out, so he had probably changed his mind or was in bed with his new girlfriend.

Schmitz persuaded her to call another friend and we overheard her imploring someone named Paulette, who replied that watching Sally's children would not be convenient right now. Finally Sally agreed to surrender the kids to California Protective Services. The boy said, "It's okay, Mom," but the little girl held her in a fierce embrace. "I just can't go," Sally said. "She gets so scared when I go away she throws up."

Schmitz offered to drive them to a motel, but on the way she began screaming in agony and changed her mind, agreeing to return to the firehouse and leave her children. As we helped her out of the squad car, she pointed to a passing pickup and wailed, "It's Bill! Bill ... Bill ... Bill ... " Her children jumped and screamed his name and all three ran after the disappearing taillights. Finally Bill's conscience kicked in and he slowly backed up. The ambulance driver said, "If she can run like that I guess we don't need to worry about her."

Afterward Schmitz wordlessly drove to a car wash where geysers of sweet San Andreas Fault–produced springwater cleaned his Crown Victoria. As we were about to turn back into the highway, a dispatcher shouted, "A five-plus earthquake has just hit Riverside!"

It is safer to stay inside a car during a quake but we instinctively climbed out. The car wash was on Palm Drive, near Roberto's barbershop, and I reckoned over the northern branch of the San Andreas.

I thought, "This is it! Maybe not the Big One, but something big enough to feel," and imagined the fault already opening the earth like a zipper in Riverside.

We spread our legs like sailors in a heavy sea and waited. We kept this position for several minutes, unwilling to give up hope. The next day the *Desert Sun* carried a small story headlined REDLANDS SHOOK BY 3.6 QUAKE, saying a small earthquake had rattled the Southern California desert without causing damage or injuries.

Here is how the city fathers of Desert Hot Springs rewarded Cabot Yerxa for discovering the springs giving their city its name and whatever small appeal it has. When he died in 1965 they schemed to demolish his house, and when his widow objected, they committed her to an institution on the flimsy pretext that (like thousands of other Californians) she claimed to have ridden a flying saucer.

His house is a four-story Hopi Indian pueblo he built with a shovel and wheelbarrow out of refuse scavenged from the desert. It is a reproach to the rest of Desert Hot Springs, easily its most attractive building, and the only one built for its climate of punishing winds and hundred degree temperatures. Its thick adobe keeps it cool in summer and warm in winter, and because its windows are small and expertly angled, the sun never shines into downstairs rooms until late afternoon. Nevertheless, Desert Hot Springs politicians considered it an eyesore and an affront to their motto, "Pride and Progress." They argued it was dangerous because it straddled the fault and Yerxa had not built to code. After his death they allowed squatters to vandalize it so they could claim they had no choice but to bulldoze it. They were thwarted by a Burbank businessman named Cole Eyraud who had known Yerxa as a boy. He bought the pueblo, moved in, and turned it into a museum celebrating Yerxa's life.

You visited it as you would a Loire château, accompanied by a guide, in this case by a sincere, gawky counterculture tomboy who introduced herself as "Lane—you know, like the road."

She resisted my invitation to explain the circumstances bringing her to Yerxa's pueblo from West Virginia, and while we waited hopefully for other visitors insisted I sample the pueblo's famous San Andreas Fault mineral water—"certified by the Mayo Clinic as the world's finest." Then she summarized Cabot Yerxa's life at breakneck speed, making it sound even more reckless, exotic, enviable, and noble than it had been, if that is possible.

His last name was Dutch and his first bestowed to honor his ancestor John Cabot who had discovered Newfoundland. He had been born in 1883 on a South Dakota Sioux reservation to the couple who ran the trading post, the beginning of a lifetime interest in Indian culture culminating in this pueblo. He joined the Yukon Gold Rush at fifteen, bringing a sack of five-cent cigars he sold to miners for twenty-dollar bags of gold dust. He met and made a lifelong friend of Theodore Roosevelt and collected the first Inuit vocabulary, selling it to the Smithsonian for fifty cents a word. Then he prospected for gold in Cuba, becoming the first diver to salvage a piece of the battleship *Maine*, and introducing Cuban cigars to the United States at the 1905 St. Louis World's Fair.

In 1913 he walked into what would become Desert Hot Springs carrying a quart of water and a small bag of food. He claimed a 160-acre homestead, built a stone cabin, and bought a burro he named Merry Christmas and taught to chew tobacco and drink whiskey from a bottle. After digging wells six hundred yards apart and discovering that because they lay on opposite sides of the fault, one produced hot water and the other cold, he called his property "Miracle Hill." Until a laboratory confirmed his water was therapeutic, the Desert Hot Springs establishment dismissed him as a crank.

He painted, prospected, collected rubbish in the desert, and in 1939 began building his pueblo out of the junk Lane preferred to call "completely recycled materials." He fashioned its door from a wagon floor and its ceiling from railroad ties. He straightened bent nails, lined cabinets with old linoleum, and mixed cement into his adobe blocks to make them bulletproof. Everything had a funhouse slant because he shared the Indian conviction that symmetry encouraged evil spirits. By the time he died he numbered among his close friends and frequent correspondents Theodore Roosevelt, Buffalo Bill Cody, Geronimo, Pancho Villa, and the ubiquitous George Van Tassel.

When I pressed Lane to make some sense of his life, perhaps to explain why he meant so much to her, she would only offer, "He was homeless, but not helpless, because he had a shovel." And "he never went to school and didn't care for stuffed-shirt society."

I suspected these were statements you could make about her, too. No one else had arrived for the $2.50 guided tour, so she led me alone up the pueblo's narrowing staircases, then through rooms with sloping ceilings and tilted floors. We lingered at every fossil and skull-filled cabinet and peered into every closet. I learned Yerxa's favorite treasures had been his World War I army jacket, a rack of aloha shirts, Geronimo's wristband (a gift from the warrior's nephew), a prayer cloth presented by the Dalai Lama during a trip to Tibet, and a statue made by the last chief of the Chuash titled "two-faced white man." She said the Indian preference for having nothing to separate you from Mother Nature explained the dirt floors, and Yerxa's desire to give rattlesnakes easy access to the premises explained the small holes at the base of the walls. They slithered in at night to feast on mice, and every morning he found them coiled by the fire and asleep on the chairs. "We *think* we have the snake holes plugged," she said.

She was particularly fond of Yerxa's wife, Portia, who was believed to haunt the pueblo. She had been a suffragette and Theosophy teacher, and her business card advertised, CHARACTER ANALYST, MENTAL ANALYST, VOCATIONAL ADVISOR. Because Yerxa had been her seventh husband she had dressed for her wedding in black.

Lane insisted I finger the Dragon Lady outfits she had acquired during a trip to China, where she was hailed as "the China Doll." Then she ushered me into Portia's top-floor office, where the walls were sticky with honey still dripping from her hives, and pointed out the window through which she had seen her flying saucer.

I saw that it faced the fault and thought, "Earthquake lights."

Lane depicted their marriage as a romantic partnership of eccentrics. But when I learned the basket of stones by the fireplace had been her antirattlesnake ammunition, and that while Yerxa slept on a mattress downstairs, she had slept on the second floor because serpents could not climb stairs, I wondered why if he really loved her so much he had not simply plugged those damned snake holes. Was it stubbornness, eccentricity, or sadism? All you could say for sure was that here was a man who preferred sleeping with rattlesnakes to his wife.

Back in the gift shop I met Cole Eyraud. He had a sun-peeled, rabbity face, glacier-white hair, and foxy prospector eyes. He had made the pueblo's preservation his life's work, for reasons elusive even to himself. He said he had met Yerxa only once in 1936 when his parents tried homesteading in Lancaster. He forgot about him entirely until reading a 1965 *Los Angeles Times* article in which the Desert Hot Springs city manager called the pueblo an eyesore that should be demolished. He bought it on impulse for five hundred dollars and moved in after selling his aerospace company that had employed 110 workers in the manufacture of centrifugal accelerators for astronaut training. He entered local politics to stop Desert Hot Springs tearing down its most historic house, and after winning election as town vice manager had the pleasure of signing the dismissal notice of the building inspector who wanted to condemn it. Now it was a state historic landmark and a candidate for the National Register of Historic Places.

When I asked why he was such a fierce defender of Yerxa's legacy, he mumbled about admiring him for being "open-minded" and "willing to take anyone in." This was all true, but so was the fact that Yerxa had left behind a first-class eccentric's retreat in turnkey condition, so that for five hundred dollars Eyraud could instantly transform himself from aerospace executive to desert character.

He tried to be a worthy successor to Yerxa. He had developed eccentric mannerisms and his first words to me had not been "Hello," but "Did you know they use DC current in prison because it kills 'em quicker?" He cultivated a group of bohemian seniors who had turned the pueblo into an informal community center. He commissioned a Hungarian artist to carve the largest wooden Indian in the world from a 750-foot redwood. He collected stray dogs, believed in UFOs, and insisted underground nuclear testing had triggered Landers, and that I would feel a sudden blast of arctic air if I waved my arm out the window as I drove across the fault. (I did not.)

He complained the pueblo was becoming like a besieged cavalry fort. Someone had scrawled graffiti and obscenities across its walls. Burglars had sprayed his dogs with arsenic and attempted several break-ins.

"Now we have more guns than Cabot did when he lived here, in the 'Wild West,' " Lane announced.

"They claim the Crips and Bloods have moved into Desert Hot Springs," he said, puffing up his parakeet chest. "Well, let them come. We have machetes, mace that sprays thirty-five feet, a .38 Special, a crossbow, and a Japanese sniper's rifle I picked up in Okinawa, and Lane is a karate expert."

He insisted I listen to a threatening telephone call he believed came from an office-supply salesman he had rebuffed. He turned on his answering machine and I heard, "Cocksucking bastard. . . You mother-fucking faggot, you got something to say to me, pick it up. I'm going down right now to get you, you son-of-a-bitch."

Read these words and they are just a string of taxi drivers' curses, but listen to them being screamed by a hysterical but educated voice and they are chilling. Had I heard them on my machine I would have slept with a loaded gun, too.

41

In the Vicinity

My street map said *Palm Springs and Vicinity*, but most of the glamour, serious money, and celebrities under seventy-five were in the Vicinity—the Coachella Valley golf resort towns of Rancho Mirage, Palm Desert, Indian Wells, and La Quinta that were strung out along Highway 111 five miles west of the fault. More specifically, they were in the forty-odd gated and guarded private country-club golf developments where celebrities, sport figures, remittance men, politicians, and current or retired captains of industry have chosen to isolate themselves from an increasingly coarse and dangerous public life that if their behavior and leadership have not contributed to, well, what has?

I had glimpsed these country clubs when the last holes of some golf "classic" delayed the weekend news. The crowds of spectators encouraged me to believe I could drive up to the clubhouses to see if the emerald fairways, sparkling water obstacles, and pink snowcapped mountains were as impossibly beautiful in real life. But in a morning of cruising down drives named for Sinatra, Hope, Shore, and Ford, I saw only iron fencing and stucco walls, and became a connoisseur of gates, coming to prefer the thruway-toll-plaza entrances to the totalitarian-state striped poles.

When I said I was thinking of buying a house, guards with the dedication of East German Vopos told me to return with an agent or an appointment. I was allowed into PGA West ("The Western Home of American Golf") because its model homes were open to the public, but when I made a run for the clubhouse I was apprehended for displaying the wrong color-coded pass.

I had known gated communities were part of the Southern California landscape, but I never expected to find so many putting so much territory out of bounds. The enormous American flags flying over the gates made my rejection even more unpalatable. So did the oldies station playing an all-day Beach Boy tribute, so that top-down, open-road California anthems like "Little Deuce Coupe" and "California Girls" accompanied my U-turns at the gates of Morningside ("A lifetime of gracious living"), Mirada ("Privacy and security . . . the ultimate desert lifestyle"), Bear Creek ("The moment you enter the private, guard-gated community, you know you are in a truly special place"), and Big Horn ("In partnership with nature").

Like everyone in the Coachella Valley, the announcer on this station made a big deal of living in the desert, going on about "desert living" and the "desert weather forecast." There was a Desert Museum, College of the Desert, Desert ExpoCenter, Hi-Desert Playhouse, Desert Breezes Tennis Club, and Desert Island Golf and Country Club. The word had the quality of a boast, as if the corporate retirees were pioneers instead of inhabitants of a cushy air-conditioned, asphalt-paved valley, where most traces of real desert had been eradicated. I comforted myself by imagining Spiro Agnew, Gerald Ford, and the other white-belt celebrity oldsters dressed in colorful golf duds and stranded in the desert, out of gas and food, real desert dwellers at last, lacking even one of the 740 gallons of water every Coachella Valley resident uses daily, ignorant that the clumps of sycamores and cottonwoods indicated a spring, but perhaps cocking an eye to the circling vultures.

I also imagined an earthquake. According to the *Desert Sun*, scientists believed a 7.5 on the Coachella Valley segment of the San Andreas could send landslides toppling onto gated communities built too close to the mountains, damage even new hotels above their third stories, cause "moderate to heavy damage" to Eisenhower and Desert hospitals, induce structural failure in the two largest shopping malls, and break the Lake Cahuilla Dam, flooding a nearby golf development. It warned that "in one worse-case scenario prepared for a government study the quake kills 5,000 people, injures another 15,000, renders 50,000 homeless." The respected British magazine *Nature* reported that because the Landers earthquake had left the Coachella Valley "highly ripe" for an earthquake of at least magnitude 7.5, the difference between the old and new odds of annihilation amounted to an annual "cost" of $64,000 to the owner of a $2 million home.

I stopped at the Marriott's Desert Springs Resort and Spa to use the toilet. Man-made canals and lakes crisscrossed the ground and its advertisements boasted, "Cruise our desert." Water gushed from fountains, lay in water traps, sprinkled fairways, and collected in an atrium lake where little vaporettos docked. The resort had been built and inaugurated during one of the worst California droughts of the century, when towns as close as Desert Hot Springs were rationing water. No excuses about how Palm Springs had its own extensive aquifer or how the water was recycled could persuade me the place did not at least violate the simple Sunday-school rule that just because you *can* do something, does not mean you should.

In the gift shop I bought a postcard showing an aerial view of the Walter Annenberg estate. I had read that it sprawled over 350 acres near the intersection of Sinatra and Hope, had 32,000 square feet of living area, an art collection worth $100 million, a nine-hole golf course, and had hosted every Republican president since Eisenhower. Nevertheless, the publisher of this postcard, Western Resort Publications and Novelty of Palm Springs, considered this information less important than that "intense security provides privacy and safety for all guests."

While I slept, the Coachella Valley's graffiti "crews" went on a "bombing run," spray-painting their tags on overpasses, strip malls, and country-club walls along drives named for politicians and entertainers. I detest graffiti but enjoyed "HA-HA-HA" sprayed across Arnold Palmer's face on a billboard advertising some golf villas.

That weekend an indignant editorial in the *Desert Sun* said graffiti had "spread like wildfire" and called for the usual "strong measures," saying it inspired "fear of increased gang activity, fear that our society is out of control." When I saw a "Gang Awareness Assembly" at the middle school in Cathedral City listed in the same newspaper among the charity auctions and celebrity tennis tournaments, I decided to see who else thought gangs were a problem in the Coachella Valley.

Cathedral City is a working-class town sandwiched between Palm Springs and Rancho Mirage. It is where people who guard gates and groom greens live in modest tracts and trailer parks alongside Social Security retirees. The middle school resembled a self-storage warehouse and the modular classrooms in back could have fallen off any container ship. Teachers at the meeting told me it was new but already overcrowded, having increased from 900 to 1,200 students in three years. Students had to pay for their own sports and the district could not afford after-school activities. Many kids went home to empty houses and played video games or joined gangs. Meanwhile, nearby Rancho Mirage was building a $24 million civic center, and farther down the valley in Indian Wells, $10 million in public redevelopment funds were subsidizing a new country club.

The school was 50 percent Hispanic, 35 percent white, and 15 percent black and others, but half of this audience of about one hundred was composed of elderly whites, and I reckoned fewer than 5 percent of the parents with children at Cathedral City Middle had bothered to attend. The guest speaker was Robbie Robinson, a thin and energetic middle-aged man who worked for the Los Angeles County Probation Department and was perhaps the most sensible and compelling black orator I have heard since listening to Martin Luther King preach in Selma on the eve of the 1965 march to Montgomery. His speech mixed passion, religion, and common sense, and he delivered it with an actor's polish and a poet's cadence. He rocked on his heels and mimicked gang language, hand signals, posture, and gestures, sucking on his teeth, pushing out his lips, flashing the "hard stare" that can trigger a drive-by, and doing the rolling "mall walk" meaning "I'm strapped, carrying a gun." But he was such a mesmerizing speaker that he unwittingly made the insistence on respect, elaborate costumes, and special gang ways sound somewhat glamorous, which they were compared with this drab library in this no-frills school.

He said the biggest trend in Los Angeles was gangs of Armenian and Irish kids. Even Beverly Hills kids were being seduced by gang music and clothing into joining gangs. Clothes could kill, and the stores, manufacturers, and parents who bought them bore some responsibility for the carnage. When he warned, "If your twelve-year-old tattoos himself and dresses in the big shirt and pants and the Raider jacket, he's already a little gang wannabe, and it's almost too late," a young couple in front of me exchanged nervous glances.

He recommended fighting back with family, religion, and community, and putting God, "whatever He means to you," into your life. He recited an Old Testament passage in which Joshua declares, "Choose you this day whom you will serve." Parents had to choose whom *they* would serve, he said. They had to discipline their kids when they talked back, praise them when they succeeded, and persuade them to look to parents, teachers, and preachers for their heroes rather than music and sports. Gangs seduced even good kids from good families, their appeal was that strong. The good families had to unite, combating gangs as a community.

"Support one another! Look to the people on your left, now on your right. Stay afterward and get to know each other," he urged. "If you don't have a community, make one. Don't let this overwhelm you! There is still hope."

He was perspiring when he finished, and I thought slightly peeved to have performed before such a small audience. "This room should be packed," he muttered after inviting questions. "When you have a small turnout, you have small solutions."

He noticed a redheaded boy of about twelve wearing CK sneakers. "Do you know some gang members buy those because they stand for 'Crip Killer' ?" he asked his mother. "Don't let him wear them outside the house, he could get shot." He turned to the boy. "Do you have a gang problem at this school?" The boy glanced around the room, checking who was here before whispering a soprano "yes."

A blond sixth grader with thick pigtails and a lisp from her braces asked in a tiny voice, "What if they say they'll kill you if you tell?"

About a dozen teachers and parents stayed behind to make a stab at following his advice of launching an antigang community group.

The teachers agreed middle school was when gang activity began, and Cathedral City's problem was increasing despite faddish programs and visits from people like Robinson. An older, hard-bitten teacher said teaching self-esteem was nonsense. It just made them feel better about being gang members. Another added, "It's hopeless. Gang clothes are glorified on MTV and sold in Bullocks." A third told me she had moved west from Wyoming because she wanted to live in California. She looked like prime California material—blond, cute, and freckly. But when I asked if she planned staying, she shook her head as if the idea was too fantastic for words.

In a 1988 *People* magazine article former mayor Frank Bogert had slapped down Mayor (now U.S. congressman) Sonny Bono for comparing himself to Clint Eastwood who was then mayor of Carmel. "Comparing Sonny to Clint," Bogert said, "is like comparing chicken shit to chicken salad."

I decided to use this standard of measurement, too, and began putting things into "chicken shit" and "chicken salad" categories. Compared with the Vicinity, Palm Springs was definitely the salad, where William Holden had seduced Grace Kelly during a moonlit ride, and Kirk Douglas watered his own front lawn and waved to tourists. The Vicinity was where a disgraced Nixon and an exiled Shah had golfed with Walter Annenberg.

Palm Springs had been created by riding, tennis, Hollywood stars, and newspaper publicity, and built for pedestrians. The Vicinity was the child of golf tournaments, television, corporate sponsors, and retired Republicans, and built for cars.

In Palm Springs, the stars staying at Darryl Zanuck's estate had played croquet and musical beds. A member of the Tamarisk Country Club in Rancho Mirage was quoted in *Palm Springs Life* as saying its residents were "either too cautious, too old, too lazy, or too satisfied."

The dramatic San Jacinto Mountains rose sharply behind Palm Springs, shielding it from the late-afternoon sun and the worst of the sandstorms. The Vicinity towns baked in a shadeless desert.

Palm Springs' main street, Palm Canyon Drive, was a desert Champs Elysées shaded by spotlit palms and lined with cafés occupying the ground floors of Mission Revival and streamlined commercial blocks. In the Vicinity, Palm Canyon Drive was a traffic-choked, billboard-blighted, shopping-center wasteland.

Palm Springs' older neighborhoods reminded me of oases in the Sahara where people lived in low-slung houses behind walled gardens, but understood the value of a community. Vicinity people lived in walled towns, and according to a Palm Desert developer quoted in *Time* wanted to "disappear behind their gates and . . . be comfortable with people like themselves."

In Palm Springs, I stayed at a bungalow motel within walking distance of Palm Canyon Drive that reminded me of a hotel I liked in Marrakech where an old Belgian couple endlessly fussed with their gardens and insisted guests turn off lights and radios at ten so everyone could enjoy the desert skies in peace. I had a kitchenette, a choice of two small pools, and a patio where I watched the mountains turn rose and lavender at sunset. Most guests came every year and gathered around outdoor tables for evening cocktails, sometimes joined by the middle-aged gay owners. When I checked out and discovered they did not accept credit cards, one said, "Oh for heaven's sake, just send us a check when you get home, that's what many of our guests do."

I thought Palm Springs' recent reputation for being an unsavory place of deteriorating neighborhoods and drunken college kids was un-deserved, perhaps spread by Vicinity boosters standing to profit from their rival's decay, and by people so unaccustomed to pedestrians and young people they found them threatening in any number. True, I missed spring break, but during my week in Palm Springs I saw only lively but well-behaved crowds of middle-class families of all races.

I dislike escorted bus tours but took one in Palm Springs because the agent promised his coach's high seats allowed passengers to peek over stars' hedges and walls. My companions were three couples from India. Our guide had speed-freak mannerisms and spoke with a hill-billy twang. He accented the wrong syllables of his words and greeted us with, "Ever had one of those morn*ings* when you shouldn't have got-ten up? I sometimes get a little sen*ile* and crazy, so *don't interrupt me*." Then he banged the door shut and screamed, "Let's rock and *roll*!"

We saw where Patty Hearst's aunt, Elizabeth Taylor's mother, Tammy Faye Bakker, Bing Crosby, Spencer Tracy, the man who had trained Lassie, and the surgeon who did Phyllis Diller's face lived, or in most cases had lived. We saw Barry Manilow's yucca tree and the pink bungalow where Elvis and Priscilla had spent six months. We were in-vited to admire the houses where George Hamilton had written his name in cement, Kenny Rogers had been spotted drinking a beer on a balcony, and Liberace had installed a king's throne over a toilet. The tour was supposed to last ninety minutes, but so many celebrities had died or moved the guide filled the last thirty showing us a Motel 6 and a McDonald's. When we passed a cactus he shouted, "Hey, tequila! That's the ticket!"

The ladies behind the desk at the Palm Springs Historical Society in the McCallum Adobe Museum said spotting celebrities had once been easy. Sally McManus had sold Doris Day a pair of shoes, and led Charles Boyer, Gregory Peck, and Alan Ladd to their seats while work-ing as an usherette in the Plaza Theater. She had watched Elizabeth Taylor, Mike Todd, Kirk Douglas, Al Jolson, and others shopping on Palm Canyon Drive. "But I never see our younger celebrities like Barry Manilow, Suzanne Somers, or John Travolta," she admitted. "Perhaps they're afraid."

"I was never afraid of *anything*," her companion Elizabeth Kieley said firmly. The Palm Springs she was born into in 1922 had been pop-ulated by a hundred whites and a hundred Indians. She denounced golf for encouraging people already living in gated communities to spend the day in small groups on the course, air-conditioning for making possible the large summer population that overwhelmed the old-timers, Bob Hope's hilltop mansion for encouraging people to live all by themselves rather than being part of the community, and a loss of open spaces for changing the young people. "We wore jeans and shorts, rode horses, went barefoot, and never complained about having nothing to do," she said. "But these kids are like any other suburban kids."

I always thought the whole point of Palm Springs was that it was *not* like any other city. Yet boosters like Kiely were on the defensive, saying things like "We're having our problems like any other city." And even Mel Haber, who owned the Ingleside Inn and told me, "in all humility," that he was known as "Mr. Palm Springs" and that his restaurant was "a reincarnation of the Stork Club with a little of Rick's Café in *Casablanca* thrown in," sometimes hedged his praise for the town he loved with "relative to," and "compared to every other place I know."

He had a rough New York charm that becomes more charming the farther you take it from New York. Despite the deep tan, resort wear, laid-back attitude, and twenty years in Palm Springs, he was still a New York fish out of water, talking with his hands, stage-whispering confidences, and taking calls over a telephone plugged into the corner banquette at Mervyn's, the Ingleside Inn restaurant chosen by *Lifestyles of the Rich and Famous* as one of "The World's Ten Best." Before California, he had invented the rear-window plastic hula dancer and become the nation's largest manufacturer of automobile novelties. He divorced, fell in love with Palm Springs during a weekend trip and bought the once glamorous Ingleside Inn. He spent $600,000 remodeling and within months of reopening in 1975 had catered Debbie Reynolds's fiftieth birthday party and Frank Sinatra's prewedding dinner. He appeared on *Phil Donahue* and *60 Minutes*, where he became famous (at least in Palm Springs) for saying that Palm Springs got the "crème de la crème," while he got the "crème de la crème of the crème de la crème."

He was a likable combination of ego and modesty. The Ingleside Inn press-kit biography began, "Haber's charismatic personality and Ingleside's old-world charm have been a successful pairing since 1975," but he had no illusions about why he had succeeded. "You didn't need to be a PR genius to figure out that if a star stays in your hotel or eats in your restaurant, you send a photograph to the press, and I know if I sold I'd become 'Melvin who?' rather quickly," he said. He thought the inn was popular because it replicated the generous space, wood paneling, and smooth service of a private club, but without the exclusivity. He was proud that unlike the Vicinity country clubs, he welcomed everyone.

It had not always been that way. The Ingleside's founder was Ruth Hardy, a legendary figure who had been Palm Springs' first councilwoman and had a park named in her honor. She kept a secret card-index file on her guests, even on guests who asked for a room but were turned away because, as her cards noted, they were "N-II" (Not Ingleside Inn), or "NG-J" (No Good—Jewish). This had been the fate of Sam Goldwyn, producer Mervyn LeRoy, and a couple from New York who had the misfortune to be "Refugee types! Possibly even J and definitely NG." People like the Grosse Pointe bank president and his wife who were "*real nice* and great friends of the Eisenhowers," got "Tops" or "Any Time." This was how you had a "gated community" in the 1950s.

Although Haber had discovered this file and would certainly have been "NG-J," he was too much of a gentleman to attack the woman who had founded the Ingleside and put lights on the trees on Palm Canyon Drive. "I don't want fat, ugly people in my restaurant, so I guess everyone's got their prejudices," he said.

He was an unabashed booster. "You can't find a more bullish person on Palm Springs than Mel Haber. Lòok how beautiful it is! Paradise! Heaven! People should *pay* to work here! It mystifies me millions aren't living here."

But he also said he had fallen in love with it "because in the mid-1970s it was unsophisticated, small-townish, and quaint." That had changed, he admitted, but Palm Springs was still wonderful, "compared to everywhere else."

When he described how the $25-million mega-casino planned by the Agua Caliente band of Cahuilla Indians on whose checkerboard reservation much of the city stood would be less than a mile away, he lowered his voice and chopped the air with his hands, the ultimate New York indication of sincerity, and confided, "I was a gambler in my younger days, so I know how gambling brings in bad elements, and I know how you tend to walk the streets afterward, debating if you should jump under a car or stick up a bank. Palm Springs is not as spread out as Vegas, so if a guy is drunk and has lost his money and is wandering the streets, he's only six blocks from my house."

Leaving Palm Springs without meeting a celebrity seemed like visiting the Grand Canyon without looking down. But unless I rented a dinner jacket, bought a jacket and tie, or spent several hundred dollars, I had no hope of mingling with celebrities attending the Republican Women's Fashion Show, the private reception for Their Majesties King Michael and Queen Anne of Romania at a private home at the Morningside Country Club, the presentation of a lifetime achievement award to Ted Grouya at the Rancho Mirage Ritz-Carlton, a speech by Margaret Thatcher on the New World Order at the Stouffer Esmeralda in Indian Wells, or the annual Desert Charities Show, an "all-star lineup of celebrities" honoring Steve Allen and Jayne Meadows at Palm Springs High School, where several months later police would be breaking up brawls between a black gang known as "Gateway," since its members lived in the Gateway Estates, and a Hispanic gang named "Dream Homes," after its tract development. A sociologist with the local Human Rights Commission characterized the rumbles as "fighting for who is going to be king of the bottom." The kids called them "Gateway versus Dream Homes."

The easiest way to meet a celebrity for free in Palm Springs was to interview Sonny Bono, so I called his restaurant several times pretending to be writing a travel article. He was always just leaving, or coming back any minute. To his credit, he left messages setting times for us to get together; to his discredit, he ignored every one. After spending six fruitless hours on three successive nights waiting at his bar while being assured he knew I was there and loved giving interviews, I arranged to see the man who had compared him to chicken shit.

My favorite photograph of Frank Bogert is a 1935 one showing him in swim trunks with his arm around Hollywood sex symbol Clara Bow. Bogert has a mop of curly black hair, perfect teeth, and a face more handsome than hers. He is staring straight at the camera, wearing the satisfied smile of a man who has made a big conquest. She is looking up at him with wide, worshipful eyes.

It is difficult imagining someone having less in common with Sonny Bono than Frank Bogert, and there are so many things to like and envy about him besides Clara Bow it is hard knowing where to begin. He is the son of a successful Montana rancher who had ridden with Buffalo Bill's Wild West Show. He played football for UCLA, and before he was thirty had been a Hollywood stuntman and professional rodeo announcer, managed a circus, traveled the country performing cowboy rope tricks, and became so clever at public relations he was known as "Mr. Palm Springs." He is a good amateur botanist, polished professional photographer, bilingual in Spanish, a decorated horseman, and one of the few North Americans to belong to the Charros, an elite riding society in Mexico where he is known as "El Grandotte"—the Tall One. He has known three generations of starlets, almost every U.S. president since the war, and has probably been photographed with more twentieth-century celebrities than anyone in the world. He enjoyed a long, happy marriage that produced three daughters, and after his wife died married a pretty Mexican attorney thirty-nine years his junior. At the age of eighty-five he still rides into the desert with her every morning.

He lived in the kind of ranch house usually found at the end of a dusty three-mile driveway. He wore beat-up cowboy clothes and was a good-looking version of what Lyndon Johnson might have become had he survived another decade. He made short work of my attempts to ingratiate myself by remarking on his testimonial plaques. "Got one every time I turned around as mayor, came from those dinner swindles they throw to make your friends come and give you money." But he was keen I should appreciate his tack room and collection of saddles, rawhide ropes, and antique spurs. His prize was his father's 1882 saddle and the woolly chaps he had worn with Buffalo Bill. I ran my hands along their soft leather and had another reason to envy him. Thirty years after my own father's death I had nothing of his except a photograph and a cigarette lighter from a bank in Toledo.

He was not shy about claiming credit for Palm Springs' reputation as a glamorous desert hideaway. When the El Mirador Hotel hired him as a publicity agent in the 1930s, he hit upon the idea of checking out the guests in *Standard and Poor's*. When he discovered, for example, that the president of Cream of Wheat was visiting from Minnesota, he took his photograph with a Hollywood celebrity and mailed it to the Minneapolis newspapers. Next winter, the Minneapolis smart set booked rooms at El Mirador. The photographs he had arranged of a horse diving into the hotel pool, Jackie Cooper kissing his wife underwater, and Shirley Temple playing Ping-Pong with Governor Lehman had helped, but it was not Hollywood that made Palm Springs, but his tycoons. The golf-playing chief executives of today were simply a continuation of that tradition.

You would expect someone who had made his career promoting Palm Springs to be optimistic about its future and Bogert was, insisting that anyone who had ever lived in the desert never wanted to leave. The city was sure to grow and grow, with more golf courses and houses filling its canyons. Why not, when there was enough land and underground water to support another century of development.

But he also wanted Palm Springs to keep its "small-town atmosphere." He was sorry the number of riding stables had shrunk from nine to two, dismissed golf as a game for old people, and complained the stars no longer lived in small houses, listed their phone numbers, and mixed with visitors.

While walking me to my car, he stumbled on the PROTECTED BY CHECKMATE sign of his security service. "Our new way of life around here," he said, pretending to kick it. I suppose it reminded him he could no longer handle the bad guys himself, and that if Checkmate ever failed him, and his thieves had any taste, he would lose his saddles and spurs.

42

"A Real Happening Place"

A side from the DURING EARTHQUAKES LEAVE STACK AREAS AND TAKE COVER signs in the public library, the most dramatic evidence of the San Andreas Fault in the Coachella Valley was the line of oases marking its route along the base of the Indio hills. In Thousand Palms and Biskra, palms grew in a straight line where the fault's shifting plates had diverted underground water veins, creating springs and raising the water table. It was the kind of desert miracle Victorian Englishmen traveled weeks to see, but at Thousand Palms there were only two cars in the parking lot and the guest register showed few weekend visitors.

South of these oases the fault skirted a bingo palace built by the Cahuilla Indians to absorb the cash and explosive boredom of the Coachella Valley retirees. I arrived too early for the first game and spent an hour with a morose Levantine bartender whose elaborate gestures made his usual Southern California complaints more affecting. When he said, "I just want to go back to the 1970s—who would have guessed those were the best times?" he patted his heart. When he said, "Next year in Seattle, God willing," he pressed his palms together in prayer.

When an earthquake finally strikes the Coachella Valley, Gerry Ford and Walter Annenberg will find themselves displaced as its most important residents by Tom Freeman, the thirty-two-year-old, $36,000-a-year head of the Riverside County Emergency Services Office in Indio. He seemed the right man for this tricky job since, according to an interview in the *Desert Sun*, he disliked "negative, pessimistic people." The memorabilia covering the walls of his basement office in the county building indicated a man experienced in handling the rich and powerful, and I found it difficult concentrating on his words because my eyes kept drifting to baseball bats signed by the likes of Reggie Jackson and Don Baylor, autographed photographs of Bob Hope and Gene Autry, and testimonial letters from Tom Brokaw and congressional heavyweights, the loot from years of working in the California Angels front office and as the U.S. Air Force liaison officer in charge of training congressmen and journalists to experience weightless flight.

Freeman believed the valley would see a Big One during his lifetime, at least a 7.5. Already it had suffered 42,000 aftershocks in the year after Landers. Before, the average for all of California had been ten thousand a year. "If fires quadrupled in your city in one year, wouldn't you be alarmed?" he asked.

For someone claiming to like "positive people," who had chosen "attitude determines your altitude" as his motto, his Big One scenario for the Coachella Valley was pretty bleak. He foresaw the possibility of cracking and buckling at the Hyatt, and structural failure at the Palm Desert Town Center trapping as many as ten thousand shoppers. He worried about an earthquake during a tourist-season weekend when thirty thousand spectators had jammed a golf course to watch, say, the "Nabisco Dinah Shore." If freeway bridges collapsed, he would find himself housing and feeding tens of thousands of stranded visitors. He also expected heart attacks and strokes. You could build a house to code, but not a seventy-five-year-old heart.

He had prepared as much as one man on a tight budget could, persuading the gated communities to store food and appoint block wardens, scattering caches of emergency medical supplies, and turning his basement into a command center. His computers linked him to every hospital in the state and his dispatching center allowed him to talk simultaneously to the highway patrol and sheriff. He had even outfitted an underground dormitory with pajamas and work shirts for disaster workers. All this was impressive until you left his office for the parking lot and noticed the Riverside County building was the kind of flimsy 1960s glass-and-concrete-block structure that has proven to be a death trap in even moderate earthquakes.

My *Fault Map of California* showed the solid pink line of the San Andreas ending on the northeast shore of the Salton Sea at the exotically named Bombay Beach. After that it became a black dotted line broken by question marks. According to Iacopi's *Earthquake Country*, this was where it turned into a confusing fifty-mile-wide zone of faulting that, although known to be active, was "difficult to define and almost impossible to trace."

I drove along the north shore of the Salton Sea to Bombay Beach past the most unappetizing large body of water I have ever seen. The shoreline was a wasteland of rotting piers and abandoned marinas. The breeze from the south smelled like rotten eggs and low tide. Twigs, guano, and algae floated like croutons on the soupy water.

A confluence of typical California impulses and mistakes had created this cesspool. In 1905 engineer Charles Rockwood and land developer Anthony Heber (who has a town named in his honor) cut a small channel from the Colorado River into a canal they had dug just south of the Mexican border. Its purpose was to divert, or more accurately steal, water from Mexico and deliver it to the Imperial Valley, where Heber was developing tracts of farmland. Their waterworks were so shoddy that when the Colorado's 1905 spring flood smashed though a headgate on their canal, water poured into the Imperial Valley, jumping the banks of their rudimentary channels to flow north into the Salton sink, a dry salt bed 230 feet below sea level that had not held water for four centuries. By the time the Southern Pacific railway built dikes to stanch the flow, the sink had become the Salton Sea, thirty-five miles long and fifteen miles wide, and the largest inland body of water in the state.

Critics have called it a "toxic toilet bowl," but at least a toilet can be flushed. With no outlet save evaporation, the Salton Sea has become progressively saltier, deader, and dirtier. Its fish are taboo for children and pregnant women, and its birds produce cracked eggs and deformed embryos. Its bottom is so polluted that were it not underwater it would qualify for a toxic waste dump.

Its sources are the New and Alamo river systems, themselves creations of the same fiasco. The New River is often cited as the most polluted in the nation. Every day it delivers to the unflushable Salton Sea the pesticide-loaded runoff of the Imperial Valley and the wastewater of a million Mexicans. When a tractor trailer of sewage sludge plunged into it, authorities prohibited the driver from reclaiming his cargo, arguing the river had "contaminated" it. Feces, toilet paper, dead dogs, and corpses float north on its lazy current, and winds sweep "foam blobs" of bacteria-loaded detergent from its surface, splattering cars and shoppers at the Calexico Plaza shopping center. It is an awesome revenge: a river created by gringos trying to steal Mexican water splattering the United States with foamy blobs of Mexican shit.

The impoverished retirees and ex-convicts of The Salton Sea's Bombay Beach lived in chicken-coop shacks and, in a sad parody of life in the Vicinity, putt-putted down its sandy streets in cast-off golf carts. An old woman with hosiery around her knees sat outside the store reading a tabloid beside a boy with a pink Mohawk and prison tattoos. When I asked people if they liked it here they said, "It's cheap," or, "It's all we can afford."

At the Salt Creek campground a middle-aged couple lay sprawled in twin plastic recliners. He had opened two cans of beer at once, she was watching a game show on a television plugged into their mobile home. They had camped near a reeking Porta-John. "Too cold for fishing, but we're enjoying the good life," he said in a flat voice. They had sold everything in Los Angeles and planned staying here until park rangers evicted them. Then they would travel slowly east until they hit the Atlantic.

I asked how they liked the Salton Sea.

"Paradise." His voice was still flat.

"Why are you heading east?"

"It's my dream."

"What about the California Dream?"

"It's my dream to leave California."

I drove a few miles back up the shore, searching for a more cheerful ending to the San Andreas.

At the Salton Sea State Recreation Area, ranger Michelle Tritt said her grandparents had managed the North Shore Yacht Club and she had been raised on stories of water-skiers, dance bands, and Palm Springs celebrities. She could not understand why tourists no longer thronged the Salton Sea, or why campers were down one third from seven years ago. Sure, the smell was unpleasant, but only if the wind blew it onshore; sure, algae blooms and die-offs had discouraged fishermen and you should only eat eight ounces of fish in six weeks, but the fishing was great! The New River might be the most polluted in the world, but salt probably killed most of the bacteria before it got this far north, although she did suggest swimmers jump into a shower afterward.

She was the first in a string of Salton Sea boosters who were among the most optimistic Californians I met. There was Pat Jordan, who cheerfully admitted that the North Shore Chamber of Commerce amounted to herself and this desk in the service station minimart. "We just took it for granted the sea would always be the same," she said, re-calling the celebrities arriving on pontoon planes. There were matching government funds available to improve the shoreline, but the area was so impoverished there were no funds to match. She conceded you had to be a "nature freak" to like it, and that when it reached 110 degrees in the summer the only people staying were those who could not afford to leave. "We *do* have one problem—the New River," she admitted. But the cacti had the most marvelous spring flowers and the night skies were unbelievable. Compared with the rest of Southern California it was "a little paradise."

I could see the North Shore Beach Yacht Club and Motel had once been a big deal. The club was ocean-liner-shaped and embellished with porthole windows and a bogus smokestack. The motel had a double carport and kidney-shaped swimming pool, although weeds had sprouted from cracks in the shuffleboard court and a pair of geese occu-pied the garden, drinking from a wading pool and crapping on the ten-nis court. Half its forty-eight rooms remained open to customers, and manager Jeffrey Platt told me he would soon be renovating the whole place, reopening the yacht club, and turning it into a "real happening place."

He was an unlikely-looking man to pull this off. He had sleepy eyes, a phlegmatic manner, and the balding, potato-shaped head of an Oriental despot. But he wanted "to put the north shore on the map" for reasons equally noble and sentimental.

He had vacationed here as a boy in the sixties with his parents and friends. They fished, raced boats, had picnics, and sang around bon-fires. "The yacht club was jammin' and jivin'," he remembered. "*Seri-ous people* came. Ralph Edwards, Jimmy the Greek's buddies. It was their ritzy hideaway, better than Palm Springs. But the rest of the Salton Sea was a working-class resort where you could have fun with-out spending a fortune."

He claimed people still loved the sea because it was so uncrowded. The water *looked* bad, but *he* still swam. So what if its temperature hit the nineties in the summer and you came out white with salt? Take a cold shower. People wanted to escape Los Angeles, didn't they? Well, he was ready for them. There would be dance bands and starlets, wa-ter-skiers, and sportfishermen again, another Lake Tahoe. "I *know* it will be packed!" he insisted. "All that needs to happen is that every-body's got to fall in line and start looking at the big picture, instead of concentrating on all this bullshit about pollution."

Here, where the California Dream seemed deadest and the danger of a great earthquake the greatest, he was planning a low-cost resort he described as "a kind of Mexico-in-California for the working man." He would keep his prices low and cultivate a blue-collar clientele. If I returned in the year 2000 I would see para-sailers gliding like butterflies, a paddle steamer making dinner cruises, and campgrounds twinkling with the fires of happy families.

Was he brave and deluded, or was his dream a sign of something more hopeful? It was certainly the kind of optimistic dream Californians have realized since the Gold Rush, one no more fabulous or impossible than that a fetid, swampy, sandy 1845 backwater of 300 could in fifteen years become wealthy and cosmopolitan San Francisco, a metropolis of 56,000 filled with luxurious hotels and stately mansions. If that could happen, then why not a few water-skiers here?

While we talked, his wife and his partner's wife, Tracy, who was also bullish on the resort, drifted into his office. She praised the Salton Sea as the only affordable place in Southern California for a middle-class family of five. "You get to love it here. I guess you kinda have to," she said.

Platt's wife shrugged and admitted being "not really into it yet."

"But don't you think it's great how laid-back the people are?" he asked.

She pouted. "Yeah, they take a half hour to tell you hi!"

"I wouldn't live anywhere else," Tracy said.

"You like it, you can have it," she replied.

When she left Platt said, "She's young. She misses the noise. . . . Aw, I'm sure she really *does* love it here. She's just bored. There'll be lots to do once the boom starts."

43

Back Along the Fault

The day after I returned to Palm Springs from the Salton Sea I found my earthquake. I was eating breakfast in my room when the air conditioner began rattling. The tremor was barely felt, lasting just time enough for my eyes to shoot to the door. The newspaper spoke of a small quake hitting the San Andreas near Desert Hot Springs.

I drove into Los Angeles to treat myself to a consolation prize, the simulated earthquake that strikes Universal Studios' back lot two hundred times a day. "An 8.3 that's a 10 on the Scale of Fun!" the publicity promised.

After ten-lane freeways, ocean-liner-sized billboards, and skyscraper power lines, Universal's Wal-Mart-sized auditoria and "420 acres of motion-picture magic" seemed built to scale. But for an amusement park, it felt curiously dead.

It was a sealed commercial loop in which every ride sold a Universal souvenir, every souvenir sold a Universal movie, and while you waited in line to see special effects from an earlier Universal film, overhead video screens hawked forthcoming ones. There was no surprise or spontaneity, just customers slapping their fannies onto auditorium seats for another lashing of special effects and kiddie vaudeville. They were as reverential as pilgrims doing the Stations, or exhausted and frantic, and in the lavatory I heard a father screaming at his son, "Ninety-seven bucks it cost and you want to leave already!"

The earthquake was the climax to a ride on the world's longest golf cart through the Universal back lot. First we rolled past sets of classic movies like *The Sting, Psycho, Harvey,* and *The Ten Command-ments,* then the set for *Coach*, and a Volkswagen shaped like a mouse that had drawn laughs in *Uncle Buck*. A mechanical King Kong lunged and the *Jaws* shark rose from a pond. For the grand finale we headed into a bunker tricked up to resemble a San Francisco BART station. Fires exploded and the ceiling pretended to collapse. It was a simulated 8.3, but after hearing Kevin Grey describe the Landers 7.4, I thought it nothing of the kind, and less terrifying than the shake table at that San Francisco museum, or the earthquakes on Mr. Stein-brugge's tape.

Had I been in Los Angeles nine months later, I would have felt the 6.7 that struck an unknown and unmapped fault under Northridge, killing sixty-one, bringing down ten bridges, and causing over $20 bil-lion in damage, but happening too early in the morning for a tramload of Universal Studios visitors to experience, simultaneously, a real and bogus earthquake.

It led to a run on $2,000 Iron Maiden beds with steel canopies, and silver pendants of Gregory the Wonder Worker, a third-century Sicil-ian saint believed to protect against earthquakes. Afterward, 25 percent of Southern Californians said they were considering leaving the state. Engineering studies revealed welded connections between beams and steel columns had suffered cracking in over a hundred Los Angeles buildings believed impervious to the strongest temblor. According to computer simulations, many of these newer steel-frame hospitals, sub-urban business centers, and malls might collapse in the large earth-quake that revised forecasts now said was 86 percent likely to strike Los Angeles by 2024.

After leaving California, I continued dialing the forecasts re-corded by Berkland and Coles. Berkland's 1-900-226-JOLT service of-fered a summary of minor quakes, missing pets, and periods of lunar and tidal risk, but never sounded an alarm urgent enough to send me flying west.

Coles called his service Earthquake Forecasters and ended every message with an earnest "keep in touch." His updates were recorded at odd times like 3:05 A.M., so I assumed he remained chained to his in-struments.

When he reported a dramatic increase in radio signals I called him in person. He said, "I'm getting ready for the worst-case scenario— evacuation!" But his main signal never arrived and two weeks later his answering-machine voice was hollow and exhausted. Then he announced a "tentative alert," a "buildup," a "yellow alert," and solicited volunteers to telephone those on his early-warning list.

Several days later my telephone rang at 1:50 A.M. It was Coles, excited and jabbering about circuit breakers and a large surge. He said a moderate quake had just rumbled through Mexico and was heading north. It was definite: a 5.1 to 6.3 somewhere in Southern California within the next four days. He was out of breath. "Gotta go. Gotta run. Lots of people to call. It's happening . . . it's coming!"

The next day our conversation seemed like a dream. There was nothing in my newspaper about a Mexican quake, but Jerry Hurley, who must have sensed it, sent me an article from the *Eureka Times-Standard* headlined QUAKES SHAKE RESIDENTS OF MEXICO CITY, and describing two moderate earthquakes the same evening Coles called. I checked a microfilm edition of that month's *Los Angeles Times* and discovered that sixty-two hours after Coles's warning a 6.0 had rumbled through the Mojave. "Had the earthquake been in a populated area," the *Times* said, "scientists said considerable damage could have been expected."

I am ashamed to admit that the warning finally bringing me back to California was an official one. Early on the morning of November 14, 1993, a 4.8 quake hit Parkfield. The California Office of Emergency Services, on the advice of the USGS, afterward issued an "A" alert for seven surrounding counties, warning there was a 37-percent chance of a 6.0 or greater striking Parkfield within seventy-two hours. It was only the second time in eight years the state had issued such a definite and high-level alert. I cashed my frequent-flyer miles, flew to San Luis Obispo, rented a car, and woke in a motel the next morning to see Parkfield Café owner John Varian wearing a sly smile and telling ABC, "It's exciting, not scary, and the exciting part is seeing the satellite trucks and doing interviews like this."

Every hour without an earthquake decreased the odds, and by the time I reached Parkfield they had shrunk to one in seven and the high-priced television talent was packing. Duane Hamann was in despair. His instruments had recorded no unusual movement along the fault preceding the 4.8. He was torn: on the one hand, an earthquake would save Parkfield from being defunded; but if one occurred, it would prove his instruments useless since they had shown no prior change in the movement of the plates.

It fell to Bill Ellsworth of the USGS to stand on a windy hill overlooking the San Andreas and tell a procession of journalists they had wasted their time. The *real* purpose of the experiment, he argued, had been to understand the physics of an earthquake. Whether this understanding led to useful predictions should have nothing to do with judging its success. The alert had not *guaranteed* an earthquake, only a 37-percent chance. People should compare it to a weather forecast promising a 40-percent chance of rain.

But the reporters only wanted to know why the prediction had failed, and as they trudged down the fault for some obligatory photographs, he said softly, "They've got more hardware here to record a quake than I've got to predict it."

When I called home my wife was laughing. That morning a 4.4 with an epicenter fifty miles north of us in Quebec had rolled through the Adirondacks, lasting fifteen seconds, causing little damage, but waking people in my town, who were now busy exchanging stories about vibrating beds.

At the time I began searching for an earthquake in 1992, a seismic drought stretching back to 1906 had been ending. Two years later the drought had become a deluge. California had experienced more destructive earthquakes than anytime in its written history and no Californian in his right mind remained blasé about the risks, not even earthquake fans like Thomas Dunklin, and certainly not people like Grey and Stockman, who had seen the earth crack open at Landers and confronted the most terrifying (although improbable) earthquake fear of all, being swallowed alive. It had been one thing to search for quakes when they elicited shrugs even from those living on the San Andreas, it was another to continue after two years of bad seismic news had culminated in Northridge. What had started as a harmless challenge suddenly seemed in bad taste, and so I gave up.

After this last Parkfield trip I drove back up the fault to San Francisco, stopping at the San Benito County Historical Park to look for Fred, Dick, and Jack. They were not there, but I noticed they had added a foundation and windows to the dance hall and built a picket fence around the schoolhouse. A leathery woman stacking firewood behind a neighboring bungalow said, "You just never know when you'll see those three. Yesterday they dropped off some floorboards, but it might be weeks before they're back." She thought they had run out of gas. It had to be discouraging. They begged for volunteers, but few people responded. They tried a cookout but the young people washed a few windows and melted away. "All they need is some help, just a *little* help. I wouldn't mind, but I'm in my sixties and I get tired," she said. "The truth is they're the only ones who give a damn about those buildings."

I arrived in Hollister in time to attend a much-publicized hearing on Mission Green, a gated 950-home golf-club development proposed for the rich farmland I had admired the year before from the mission church of San Juan Bautista. The county planning commission had already rejected the plan, but the county supervisors had the last word, so the developer had marshaled lawyers and supporters to argue for more time to submit a scaled-down proposal.

They claimed Mission Green's wealthy retirees would be a "crime-free" population, desirable as neighbors because they could be milked for taxes. The project was a blessing because it would replace lower-income (Hispanic) migrant workers with a population of wealthy (white) consumers. Population growth, new roads, and the Bay Area sprawl made developing this farmland "inevitable."

One real-estate agent even made it sound like an act of compassion, saying, "My buyers see this beautiful land and ask, 'How about building up there? What's up there for *me*?' "

The rest of the hearing was good news for anyone preferring to be optimistic about California. The Mission Green opponents were a lively cross section of ranchers, farmers, academics, politicians, Native Americans, Hispanics, and busybodies. They ranged from the head of the San Benito County Farm Bureau, who announced his organization was taking a political position for the first time in its history, to San Juan's Becky McGovern, who delivered a rather good speech beginning, "This project would begin the destruction of what is considered one of the world's richest agricultural valleys. . . ." They argued the world's exploding population placed a moral responsibility on San Benito County to keep productive land in cultivation, and urged the supervisors to consider a future when prime farmland would be a more important resource than a golf course. They pointed out that only one valley in Chile had the same fortuitous combination of moderate climate, productive soil, and water. The visual beauty of the valley was also "no small good." San Juan did not need a "fortified city" for people who would be unlikely to join in community activities, but would vote down all but the meanest school budgets. Too much of California had already been lost to developments like this one, one woman declared, "and if they can build here, California is lost."

Since Mission Green was the kind of tax bonanza of a project usually winning easy approval, particularly in hard-up counties like San Benito, I was surprised when the supervisors unanimously voted it down. Perhaps the much-publicized California decline had given new credibility to the arguments of its opponents. If so, and if this is a trend, which I think it is, then Californians may soon consider this apparently gloomy decade as a correction to years of pathological optimism, the bottom that needed to be touched before the Dream could be rescued by the kind of unconventional California dreamer I had been meeting everywhere along the fault.

Before arriving in California, I imagined the San Andreas as a line of scarps, furrows, landslides, and offset streams. But now, when I ran my finger down its curving pink line on my map, I saw Jane Cryan crusading for her shacks, Bob Valenzuela amusing Hollister, Rondal Snodgrass rescuing redwoods, Duane Hamann letting his kids soar, Nancy Vogler preserving Lawson's Landing for the middle class, Reverend Nevins preaching to fishermen, Sonne Reyna reminding visitors Indians had once lived in San Juan, Bob Coles running up his phone bill to warn people of impending quakes, Roger Stockman sitting down to an Iowa Christmas dinner with his extended family of former misfits, Harry Lee Curtis providing a forum for beleaguered Santa Cruz conservatives, Bill Platt agitating for community facilities at Sea Ranch, the Robbs sweeping trash off their beloved desert, Fred, Dick, and Jack hammering San Benito's history back together, Albert James crusading for the Wiyot to be recognized as a tribe, Art Rogers photographing Wallace Stegner's "deeply lived-in" community, Viola McBride saving Ferndale's main street, Georgia Marino leading students through her scrapbooks, Lanty Molloy providing a comforting venue for wakes, Nancy Sullivan installing an impecunious genius in her downstairs room, and Robbie Robinson urging parents to "look to the left and look to the right, and form a real community."

I saw the Wizard and his counterculture campers capturing flags on wildflower-carpeted Oz meadows, Obie Bowman designing walk-in cabins for Sea Ranch, Father Riker turning ragged hobos into a well-fed community of disciples, Llano colonists gathered for Sunday-evening recitals in their community hall, A. S. Murphy holding ancient redwoods in trust for future generations, Martin Murphy serving boxcars of champagne to all comers, and Goldsborough Bruff keeping his community of tenderfoot civil servants united and safe during their journey.

I had not gone looking for these eccentric community builders, and not until afterward did I realize I had found so many. They were simply thick on the ground in California, as hard to miss as scars left by the San Andreas.

Although I met them along the fault, they had more than this location in common. Most were optimists, but none exhibited the lethal optimism of San Francisco's post-1906 earthquake politicians and businessmen. Most were the kind of eccentric freethinkers who give California its distinctive whimsy and fizz.

They nurtured a Dream larger than the "major appliance" or "new/bigger house" of Young and Rubicam's *California Dream Report*, a Dream that was the antithesis of the gated, solitary, privacy-obsessed one that had produced Stonegate, Shelter Cove, the Vicinity, and the indifferent neighbors of Cupertino. In their California Dream, no one was erecting fences or filing lawsuits to prevent others from making "stationary use of the sand" on Stinson Beach, building a new prison while closing a library, or refusing to look after Sally's sweet children while an ambulance rushed her to the hospital.

Their Dream incorporated California's tolerance, love of nature, and optimism, and offered the best hope for producing the satisfying communities and protected landscapes that will have to replace an antiquated Dream based on unlimited resources and material rewards that is becoming increasingly difficult to deliver as California sprawls and grows. Perhaps the people I met along the fault bewitched me, but after my journey I believe their California Dream, rather than the "tortured place" of the CALIFORNIA ONE scenario, will be California's future.

One of the reasons for my optimism is, oddly enough, the inevitability of a great California earthquake. The phenomenon of "earthquake love" may be a fleeting one, but after hearing how Loma Prieta spooked the most independent loners and elicited such comments as, "I need people and to be a part of my community—not a separate entity living in it," and learning how Joe Scaramella's mother, the lonely Hispanic workers of Big Bear who flocked to COPE, and other people without a community to fall back on suffered the greatest psychological aftershocks, I am convinced the Big One will persuade Californians to create the kind of deep-rooted communities that can withstand the destruction of the material possessions that have become their Dream's precarious foundation.

Postscript
At Bruff's Camp

I returned to the West Coast to meet Wendy Lucas, the woman I had located through the Oregon–California Trails Association who was the great-granddaughter of Washington City Miner John T. Coumbs and possessed the diary of Washington Miner John Bates. She lived in Lakeview, a county seat of 5,000 people that is the highest town in Oregon, and largest in that vast region where the emptiest corners of Nevada, Oregon, and California meet.

When I arrived on an early December afternoon there was a foot of snow on the ground and it was only 10 degrees, but the sidewalks were busy around Lakeview's department store, one-screen cinema, and Safeway with a sign saying HERE SINCE 1932. Because of the altitude or my excitement at meeting a Washington Miner descendant, I spent a restless night, waking early to a heavy snowstorm. I scraped my windshield with a credit card and drove down a narrowing dirt road past increasingly isolated homesteads. Squalls swept the high plateau like tornadoes and I was blinded by snow, then by a winter sun hanging low over the Fandango pass.

The Lucas ranch was three miles north of the California border and less than twenty miles from the Lassen Trail. Dan Lucas greeted me in his yard and said he had enough cattle, sheep, and horses to make a fuss about, "but if we never sold any cattle, McDonald's sure wouldn't go out of business."

His low-ceilinged parlor was cozy and cluttered. A dog slumbered, a woodstove blazed, and a blizzard of old notes covered the refrigerator.

Wendy Lucas had a crinkly smile and a helmet of short white hair. She apologized for the disarray, but explained she was suffering vertigo after a kick from a horse that had interfered with her genealogical research. Learning about her family had become her "avocation," she said, and she enumerated her computers, databases, and programs giving her access to millions of names in the brisk, commonsense manner of any good research librarian.

I had imagined exchanging pleasantries before easing into her great-grandfather Coumbs, but she turned to him immediately. His story was that of a plucky orphan making good. He had run away from the private school in Maryland where his guardian had enrolled him, supported himself as a carpenter, married at twenty-two, and fathered a son before joining the Gold Rush. He stayed in California only a few months longer than Bruff, running a Sacramento store and returning to Washington in 1851 via the Panama Canal. But unlike Bruff, he carried home a gold nugget that became the foundation for his comfortable upper-middle-class life. He bought a cemetery plot to bury the son who had died in his absence, attended medical school, acquired property in Virginia, and had eight children. When he died at seventy his remains were interred under an impressive black granite memorial Wendy Lucas had photographed on a trip to Washington. She also had a daguerreotype of his wife and infant son, a picture of his six sons, and his laissez-passer for the Panama Canal, describing fair hair, hazel eyes, a Grecian nose, and "rather small chin."

The only mention Bruff made of Coumbs in his diaries was that he "slept on post" during the night of July 13, 1849, and that he encountered him later in Sacramento.

Lucas had her opinions about why Coumbs was among the men abandoning Bruff. "Bruff had a quick temper," she said sternly, as if I were somehow responsible. "He had military training and brought them across because he was a strong, determined man who—"

"You call that a leader, dear," interrupted Dan Lucas, who had come inside and was hanging his wet hat on a pair of antlers.

They discussed Bruff and Lassen for several minutes. She admired Bruff for his "tremendous willpower." He admired him for not eating that Indian. He had little use for Lassen, "a combination of avarice and foolishness, and not a good trailblazer," and while describing how he was killed by Indians while searching for gold, shook his head as if to say "good riddance." Finally they looked at me and laughed. "That's right," she said, "for us it's like it happened yesterday."

I had come hoping to find generations of Coumbs living near the Lassen Trail, but she was the only one, and had landed here by chance. Dan had worked for the Soil Conservation Service, transferring every two years between towns in Nevada and California and at one point living in nearby Alturas, California. They liked the area so much they bought this ranch when he retired. For a while he taught junior-high-school history to the children of Lassen Trail pioneers in Cedarville, California. He was shocked how little they knew about the wagon trains. While his wife was fetching Bates's diary from the safe he said, "The greatest mass movement in our nation's history, but people living on the trail, whose ancestors traveled it, don't know about it. We've lost our roots, and it's probably the source of lots of our problems."

She pulled the diary from a worn plastic bag. Her aunt had sent it to her fifteen years before, thinking it had belonged to Coumbs. She assumed Coumbs brought it back to Washington after Bates died in California, then kept it after being unable to locate any members of his family. It was a two-by-four-inch leather-bound notebook fitting easily into a palm or breast pocket. The writing was cramped and in pencil that had been smudged and erased. The pages were spotted by food, rain, and God knows what else.

I turned its brittle pages carefully but still the binding loosened and broke, showering scraps of paper into my lap. I stopped after a few pages when Dan muttered it should really be in an airtight case. He was right: to read John Bates's diary was to destroy it.

Wendy Lucas had a typed transcript so I began reading that instead. But once I did, the intimate communication from Bates's hand to my eye was broken, and his words had less impact. The early pages were literate and precise, but dispassionate, their descriptions of weather, food, animals, and other emigrants delivered in telegraphic style. A typical entry went, "Rose at 2 am pleasant morning moved on briskly over rolling prairie similar to that of the day before."

But I was glad to see Coumbs confirmed Bruff's account of the happy July Fourth celebration, describing polishing the silver and eating "all the best our camp can afford." On August 14 he noted, "Election took place at 4 pm G Bruff—President."

Before California, his descriptions seldom rose above "The scenery every day became more interesting and I began to enjoy it much." But once he crossed the Fandango Pass, his diary, like Bruff's and Austin's, gushed with ecstatic praise: "[I] beheld the scenery which surrounded me and felt the invigorating mountain breezes. I was soon filled with animation and with a heart swelling with emotion at the grandeur of the surrounding country [and] felt as though I would like to climb one of its loftiest mountains. . . . Got a glance for the first time of the great Sierra. . . . Oh I beheld it with an excitement [that] seemed [to] move every impulse of the soul and filled the heart with gladness."

Bruff held Bates blameless, and when he saw his obituary in a San Francisco newspaper remembered his kindness in leaving him a ration of tobacco, calling him "an estimable member of the company."

He made an earlier appearance in Bruff's diary on October 24, 1849, when he unexpectedly reappeared two days after leaving the camp with the rest of the company because he had forgotten his baggage. Bruff wrote, "Bates breakfasted with us, packed his pony and bade us adieu, taking a message about my horse." (The message was to the company's treasurer, Brooke Edmonston, who had packed Bruff's horse with flour but ridden past without offering him any. Bruff must already have suspected him of planning to keep the animal.)

Bates described this breakfast in one sentence: "The captain received me with much surprise and furnished me with an excellent repast which I enjoyed much as I had almost starved."

His diary ended two days later with his arrival in the Sacramento Valley. Its last entry was, "Moved down the valley 7 miles." He totaled his mileage on the back page and never wrote another word about gold, California, or Bruff.

I reread his October 24 entry, seeing in it an explanation for how Bruff's comrades might have justified abandoning him. Bates had no way of knowing Bruff could feed him so well only because another emigrant had just made him a gift of several pounds of bacon. In their hurry to join the Gold Rush, Bruff's men had naturally seized on any pretext to believe he could survive the winter or walk into the valley when he chose. Some probably never intended to return, but others must have struggled with their consciences, and found in Bates's description of the "excellent repast" evidence Bruff was well provisioned.

I had more reason to understand the Washington Miners' reluctance to help Bruff after driving the two-hundred miles from Lakeview to Redding in the Sacramento Valley on a road that in places shadows the Lassen Trail. I left in light snow and arrived in Redding in a downpour nine hours later after fishtailing through thick fog, hard rain, and snow squalls down a roller-coaster highway that climbed over three high passes and fell through canyons so narrow there was scarcely room for two lanes and a narrow shoulder. I am accustomed to difficult winter driving conditions in the Adirondacks, and I have driven for days on rutted tracks in the Sahara, but this was the hardest and most terrifying drive of my life, and I would seize on almost any excuse not to repeat it.

I sometimes paused to read the cream-colored historic signs marking Lassen's Trail. He had also given his name to a nearby mountain, national park, state forest, and county. The libraries I visited the next day in Chico and Red Bluff had shelves of Peter Lassen histories, monographs, and biographies, all making it clear the biggest accomplishment of this Danish immigrant had been arriving in California a few years ahead of everyone else and finagling a sizable Mexican land grant that enabled him to build a lumber mill, blacksmith's forge, and trading post.

In 1848 he had traveled eastward along the California Trail to promote his trail as an excellent shortcut to the goldfields, even though he had not yet taken it himself. As a local historian who is a Lassen apologist concedes, "An important motive for this trip was the hope of persuading California-bound emigrants to settle on his land, thus increasing its value. As part of this plan, Lassen determined to open a new trail to the upper Sacramento valley, one which would bring travelers through his embryo town."

Lassen attempted his own "shortcut" for the first time while returning west that summer at the head of a twelve-wagon train. His party wandered into dead-end canyons, hacked trails up steep slopes, and chopped wagons into handcarts, becoming so hopelessly lost the pioneers threatened to lynch him. They might have perished if settlers coming south from Oregon had not seen their confused meanderings, tracked them down, shared their provisions, and guided Lassen to his own ranch.

Despite this fiasco, he promoted his route again in 1849, even sending paid agents down the California Trail to urge it on overland parties. A Wolverine Ranger charged it was advertised "expressly to bring the rear emigration into the northern settlements, to their utter ruin." Survivors called it the "Death Route" and the "Holy Terror," and suspected it had been blazed to funnel customers to Lassen's store and his planned Benton City subdivision.

Even more unsavory than Lassen's promotion of his trail was the behavior of his "shingle men," former emigrants he hired to cut wood to build Benton City. Bruff encountered them around his camp and believed their shingle cutting was a cover for scavenging whatever property they could persuade emigrants to abandon. They were, he charged, "determined to prey on the misfortunes of the brethren; and make a harvest of their calamities." They exaggerated the difficulty and distance of what lay ahead, and "the poor Emigrants were at once disheartened, and in despair, left wagons, cattle, and all their effects, except such as they could pack on their backs, and pushed on."

At best Lassen was a stubborn fool; at worst, a mountebank determined at all costs to bring emigrants to his holdings. His trail may be the archetypal example of the boosterism bordering on fraud, and optimism bordering on delusion, that runs through California history to the shoddy rebuilding of San Francisco after the 1906 earthquake, and Scott Dickerson's death in 1989.

Bruff had a curious blind spot about Lassen, describing a man who was pigheaded, but not smart enough to be venal. He even agreed to survey his Benton City subdivision for two ounces of gold dust a day. He complained of exhaustion, heat prostration, and Lassen's meddling. The project was suddenly suspended when Lassen heard rumors of a "Gold Lake" scattered with nuggets, and persuaded Bruff to join him on a fruitless expedition to find it.

There is no evidence that as Bruff laid out Benton City he saw himself as a victim of California's first land scam, or, as assisting in the very scheme that, by prompting Lassen to promote his trail, had contributed to his sufferings.

Perhaps he was too grateful to have survived to reflect that had he not taken Lassen's cutoff, his men would have arrived in California a month earlier as part of the most intact, well-equipped, disciplined, and healthy company of the Gold Rush. He would have been hailed as the most skillful leader of that year, the kind of reputation other pioneers turned into a fortune and, later, a cemetery plot in Colma among the Hearsts and Crockers.

I stopped at the Benton City site to see what had survived of Bruff's efforts. It was off Route 99 and marked by a concrete monument the Masons erected in 1923. The physical surroundings were lovely: fast-moving Deer Creek, pleasant pastures, and groves of trees old enough to have shaded Bruff. But the ground was littered with Dunkin' Donut boxes, car parts, and household garbage, and the bridge defaced by typical lovers'-lane scrawlings of phone numbers, initials in hearts, and promises of oral sex. People in nearby Vina confirmed my suspicion that this ground lay empty because the river frequently jumped its banks in the spring. It was more evidence, if any is needed, of Lassen's stupidity, or his lethal optimism.

During another trip into Northern California I finally visited Bruff's camp. I called from Red Bluff to the Lassen National Forest office in Chester and was told a firefighting pilot named John Little was the "resident Bruff expert." When I met him the next day and he saw my flimsy rental car and confusion at directions beginning "follow Ponderosa Way to Lassen Trail and look for a blank wooden sign hanging half off a tree," he volunteered to drive me. He said the camp looked close on a map, but the road was so bad the drive took two hours even in a four-wheel-drive vehicle. Besides, Bruff was one of his heroes and his camp lay at the edge of the newly declared Ishi wilderness, one of the prettiest and most unspoiled places in Northern California.

Little was a forty-niner out of a Bruff sketch—short, round-faced, and gray-whiskered. He was certainly the calmest Californian I met, a quality useful in a job he compared to piloting a spotter plane in wartime. He flew above fires, selecting targets, coordinating the attack of planes, helicopters, and trucks, and reporting on the battle's progress. During the summer he spent seven days a week over northeastern California and northwestern Nevada, a landscape so empty he could see ruts left by emigrant wagons. He, too, had been bewitched by the story of the Wolverine Rangers, and when he drove through the Fandango Pass he imagined them dancing around that campfire. He had become a Bruff fan when he noticed how perfectly his topographical descriptions matched what he saw from the air. This convinced him everything else in the diary was probably true. He also admired how Bruff had cared for the Lambkin boy, "and the way he tried to create a community even after he was abandoned, turning his camp into a kind of village, and helping the stragglers."

As we drove to Bruff's camp, we followed Ponderosa Way, a rutted track laid out in the 1930s by the Civilian Conservation Corps. Little pointed to where the Lassen Trail ran along a steep ridge that looked scarcely wide enough for a man to walk down, much less a team of oxen. Forest Service employees and archaeologists from the Oregon–California Trails Association [OCTA] still recovered emigrant wagons that had tumbled into the canyons.

The same harsh geographic features causing the emigrants such hardship now attracted marijuana growers. Road crews saw the headlights of cars winking as they bumped along logging roads to remote patches where federal agents found even the hammocks and whiskey bottles covered in camouflage cloth. The only vehicle we passed in an hour was a clunker driven by a pasty-faced couple Little believed were growers for sure. He said the logging roads had transformed the back country by making it accessible to dopers and recreational vehicles. From his plane he sometimes saw circles of Winnebagos on land that the year before was trackless wilderness.

Without Little I never would have found Bruff's camp, and even he missed the path at first, forcing us to double back. He said that in 1948 California Trail buffs had found the remains of the oak that killed the Alfords, and the one on which Bruff carved a Masonic square and compass, but both were lost when the area was logged in 1985. Recently a fire had burned twenty thousand acres nearby. Lumberjacks salvaged the surviving trees, and the camp attracted scavengers who, having read descriptions of emigrants burying household goods, swept the ground with metal detectors, thereby becoming modern versions of Lassen's shingle men.

Despite all the digging and logging, it remained a delightful spot—breezy, fragrant, and the only ground for some distance suited for pitching tents and building fires. In 1967, OCTA had erected an imposing cenotaph of boulders set in concrete. A plaque said *Bruff's Camp, Lassen's Trail. J. G. Bruff, leader of the Washington City Mining Company, camped on this site from October 21, 1849, to December 31, 1849. While here guarding company goods at what he called "his mountain lodge in prosperity," he aided, fed, and cheered many weary, hungry, and sick emigrants, struggling to the goldfields.*

A smaller marker commemorating the Alford family began, *In a common grave at this site or in close proximity to it there are buried four emigrants who were killed by a falling tree. . . . Thanks to the detailed account by J. Goldsborough Bruff, the man for whom this campsite is named, we know the full story of this tragic event. . . . This is part of your American heritage—honor it, protect it, preserve it for your children.*

On December 31, Bruff moved a mile south down the Lassen Trail to winter at Obie Fields, where an emigrant named Roberts had built a log cabin. Bruff raised his tent nearby and developed an instant dislike for Roberts, who seemed willing to be a spectator to Bruff's starvation, and kept busy digging up caches of valuables buried by emigrants, filling his cabin with what Bruff called "plunder." Obie Fields now lies just inside the newly declared Ishi wilderness, so it will probably remain undisturbed for centuries. It is on the edge of an open ridge and surrounded by groves of oak, so perfectly proportioned and landscaped it resembles a park. Little called it "one of the most beautiful small-scale places in California."

The view of the Sacramento Valley was so spectacular he often brought his son camping here. When he looked down on the twinkling lights only a long day's hike away, he wondered if Bruff had seen the distant campfires of his former companions.

We walked a mile down the Lassen Trail so Little could check on a trail crew that was breaking a new loop for recreational hikers. An earlier crew had become hopelessly lost in the tangle of gullies. A rescue party found them the next day, exhausted and scared.

The land had never been logged so the ruts under our feet had been carved by emigrant wagons. Little said it was about as pure Lassen Trail as you could find. It was the same path the Washington Miners had followed into the settlements in October, and that Bruff stumbled down six months later.

We turned around when we came to a fresh bear print. On the way back I caught my boot in a wagon rut, twisting my ankle and tripping forward. "Don't break a leg," Little joked, grabbing my arm. "I might leave you. Remember, you're a Bruff."

Back at Obie Fields we rested under the pines where Bruff had made his winter camp. There was a marker here, too, noting it had been his home between January 1 and April 4, 1850. While I picnicked on smoked turkey on pumpernickel and drank a bottle of diet raspberry iced tea over the ground where he had almost starved, Little argued the Fandango Pass showed Bruff "just didn't get it," and had not understood that when you arrived in California the rules changed, and you burned your constitution and danced a fandango. Instead, he had remained an Easterner, trying to hold his men together in an organized community. He had been more interested in his notebooks than gold, in helping stragglers than striking it rich, in his journey than its destination. He was, if I had to summarize Little, the wrong man for California.

Gesturing to the valley, he said, "After they arrived here, and after the ordeal of the trail, they finally said screw him. Why not, since they'd arrived in the Promised Land?"

I could never hope to know what had gone through the minds of the Washington Miners without finding their letters, or a more forthcoming diary. Some, no doubt, nursed grudges fostered by the military discipline Bruff imposed on them. Some perhaps resented his slow, deliberate pace across the continent, his insistence on burying the dead left by others, and his frequent stops to sketch the landscape and take notes. Some must have been in poor health themselves and convinced a two-day journey back to rescue him would finish them. Some must have reasoned that if he only abandoned his notebooks, surveying equipment, and other possessions, he could, despite his infirmities, stumble into the valley on his own (conveniently ignoring that his offer to remain and lend them his horse had made it possible for them to salvage their own possessions). And some surely assumed they would never be called to account for what they did in California.

This was speculation. But what I knew for sure after seeing Bruff's camp and Obie Fields was that the disciplined community he brought across the continent had shared this spectacular panorama of California's fault-created landscape, stretching unoccupied and unexploited, and then shattered, its members scattering to pursue their individual dreams.

Bruff's men were by no means the most despicable emigrants to travel the Lassen Trail that autumn. Some set grass fires after their livestock had grazed, hoping to starve the parties behind them and reduce the competition for California's riches. Bruff described an old man nearly dead with scurvy whose "friends" had ejected him from their wagon and "abandoned him to his fate," and he encountered a Dutchman breaking up tools he could no longer carry so others could not use them.

Yet even in 1849, and even on the Lassen Trail, you could find evidence of the contradictory California Dream of community and sacrifice. It was there in the food and shelter Bruff supplied to stragglers passing through his camp, and there in Major Rucker's relief column, organized by California residents to ride back along the trail with food and prevent a repetition of the Donner Party disaster. If this contradictory dream ever becomes the principal California one, as may happen in the aftermath of a great earthquake, then Bruff may someday be seen as the right man for California, but one who simply had the misfortune to arrive 150 years too soon.

BIBLIOGRAPHY

EARTHQUAKES

I relied on Bruce Bolt's *Earthquakes* (New York: W. H. Freeman, 1988), Peter Yanev's *Peace of Mind in Earthquake Country* (San Francisco: Chronicle Books, 1991), T. A. Heppenheimer's *The Coming Quake* (New York: Paragon House, 1990), and *The San Andreas Fault System, California*, ed. Robert Wallace (Washington D.C.: U.S. Government Printing Office, 1990) for background on the fault and earthquakes.

I found two books invaluable in locating the fault: *Roadside Geology of Northern California* by David D. Alt and Donald W. Hyndman (Missoula, Mo.: Mountain Press Publishing, 1975), and *Earthquake Country: California*, ed. Robert Iacopi (Menlo Park, Calif.: Lane Publishing, 1976).

Assembling California by John McPhee (New York: Farrar, Straus and Giroux, 1993) is as elegantly written and engrossing as John McPhee's other books about geology and will interest anyone looking for a more scientific journey along California's faults than I have provided.

CALIFORNIA

Kevin Starr's three-volume cultural history of California, *Americans and the California Dream*, *Inventing the Dream: California Through the Progressive Era,* and *Material Dreams: Southern California Through the 1920s* (New York: Oxford University Press, 1973, 1985, 1990) is a towering achievement and no one can truly understand California without reading it, or write about California without being influenced by it.

Among the other general surveys of California culture and history I found most useful were *California—The New Society* by Remi Nadeau (New York: David McKay, 1963), *The Fall into Eden* by David Wyatt (New York, Cambridge University Press, 1986), *Californians* by James D. Houston (New York: Alfred A. Knopf, 1982) *Southern California: An Island on the Land* by Carey McWilliams (Santa Barbara: Peregrine Smith, 1973).

Herbert Gold's *A Walk on the West Side* is as entertaining and perceptive as all of his California fiction and nonfiction, and *Where the Bluebird Sings to the Lemonade Springs* by Wallace Stegner (New York: Random House, 1992), a collection of essays about the West, helped to crystallize my thinking about the importance of "lived-in" communities.

The Northern California Handbook by Kim Weir (Chico, Calif.: Moon Publications, 1990) is as good as a guidebook can be, filled with excellent background information about even the smallest North Coast towns. *Mysterious California* by Mike Marinacci (Los Angeles: Panpipe Press, 1988) was a good source of offbeat information about the state, as was *Only in California* by Janet Hearne (New York: Plume, 1993) and *California the Curious* (Arroyo Grande, California: Bear Flag Books, 1989).

BRUFF

Bruff's diaries and drawings were published by Columbia University Press in two volumes in 1944, and five years later in an abridged one-volume edition: *Gold Rush: The Journals, Drawings, and Other Papers of J. Goldsborough Bruff*, ed. by Georgia Willis Read and Ruth Gaines (New York: Columbia University Press, 1949).

Among the many histories of the California Trail and Gold Rush that mention Bruff, and that I used, are George R. Stewart's *The California Trail* (New York: McGraw-Hill, 1962), J. S. Holliday's *The World Rushed In* (New York: Touchstone, 1981).

***

PART ONE

Ray Raphael's *Edges* (Lincoln: University of Nebraska Press, 1986), *Tree Talk: The People and Politics of Timber* (Washington D.C.: Island Press, 1990), and *An Everyday History of Somewhere* (Covelo, California: Island Press, 1980) were invaluable in understanding Humboldt County, and I drew on them for my summaries of the county's recent history. I also used back issues of *Ridge Review* (Caspar, California), Owen C. Coy's *The Humboldt Bay Region 1850–1875* (Eureka: Humboldt County Historical Society, 1982 [reprint of the 1929 edition]), Mary Siler Anderson's *Whatever Happened to the Hippies?* (San Pedro, California: R. & E. Miles, 1990), and Lynwood Carranco's *Redwood Country* (Belmont, California: Star Publishing, 1986).

PART TWO

There was useful background material about the Anderson Valley in David and Micki Colfax's *Hard Times in Paradise: An American Family's Struggle to Carve out a Homestead in California's Redwood Mountains* (New York: Warner Books, 1992). If you find the *Anderson Valley Advertiser* as much fun as I did you might consider subscribing (*AVA*, Booneville, California).

PART FOUR

For the Great San Francisco Earthquake and Fire of 1906 I relied on *The San Francisco Earthquake* by Gordon Thomas and Max Morgan Witts (New York: Stein and Day, 1971), *The Earth Shook, the Sky Burned* by William Bronson (San Francisco: Chronicle Books, 1986), *1906 Remembered: Firsthand Accounts of the San Francisco Disaster*, Patricia Turner ed. (San Francisco: Friends of the San Francisco Public Library, 1981), and *The San Francisco Calamity by Earthquake and Fire* (Secaucus, New Jersey: Citadel Press, 1986), a reprint of the 1906 eyewitness account of the quake by Charles Morris.

I am in debt to Gladys Hansen and Emmet Condon for their research into the 1906 earthquake. Their book, *Denial of Disaster: The Untold Story and Photographs of the San Francisco Earthquake and Fire of 1906* (San Francisco: Cameron, 1989) is a great achievement of scholarship and persistence.

PART FIVE

For material about Father Riker and the eccentrics of the Santa Cruz mountains I was helped by John V. Young's *Ghost Towns of the Santa Cruz Mountains* (Santa Cruz: Western Tanager Press, 1984), Betty Lewis's *Holy City: Riker's Roadside Attraction in the Santa Cruz Mountains* (Santa Cruz: Otter Books, 1992), and Richard A. Beal's *Highway 17: The Road to Santa Cruz* (Aptos, California: The Pacific Group).

PART SIX

It is hard to imagine anything more to say about Parkfield that has not been said by D. (Donalee) I. Thomason in her *"Cholama": The Beautiful One* (Tabula Rasa Press, 1988).

The story of Jesse Whitton comes from Marjorie Pierce's *East of the Gabilans* (Santa Cruz: Western Tanager Press, 1976).

PART SEVEN

I liked *City of Quartz* by Mike Davis (New York: Vintage, 1992) because he agrees with me about Palmdale. Anyone wanting to learn more about Llano should read *Bread and Hyacinths: The Rise and Fall of Utopian Los Angeles* (Los Angeles: California Classics Books, 1992), and anyone wanting to gorge on fifty years of Palm Springs gossip will enjoy, as I did, Ray Mungo's *Palm Springs Babylon: Sizzling Stories from the Desert Playground of the Stars* (New York: St. Martin's Press, 1993). Frank Bogert's *Palm Springs First Hundred Years: A Pictorial History* made me sad I had not visited it a few decades earlier.

ACKNOWLEDGMENTS

During my travels many people told me they thought Californians had become less friendly. This was certainly not my experience and I would like to thank the many people, most of them mentioned in the text, who invited me into their homes, guided me around, and spent hours with me in conversation. I am sure not all will agree with everything I have written about their hometowns or their state. I can only argue that the impressions of the traveler and resident are often quite different, and the truest insight is rarely a monopoly of either one.

I am grateful to John Coyne for having the clever idea that led to this book. Without the hard work of my wife, Antonia, I would be looking at a manuscript still several drafts away from completion. Linda Grey's encouragement and enthusiasm, Ginny Faber's perceptive criticisms and suggestions, and Kathy Robbins's wise counsel and unflagging support are reflected on every page of this book.

ABOUT THE AUTHOR

Thurston Clarke has investigated Wall Street crooks, traveled with Tuareq nomads in the Sahara, sold encyclopedias in Beirut, and followed the equator around the world. He has written eight widely acclaimed works of fiction and nonfiction, including *Equator, By Blood and Fire, Pearl Harbor Ghosts,* the basis for the CBS Pearl Harbor documentary, and the bestselling *Lost Hero,* which was made into an award-winning NBC miniseries about Raoul Wallenberg. He has written for *Vanity Fair, Glamour, Outside, Travel Holiday, Condé Nast Traveler,* and numerous other magazines and newspapers. He is the recipient of a Guggenheim Fellowship, the Publication Award from the Geographic Society of Chicago, and a Lowell Thomas Award for travel literature. He lives with his wife and three daughters on Lake Champlain in upstate New York.